Robert Crichton

Ontario history

vol. 18-19

Robert Crichton

Ontario history
vol. 18-19

ISBN/EAN: 9783741135347

Manufactured in Europe, USA, Canada, Australia, Japa

Cover: Foto ©ninafisch / pixelio.de

Manufactured and distributed by brebook publishing software (www.brebook.com)

Robert Crichton

Ontario history

Ontario Historical Society

PAPERS AND RECORDS

VOL. XVIII

TORONTO
PUBLISHED BY THE SOCIETY
1920

CONTENTS

I. President's Address, June 10, 1920. GEO. H. LOCKE, M.A. 5

II. Reminiscences of the First Settlers of Owen Sound. M. KILBOURN 7

III. Impressions of Owen Sound in 1851. ROBERT CRICHTON 10

IV. Reminiscences of Owen Sound and its District. JAS. McLAUCHLAN, SR. 12

V. Early Navigation on the Georgian Bay. JAS. H. RUTHERFORD 14

VI. Bruce County, and Work Among the Indians. REV. J. C. CADOT, S.J. ... 21

VII. Ship and Shanty in the Early Fifties. REV. CANON P. L. SPENCER 25

VIII. A Warrior of the Odahwahs. HARRY G. TUCKER 32

IX. Early History of the Beaver Valley. CLAYTON W. HARTMAN 37

X. Early History of Meaford and its District. DR. J. D. HAMMILL 42

XI. The Municipal Loan Fund in Upper Canada. J. MURRAY CLARK, M.A., LL.D., K.C. 44

XII. A Trial for High Treason in 1838. HONOURABLE JUSTICE W. R. RIDDELL... 50

XIII. Col. Joel Stone, A. U. E. Loyalist and the Founder of Gananoque. JUDGE H. S. McDONALD 59

XIV. Pioneer Schools of Upper Canada. FRANK EAMES 91

XV. Genealogical Tables and Their Right Uses in History. A. F. HUNTER, M.A. 104

I.

PRESIDENT'S ADDRESS, JUNE 10, 1920.

By George H. Locke, M.A.

In accordance with an ancient custom the President of the Ontario Historical Society is expected to make an address. The extent of that address is fortunately left to himself to decide. That decision was greatly helped in my case by the kindness of my friend, Father Cadot, in complying so heartily with my request that he share the programme with me this evening. Therefore my position is made much simpler and your patience is subjected to much less strain.

I belong to the Ontario Historical Society because I believe that history is the most important and the most interesting of all subjects not only in the curriculum of a school but in the world of affairs. It is the most important because it reveals to us what has happened, and only from a study of that can we understand what is happening or likely to happen. History is not mere historical material: it is life, and living men make it according to the ways they think and act. Therefore, if one would be an intelligent citizen he must know how the citizens who have preceded him have acted and whence was the origin of the political problems with which he is faced.

An example occurs to me in the story of a man who has been in Canada only a few years, and who was holding forth in an impassioned way against the French-Canadians and what a menace he thought they were. He was fairly intelligent in other respects and when I talked to him about this particular subject I found that he knew nothing of the history of our country but his information was obtained wholly from the newspapers, and he imagined that the French were but late arrivals on our shores. This is an example much too common, and so many of such did I find that being in charge of the largest educational institution in Toronto, I determined to offset this sort of ignorance by beginning with boys and girls and giving them the background of our national life in such a form that it would remain in their minds, and when they grew up they would be intelligent citizens because they would be learned as Lucretius says we all ought to be, in that they would know " the causes of things." Therefore we began Story Hours for boys and girls and made Canadian history the centre of interest. There was no inducement of a material nature held out to them, and there was no compulsion. We announced the stories and they did the rest. When we told the story of Champlain and where he had been in the Province of Ontario, one little boy in a pathetic way said: " Was this Champlain the same man the history book in school tells us about how he founded Quebec on the site of an ancient Indian village named Stadacona?" It was hard for him to believe for the history book had taken pains to devitalize and pan dry all the historical food in such a dessicated form that the process of examinational digestion might be more easily accomplished.

You will notice we gave this story as we do all our stories as much local colour as possible. It is only by a study of local history that we can hope to understand the development of human society, and it is human to be interested in one's local surroundings. The abstract term "citizen" means but little, the concrete term "neighbour" is readily understood and appreciated. And so we have gone on until we have each year over 10,000 boys and girls crowding in to hear stories of early Canada, the land where they live. The work is not spectacular. It is a slow steady progress just like the growth of the children themselves. We are not cultivating radishes; anyone can do that. We have courage to plant acorns because we believe in oaks. We work among boys and girls because we believe they are the hope of the country. Grown up people are often called mature persons. What can you do with a mature person? He is ripe and complete and very often acts as if he were.

We are a nation, a nation within an Empire. We have a history of three centuries and isn't it reasonable to think that if we are to develop patriotic citizens they should know why they are patriotic? They should have knowledge of the facts that have concurred to build up what we call Canadian civilization. This can be accomplished through the study of history which deals with what man has done and how he has done it.

The dangerous revolutionist is commonly a man with little knowledge—especially of history. He cares nothing for the past. He evolves a new earth and sometimes a new heaven out of his inner consciousness, which accounts for its narrowness and impracticability, and nothing answers him so completely as illustrations from history. History no longer deals merely with the soldier and the statesman. The farmer, the trader, the inventor, the poet, the missionary and the mechanic have their rightful places in this social world and the recognition of this fact has broadened our conception and deepened our interest in the achievements of our fathers.

The misunderstandings that arise among the different parts which make up a young nation like ours are due in a very large measure to ignorance of our history. These misunderstandings disappear when we trace them back to their origin and find a historical reason which explains them away. It was old Socrates who said to his sceptical pupil—and we have many of these sceptics to-day—" If beneath all our differences there were not a sameness of feeling present to the mind of each one of us no man could tell his feeling to another." And it is that sameness of feeling that some of us who are interested in a united Canada are trying to develop in our boys and girls through the medium of the Story Hours of Canadian History. Out of such work we hope there will emerge a largeness of vision that will develop in Canada great men who will be leaders, a commodity of which we stand in great need to-day. "Who is a great man?" asked Ibsen and answered his question by saying: "He whom the cravings of his time seize like a passion begetting thoughts he himself cannot fathom and points to paths which lead he knows not whither, but which he follows and must follow till he hears the people shout for joy, and looking around him with wondering eyes finds himself the hero of a great achievement."

II.

REMINISCENCES OF THE FIRST SETTLERS OF OWEN SOUND.

By J. M. Kilbourn.

The Town Plot, as I first recollect it, was called the Town Plot of Sydenham. The Township of Sydenham, among the first surveyed townships, lay along the eastern side of the Bay, also first called Sydenham Bay, extending northeastward about twelve miles to where it joined on to St. Vincent, settled still earlier than the site of Meaford, which was then called Stephenson's landing, with a post office and store. The Town Plot of Derby adjoined the Town Plot of Sydenham. Perhaps I could best help to preserve the names of those whom I remember by giving them in order as I first remember them.

The first wharfinger and forwarding agent was William Carson Boyd who brought here some merchandise and served the community by affording means for its exchange into such articles of commerce as might be offered for barter or sale. Mr. Boyd brought with him a young and energetic family who at once took an active part in all the work of the hamlet. Mr. Boyd built a two-storey wooden building on the corner of Union and Scrope Streets where he lived and did business. If any part of this structure remains, it will be as part of the Queen's Hotel kitchen apartments, and it was long the best and most pretentious building of any description in the town.

Messrs. A. M. Stephens, R. E. Stephens, Thomas C. Stephens, William A. Stephens; also younger members, Marshall and Henry Stephens, came a little later.

Among the early important enterprises established were the Inglis Grist and Woollen Mills at Inglis Falls in Derby about two miles south of the town. A number of skilled carpenters, millwrights, iron workers and others were brought here from Toronto and established themselves in business when the mill was completed.

About the same time, John Telford, who was the local agent for the sale of Crown Lands at this point, established another saw mill at Leith on a little stream known as Leith Water, and there later developed it into a distillery and sold it to John Ainslee, a lawyer and capitalist who was then residing at the Town of Galt, and brought quite a large amount of means into the County with him. He hoped for a time to establish a wharf and grain market at Leith, there being no prospect of a railway to the Town of Owen Sound and no other means of getting the grain from the port to market than by sailing vessels around through the Great Lakes and via the Welland Canal to Detroit and Toronto.

In the month of June, 1845, Hiram Kilbourn and his family came in by way of a sailing sloop via Penetanguishene and Sturgeon Bay. The vessel was of considerable size, and in addition to carrying a cargo of maple sugar to be traded with the Indians, had room on board for Mr. Kilbourn's family, and for the family of another settler, one Joseph McFarlane, who had removed from the Town of Smith's Falls along with Mr. Kilbourn.

Mr. Kilbourn brought with him all the necessaries for the establishment of a tannery and at once proceeded to erect a very considerable building at the mouth of the little creek which crosses Poulett Street underneath the American Hotel, and which finds an outlet at the sewer, now Tenth Street. Mr. Kilbourn brought also with him a considerable stock of ready-made boots and shoes and shoe findings and all the necessaries for the establishment of a shoe manufacturing business, on such a scale as it was then carried on, employing in the shoe shop from six to eight men for several years when it was finally sold out to Charles Hall, who erected a fine structure on Poulett Street, now forming part of the Patterson House.

In the same year there settled in town from Ottawa, John Frost, with his small family. He also brought a stock of merchandise and established himself in a retail general store. Mr. Frost engaged also in a number of enterprises, among them being brick making, in the early days. Mr. Frost having somewhat of an ambitious mind and being somewhat disappointed in the election of a member to represent the constituency in the old Legislative Assembly of Ontario, became dissatisfied with the Town and removed to the Town of St. Catharines where he remained for several years, but later returned with his family who all settled and finally died here.

Among the early settlers of that period was John Mills—"Commodore Mills," as he was generally known in later years—a jovial, public-spirited citizen whose initial enterprise consisted of a small distillery. This he carried on for a year or two, when he finally sold it out to Thomas Scott, afterwards M.P.P., who carried it on until it was absorbed in the Douglas Riddell Brewing Company.

The chief merchant of that date was Robert Patterson, who kept a general store and who amassed a very considerable amount of money, being afterwards commonly known for many years as "Bobby Cash." In the year 1852, Patterson retired from business, selling out his store goods and stock-in-trade and leasing his store premises to Richard Carney, who had recently removed from Barrie, and who was a painter by trade, a very active, energetic citizen, inclined to be domineering and dictatorial, who for many years filled a prominent place in the public life of the town.

After Mr. Patterson retired from business, he and his wife took an extended journey to Scotland to see old friends there. On his return from Scotland, he again took up store-keeping on a more extensive scale than before and carried it on for many years until his final retirement about 1870.

It so happened that Richard Carney was an influential character at the time the proposal was made for the building of the Northern Railway to the Town of Owen Sound. There was a rival scheme to build at what was called "Hen and Chickens," being an exposed point without shelter on the eastern shores of Georgian Bay some ninety miles from the City of Toronto. It was thus much more easily reached than the more distant and hilly country which would have to be traversed, to get to the Town of Owen Sound. Mr. Carney's idea was that there being no harbour at

"Hen and Chickens," a bonus to assist the establishment of the Northern Railway to Owen Sound need not be given on the ground that the company must be obliged to build to Owen Sound for the lack of harbour at the other place. However, this prediction proved erroneous. The road was built to "Hen and Chickens," which became known as Collingwood, and Owen Sound was for about twenty years afterward without a railway.

About the year 1850, there settled in the town, James Butchart and Sons, consisting of George, a tinsmith, David, a tailor and James, a carpenter. These proved successful citizens, and have ever since remained and have taken an active part in everything that promotes the advancement of the place.

A public man of that period, who will still be in the recollection of a good many, was George Jackson, local Crown Land Agent for the County of Grey, whose residence was fixed at Durham. Mr. Jackson was a typical English gentleman, well educated, well read and lived largely the life of an English country squire. He carried on the small duties of his land agency as his chief occupation for many years, and for successive periods represented the county in Parliament.

I say nothing of the recent life of the City of Owen Sound. That is all too fresh in the memories of persons living to be styled historical, which will remain for the later activities of the Society to give whatever degree of prominence they may think proper.

III.

IMPRESSIONS OF OWEN SOUND IN 1851.

By Robert Crichton.

Coming from Caledon Township in Peel County in April, 1851, on the way up we passed through Erin, Fergus and Arthur. Where Mount Forest now is, the only sign of welcome was a log shanty and an Indian wigwam. My older brother took sick on the trip at Durham and I had to take the old mare along and finish the journey alone, although only twelve years old.

Owen Sound was quite a village, with a population of 150 or 200, and it had made a surprising growth since the Government House, or dwelling of the Government agent, was built in 1840. At first the village was attached to Sydenham Township for municipal purposes, although it was often called "Owen Sound." The Government House was the schoolhouse and the public hall for political meetings. In those days politics seemed to run harder in men's veins, and many fiery speeches were delivered by such local orators as John Frost and Richard Carney. The first hotel was built in 1842, and there were several other hotels. The liquor traffic had itself pretty well established in those days. Churches were fairly well established then too. The Presbyterians were in a log house upon the hill under Rev. John McKinnon in 1849, after a meeting was held of many of the old settlers petitioning for regular services. There was not a Methodist Church but they worshipped in a log building on what is now Third Ave. East. The English Church, near where it now is, was the first church to have a bell. The Congregationalists were also represented, under Mr. Cribbs, an excellent man. St. Mary's Church, then under Father Granothier, was standing on the east hill where the convent now is.

The County was at first united to Wellington County for judicial purposes, but later it was separated when the Court House was built. The old stone school on Fourth Avenue East was built as a combined High School and Public School. For two or three seasons wild pigeons were very numerous, especially in 1853 and 1854. The sportsmen used to range themselves along the edge of the hill, and in the morning the shooting seemed like infantry practice, as the pigeons flew over the village from their nesting places on the hills to the westward. I remember the pigeons so numerous that they almost darkened the sun with the immense flocks. Large rookeries of them were in the neighbourhood, and they supplied the family pot of many an early settler. It is one of the strange things of nature that they have all disappeared.

There were a number of stores at that time, chiefly general stores, with the one exception of Mr. Butchart. Richard Carney was also in business then. Another in business was John Frost. Things were pretty dear in those days, owing to the long transit. I remember my father could buy a pound of tea for 50 cents in Toronto while in Owen Sound it was $1.25. The first gristmill in the district still stands as part of Harrison's woollen mill. Before this, Inglis' mill at Inglis' Falls had supplied a vast tract of country.

Dr. Wm. Lang and Dr. Henry Manley were the first doctors in the village, along with another doctor, who worked among the Indians and also started the first drug business. Soon afterward, Parker and Catto came and Dr. Allan Cameron. This part of the county has always been supplied by skilled medical men.

Owen Sound was not nearly so beautiful then. There were trees but they were not nearly so ornamental as now.

The village in those days was mostly along Second and Third Ave East, and Tenth Street. Much of the place was a dense thicket or swamp of cedars which originally occupied the whole site of the present city. The late Ezra Brown, when he was building the tannery where the Bank of Hamilton is now, went up to the Government House, on the present Market Square, to get men to help him. In coming back through the bush some of the men got lost, where our present main street is, and it took them some time to get out. That happened in the early 40's. All the district around both railway stations was a vast marsh with willows and black snakes. At the mouth of the river was a sand bar that kept shifting, over which only vessels of very shallow draught could sail.

Nearly all the present beauty of ornamental trees has been promoted by the early settlers, till they made this young city one of the most beautiful in Ontario. Lord Elgin visited Owen Sound before 1851; and in the late months of 1850 a distinguished visitor, Sir John Ross, who had been leader of an Arctic expedition in search of the ill-fated Franklin expedition and was on his way back to England, spent a night in Owen Sound.

Owen Sound has been noted for its work in prohibition. Temperance principles were firmly rooted here in 1851, when a temperance union was held.

When the Northern Railway was projected, the people fooled themselves by refusing any aid, and it went over to Collingwood, a place we used to laugh at as Hen and Chickens harbour. The Indian village of Newash was where Brooke now is. That same fall the Sydenham Agricultural Society held their first fair.

IV.

REMINISCENCES OF OWEN SOUND AND ITS DISTRICT.*

BY JAMES MCLAUCHLAN, SR.

The narrator was a native of Dumfries, Scotland, and landed in Quebec, May 26, 1854, when he was nineteen years of age. On the trip out from Ayrshire in a sailing vessel with a passenger list of 98, in mid-ocean they picked up the passengers from a shipwrecked vessel, the *Berkshire*. On landing in Canada he and his friend, George Bell, went to Hamilton where for some time they worked. Then they decided they would go into the Queen's Bush and take up land. They left Hamilton at 8 o'clock of a Monday morning in the fall of 1854, on a "rock away" stage. The trip to Guelph took ten hours, and there were thirteen other passengers besides the driver. From Guelph the trip was made on foot through Elora, and Fergus. Between Fergus and Durham they came up with a man driving a yoke of oxen to whom they gave $1.00 to ride five miles. At the end of the first mile he decided walking was best, but Bell stuck with it, determined to get the worth of his money. On arriving at Durham they put up at a first class stopping place. Here, for fifty cents they got a night's lodging, and supper consisting of bacon, bread and tea. When they went to bed at night they climbed a ladder to the second storey and stretched themselves out on sheepskins. There were hotels about every two miles along the road, and stopping at one of these was a number of men sitting around. He decided that the polite thing to do was to treat the crowd. Each man had what he wanted and it cost the treater just one York shilling or about 12 cents. On Friday night they reached McIntosh Corners near Dornoch, and spent the night there. The following day Bell was not very well and Mr. McLauchlan spent the day tramping through the bush, finally locating a farm for his friend Bell in Bentinck and later taking up land for himself in Sullivan. Saturday night and Sunday he spent at Mr. Halliday's. The Halliday family were amongst the most prosperous settlers and lived in a log house of a single room, east of Dornoch. Mr. Halliday had the only team of horses north of Arthur. In the middle of Saturday night the household was aroused by the noise made by a bear as it ran off with a young pig.

On Monday morning in company with one of the Halliday boys, each of them mounted on horseback, they came into Owen Sound. From the Lime Kiln Rock nothing could be seen of the town but the long line of burnt hemlocks along the top of the East Hill. On coming into town there were very few houses, and the main street, now Second Ave. East, was a mass of mud. A single plank ran up and down each side of the street. In stepping off the plank to let a lady pass he went so deeply into the mud that he pulled his boots off in getting out.

---

*An address to the Society, June 10, 1920, at Owen Sound, as reported in the local press (the *Sun-Times* and the *Advertiser*) and by the Secretary.

That night they put up at a hotel on the site of the present Comely House; it was owned by a Mr. Orr and was a fine hotel for those days. A number of men were sitting around the fire when Mr. McLauchlan took his tallow dip and retired at 8 o'clock in the evening, and at 6 o'clock the next morning they were still there when he came down.

Mr. McLauchlan's next visit was in 1855 when he came by way of boat (the *Canada*, owned by Capt. Smith) from Collingwood. The trip was the roughest he had ever made, being worse even than that across the ocean. For four hours the boat lay off Craigleith without making any progress. However, Owen Sound was reached finally and the next day he was married.

He made another visit to Owen Sound in 1857, driving the first peddling waggon selling candies and crackers, and also about once every year afterward.

In 1869 Mr. McLauchlan, who had been living in Hamilton, decided to take up permanently his homestead in Sullivan. He moved to Williamsford, built a little bakeshop and started to make candies and crackers. In 1869 he drove into Owen Sound with his first load of candies and biscuits and sold them for $125. His business grew gradually and with a double-decked waggon he sold his confectionery all through Bruce County and the biggest part of Grey. He moved to Owen Sound, and to-day has one of the biggest confectionery establishments in the Province of Ontario as a result of his untiring work.

In 1883 it was reported that the C.P.R. boats were to come here if the harbour could be dredged and made deep enough for them. Early in April he with David A. Creasor and several others, got together and decided that the harbour must be put into shape. He suggested buying dredges, going into their own pockets if necessary to buy them. It was learned that in Collingwood there were two dredges, four scows and one tug for sale. The following Monday the sale of dredges, scows, and tug was to take place in Collingwood. On Sunday afternoon through mud, rain, and melting snowdrifts, Mr. McLauchlan went to Meaford, arriving in Collingwood the following morning. Dropping off the train in Collingwood before it reached the station, Mr. McLauchlan bought No. 9 dredge and two scows and then the tug. Then it struck him that the others in Collingwood might buy the other dredge and get their harbour dredged first. So he bought the other dredge also and the remaining two scows, and then found that he had no money to pay off the required ten per cent. of the purchase money but he was able to borrow it. Then the moment the ice moved out, inside of two weeks, dredging operations were started in the harbour and by the time the C.P.R. boats arrived the harbour was ready. The coming of these boats marked a great era in the growth of Owen Sound.

In the small towns the people were more friendly than in the cities, and it is hoped that its becoming a city will not destroy the old feeling of neighbourliness which existed in smaller towns.

V.

EARLY NAVIGATION ON THE GEORGIAN BAY.

By James H. Rutherford.

Removed from the Great Lakes trade route between the East and West and from the international boundary with its early complications and war strife, Georgian Bay, which hangs like a bundle on the back of old Lake Huron does not seem to have secured the prominence in Canadian history that has been the part of Lake Ontario, Lake Erie or Lake Huron. True, the hardy Canadian voyageur found in it a convenient and often pleasant break in the passage from Eastern Canada and the hunting grounds in the wilds to the north and west. In it they welcomed the escape from the heavy portages, perilous rapids and other dangers of the rivers and lakes while crossing from the St. Lawrence or Ottawa Rivers to its shores, and gliding through the thousands of islands made their way to the Northern Channel, and thence to the "Soo" and the lands beyond. There were the dangers of storm and the attendant tragedies, but in their stout batteaux the journey was made in safety and comparative comfort more often than otherwise. Whatever of traffic or conflict there may have been in the days when the Indian roamed the wooded wilds which enclosed its shores and fought in his war canoe, it was not until the early settlers came through from the southern sections of the Province and settled in the Queen's Bush and along the eastern shores that the enterprises of navigation had their initial steps. The batteaux which carried many of these early settlers to their destination and often landed them where the prow of the boat could best find a spot to run up on shore, began to give place to the little sailing vessels which in turn were replaced by larger craft of the same class as freights developed, following as a result of the industry and enterprise of the citizens who were grouped in settlements along the shores. As this fringe of civilization expanded the steamboat came on the scene and more rapid and regular connections were maintained as the importance of the ports of the bay increased. This was particularly marked in the case of the opening up of the copper mining regions on the North Shore and the settlement of the Manitoulin Island, steamboats then becoming a factor in the handling of supplies. Before the railway touched the shores of the bay the out-ports for the traffic developing in the vicinity of Toronto, and in the eastern sections of the country, were in the Matchedash Bay. The arrival of the iron horse changed this and Collingwood became for several years the southern distributing point for the freight and passenger traffic originating in the southern section of the Province. To the north of the bay the inner channel was the accepted route for almost the entire traffic. Whether this was because of the growing business along the North Shore or for the purpose of avoiding the channel at the Lake Huron entrance to the bay is uncertain. The fact that with sailing vessels in particular the channel entrance to Lake Huron was not popular may have been due to a tide current which at some times runs strong there. On a map of the bay made in the 18th century this channel is marked dangerous and advises that its passage be only attempted by the stronger vessels and then under the most favourable conditions. A portage from Lake Huron across the Bruce Peninsula is shown on the same map as the alternative to attempting the dangerous passage.

The earliest recorded vessels which did business on the bay were the sailing craft. Owen Sound being the oldest and largest settlement, it attracted the majority of this kind of vessel and became the headquarters of a considerable number of these craft. In fact, the first shipbuilding which took place in this part of the shores of Georgian Bay was probably that of the *Ann Mackenzie* built at Owen Sound in 1848. She was, as compared with modern craft, a small vessel with not over 100 feet keel and a beam of 24 feet. But that she was staunchly built may be accepted in the fact that after facing varying financial situations in the bay traffic she was loaded for Toronto and from that port was sent with a cargo of lumber to Quebec. From information secured by the lawyers of one who was a creditor, the *Ann Mackenzie* was sent across the Atlantic to a British port and from there despatched to Rio de Janeiro, South America, from which point all trace was lost. She may be sailing yet somewhere in the Southern Seas. At any rate the creditor, Mr. Henry Wood, a ship carpenter who helped build her and who is now a resident of Buffalo, N.Y., never realized on his claim.

The second vessel of this class was the smaller schooner the *Elizabeth Broder*, which was built on the east bank of the Sydenham River, and which served her day and generation, trading out of this port until she was lost, fortunately without loss of life, on the shore of the Manitoulin Island.

The schooner *Belle McPhee* was the third vessel to be built at this port. She was built by her owner on the site of the Dorie cement plant on the west side of Owen Sound Bay, and after sailing three years was hauled out at the basin of the harbour, and, after having had thirty feet added to her length and an additional mast, was re-launched. Her good service was terminated when on a voyage from Owen Sound to Collingwood in the following spring she ran too close inshore off Thornbury, and striking a boulder or rock ledge went down, her crew escaping in a fishing tug the captain of which hastened to the rescue.

Other sailing craft which did service in Georgian Bay waters, often taking cargoes to Lake Michigan and Lake Huron ports and around through Lake Erie and Lake Ontario, were the *Prince Edward* owned by Capts. Charles Anderson and James McNab, the *Maple Leaf*, owned by James Sutherland, *Phoebe Catherine*, owned by John Pearson, *Mountaineer*, owned by Capt. Lawson, *Ann Harkley*, owned by Capt. Harkley, *Restless*, owned by Thos. Maitland, *Clyde*, owned by Capt. Johnston, *Neechee*, owned by T. C. Stephens, besides the *Garibaldi, Stanley, Ariel* and others. All of these craft have disappeared from off the scene of action, some having gone down on the bay while on service, others going to the lower lakes where they were converted into tow barges, while others found places in the proverbial boneyard of discards. That their navigators were willing to take long chances is evidenced in the statement that the *Ann Harkley*, which had been converted from a propeller into a schooner after the engines had been removed, made the trip from a Georgian Bay port to Chicago and then back to Port Colborne with a large hole in her bow plugged with blue clay. A mutiny on board while in Lake Huron was a result of the discovery. But the captain and crew went through to the Lake Erie port where the crew left with the exception of the mate. After repairs had been made, the journey back to Georgian Bay was undertaken, the cargo being barrelled whiskey. While the man in charge was coming through the gap and the crew below sampling the cargo, the *Ann Harkley* was carried off her course off Lonely Island by the current referred to in the 18th century map. Running ashore she became a wreck, but her cargo was salvaged by two smaller vessels and brought to Owen Sound.

The dimensions of these craft varied. The largest, however, would not be more than 125 feet on the keel with a maximum of 30 feet beam. The lines of some were exceedingly graceful and they were masterpieces of the shipbuilder's art. Others were but floating boxes, with their two masts and a set of canvas suggesting little more than a floating lumber pile. The carrying capacity was a variable matter; but as an example, the *Maple Leaf*, one of the better class of craft, would carry 10,000 bushels of wheat when fully loaded while the *Prince Edward* would carry 12,000 bushels. As a matter of comparison, the average bulk carrier of to-day would absorb thirty such cargoes and still leave room for a train load of grain. Many of these wooden craft were built at the Lake Ontario shipyards and with few exceptions were creditable specimens of marine architecture. In addition to those named, a complete record would include several others of this class which plied on the waters of Georgian Bay.

There were also numerous smaller vessels, most of them open boats or partially decked. These were largely traders' vessels which visited the villages along the shore and served the settlers and Indians with commodities which the absence of stores and mercantile houses made difficult, if not impossible, to procure.

But there was development in shipping as well as in all other avenues of life, and the club-sail two-masted vessel gave place to the more certain means of travel and carriage, and the steamer made its appearance on the waters of the bay where comparatively few years earlier the batteaux and the mackinac served the requirements. Small settlements grew into towns, and found places on the map. The railway touching at one point on the bay made a change in the traffic routes, and instead of the teamed freights which followed the shortest overland routes, cargoes accumulated at the railway terminal and were despatched to their destinations by steamers.

The first steamer to have a definite place in the traffic was the *Gore*, a small sidewheeler, to which Rev. John McDougall refers in one of his books ("Forest, Lake and Prairie," p. 27) describing a trip made in 1851 when travelling from Coldwater to Owen Sound. She was a craft of 189 tons and her operations were confined largely to the south shore ports. The growing trade of the North Shore resulted in the placing on the route of the *Kalloola*, a vessel considerably larger, 250 tons. Though by no means a new vessel when coming to the service, the *Kalloola* proved a staunch sea boat and weathered many a gale, coming through at times when to save her seemed beyond the possibilities. In time she was superseded by the *Ploughboy*, which in addition to making the run to the "Soo" by the North Channel, entered Lake Superior and went to the head of navigation every third trip. She, however, was past her best days when on the route, though she did service at Detroit and Lake St. Clair for years afterwards, until destroyed by fire in 1870. While these steamers were engaged in the traffic around the bay, the growing importance of Owen Sound attracted the attention of Capt. W. H. Smith, of Chatham, and he brought up the steamer *Mazeppa* and placed her on the Owen Sound-Collingwood route in the early fifties, and he was joined in the enterprise by his brothers-in-law, Messrs. Eberts, who placed the steamer *Oxford* on the route running opposite to the *Mazeppa*. The enterprise of the brothers Eberts was not a success and after a few trips the *Oxford* was withdrawn and she returned to the lower lakes. An advertisement in a local paper of June, 1855, announces the arrival of merchandise by the *Canadian*, which steamer evidently came on the Collingwood-Owen Sound route in 1854. The day of the propeller had not yet arrived, and though there was a growing number of steamers with this form of propulsion, it was generally regarded as unsuited for passenger service, as vessels having power of this type did not afford sufficient beam to meet the stateroom requirements. The *Canadian* spent about 10 years in the service on the route and was followed by the *Clifton*, another sidewheeler built at the Niagara River shipyards, the *Canadian* going back to the Lake St. Clair field of operations. The *Clifton* was celebrated on the bay as the craft which demonstrated that the River Sydenham was a navigable stream when her owner, Capt. Smith, had her lightened of everything movable, even to the water in her boilers, and with an anchor out over her bows hauled her over the bar at the mouth of the harbour and thence up the stream to her landing place at the foot of Eleventh Street East, then Peel Street. The demonstration resulted in the fulfilment of a promise by the Government to have the bar at the entrance dredged and from that beginning the present unequalled harbour facilities have been developed.

With the completion of the railway in 1855 to Collingwood an added impetus was given to shipping on the bay. A line of steamers was established between Collingwood and Chicago, and four steamers, the *Montgomery, Ontonagon, Hunter* and the ill-starred *Lady Elgin*, were engaged in this service. An important traffic grew as a result and was maintained for years.

The east shore interests of the Beattys, of Thorold, resulted in the placing of the small sidewheel steamer *Waubuno* on the Collingwood-Owen Sound-Parry Sound route in 1864 in which service she plied for 15 years until she foundered in an autumn gale in 1879 with all hands on board.

The *Clifton* having served her day was replaced by the *Frances Smith*, built at Owen Sound and launched July 1st, 1867, and admittedly in her time the finest passenger steamer on the upper lakes. The machinery of the *Clifton* was installed in the new boat. Capt. Smith's enterprise in her construction was generally commended, and the steamer did excellent service on the Owen Sound-Collingwood route until conditions became changed in 1874 by the completion of the Toronto, Grey and Bruce railway to Owen Sound, reducing the traffic between these ports to an unprofitable degree, and the steamer went to the Owen Sound-Sault Ste. Marie route and later to the Owen Sound-Prince Arthur's Landing route.

With the railway touching several points on the south shore, and the growing importance of the north shore ports, came the incorporation of several shipping companies. Among the earliest was the Georgian Bay Navigation Co., which had brought the steamer *Northern Belle* up from Lake St. Clair and placed her on the local route, as the service to the Georgian Bay ports came to be known, in distinction from the Lake Superior route. Later the amalgamation of the Beatty interests brought the *Waubuno* and the *Belle* into the same company, forming the nucleus of what eventually became the Northern Navigation Company, now a division of the great merger, the Canada Steamships, Limited.

About the same time as the initial steps in the organization of the local service, other steps were being taken. A Lake Superior Service, which included the steamers *Algoma* and *Cumberland*, was established by the Toronto and Lake Superior Navigation Company, in which Col. F. W. Cumberland of the Northern Railway had a large interest. Later, the steamer *Chicora*, fresh from her service as a blockade runner in the American Civil War, and still retaining the tracks for her guns on the main deck, came from Toronto to join the fleet. She was the first steel or iron hull on the upper lakes. As speed was estimated in those days, she was classed as amongst the crack runners of the lake; and amongst the most exciting incidents in her career in the upper lakes were the races she had with the *Frances Smith* over the fifty mile course between Collingwood and Owen Sound. The *Algoma* found her last berth in the Collingwood harbour, the *Cumberland* was lost on Isle Royale in Lake Superior, and the *Chicora* went back to Toronto, where she became the nucleus of the present Toronto-Niagara fleet.

In 1878 a company which included the interests of Smith and Keighley, wholesale grocers and commission men, was formed as the Canada-Lake Superior Transit Company. Their first vessel was the *City of London* which was burned. Her engines were then placed in the *City of Owen Sound* which had been built at Owen Sound for the company. The latter vessel made the first two years on the Chicago service. The company also acquired the steamer *Annie Craig* which was renamed under the Canadian register as the *City of Winnipeg*. In 1881 the *Winnipeg* was burned at her dock in Duluth. The company then created an innovation by going to Great Britain and purchasing the twin-screw steamer *Campana*, joining the *North* which had been employed in the Rio de la Plata cattle trade. She was brought to the upper lakes and was the first of the steel bulk carriers to be engaged in the upper lake traffic, continuing in the service until 1886 when she was leased to the C.P.R. to replace the lost steamship *Algoma*. Finally she was returned to the ocean service and was a total wreck after grounding on the Gaspe shore in the Gulf of St. Lawrence.

Other incorporations followed, and amongst these was the Owen Sound Steamship Company in which the Smith and Keighley interests were merged. The fleet included the sidewheel steamers *Spartan* and *Magnet*, brought up from the Toronto-Montreal service, and the propeller *Africa*. The construction of the Canadian Pacific Railway link along the north shore gave an impetus to lake traffic in carrying labourers and supplies, but the rates were not remunerative, and the stockholders had their stock certificates as mementos of their venture.

Individual enterprise was not entirely eliminated by the Corporative interests, and several vessels at varying periods operated on the Georgian Bay. These included the *Silver Spray*, the *Seymour*, the *Jane Miller*, the *Hero* and others. The *Cambria*, a rebuilt ocean going sidewheeler tug, and the *Carmona*, operated under a local partnership, were amongst the last of the steamers placed on the local route.

The opening up of the Bruce Peninsula ports and settlements created a new route. This was first served by the *Okonra*, a small steamer built and owned by the Dunns of Owen Sound. The traffic gradually outgrew the dimensions of this vessel and she was replaced by the *Wiarton Belle*, additional capital being taken into the management. The *Alderson* was the immediate successor to the *Belle*. The arrival of the Grand Trunk Railway at Wiarton spoiled this as a trade route, and in time the *Alderson* went to Lake Erie, leaving the remnants of the traffic to be taken care of by the smaller craft.

This brings the story of navigation on the Georgian Bay up to the early eighties, viz., the first forty years in which it was a factor in the business of Canada. Since that time came the Northern Navigation Company, one of the strongest corporations doing business on the bay, whose fleet included the city line of steamers, *Cities of Midland, Collingwood, Toronto, London, Meaford*, and *Parry Sound*, and after the absorption of the Great Northern Transit Co.—its only rival in the field—the *Majestic* and the *Germanic*. All of these steamers have passed off the scene of action, the majority having been burned, and the company has not for some time had a steamer operating on the Georgian Bay route.

In 1884 the Clyde-built Canadian Pacific Steamers, the *Alberta*, the *Algoma* and the *Athabasca* were brought to Owen Sound. Their arrival marked a new era in lake navigation in that they formed a link in a great transcontinental railway service and were operated as a portion of that system. Originally intended to ply between Algoma Mills on the North Shore and Port Arthur, the facilities promised by the Government at the former port were not forthcoming as the time for the operations of the steamers approached, and this turned the attention of the C. P. R. Board of Management to the fact that the lease of the Toronto, Grey and Bruce Railway was on the market. On the recommendation of the late Henry Beatty, who for several years was General Manager of the C. P. R. steamship lines, the lease was acquired, and with the newly constructed Ontario and Quebec Railway between Montreal and Toronto, the great railway enterprise found its connection between Montreal and Port Arthur complete. Later to reduce the rail haul to the seabord a harbour was constructed at a port on the Matchedash Bay, where nearly half a century before traffic had seen its first development, and Port McNicoll became the principal Georgian Bay port for Canadian Pacific steamships.

In more than half a century the tragedies on the Georgian Bay have been comparatively few, when the fact is taken into consideration that no portion of the chain of the great lakes is more susceptible to storms than this eastern area of Lake Huron. The *Waubuno*, the *Asia*, the *Mary Ward*, the *Jane Miller*, the *Jones*, were disasters of no small proportions, and only when the sea gives up her dead will the facts in some of these calamities be known. But when it is considered that many of the vessels which have been in the service were discards from other routes, the wonder is that more of them did not prove to be floating coffins. The fact that so many of the boats went up in smoke, the victims of the flames, is remarkable as well as the fact that the loss of life has been infinitesimal.

Reference might be made to the development of the aids to navigation which the three-quarters of a century have produced. The lighthouses, the gas buoys, the spar buoys and other guides for the mariner are nowhere more adequate than on Georgian Bay, and the navigator is for no great length of time out of sight of some of these safety indicators. This could be the subject for another paper, however, and would prove to be highly interesting.

To-day the conditions for a return of the influence and importance of the navigation of the bay are not in evidence. Skirted by railways which give summer and winter service, there are no great inducements for capitalists to invest in tonnage for the increase of the local service. One cannot forget the remark of the President, Sir Thomas Shaughnessy, of the C. P. R., when he said, "While changes may take place at intervals one should not overlook the fact that the development of the Canadian West will tax every outlet to the seaboard in the very near future—and every port in the Georgian Bay will be needed to accommodate the traffic." With this vision, it is quite conceivable that the Georgian Bay trade routes will be crowded with carriers beside which the vessels of the past would appear as yawl boats. This fact, however, should not let us overlook the debt of gratitude we owe to the hardy mariners who in the early days risked all to provide comforts and conveniences to the early settlers who were the pioneers in the settlement of this great and important section of the Dominion of Canada—the Georgian Bay District.

VI.

BRUCE COUNTY AND WORK AMONG THE INDIANS.

By Rev. J. C. Cadot, S.J.

The study of the early years makes us love our country more because it makes us understand the cost of the country and how our ancestors had to toil hard and to suffer to hand down to us such a beautiful inheritance. And when we see and understand what they have done we love them and our country more and more. But there is something more that makes us broader minded, more just to one another, and more fair to the descendants of the first settlers. Whether they are Indians, Irish, Scotch, or any other nationality, we should love them for what they have done. So we cannot give too much praise to the Historical Society. They help to foster, not only a better understanding of what our early settlers have done, but in doing so foster a better understanding and harmony between the citizens of the country no matter to what creed they belong.

(Father Cadot divided his address into two parts. The first dealt with the origin of the County of Bruce, the second with his work among the Indians.)

I.

The first white men to come into the Georgian Bay region were Champlain, Le Caron and Etienne Brule. Even some of our editors and members of Parliament do not seem to know of these Frenchmen. They think the French came to the country about twenty years ago instead of over three hundred years ago, and that they should be put out. After Champlain came Nicolas Perrot.

Then followed two hundred years before Pierre Piche in 1818, hearing of the number of furs to be obtained on the east shores of Lake Huron settled at the mouth of the Saugeen River, where he built a house and store and traded with the Indians. Ten years later came Edward Sayers, an Englishman. Then two French Canadians, Cadotte and Loranger, succeeded Sayers. This was the story of the first settlers.

By a treaty in 1836, the Indians ceded their rights to the land to the Government. The Indian trait of kindness and generosity was never more clearly demonstrated than by the readiness with which they surrendered their rights to their ancient hunting grounds. But too often their generosity has been abused by the meanness of the whites. The first two townships to be formed were Kinloss and Huron. At first it was an unbroken wilderness from Meaford to Goderich, but little by little settlers came in and new townships were formed, all at the south of the present county. In 1850 there were eleven organized townships, and by an act of Parliament it was called Bruce.

At that time there were three counties (Bruce, Huron and Perth) with one Council. The first Warden was Dr. Chalk, of Tuckersville, Huron

County. The County Clerk was F. W. Otto, of Walkerton. The first representative from Bruce was in 1853 when they had three men on the Council. Only in 1856 was there a representative from each township on the County Council. In 1853 Perth withdrew. In 1857 Bruce and Huron had a dispute over a bridge at Kincardine and parted company. In 1867 the county town was finally located at Walkerton. The first Warden was Mr. Brocklebank and the Clerk, Geo. Gould. The first permanent settlers were at Kincardine and Southampton. In 1848 James Withers and Allan Cameron settled where the station now stands at Kincardine. Capt. John Spence and Capt. Wm. Kennedy were Southampton's first settlers. Captain Spence died in 1904, and his widow passed away only a few years ago.

II.

Mission work is carried on among seven different bands, but all of them belong to the Ojibway branch of the Great Algonquin family. With headquarters at Cape Croker the missionary serves the Indians at Saugeen, Cape Croker, Christian Island, Honey Harbour, Parry Island, Moose Point and Shawanaga.

In Canada there are 106,000 Indians; of these, 26,000 live in Ontario. In Ontario three-fifths of the Indians are Protestants and the rest Roman Catholics. The Indians of Canada are estimated to be worth $10,000,000, half of which belongs to the Ontario tribes. The value of all the Indian land in Ontario is $115,000. The Ojibways with whom the missionary works are all descendants of the warriors who fought under Tecumseh in the war of 1812.

The Cape Croker Band came from Newash or Brookholm, now a part of Owen Sound; before that they had lived around Coldwater, Rama, and Orillia, but moved west before the advancing tide of civilization. Many of the original Saugeen Indians have also moved north to the Cape Croker settlement.

To speak of the Indian character, their faults are not few, but these are far outbalanced by their virtues. In the first place they are stubborn. No amount of coaxing, pleading, or force could make an Indian change his mind once it was made up. To illustrate their improvidence: an Indian at Garden River tore down one-half of his house to provide fuel to keep the other half warm. The Indian often not only does not pay any heed to the morrow; he even lets the afternoon look after itself. A great number of them, are, through all their life, children; an Indian graybeard of sixty is but a mere infant. Of their extravagance, within a week after the Government allowance has been issued practically none of it would be left in the possession of the Indians, and the things it was spent on were so childish. They are untidy about their homes. Eight years ago we offered prizes for the tidiest houses on the Reserve. The result was astonishing. All the homes were as neat as a pin till the prizes were awarded, when, without an incentive to work for, they dropped back into their old slovenly state. They are very suspicious of strangers and a new missionary is not a welcome visitor at their homes till he is thoroughly tried out.

The Indian has very little will to resist temptation and many are disinclined to pay their debts. A most amusing incident occurred of a collector going to the Saugeen Reserve to collect a debt owed his firm by an Indian. He accosted the first Indian he met and asked him where the party he was seeking lived. After inquiring the purpose of the traveller's visit, the Indian assumed a very doleful expression and shook his head sadly. He told the collector of what a very fine man the debtor was, how he always paid his debts, and was very highly thought of in the community. Unfortunately he had died the week before and the whole Reserve had attended the funeral; there had been a brass band, and much sorrow over the death of so good a man. It was most unfortunate the collector had not come a little sooner as his debt would most certainly have been paid. The traveller was deeply chagrined and went away, only to find out later that his informant, who had related so touchingly the story of the demise of the man he sought, was that very man himself. Strange to say, these defects are more pronounced among the women.

But the Indian has many good qualities that cover their defects. Their physique is magnificent. They have a most dignified carriage and look like princes. They are always courteous, and always true to you if they like you. Indians are good at the fine arts and can draw and sing as well as, or better than white men. The brass band on the Cape Croker Reserve has never had a white man to lead it. Music is bought, and the band simply stays with a piece until they know it. The Bishop said it was the best band he had heard in the whole Diocese. They never forget a wrong, but if an apology is given an Indian is always ready to become your friend. They are generous.

We feel justly proud of the Indians in the Great War. Out of sixty-seven men on the Reserve who were eligible for service, sixty-three enlisted and went to the war. This included married men as well as unmarried men. Every man who could go served his country. Six will never come back, but sleep in soldiers' graves. Two have brought back Military Medals and one has lost his right arm. Many of the returned men have accepted the Government's aid and have taken up land. The Indian Agent, who is a returned officer, has lent every assistance in his power, and during his term of office has greatly helped the Reserve. The Indian soldiers are not naturally fond of farming, but have learnt overseas the lesson of patience and are staying with it.

Cape Croker has three good schools, all of them public schools. One of these is taught by Miss Moffitt who has been at the Reserve for a long time. Besides the usual curriculum, Miss Moffitt teaches music, gardening, house-keeping and carpenter work.

There are two churches on the Reserve, a Methodist Church and the Roman Catholic, and there is not the least bit of friction between the two churches. The present Catholic Church was built in 1907 and paid for in five years. There is a hall in which the boys meet and play pool, or cards, every evening till ten o'clock. At nine o'clock the curfew rings and all the school children go home at once and to bed. The missionary's house is always open as a club house for the soldiers. The returned men are free to come and go at will.

Of the Saugeen Reserve there must be told the story of a young Indian who since has been overseas and returned. Young Lavalle was the missionary's guide and a companion on many a weary journey to and from the Saugeen and other charges. One winter day coming from Saugeen they were caught in a blizzard. Food had been scarce on the Reserve and they were none too well nourished. The last three miles, till they came to a house near Hepworth, were done on hands and knees so weak were they that they could not stand upright. Such hardships as these are what the missionary has endured for over twenty years and will probably endure till he is called to the last reward. The Saugeen Reserve has a war record the equal of Cape Croker. Its Indians are much poorer than those of Cape Croker.

In the winter time the missionary, to reach his charge at Christian Island, must travel 255 miles by way of Toronto and Midland. In the summer it is but 70 miles by boat. The Christian Island Indians were not as eager to enlist as their brothers of the Cape Croker and Saugeen Reserves. They said they did not want to be killed. But the judgment of God was upon them, and in three weeks He had killed seventy with the influenza, many more than the other reserves lost in the war.

At Parry Island there are about one hundred and fifty Indians in the charge. At Honey Harbour there are not many Indians now. But eight years ago they raised sufficient money to build a church, and the church was built within one week.

Huronia extended from Coldwater to Orillia and from the Nottawasaga River to Barrie. There were 30,000 Hurons living there who were becoming well civilized under the instruction of the Jesuits. In 1649 the Iroquois hordes swept down on them from the south and exterminated the Huron nation, root, trunk and branch with the exception of a few who reached Christian Island. Here in 1650 a fort was built whose walls may still be seen. It was seventy-two feet square and in 1875 its walls were quite high; now they are only about six feet.

We stick to our work because we see it is patriotic. We want to give to our country good citizens. When my boys went to the war I saw I was not working for nothing. Another reason is the example of those Jesuits who gave their lives so stoically and nobly when the Huron nation was annihilated. Our hardships are only a trifle compared to theirs, and we need only to remember them to stay with our work. We ask God to give us some of their constancy and ability to stay with the task till the end.

VII.

SHIP AND SHANTY IN THE EARLY FIFTIES.

BY THE REV. CANON P. L. SPENCER.

On the morning of the 22nd of September in the year 1853, a mother and her two youthful sons embarked on board the sailing ship *Prince Albert* in the harbour of the old walled town of Portsmouth with the hope and expectation of joining in due time five other sons of the same mother, who had seven years before, with one exception, emigrated to North America and settled on bush land a few miles south of the small village of Owen Sound in the Province of Upper Canada. The vessel was bound for New York, the majority of the passengers of all three classes having booked for various places in the United States. As might be supposed, the voyage, beginning with the autumnal equinox, proved to be almost continuously rough. The steerage passengers, chiefly foreigners from continental countries, had in accordance with the rule or custom then prevailing, brought provisions with them; but as the food was of an inferior quality and as, owing to the stormy weather, cooking could be performed only with great difficulty, they suffered much hardship, sickness, and discomfort.

Soon, moreover, was their pitiable plight aggravated by an outbreak of the justly dreaded disease, cholera. This fatal malady could not be effectually overcome by medical and sanitary treatment before forty-seven persons had yielded up their lives as its victims, one being an able seaman, who contracted the disease while performing the tender and merciful act of sewing the first corpse in a sail-cloth shroud.

During the epidemic only a rope stretched from bulwark to bulwark separated the exempted from the infected on deck. After the loss of this member of the crew, Capt. Bradish was reluctantly compelled to omit the enclosing of the bodies of the dead in canvas shrouds and to require their committal to be performed as simply and speedily as possible. The garments in which the deceased person had died were not removed, but were bound to the body. A weight of iron was then fastened to the feet. A brief service was read; and at the words, "We therefore commit his body to the deep, etc.," the inner end of the plank on which the body lay, was lifted, and the corpse was permitted to slide through the open gangway and drop into the sea.

A remarkable experience of a very different nature followed in mid-ocean, viz., the capture of a huge sea turtle, which the mate and a few sailors surprised as it peacefully slept on the tranquil bosom of the deep, quite unaware of the ability of human watchers with the aid of a telescope to discern it, though to the unassisted eye the creature might have been invisible. After a zoological exhibition, to which the passengers were admitted without the payment of an entrance fee, the marine shell-clad animal of amphibious habits was consigned to the butcher and by him transferred to the master of the kitchen, who produced from its flesh a sufficient quantity of genuine green turtle soup to please the palate of each of the first and the second cabin passengers.

At the end of a period of 43 days, the welcome call of "land in sight" came from the "crow's nest." Soon a pilot boat was hailed, and then followed the heaving-to of the *Prince Albert* and the boarding of the vessel by the important personage who was to direct our course to the place of anchorage within New York harbour. Night intervened before a clear view of the shore could be obtained, but rising betimes on the following morning we beheld a fairy-like scene, never to be obliterated from our memory—the terraced slope of Staten Island with its white houses and green grassy plots.

The health officers of the port, after careful investigation and inspection, allowed us in common with the other cabin passengers, both first and second, to go on shore, although the ship was ordered to proceed, with its full complement of third class unfortunates, to the quarantine station, there to undergo thorough fumigation and disinfection. The heavy luggage of all passengers was detained on board.

At the hotel known as Gunter's Arms we lodged while waiting for our family effects, which comprised the contents of heavy boxes and a chest of drawers, besides articles too numerous to mention, packed within a feather bed. The fire-bells having one night rung out their wild alarm, our mother, upon making inquiry regarding the nearness of the danger, was reassured by the watchman of the hotel complacently saying: "Madam, you need not be in the least alarmed, unless you can feel the walls growing hot." A ride in the street horse-cars to visit a brother of an aunt in England and a taste of hot oyster stew procured from a street vendor were the other chief experiences that have impressed themselves on my memory as being at the time quite strange and novel.

To reach our first objective in Canada West our route included a railway journey through Rome and Albany to Rochester. At Rome through a mishap our mother was left behind, and her two small boys were carried every minute farther and farther from her care and comfort. A reunion was, however, some hours afterwards effected, the boys at a certain place boarding another train and in each car in succession calling, "Is Mrs. Spencer here?" The resulting scene was not devoid of interest to the other passengers. Being obliged at some place to break our journey and arrange for staying in the town all night, we found the representatives of the various rival caravansaries so demonstrative in their attentions and so forcible in their endeavours to win us as guests that for a few moments we incurred the danger of being dismembered, or "quartered," as were criminals in early times, a treatment which as harmless intending colonials we not unreasonably resented. At another place, being directed to change from one train to another and have our household effects transferred, we perceived that the baggage-men were not enamoured of the weight of some of the packages comprising our equipment. When handling a ponderous chest one man remarked to his comrade, "I guess this is where the gold and silver are," an observation which amused us not a little, since we were far from being burdened with a superfluity of either of the precious metals.

Upon our arrival in Rochester we changed our mode of travel, from train to steamer. Lake Ontario was at the time in a somewhat turbulent mood. During the few hours' delay that in consequence ensued, my brother and I summoned sufficient courage to sing at intervals some English songs that we had in the Old Country committed to memory. This vocal performance, though of a very humble nature, met with a very kind reception on the part of the other passengers. It certainly helped to while away the time. Ontario's "sullen billows having ceased to leap," we bade good-bye to the United States and in the course of a few hours planted our feet on the soil of one of the richest possessions of the United Kingdom. Toronto, containing a population of about 35,000, seemed to us a pleasant place, thoroughly British and very English. No friendly hand, however, was extended to welcome us. A brother of mine from the County of Grey was to have greeted us; but the uncertainty of travel, the irregularities of postal communications and the absence of telegraph facilities in the north country combined to cause his non-arrival at the hoped-for moment. When after a day or two he arrived, and in one of the rooms of the "Masonic Arms" near the central market announced his relationship, but withheld his Christian name, our mother was at first unable to identify him, so great a change had seven years wrought in his face and figure. He proved to be the third in order of age and experience.

No time was lost in making arrangements for our journey to the north. Instead of using the railway which then led as far as Barrie, we took stage for Hamilton and arrived after a day's travel at the Saint Nicholas' Hotel in that small but pleasantly situated city.

From Hamilton we journeyed in a similar manner to Guelph. Thence we pursued our way by mail coach to the village of Fergus. Here our further progress by public conveyance was barred, the road through the "Queen's Bush" being devoid of gravel or broken stone, and therefore liable in the fall of the year to be converted into an elongated "Slough of Despond," and the settlements along the way being too few and small to tempt any stage proprietor to maintain a continuous service. An uncovered wagon drawn by a team of stout horses under the control of a reliable resident of the village became our means of locomotion for the remaining fifty miles. Fortunately the weather continued comparatively mild and calm; and the road, alternating between bare earth and corduroy, the latter in some places as bare as the earth, was fairly dry. Under these favourable conditions we were able to advance at the rate of about twenty miles a day, passing a branch of the Saugeen at a point now within the bounds of Mount Forest, and spending one of the nights in Hunter's Hotel in the village of Durham, a hostelry which contrasted strongly with the average wayside log public house, since it was built of well-mortared and well-laid stone, material as solid and immovable in the building to-day as when it was placed there probably 70 years ago.

Our first view of Owen Sound, obtained from the top of Union Street Hill, revealed to us a scattered village of log or frame dwellings and two buildings of red brick, one of the latter being the place of worship used by the Disciples of Christ, and the other being a house of merchandise kept by Mr. Brodie and commonly known as the "brick store." The general aspect of the place was decidedly picturesque, the Sydenham River, a perennial and copious stream of then unpolluted water, flowing midway through the valley-enclosing hills and giving promise of future busy scenes of trading and navigation. Passing through the village, we ascended the north-eastern hill which was partly paved with corduroy, and made as our final objective the temporary home of the eldest member of the family, he having recently laid aside the implements of forestry and agriculture and applied himself to the less strenuous and probably also less remunerative vocation of rural school teaching. I say, probably less remunerative, because when I myself ten years afterwards adopted the same profession and made a rural school, near the fishing hamlet of Cape Rich, the scene of my first endeavours, the salary was at the rate of $200 per annum. My brother, although a married man, did not probably receive more than $300. His house, situated about two miles from Owen Sound, was finally reached, becoming, although diminutive in size, the meeting place for a family conclave of ten persons old and young, some of whom had not seen each other for years. The trustees of my brother's school, upon learning that the mother of so many big sons had arrived at the residence of the teacher of their section, expressed a wish for an interview, asking at the same time among other inquiries the question, "Can she walk?" A person of fifty years of age was, in those days, regarded as old. Very few men or women of that age were to be met with in new settlements. The trustees, reflecting upon the general rule with regard to the age of the hard-working settlers, could with difficulty imagine health, strength and activity continuing after the half-century mark had been passed. As a fact my maternal parent years after this time often walked from the old farm in Sydenham township to Owen Sound, a distance of eight miles.

With the arrival of snow and the commencement of sleighing, the order came for the removal of the latest family contingent by ox-sleigh to the heart of Holland Township, a region which was an almost unbroken forest, settlers having only just begun to take up land therein. In this quiet, secluded part of Grey County, fourteen miles from Owen Sound, in a small clearing perhaps about two miles distant from that of our nearest neighbour, we spent our first Canadian winter. Neither church nor school was within reach. So deep was the snow that trampling it down was necessary before the oxen would venture to go forward on an infrequent blazed path. So calm was the atmosphere that the snow which fell on the roof of our humble log dwelling, put the rafters to a severe test of strength, and we had to lighten the weight by the use of shovel or spade.

Stoves were unknown in that sylvan retreat, but the huge open Dutch fireplace, built in an end wall with timber arms or brackets to support the sides of the chimney, received the fire's main support—the big back-log, and frequent smaller contributions from nature's immense woodyard, and it thus gave forth ample heat and much "light at eventide." The cooking utensils were, however, ponderous, clumsy and awkward to handle. Soot and ashes clinging to their exterior did not improve their appearance or lend charm to the gentle art of preparing toothsome viands for the family board. A fire above the average of normal strength would, moreover, ignite the chimney's side supports, necessitating the sprinkling of water upon them.

The larder of the log cabin included, as one of the chief contents, the flesh of swine that had during the preceding autumn fed freely in the bush on beechnuts. This grade of pork, owing to the softness of the fat, seemed, while in the frying-pan, to shrink to less than half its original bulk, the remnant floating in a miniature pool of oil. The lean part, however, was wholesome and palatable. The simple life was certainly the rule in Holland Township. As an illustration I may relate that visiting one Sunday afternoon our neighbours, the R——s, we were invited to stay for tea. The meal consisted of tea (real store tea), and bread,—the product of flour, water and salt rising. The usual accompaniments of the latter, butter and jam, and the customary trimmings of the former, milk and sugar, were conspicuous by their absence.

While the winter of 1853-54 was still with us, news reached us from England concerning the return voyage of the *Prince Albert*. The following brief official entry in the register of the famous Marine Insurance Office of Lloyd's, London, England, tells the tale:

"Queenstown, Jan. 11th, 1854.

"*Prince Albert*, American ship, Captain Bradish, New York, for London, was fallen in with, in a sinking condition, in lat. 48, long. 15; and the crew and passengers taken off by the *Norfolk*, arrived here."

The *Prince Albert*, laden with wheat, encountered, when 250 miles from the south-west coast of Ireland, a furious storm. The signals of distress were observed by Captain David Baird Brown, of the sailing ship *Norfolk*, whose brave sailors at great peril came to the rescue and saved the forty-three men, women and children on board. Captain Brown was the husband of my eldest sister. Their youngest son, Percy Brown, has for many years been a resident of Owen Sound. When we learned the fate of the *Prince Albert*, although we were sorry, we were not surprised, for we could remember the frequent utterance of the sailors during our own voyage: "We'll never sail in this old tub again."

On account of the extreme loneliness that marked our life in Holland, our mother persuaded her big boys to remove to an old cleared farm in Sydenham Township, owned by them but abandoned, for the reason that boulders huge and abundant disputed with the hardwood stumps the occupancy of the soil. To this open country "estate" we accordingly in the spring of '54 migrated. Neighbours were there; schools were accesible; even a church was not more than four or five miles distant. During the three years of residence here, my education, at least during the summer months, made some moderate headway. Occasionally I accompanied my elders to St. Paul's Anglican Church on the Garafraxa Road in the neighbourhood of Chatsworth. In the absence of a reed organ, called in those days a melodeon, my brother, W——, would sometimes play the tunes on his English accordeon. On the occasion of the visit of Bishop Strachan from Toronto for Confirmation, the organist and choir of St. George's Church, of this city, drove out to St. Paul's Church, carrying the melodeon with them, and rendered the musical parts of the service with due earnestness and surprising vigor. The clergyman was Rev. A. H. R. Mulholland, who successfully in the course of his long and faithful ministry filled the offices of missionary, incumbent, Rural Dean, Canon, and Archdeacon, and enjoyed such honours as accompany such ecclesiastical titles.

In 1857, the eldest son, and two other members of the family, being already residents of Owen Sound, the family council decided that the mother and the two youngest boys also should move thither. This brought great advantages within the reach of the writer. The log building at the north of the village, originally used as a store and subsequently converted into a temporary place of worship, had been exchanged for the newly erected Church of St. George, a roughcast structure which stood at the foot of the hill on what was known as Division Street. The Methodists and Presbyterians had fairly substantial edifices. The Roman Catholics met in a private house. The Disciples had a neat brick building on Division Street, as previously noted.

Of incidents connected with St. George's Church and indelibly impressed on the memory two are worthy of recital. An infrequent attendant, having come early to morning service, and having observed that a certain pew was wholly unoccupied, took a seat in the same at a point most remote from the pew door. After a few minutes three ladies entered the church, advanced to this pew and seeing a stranger occupying part of it, paused at the door and apparently waited for his withdrawal. The awkward situation was relieved by the uncomfortable visitor nimbly vaulting over the pew back and taking a seat one place to the rear. Here he was not again disturbed. The old pew rent system now happily passing away, was responsible for many unseemly episodes.

In the event of the melodeon being out of commission or some other untoward circumstance occurring to interfere with the regular performance of the musical part of the service, Mr. G——, one of the churchwardens, was wont to "raise the tune" for the psalm. On one occasion the worthy man unfortunately chose a tune whose metre did not match the psalm. The first line of the words fared fairly well, precentor and congregation lifting up their voices with one accord and making a joyful noise. The second line, however, fell lamentably short of the tune's requirements, the only recourse being the abnormal lengthening of the last syllable. Rather than tolerate such an absurdity a lady vocalist in the gallery courageously interrupted the melody with an entirely new tune and after a few seconds' confusion and discord triumphed over error and won the congregation to harmony, order and reverence.

The clergyman sometimes held a service in a schoolhouse in the Township of Derby, depending on a musical woman of the congregation to lead in the singing. One afternoon he announced the psalm or hymn as usual, but there was no response. Supposing that he had failed to make himself heard or understood, he repeated the announcement, whereupon a male voice from the rear exclaimed, "Please, sir, she isn't here to-day."

The Public School of Owen Sound, or Common School, as it was termed, was an oblong log building of two original sections or parts, and stood where now one finds the city hall. I think that originally it had served as an immigrant shelter. For a short time my eldest brother, previous to my entrance within its walls had been the principal. He was wont to relate that when for some reason a special holiday was at one time granted by the board of trustees, one of them undertook to make a fitting announcement early in the morning. This he did by chalking on the door, "No Skule to-day."

A private Grammar School was at first for a year or two maintained by a brother of Rev. A. H. R. Mulholland, the teacher himself being a clergyman. This was followed by a Government Grammar School, held in a part of the long log building just mentioned. The first teacher was Mr. John Gibson, eldest son of the pastor of the Presbyterian Church on Division Street, a scholarly man, who subsequently distinguished himself in modern languages at the Toronto University, and later as a Presbyterian clergyman filled important positions in Hamilton, Chicago and London, England. Besides the ordinary branches of education, some of the pupils took French, Latin, Greek, algebra and geometry, there being two classes, senior and junior. Prayers were said, the Bible was read and a good moral tone pervaded the institution. The English reading books were those of the Irish National Series, No. 5 of which contained the history of the Kings of Israel and Judah. The scholars therefore by using this reader gained not a little knowledge of Scriptural history.

The examination which served as a test of a Common School pupil's fitness for entrance into this academy of a higher grade was of the simplest possible nature, consisting of a specimen of his or her reading and writing, and a few oral questions in other subjects, of the quality of which Mr. Gibson himself was judge.

Although corporal chastisement was not an unknown quantity, very seldom indeed was it considered necessary, Mr. Gibson being patient, kind and considerate, and able to infuse into his scholars a spirit of ambition. An incident illustrative of his forbearance may be related. For lack of a town bell, the blowing of a certain mill steam-whistle served as the signal for the noon dismissal of the pupils, a sound which was always eagerly waited for by them. On a certain day when this welcome signal was heard, one of the boys made some remark with reference thereto. Mr. Gibson, addressing the lad by his Christian name, said: "P——, is this the first time you've heard that?" "No, sir," replied the audacious youth, "it's the last time." On account of the previous record of the embryo wit the offence against due respect for authority was not followed by a reprimand.

Attention may be drawn to Grammar School public examinations, to the way in which advanced scholars might appear before the County Board and obtain teachers' certificates, to the promotion of the village to the status of a town, to the first dredging of the river to facilitate steamboat navigation, to the building of the Court House and the holding of the first court therein, to making of good roads leading into the town, to the introduction of the telegraph and to other proofs of a steady advance from the common, simple life to the enjoyment of the comforts and conveniences of fuller civilization. With a return to backwoods or cleared land experience, one might tell about the countless hosts of wild pigeons that flew over the settlements, the flocks of wild geese that in triangular formation migrated northward or southward, according to the season, the sparkling myriads of fire-flies that flitted in the evenings in kaleidoscopic manner among trees and bushes, the groundhogs, or woodchucks, porcupines, squirrels and chipmunks that frequented the groves and slashings, the saucy, richly-tinted blue-jay, the gorgeously-adorned, red-headed woodpecker, the invisible but unfailingly recognized whip-poor-will, the flashing, brilliant, but tiny, ruby-throated humming-bird, living things that helped to make the settler's lot endurable, and to some extent, indeed, enjoyable. One might also, on the other hand, relate facts concerning the nightly howling of wolves and their depredations in the sheepfold, and the screeches and shrieks of the lynx, or wild-cat, sounds and sights that made the land-clearer almost envy the village merchant or mechanic. Enough, however, has been said to show that the old times, though good, have yielded to times that are better. The writer feels happy and thankful that he has lived to see the humble Canadian village of his early years grow into a prosperous city, and he joins with the other members of this Historical Society in the fervent hope that the future career of Owen Sound will be marked by unbroken progress and improvement.

VIII.

A WARRIOR OF THE ODAHWAHS.

By H. G. Tucker.

"There is a beautiful maple grove in my people's old camping ground on the Isle of the Manito. To it I will go, and under the blue sky of the Northland end my days."

The speaker was a young interpreter of the Indian Department in Toronto, Canada. His companion, an old man of English birth, white haired and ruddy cheeked, looked at him with compassionate countenance, but said nothing. What could he say? Francis Assikinack was dying of consumption, and to the chief clerk of the Provincial Indian Department it was as if death were snatching from him a beloved son. The young Indian had been much with him from the time he first came, a mere lad, to Upper Canada College, sent there through the interest taken in him by the Superintendent-General of Indian Affairs. Holidays and Saturdays the boy had usually spent at the Indian Office, the one place in the city where he stood a chance of hearing his own tongue spoken. Soon he had begun to do a little work for the chief clerk. The little had increased to more, until, when Assikinack left school for good, he had been appointed Interpreter.

Everyone had liked and admired him as a boy, and there are those still living in Toronto who can recall his feats of prowess and endurance. If you begin to talk to those old men of their school days they will tell you of this Indian fellow-student who could shoot a robin on the wing with his bow and arrow, or who ran a race through Queen's Park and down University Avenue with a mounted English officer and reached Queen Street first.

As he grew to manhood his friends' delight in his intellectual achievements was as keen as it had been in his proofs of Indian skill, and when, after finishing his studies at Upper Canada College, he was appointed to the position of Interpreter, more than one Toronto fireside rejoiced, for he was as much beloved as he was admired.

Francis Assikinack was an ideal Indian in appearance, tall, lithe, with jet black hair, aquiline nose, piercing eye and—a mark of good family in either man or woman of Indian race—small and beautifully shaped hands and feet. A descendant from an illustrious line of Indian chiefs who had left their mark on American and Canadian history, and belonging to an apparently fast disappearing race, it was small wonder that romance came early to the handsome and gifted young Indian. Shortly after he began his work as Interpreter he met a beautiful English girl of noble family to whom he soon became engaged.

But before the time set for the marriage, Assikinack began to show signs of that disease which so often attacks those accustomed to the freedom of life in the wilds when subjected to the confinement of civilization. A doctor was called. He found the Indian suffering from decline, but feared the effect should he speak the truth. Assikinack, however, looked searchingly into his face—"I see, my friend, I must die," he said simply.

He broke his engagement, gave little gifts of remembrance to his friends, put his affairs in order—all without apparent emotion. It was not until he was back on the Manitoulin Island that the real test of his power to endure his fate with stoicism came to him.

It was a day in midsummer. Before his wigwam on the shore of the bay the Indian sat, gazing at the beauty of woods and water asleep in the noon sunshine. Here in the camping ground of his forefathers he had hoped to find the quiet peace he knew best prepared the soul for its long journey to the spirit land. Instead of that preparatory peace he had found only restlessness and bitter rebellion. For, since his return to the Island, a certain passion of his boyhood and manhood had been constantly in his mind, an ever present torment of never-to-be-fulfilled desire.

He was recalling now the birth and growth of that passion. He remembered how his father, the great Blackbird, according to the custom of his nation had, in the days of his early youth, made him fast for the vision of his destiny, bringing him from time to time while he lay as one dead in his wigwam, only the sips of water necessary to sustain life. At last the vision had appeared. Out of the confusion and delirium of the dreams of his fast had gradually emerged the form of a fair girl. She came to him with song on her beautiful lips—tales of glory, legends and traditions of the Algonquin people. The youth, listening eagerly, believed she foreshadowed the realization of his secret desires; for, from a child he had not only loved to listen to the valorous tales of his race, but he had longed to tell them to those who neither knew nor cared about them. After the vision the longing strengthened, and as he grew into manhood the hope was born that he might be the means of making his tribal history and traditions better known to his white brothers. This is the hope that had made his life in Toronto seem to him the beginning of the fulfilment of his prophetic dream, that made the learning of his lessons, and especially of the difficult English, a constant delight. And now just when his words were beginning to gain the ear of the white man, fatal, quick-destroying disease suddenly claimed him for its own. All other sacrifices—love, friendship, delight in his work as Interpreter—all had seemed easy to make in comparison with the sacrifice of this long-cherished dream. He knew that his people were fast disappearing, and he had believed that his was to be the work of preserving to mankind the story of the valour and beauty and poetry that had always echoed round the campfires of the Algonquins.

He recalled, bitterly enough, the defeat of his hopes. Certain words from one of his teachers at Upper Canada College came unbidden to his mind. As a boy rejoicing in his strength, he had often called himself—much to the delight of his father, the valiant Blackbird—"A Warrior of the Odahwahs." Once, while at school in Toronto, in spirit of playfulness, he signed a composition—"A Warrior of the Odahwahs." The English master had not laughed at him for using the name, but had asked him questions about the change of "Ottawa" to "Odahwah," and then had talked with him about the possibility of his still being a real warrior—although not now with scalping knife and tomahawk—a real warrior in the cause of brave, manly living. He had never forgotten his teacher's words, but to-day they came to him with a new and accusing meaning. Was he putting up to the end as brave and manly a fight as would that ideal "Warrior of the Odahwahs"? He asked himself the question, only to be met by an answer from which his soul shrank.

The long hours passed, and at last the blue of sky and water turned to the opal tints of evening. In the woods above and behind the wigwam the shadows deepened and became full of mystery. Across the bay on the high shore the glow from the western sky touched the trees with reddish gold and made rocks and stones shine like burnished steel. The air suddenly fell cool and keen, bringing renewed strength to the slowly dying Indian. Assikinack's canoe was on the shore. He launched it and went far out over the darkening waters. Lying face downward in the bottom of the little craft he drifted for hours, wrestling the while against the demon of rebellion within him. How death and defeat mocked him. How life and its attendant success lured him. He cursed the fate that had made death and defeat his. Writhing in his agony as if in physical pain, he turned, and his eyes met the panorama above him. The glory of the over-arching heavens struck on his senses with a new and overpowering revelation of wonder and beauty. Here and there white pathways of light crossed the clear dark blue vault—the Aurora—and everywhere—even shining through the pathways—were the stars. It was night. As he gazed, their multitude, stretching on and on, star beyond star, into the furthermost fields of heaven, made him faint and dizzy. His canoe, rocking gently on the bosom of the water, was a mere speck under the arch of mysterious splendour. And he? How poor and mean seemed his whimpering soul amid the eternal vastness and power that encompassed it. Long he lay with his face upturned, drifting in the summer night. To his imagination the white pathways became peopled with spirits. At times the radiance seemed to grow vocal, and he fancied he heard the triumphant shouts of victorious warriors—victorious, not over human foes, but over sin and death. Sometimes he fancied he heard singing, and the voices told him of happy scenes amid which all earthly disappointments were forgotten. Listening, he felt the peace of submission steal over him, only to be followed, again and again, by renewed rebellion and anguish of spirit, while at such times the pathways—the ghost walks from the West—seemed for a moment to be alive with those who taunted and gibed at him for his failure on earth, for his dying like a weak woman, without having accomplished his desire. But always the stars looked down upon him and gave him their message of obedience to a power not his or their own, a message that, in Assikinack's mind, blended with and became a part of his teacher's words. At last, under the stars Assikinack learned submission. When morning dawned the "Warrior of the Odahwahs" had fought his fight and had conquered.

A few hours later Assikinack made his way very slowly through the woods to the Mission at Wikwemikong, there to ask of the holy father Extreme Unction. The latter wished to keep the Indian with him until the end, but Assikinack refused to stay. Leaving an assistant in charge, the priest returned with him to his wigwam. The following extracts from the priest's journal, translated from the French into English, are of interest.

'Priest as I am,' the diary reads, 'Assikinack is daily teaching me lessons of saintly patience. I have seen Indian fortitude before, but never have I seen it combined with so much reasonableness and sweetness—qualities rare in the Indian character.

* * * * *

'Surely Assikinack has in him the stuff out of which poets are made. To-day as he lay watching the sky he said, "How unfathomable and mysterious is that wonderful canopy of blue above us. How wonderful are God's colours in sunlight or in shadow. It seems almost like mocking the Creator to try to reproduce them. Who can paint the softness of yonder cloud, or the ever-changing water with its crests of white, its paths of gold, its great patches of silver, its blues and greens and greys? When I first learned of the white man's God, he seemed to my boyish mind a magician who, with wondrous dyes, made beautiful the earth. And as I watched the greys of winter turn to the first faint blushing of the verdant hues of spring, or as I saw the autumnal colours touch the trees until they flamed in scarlet or shone in gold, I seemed to become, in my own desire for beauty, one with the God who so loved it that always and everywhere He places it for the delight and solace of mankind." After a while he added, "But I fear the eyes of most are sealed to the loveliness everywhere about them. I wish they might learn to look at earth and sky and see."

'To-day Assikinack spoke of the waning eloquence of his people:—"I have often heard it said that my father, the Blackbird, was the last orator of the Ottawas. Yet there are many clever young men in our tribe to-day. Is it because they do not go to the true teacher of eloquence that they do not learn its secret? I think it is, they forget that nature is the teacher. It was owing to their deep contemplation of her in their silent retreats in the days of their youth that the old Indian orators acquired the habit of carefully arranging their thoughts; when instead of shouting to drunken companions, they listened to the warblings of birds, whilst the grandeur and the beauties of the forests and the majestic beauties of the clouds which appear like mountains of granite floating in the air, the golden tints of the summer evening sky, and all the changes of nature, which then possessed a mysterious significance, combined to furnish ample matter for reflection to the contemplative youth.

* * * * *

'All day Assikinack had been strangely restless, yet it hardly seems the restlessness of approaching death. Twice he has said to me, "There is trouble somewhere, there is a great battle going on. I feel it in the air."

* * * * *

'It is two weeks since I wrote the above. Since then I have had to be at Wikwemikong. On my return to Assikinack to-day I found him much weaker. A steamboat came to the village opposite the place where Assikinack has his wigwam at Bushwa, and I went over to see if I could get alleviating medicine for the sick man. From the captain I learned the most extraordinary thing. Two weeks ago to-day—the very day when Assikinack insisted that a battle was going on somewhere—a terrible conflict between the North and South in the war that is now going on took place at Antietam. When I told Assikinack his eyes flashed with martial spirit. After a while he said: "I hope the North will win. But after all, slavery needs be only of the body. The man who can gaze into the far sources and depths of the sky above him need never be a slave in spirit. God placed the wide heavens above the earth as a symbol of the freedom of our souls."

* * * * *

'This morning Assikinack asked me to take him in the canoe to that part of the bay where, it is said, bottom has never been found. It is called "Waning," meaning hollow or cave, and this added to the Ottawa for God, "Manito," gives to the bay its peculiar name of "Manitowaning." I took the poor fellow, fearful though I was that he could not live through the effort of getting in and out of the canoe. When I reached the place which he indicated, I stopped paddling. Assikinack listened attentively. "You hear no voices from below the water?" he asked me. When I assured him that I heard nothing but the gentle lap of the waves against the canoe he seemed relieved. "This bottomless part of the bay is the abode of evil spirits who cease not to tempt a human soul as long as there is hope of gaining it." "You are sure no voice comes?" I crossed myself and listened. No voice could be heard. In this gifted Assikinack what a strange mixture we have of Indian superstition and Christian grace.

'For the rest of the day Assikinack seemed strangely comforted. He was very weak, and lay on a blanket looking up at the flying clouds of the autumn sky. Often I held the crucifix before him and prayed. Frequently he turned his eyes to it but the only word he uttered was "victory." When twilight came he asked not to be moved. I covered his body with a blanket and tried to raise him in order that he might look on the emblem of our crucified Lord, but he kept his face turned toward the stars which shone clear in the cold November night. Suddenly a stream of dancing light shot up from the northern horizon. Then another and another. With a loud shout of joy Assikinack, raising himself, cried as in greeting "Manobozho's fires. The warrior of the Odahwahs has conquered." And fell back—dead.'

* * * * *

In the graveyard of the Jesuit Mission at Wikwemikong on the Grand Manitoulin Island may be seen the white cross which marks the resting place of Francis Assikinack, who still lives in the memory of a few men and women, now old, as one whose inherent gentleness and whose delight in the ways of peace and in the things of nature made his self-selected title "A Warrior of the Odahwahs" seem, to them, strangely inappropriate. Perhaps this little history of his fight and victory over the rebellion of his spirit against what, at first, seemed God's untimely call, will reconcile them to it.

IX.

EARLY HISTORY OF THE BEAVER VALLEY.

By C. W. Hartman.

Collingwood Township is the north-east municipality of the County of Grey; its northerly limit is the south shore of the Georgian Bay and it adjoins the County of Simcoe to the east. When first surveyed it was called "Alta" from the great height of land within it known as the Blue Mountains, but Captain Moberly, a retired naval officer, when drawing his grant of land within the township, disliked the name "Alta" and persuaded the Governor, Sir John Colborne, to change it to Collingwood and the adjoining township called Zero to St. Vincent, after the two great naval heroes.

Associated with this part of Grey County is the fertile fruit and farming district known as the Beaver Valley, along the line of the Beaver River whose southerly branch comes through Flesherton, and five miles northward unites with the main stream below Eugenia Falls. This branch takes its rise near Rob Roy in Osprey Township, flows through Feversham, supplying power for mills at that point, and six miles west at Eugenia drops four hundred feet into the Beaver Valley, thence flowing on a course north and east through the villages of Kimberley, Heathcote, Clarksburg and Thornbury, it empties into the Georgian Bay. The business places of Clarksburg and Thornbury are the gateways to the valley from the northern end. It has a natural roadway, with little or no grade, extending twenty-five miles southerly to Flesherton. The County Council are now building a permanent road that will be the recognized highway connecting the southern part of the county with the Georgian Bay, and giving the citizens of the northern district easy access to the country lying south without going over the mountain roads, and an alternative road to reach Owen Sound and the West. The Hydro-Electric Commissioners have at present an artificial lake of twenty-five hundred acres and power house at Eugenia, supplying light and power along the line from Collingwood to Owen Sound.

The first historic reference to the land that now constitutes the County of Grey that I have been able to find is in February, 1616, when Champlain, after reaching the Georgian Bay by way of the Ottawa and French Rivers, spent the winter among the Hurons near Penetanguishene and visited an Indian village located in a valley of the Blue Mountains.

The next (and it is traditional history) is during the war of 1812, when a force of British with a small gunboat were located at the mouth of the Nottawasaga River. A young army surgeon with others skirted the south shore of the Georgian Bay in canoes and were much impressed with the natural beauty of the lake shores at the foot of the Blue Mountains, nine miles west of what is now Collingwood, where they also discovered a mineral spring at the point, whose waters are very similar to the celebrated Harrowgate waters of England. The location possessed a small harbour with an excellent bathing beach. Dr. Wm. Rees later became possessed of this property, erected a substantial building and established a sanatorium, which he named "Delphi," but did not live long afterward, being at that time an old man. The original sanatorium was destroyed by fire, after the death of Dr. Rees, in about the year 1880, but it was rebuilt by the late Thomas Fields for a summer resort and was recently purchased by the Dominion Council of the Young Women's Christian Association as one of their summer camps.

In the year 1833, Charles Rankin was employed by the Government to survey the wild land west of Simcoe County. He at once procured supplies and moved his family (temporarily) to Lora Bay, a pretty spot a couple of miles west of Thornbury, and he thus became the first settler in the township. An incident of the survey is worth preserving. Chief Wahbatick, of the Ojibways at Cape Croker, called upon Mr. Rankin and ordered the surveying party to desist and leave "his land." Mr. Rankin reasoned with him, showing him that the Government did not profess to claim the land further west than Vail's Point, but that up to that headland they had bought out the Indian rights. Wahbatick had probably never consented to the transfer, as, in after years, when no longer considered as a chief, he dissented from the surrender of the Saugeen Peninsula to Lord Bury. Be this as it may, he threatened the party, but having implicit faith in his "Great Father" at York, Sir John Colborne, the Lieutenant-Governor of Upper Canada, he would first try peaceful terms. He departed, and within the short space of about ten days reappeared having been by canoe and on foot to York (Toronto) in the meantime. The clerks at the Crown Land Office had imposed on the fiery chief and had given him a paper which they asserted would cause all unauthorized trespassers to decamp, and thus got rid of him. The paper was but a printed handbill, "Lands for Sale," and this he carried carefully folded in his bosom all the way from York. He "served it" upon Mr. Rankin with all due ceremony, but seeing no immediate effect, grew confidential and admitting he was "buckatae" (hungry) got something to eat and drink, and made peace with the party. It is largely to an article by Richard Carroll that I am indebted for being able to present many details of the early history of this part of Grey.*

In the same year (1833), Richard Maguire . . . . located on the base line near Lora Bay and began clearing a farm. A man named Brazan (Brazier?) shortly afterward settled at Craigleith and was Maguire's nearest neighbour to the east, ten miles away. The nearest mill was at Holland Landing over eighty miles distant . . . . In 1839 a man named Grady settled on a lot north-east of Maguire's, made a small clearing, but did not live long to enjoy it . . . . His was the first death, as far as known, in the Township of Collingwood . . . . Charles Maguire was born at the old homestead in the winter of 1837, and was the first white child born in the township. He became an industrious farmer, owned a splendid farm,

*The reader is referred to the original article by Richard Carroll, in the Xmas number of the *Standard Reflector* (Thornbury and Clarksburg), 1901, for various items respecting the history of the locality, quoted by the author, and not reprinted here.

part of the homestead of his father, only retired a few years ago, and is still alive and residing in Calgary with his children . . . . In 1846 Mr. Chas. Rankin sold his claim at Lora Bay to his uncle, Major Stuart, who wished to settle down in this part of the British Dominions . . . . In 1847 Mr. Heman Hurlburt . . . . settled on the town line between Collingwood and St. Vincent, about three miles west of the Maguires. He took a deep interest in the spiritual as well as the temporal welfare of the early settlers. It was his custom . . . . early Sunday morning to start on foot for the Whitelaw settlement and another small settlement on the 9th line of St. Vincent, preach two sermons and return home the same night . . . . In the following year Mr. Richard Rorke settled near Heathcote (then called Williamstown) some six miles from the Maguire settlement . . . . He was the first school teacher in Heathcote and the first Clerk of Collingwood Township, which office he held for many years, giving the public a splendid service. His son, the late Major Joseph Rorke, was afterwards Reeve of Collingwood Township, Warden of the County of Grey, and member of the Ontario Legislature. Another son, Colonel Edward Rorke still survives.

In 1848 Solomon D. Olmstead came to Collingwood Township. When surveying the Township Mr. Rankin left a block of nine hundred acres at the mouth of the Beaver River, where there was a splendid water power, for a town site, and Mr. Olmstead took up the water power claim at Thornbury . . . . The settlers were so pleased at the prospect of a mill that they turned out and built a house for Mr. Olmstead and in two weeks had him comfortably housed . . . . In 1851 Mr. Sol. Olmstead induced his brother, Rufus, to sell his farm in the old settlement and take a half share in the milling business, which he did, and brought with him the next spring a lad of sixteen years, named Richard Carroll who later became the principal builder in the district, as well as one of the leading citizens, and whose article on the early history of this part of Grey has been already referred to . . . . At the entrance of the Beaver River west of the point of the Blue Mountains, where they arrived in due time, they met a company of surveyors under direction of a Mr. Gifford, P.L.S., who were surveying the town plot afterwards called Thornbury. The next year a small store and post office was established by S. D. Olmstead. The mail came at that time once a week from Barrie by way of the Brock Road to Williamstown, Thornbury, Meaford and Owen Sound . . . . In 1860, Collingwood Township produced one-half of all the fall wheat in the county . . . . In 1856 a Mr. Donough opened a store on the east side of the river . . . .

In 1858 Mr. W. J. Marsh purchased the business of Mr. Donough and induced Mr. Henry Lyne to open another store. Both these men were of a high type and came from the County of York, but Mr. Marsh was born in England. He founded the Village of Clarksburg, one mile inland among a number of splendid water powers on the Beaver River, bringing in W. A. Clark, after whom Clarksburg was named, who built a large woollen mill that was a leading industry of the locality until 1909 when it was destroyed by fire. Mr. John Tyson purchased a water privilege adjoining the woollen mill and erected a first class mill which has been refitted from time to time and to-day is one of the up-to-date mills of the county.

The Thornbury mills . . . . after the death of Mr. T. Andrews a few years ago, were bought by the Town of Thornbury and leased to the

Georgian Bay Milling Co., but unfortunately, like many frame mills, were burned shortly afterward.

The early settlers had the luxuries of fish and game that can only be found in limited numbers now. Wild pigeons, then plentiful, are now extinct; speckled trout five pounds and under were plentiful. The late Chief Justice Falconbridge, who was an enthusiastic angler, spent some of his early days in the section when the country was new, and in conversation not long before his death he said that the Beaver River was one of the best trout streams that he had ever known, and that he knew every trout hole from the mouth of the river for five miles up.

In 1862 the villages of Clarksburg and Thornbury united in purchasing a beautiful site for a cemetery which has been enlarged and beautified since then. The by-laws provided that all money received for sale of plots should be expended in improvements and that no dividends be paid to shareholders. It is to-day one of the best kept cemeteries in the county, and is a monument to the wisdom and foresight of its founders.

Collingwood Township has large deposits of oil producing shale at the foot of the Blue Mountains on the shores of the Georgian Bay. As long ago as 1859 works were erected for obtaining illuminating and lubricating oils—a building 100 feet long by 48 feet wide; 24 longitudinal cast iron retorts were set in two ranges and heated by means of wood, of which 25 cords were said to have been required weekly. The shale broken into fragments was heated from two to three hours, from eight to ten charges being distilled daily and made to yield 250 gallons of crude oil corresponding to about three per cent. of the rock. By a further continuance of the heat a small portion more oil was obtained. The broken shale cost twenty cents per ton and the crude oil cost the producers fourteen cents per gallon. When rectified and deodorized there was about 50 per cent. waste, the remainder being heavy and suitable for lubricating purposes. The owners were in successful operation in 1860, but the discovery of petroleum in other parts rendered the works unprofitable and shortly afterward the buildings were destroyed by fire. Since that date shale oil has been produced in other parts of the world at a profit and it is asserted that there are by-products in the distillation of the rock that will pay the cost of the oil. It was largely due to the enterprise of the late Colonel W. D. Pollard that the oil works were started. The retorts were cast in Good's foundry at Hamilton, and the fire bricks were imported from Wisconsin, and together with all machinery were brought to the site of the oil works near Craigleith by boats.

The late Dr. G. W. Hurlburt, of Thornbury, was the first physician to commence practice in the locality. He was succeeded a few years later by Dr. R. H. Hunt, who was a gold and silver medallist at Toronto University, and who became known far and wide not only as a skilful physician but the personal friend of everybody. He died in 1894 after practising here for 25 years. Both of the early physicians were men of skill and sympathy whose good works still live although they have passed out. Jerome Farewell established the first newspaper called the *Union Standard* in 1870, and Mr. T. H. Dyre, present Crown Attorney, was the first barrister.

In 1855 Andrew G. Fleming, a Scotchman, with a family of eight children all gifted with abilities far beyond the average, settled at Craigleith.

One son, Mr. Alexander Fleming, now over eighty years, and one daughter, Mrs. Jos. Goodchild, still survive. The late Sir Sandford Fleming, at one time Chief Engineer of the Canadian Pacific Railway, and later Chancellor of Queen's University, was one of the sons.

Among other early settlers were the Creelman family, of Scotch descent but coming here from the Maritime Provinces, a family of twelve children, brilliant men and women. Among the best known were Adam Creelman, K.C., Solicitor for the Canadian Pacific Railway and Dr. G. C. Creelman, President of the Ontario Agricultural College.

The farms on the Blue Mountains of Collingwood Township were settled largely by Highland Scotchmen, while the hills on the west side of the Valley in Euphrasia Township were early occupied by men from Ireland who brought with them industry and thrift and occasionally some other characteristics from the Emerald Isle.

The first reeve of Euphrasia was the late James Kerr, known to everybody as Squire Kerr. He was for a long time the principal Magistrate for the district and was called upon to settle disputes of all kinds usually dispensing justice tempered with mercy. James Patterson was also an early reeve of Euphrasia and held the position for some years. He was also Warden of Grey County and an excellent citizen. Mr. Robt. Myles was later Chief Magistrate of Euphrasia for many years.

The Beaver Valley, including parts of Collingwood and Euphrasia, has long been known as an exceptionally good agricultural part, but also one of the leading fruit districts of Ontario. Peaches grown in Clarksburg were awarded first place at the World's Fair in Chicago, and in "Picturesque Canada" (Vol. II, p. 574) the Beaver Valley is referred to as possessing the finest climate and being the best peach-growing district in Canada. It has produced the best quality of peaches, and the Northern Spy apple is grown here to perfection, but so far the peach trees are not sufficiently hardy to make orchards of this fruit (exclusively) a profitable investment. Apricots and the best quality of plums are, however, grown in abundance.

Many of the early settlers were men of the highest type, the names of White, Shore, Parkinson, Irwin, Wright, Hewgill, Eaton, McDonald, Lougheed, Malcolm, Carscadden, Vickers, Cruickshanks, Reekie, Dinsmore, Milne, Spaul, Marsh, Foster, Walters and many others in addition to the public men already referred to having been indelibly stamped in the community in which they lived. Although they have long since passed over to their reward it is the privilege of those who enjoy the fruits of their labour to measure up as far as possible to the high standards of citizenship of some of the men who hewed their homes out of the forests of Collingwood Township and vicinity.

X.
EARLY HISTORY OF MEAFORD AND ITS DISTRICT.
By Dr. J. D. Hammill.

The Town of Meaford separated from the Township of St. Vincent on March 30, 1874. So Meaford is not an old town, and to give the early historical events we shall have to include the township.

The Township of St. Vincent was surveyed by Deputy-Surveyor Chas. Rankin in the year 1833. The block of land for the town site of Meaford was afterwards surveyed in 1845 by the late W. Gibbard. Mr. Gibbard, it is said, deemed it fitting to name the principal village after his country seat, which was called Meaford. And the authorities named the principal streets after admirals and naval heroes, as follows: Trowbridge Street, Bayfield Street, Nelson Street, Collingwood Street, Parker Street, Cook Street, Sykes Street, Boucher Street and St. Vincent Street.

Meaford did not grow very rapidly. In fact, it was nothing more than a wilderness up to 1848. George Chantler, who is still a resident of the town, and who will be 94 years of age in October, 1920, landed in Meaford on April 30, 1844. For him and others milk and potatoes was the only diet, straw was used for bed and anything they could get served as a cover.

Capt. Workman is said to have been the second settler. He received 900 acres of land along the Georgian Bay from the Crown Lands Department. The deed was issued in 1856 and signed by Lieutenant-Governor Head. I mention the above because a part of this land is within the town limits and a large portion of it belongs to the late C. R. Sing's estate.

Mr. Sing came to this vicinity in 1846, and in 1847 started a carding mill in the basement of Purdy's mill. Then he built a mill of his own, and George Chantler built a fulling mill for him, the first in this part of the country.

The first postmaster in Meaford was Wm. Stephenson, and the post office was just north of the late W. F. C. Arlidge's residence. But it is said that the first post office was really at Workman's Point, and was moved later to Bayfield Street as described above. Mr. Stephenson's and his wife's remains are buried at the end of the lot, and the grave is still protected by a little board fence. Mr. Stephenson died about 1850. Then there was a race between the late Jesse Wright and the late D. L. Layton for the position of postmaster.

In 1845 the wharf was started by Wm. Stephenson, the late postmaster. It is said that George Chantler's father had the first mill.

The Corley family and the McFarlane family came to Meaford about 1848. Wm. Carnahan and his family settled in St. Vincent the same year.

In 1855 Alexander Milne came to Meaford. Mrs. Alexander Thompson was then about twelve years old. Her brother, Alexander Milne, was the first wharfinger.

The Raymond family came in 1855. The late James Cleland came in 1856, carrying his outfit on his back. James Randle settled here in 1863 and Wm. Butchart in the same year, and J. S. Wilson in 1868. James Randle says that in 1863 the village contained less than 500 in population.

A survey of Cape Rich for a town site was made by the late Wm. Gibbard, the plan of which is still in the office of the Town Clerk, Mr. G. C. Albery, and may be seen by anyone. However, as the plan provided no protection for boats, it was not considered.

In 1863 Meaford's business places, as well as the post office, were on Bayfield Street, but building was commencing on Sykes Street. The *Monitor* of June 19, 1873 (Watt and McLaren, proprietors), gave an outline of the progress of Meaford since 1868, and mentions the names of those in business then located on Sykes Street. Among them are the names of the following deceased citizens and of business places: T. W. Stubbs; Peter Fuller; Mr. Soper, gunsmith; T. Bradford, hotelkeeper; Mr. Jordan, saddler; Dr. Hall; Mr. Blanchard, baker; Matthew Robinson; Hector McDonald, saddler; Samuel Carson's shoe shop. Mention is also made of the splendid block on the corner of Nelson Street, built by H. Chisholm and Co., and of the British Hotel, owned by John Lang; the two storey brick building owned by Peter Fuller, then occupied by the Molsons Bank; the Trout block; the Milne block; Thomas Punkett's block; James Stovel's shop; the *Monitor* office built in 1867 by Mr. Pilgrem; Mr. Hurd's building; Joseph Bell & Co.'s drug store of two storeys and McIntosh's surgery.

The large addition to the Meaford Hotel was barely finished when the sad death of the late John Paul took place, his age being 69 years and 10 months. His first hotel was the one built by the late Mr. Stephenson, postmaster, and stood just to the north of the late Mr. Arlidge's residence, but was burned in a few weeks after it was completed. Mr. Paul then moved to Nelson Street, where after about three years, his property was also burned. The late Mr. Paul then purchased the hotel site now occupied by the Paul House. The late E. Sewell also built a two storey building with residence above. Other business houses were those of W. H. McCartee, W. H. Tait, A. Tait, Monk & Green's marble works; F. Livingstone's hotel, Law's factory on the site of the present Methodist Church, H. Helstrop's wagon shop and many others.

Meaford was incorporated March 30th, 1874, and at once elected a council with the late Col. W. D. Pollard, barrister, as its first mayor. Lorenzo Londry, was a member of this council, as also was J. J. Johnston, who will be eighty-five years old next September. Other members were D. L. Layton, Thos. Harris, Frank Law, Elliot Thompson, Jas. Stewart, Reeve; Alexander Thompson, Deputy Reeve; also John Hill, Councillor.

The above council at once set to work to improve the streets and sidewalks, and the town was built up very fast. In 1882, however, the west side of Sykes Street was burned. But before the ashes were cold, building operations commenced, and the present fine brick buildings were the result of the fire. In 1883 the block on the east side of Sykes Street was also burned and the buildings now standing were erected.

The late John Albery was appointed clerk of the town and the late C. R. Sing was reeve of the township, and some years later was elected mayor of the Town of Meaford.

There is yet much to be told of the progress of the town, but I do not want to weary you.

The extension of the G. T. R. from Collingwood and the improvement of the harbour and wharf are subjects which, perhaps, some one will take up and add with what I have left out.

XI.

THE MUNICIPAL LOAN FUND IN UPPER CANADA.

By J. Murray Clark, M.A., LL.D., K.C., Toronto.

The terrible collapse of Russia, where many of the pernicious fallacies, loudly advocated in Canada, were put into practice with disastrous results has, when rightly interpreted, many needed lessons for us. The conditions in Russia are, however, different from those in Canada, and the genius and traditions of the Slav quite different from those of the Anglo-Celt, so that perhaps we can learn more readily the lessons we need from our own long history and varied experiences.

Since the beginning of the present era of waste and extravagance I have often felt there is much to learn from the forgotten experience of our fathers with what was called the Municipal Loan Fund. The author of this disastrous scheme was Sir Francis Hincks, one of the outstanding public men of that day. He had in some respects genuine ability and, in matters which he understood, rendered considerable useful public service, but he was an idealist and a theorist without any practical grasp of the rigorous laws and unyielding facts of finance. He was patriotic and well-meaning, but his patriotism and good intentions did not save the country from the inevitable consequences of his scheme which those able to think clearly on matters of finance perceived from the beginning. He possessed in an eminent degree that fatal fluency of persuasive speech with which so many of our politicians are endowed, and swayed the people for whom he expressed, and probably felt, sincere devotion, with superficial catch-words and glittering generalities not founded on the stern realities of economic laws. The confidence he inspired only enabled him to do infinitely more mischief than would otherwise have been caused by his scheme, and did not protect the people from the losses and distress resulting from disregard of sound business principles.

The enterprise was inaugurated with great eclat on the 10th November, 1852, by the statute known to lawyers as 16 Victoria, Cap. 22, which provided credits for the municipalities of Upper Canada, now Ontario, on certain terms and conditions.

The municipalities were to pass by-laws which were advocated by the demagogues of that day.

Upon the passing of such a by-law as was provided for, the municipality borrowed the money specified from the Province which, in turn, borrowed from abroad. Those who warned the people that borrowed money would have to be repaid with interest were denounced as pessimists. By-laws were passed in many municipalities and those who shouted for lavish expenditures, for the time being, prevailed. It was not popular to point out that permanent prosperity could not be achieved by spending borrowed money. Indeed, as was said by an observant contemporary, no one in those days could be elected a poundkeeper in certain parts of this Province unless, to use his own picturesque language, " he shouted with both hands for the Loan Fund."

The moneys were borrowed and spent but the day of inexorable reckoning duly arrived. Some municipalities could not, and some would not, pay the interest due the Province, but the Province had to pay the interest due its creditors and to raise the necessary funds by taxation. On the 1st January, 1873, less than twenty-one years after the scheme was started with a great hurrah, there were arrears amounting to $12,628,657.05. We now talk in billions, but in those days debts amounting to over $12,000,000 were serious. The municipalities where wise counsels prevailed, and which had not borrowed from the Fund, complained that they were compelled to pay heavy taxes to meet the interest on moneys in respect of which other municipalities were in default.

Speaking on the subject in 1873, Sir Oliver Mowat (Mr. Oliver Mowat he then was) said: " The effect was to diminish the value of municipal securities generally, and to corrupt the moral sense of the people with reference to moral obligations." Sir Oliver Mowat did not overlook the material loss, but rightly regarded the moral loss as tremendously more vital.

In several Ontario constituencies candidates appealed and, sad to relate, appealed successfully for support on the ground that they would defy the Government to collect the amount due in respect of such loans, and the disastrous habit was formed of repudiating just obligations.

This habit persists and fundamentally is of the same nature as the act of the Germans in regarding the Treaty guaranteeing the neutrality of Belgium as a " scrap of paper."

The United States Constitution forbids legislation impairing the obligation of a contract; but in Canada, apart from the power of Disallowance, the security against such vicious legislation depends largely on the " moral sense of the people with reference to moral obligations."

In dealing with this subject one of our ablest jurists made the significant remark that our Provincial Legislatures within the sphere of their jurisdiction " are bound by no law, human or divine." This constitutes an additional reason why the statesmanlike and sagacious observation of Sir Oliver Mowat should be studied by the present generation.

The injustice of making the thrifty and wisely guided municipalities pay for the default of those who had been misled by the demagogues of the day, was so keenly felt that the plan was devised of forgiving certain municipalities which had borrowed more moderately, reducing the indebtedness of those which had borrowed heavily, and of voting $3,388,777.40 to be distributed among the other municipalities. The total net loss to what is now Ontario was over $13,000,000, though the taxpayers had been solemnly assured the Province would not lose a cent.

Of the first class was the Town of Woodstock which borrowed $100,000. The authoritative comment made about twenty years after in regard to Woodstock was " Its investment became an entire loss and the work in aid of which the stock was taken has been abandoned, and there is no probability it will ever be revived. The company is hopelessly insolvent and the whole undertaking has collapsed never to be revived."

The loss was assumed by the Province and the debt of Woodstock cancelled by the Municipal Loan Fund Act.

In the second class was St. Catharines which borrowed more heavily. Only part of its indebtedness was cancelled and the municipality had to pay the balance of $160,571.52. The municipality loaned $166,000 of borrowed money to six local companies. In the official return it is stated as to four of these, "No revenue derived and stock worthless." As to the fifth, the record is, "Road sold by Sheriff in 1862." All these enterprises which ended in disaster had been only ten years before confidently commended to the electors by those who guided the destinies of the municipality and boasted of their devotion to the interests of "the people."

Toronto was not affected by the prevailing madness of the time and did not borrow from the Municipal Loan Fund, and, in consequence, received a considerable sum ($165,984.08) in the final distribution.

On inquiring as to the reason for this good fortune I find that in 1852 Mr. John George Bowes, a successful wholesale merchant, was Mayor of Toronto. Indeed, for many years thereafter the municipal affairs of Toronto were directed by men of high reputation and large calibre who each had made a success of his own business. The list of the Mayors of Toronto during those years included John Beverly Robinson, George William Allan, William Henry Boulton, Oliver Mowat and William Barclay McMurrich, who each did his part in laying deep and true the foundations of Toronto's prosperity and greatness.[*]

In Hamilton, the demagogues of the day won, though the borrowing was not from the Government but from British investors. In less than ten years Hamilton made default and could not pay the coupons which matured on 1st July, 1861. This, it will be observed, is less than ten years after the by-laws authorizing the expenditures were carried with great enthusiasm.

The municipal authorities of Hamilton requested the Government of the Province of Canada, which then included what is now Quebec, to come to the rescue and to save the credit of the country. The interest was paid by the Government of the day. On the 6th March, 1893, the Dominion, as the successor of the late Province of Canada, filed a claim before the Board of Arbitrators appointed to deal with the accounts as between Ontario, Quebec and the Dominion arising out of Confederation; Ontario acknowledged liability for the amount which a few years later was paid by this Province, nearly half a century after the folly of the fifties.

There were further defaults, judgments were recorded against the corporation, and in 1863 Hamilton was in the hands of the Sheriff. The levying of a rate to pay its creditors was delayed by the zealous City Clerk who took the books, assessment rolls, etc., to White Sulphur Springs (now Clifton Springs) in the State of New York, beyond the jurisdiction of the Canadian Courts.

The time so secured was wisely utilized by the able City Solicitor, Mr. Burton, afterwards Mr. Justice Burton, who negotiated a compromise with its creditors afterwards embodied in "The City of Hamilton Debenture Act, 1864," 27-28 Vic., Chap. 72, assented to on 30th June, 1864. This Statute passed by the Parliament of the late Province of Canada recited a

---

[*]Some comments on the fundamental principles involved and on the relation of the developments to Socialism and Bolshevism, and to British ideals of liberty and justice, are omitted.

Petition of Hamilton representing that the City had issued debentures for £104,600 Sterling, and £91,470 Currency, in all nearly a million dollars for various objects "which from various causes have proved to be unremunerative;" also debentures for about another million dollars, for waterworks (substantially constructed under the direction of the late Mr. T. C. Keefer), and for "other local improvements from none of which is any adequate return at present received." The Petition of Hamilton stated that there were "considerable arrears of interest," "judgments," "much litigation," and that "the finances of the Corporation have consequently become embarrassed."

The Statute authorized debentures payable in 30 years (1894) at a reduced rate of interest (gradually, however, to be increased) which the creditors, or at least a majority of them, were willing to accept.

By the City of Hamilton Debenture Act of 1893, 56 Vic., Cap. 65, the City of Hamilton was authorized to renew some of these debentures for a further period of 40 years, i.e., until April, 1934.

An elaborate report on the Municipal Loan Fund prepared by the Hon. E. B. Wood, was presented to the Ontario Legislature and printed as Sessional Paper No. 8 of 35 Vic., 1871-2, and the details of the scheme by which the Fund was wound up appeared in the Sessional Papers of 1874, No. 13. Both of these historic Sessional Papers are worthy of careful study by all interested in, and especially by all responsible for the financial affairs of Ontario municipalities.

A few years after this closing of the matter, viz., in 1883, when the details were fresh in the minds of all, the results were described as follows: "Important sections of the Province were retarded in the march of improvement and property there was depreciated in value."

It is to be borne in mind that before the disastrous Municipal Loan Fund was inaugurated, Upper Canada was making steady and indeed rapid progress. It was being settled by an energetic population, and, before the retardation above referred to, was making as satisfactory progress as, for instance, Ohio. The fact that some Ontario municipalities have now to pay about double the rate of taxation in such Ohio cities as Cleveland, is a serious handicap in the keen competition we must shortly face.

Some of the lessons to be gathered from a consideration of the history of the Municipal Loan Fund are:

(1) That moneys borrowed or guaranteed by municipalities as well as by individuals must be repaid, and with interest.

(2) That permanent prosperity cannot be founded upon the extravagant expenditure of borrowed money.

At the present moment expenditures of public money are popular, and professional politicians, who can bring great pressure to bear upon the authorities, are able, in the present state of the public mind, to secure more votes by advocating the expenditure and waste of public moneys than by advocating the saving thereof. For the time being, economy is unpopular, but, judging from the experience above referred to, this will not last many years, because the time for repayment of the moneys now being borrowed with interest is arriving with sure and steady foot.

Many people are at present under a complete misapprehension as to the effect of such public debts and are acting under the delusion that they can throw the burden of taxation upon other people. They forget that all taxes must, with exceptions which are not really important, be paid by the producers and consumers. The producers, in order to continue to produce, must throw the burden of such taxation on the consumers who ultimately must certainly pay. Sound reasoning should convince everyone that the burden of taxation caused by the prevailing extravagance will be seriously increased and that such taxation will inevitably increase the present high cost of living. This, however, will certainly appear by experience, and it may safely be stated that in a very short time extravagant expenditures of public money will not be popular in this country.

People have not yet sufficiently reflected on the fact that now, as in the days of the Municipal Loan Fund, as a general rule (of course there are exceptions) it costs a municipality or other public body from 30 to 60 per cent. more than a private company to do the same amount of work. One of the reasons for this is that a glib talker can often secure the management of public business without much regard to his competency.

An illuminating example of this occurred some years ago in Toronto. According to the opinion of an expert alienist, the speech of a candidate for the office of Mayor contained evidence of incipient insanity and the alienist predicted that the candidate would be in the asylum in so many months, and added that the speech containing the evidence of insanity would elect the candidate Mayor. The candidate was in an asylum within the time specified, and died there, but after the speech, animated by the undue optimism of incipient insanity, the voters elected him Mayor. The people of Toronto are still paying the penalty in the shape of burdensome taxation, and will continue to pay to the third and fourth generation.

Generally, people pay little heed to a waste of from 30 to 60 per cent., but do express some temporary alarm when there appears a waste of public money of from 90 to 95 per cent. of the amount expended. It is well, therefore, to emphasize that, as in the case of the Municipal Loan Fund, the grievous burden caused by such waste is largely borne by the small property owners and by consumers in general. Very few benefit by the waste of public money; but whether they realize it or not, the mass of the people ultimately pay and then wonder why the cost of living is so high. The cost of living must, of necessity, become higher and higher until the prevailing waste and extravagance are replaced by thrift and economy,* the excessive exodus from the farm to the city checked, indeed, superseded by a considerable movement from the city to the farm, and production, especially of foodstuffs, greatly increased. Sooner or later the majority of the people will discover that the plans of the agitators to throw the heavy burden of taxation on others are futile. We shall all, sooner or later, if not by logic, then by stern experience, learn that if we sow the wind we shall reap the whirlwind.

In the case of a private company the consequences of waste and extravagance speedily manifest themselves, and if competent management is not provided, insolvency ensues. There is no patient taxpayer to make good any deficits that may result from lack of foresight or energy, or from disregard of business principles. But economic laws are as inexorable as the laws of chemistry, and, after all, no more in public than in private matters

---

*This was written in May, 1919.

can people escape the consequences of their acts, and that is the real lesson of the Municipal Loan Fund.

Far-sighted men perceived the results of what was proposed, and warned the people. In the course of years what they said was proved true. Similar warnings now go unheeded; the exhortations of the Minister of Finance to "work and save," and similar warnings by his predecessor, Mr. Fielding, are by many (perhaps at present by the overwhelming majority) treated with unconcealed derision. We profit less than we should from the lessons of history, but we of this generation will again learn for ourselves that the consequences of waste and extravagance can by no devices be avoided.

XII.

A TRIAL FOR HIGH TREASON IN 1838.

BY THE HONOURABLE WILLIAM RENWICK RIDDELL, LL.D., F.R.S.C., ETC.

The extraordinary fiasco of Mackenzie's Rebellion in 1837 had unhappy results for many real lovers of their country: some misguided persons lost their lives, many were exiled, many lost their lands, and not a few were in deadly peril of death or exile, but fortunately escaped the worst.

It is of some of these last that this paper is intended specially to deal.

Mackenzie's attempt to take possession of Toronto occurred early in December, 1837,[1] and rumours of his operations ran like wildfire throughout the Province.

In the Township of Eramosa a meeting was called of the inhabitants at the Central Schoolhouse about seven miles from Guelph to consider what was to be done. The meeting, held on December 7, was attended by some sixty or seventy persons of all politics. James Benham was called to the chair—a man of high standing in the community and one who desired reform in the Government; he appears to have called the meeting. James Peters was appointed secretary—the Township Clerk and of equally high standing and like views.[2] Benham addressed the meeting and a paper was largely signed by those present. At once the story went abroad that some of those who had been at the meeting had there plotted armed insurrection and were about to carry out their treasonable scheme.

Walter King, who had spoken at the meeting, laid an information against James Benham, James Peters and others before "Squire" John Inglis, a Justice of the Peace in Guelph.[3] Inglis was a warm supporter of the Government and took proceedings at once. Following the old practice of Fielding and other English magistrates he gathered some thirty men under arms to "break up the rebel nest in Eramosa." Before daybreak, December 14, 1837,[4] a detachment under Inglis arrested Peters and scarcely gave him

---

[1] The outbreak was arranged for Thursday, December 7 1837; but Monday, December 4, the Rebels were advancing and Col. Moodie was killed. Tuesday morning was spent in parleying and that evening all was over.

[2] Of James Peters it is said that he was one of the very few in this most drunken Province who never used alcoholic beverages, even at "bees." An "active, energetic, consistent Congregationalist, a Deacon in the Church at Speedside from its formation, always in the front ranks of the progressive, liberal-minded citizens of his time." *Guelph Weekly Mercury and Advertiser*, Aug. 2, 1906. The late Dr. George Peters, of Toronto, was a grandson; and Dr. Janet Armstrong, of Cobourg, is a granddaughter.

[3] At that time, and for years thereafter, in the country places of this Province the title "Squire" was given popularly to an active Justice of the Peace; the custom is not yet dead. They have not yet attained the title of "Judge."

[4] James Peters, in an account in the *Guelph Weekly Mercury and Advertiser*, Aug. 2, 1906, says he was arrested "before daylight one morning, that is on the 13th of December, 1837"; but Benham in an almost contemporary statement says, "on the night of the 13th or the morning of the 14th December, 1837, John Inglis, Esquire, one of Her Majesty's Justices of the Peace, with a body of armed men amounting to 30 or more entered our dwelling houses, with fixed bayonets and arrested James Benham," etc.

time to dress. Next the cavalcade of two sleighs went to the residence nearby of James Parkinson, and after getting breakfast there arrested one of his sons of the same name. The elder Parkinson had been a staunch supporter of the Government, but that did not help his son. James Benham, John Butchart, Hiram Dowlan, Calvin Lyman and William Armstrong were arrested in the same way. They were taken to Guelph and four of them, Parkinson, Dowlan, Lyman and Armstrong, had a formal examination there before Inglis and were admitted to bail;[5] but those who were considered the ringleaders received no such courtesy; they were sent at once without examination of any kind to Hamilton Gaol, and Benham, Peters and Butchart, after a long sleigh ride, arrived at Hamilton at 10 o'clock p.m. There they lay until the session in April, 1838, of the Commissioners under a Special Commission of Oyer and Terminer and General Gaol Delivery for the District of Gore.

We are so fortunate as to have at Osgoode Hall the original notes made by the presiding judge.

The Honourable James Buchanan Macaulay was the presiding Judge at this Special Assize; he had been a Puisne Justice of the Court of King's (Queen's) Bench since 1829 and was in 1849 to become Chief Justice of the Court of Common Pleas when it was formed in 1849, and Sir James and a Judge of the Court of Error and Appeal in 1857. He was a sound lawyer and a fair and impartial judge. When the Special Court of Oyer and Terminer and General Gaol Delivery for the District of Gore opened at Hamilton, Thursday, March 8, 1838, Mr. Justice Macaulay had as his associates, Hon. James Crooks, James Racey and Richard Beasley, but these gentlemen had no real authority or voice in the proceedings. A Grand Jury was sworn, Mr. Kirby chosen as foreman; the Grand Jury was charged and the Petit Jury sent home until Friday, March 23. The Grand Jury began at once to find True Bills amongst them—one against the seven men from Eramosa; while fifteen accused were released as nothing was found against them.

The first of those accused of High Treason to come before a Petit Jury were the seven from Eramosa who on Tuesday, March 27, 1838, were placed at the Bar to be tried for their lives.

The Crown Counsel was the new Solicitor-General, William Henry Draper;[6] of English birth and descent he had run away to sea when a lad and arrived in Canada in 1820, not yet twenty years old. Abandoning the sea he came to Port Hope and entered the Law Society: by diligence and natural ability he achieved his call in 1828. Almost at once he obtained a place in the office of the influential Attorney-General, John Beverley Robinson, and soon entered politics on the Tory or Government side. He was a very sound, if somewhat narrow and technical, lawyer; and he

---

[5]Peters in the *Mercury* article says, "after being bled, in the pocket of course"—I assume he means paying costs of the Bail-bonds, etc.

[6]He had succeeded Henry John Boulton as Solicitor-General in March, 1837, when Boulton succeeded in the Attorney-Generalship Robert Sympson Jameson, who was made our first Vice-Chancellor.

prosecuted these treason cases with vigour. With him there were no extenuating circumstances; the accused was either guilty of treason, or he was not.[7] The Solicitor-General was ably and strenuously assisted by Allan Napier MacNab a comparatively young practitioner; he was called in 1826; but an old soldier—he had fought in 1812—and one who had done magnificent service to the Loyalist cause during the ill-timed, ill-considered, ill-fated rebellion. He had in January, 1838, been created the first Queen's Counsel for Upper Canada and was to live to be knighted and to become Prime Minister of the United Canadas.

The men of Eramosa (and others) had engaged Miles O'Reilly, a young lawyer practising in Hamilton; he had been called in 1830 and had a high reputation for ability and eloquence[8]—and they paid him a fee of "$10 each or $70 for the job."[9]

By the Statutes of 7 Will. III, c. 3, and 7 Anne, c. 21, the accused were entitled to receive ten days before arraignment a copy of the indictment, a list of the witnesses and of the jury summoned, and this they did; but not only the three who were in Hamilton Gaol but also the four who had come from Eramosa to answer according to their recognizance were compelled to stay in gaol until the day set for the trial.

The tremendous indictment was read;[10] they were all charged with conspiring to subvert the Government, to levy war against the Queen and to put her to death, and such like wicked and traitorous compassings, imaginings and intentions; they were false traitors, etc., etc. Of course they pleaded not guilty.

The evidence was very contradictory. William Campbell, of Eramosa, told of all the accused being present at the meeting and that Benham had spoken saying that Lower Canada was in possession of the rebels and that "we should keep in favour with the Lower Province and do the best we could for ourselves;" that the Reformers were in possession of Toronto, and such like. There is considerable insinuation but nothing that can be called evidence of treason in this testimony. Walter King was the next witness; his evidence, if believed, was almost conclusive: he said that Benham said that "Canada should throw off her allegiance to the British Crown;" that the meeting was called because of the news that Mackenzie had taken Toronto and to assist Mackenzie in the insurrection, all but five or six

---

[7] In an article in the *Guelph Weekly Mercury and Advertiser*, Aug. 2, 1906, James Peters says: "The late Sir Allan McNab and the Solicitor-General, afterwards Judge Draper, were Queen's Counsel, and if we did not get our necks stretched it was not their fault."

Draper became Solicitor-General 1840, Puisne Justice of the Court of Queen's Bench 1847, Chief Justice of the Court of Common Pleas in 1856, Chief Justice of the Court of Queen's Bench and President of the Court of Error and Appeal in 1863; he died in 1877.

[8] Miles O'Reilly, Q.C., succeeded William Leggo (of Leggo's Chancery Practice and Forms) as Master at Hamilton, 1872; this office he held until 1890; he was a Bencher, 1871-1875; he had a respectable practice when at the Bar.

[9] The language of Mr. Peters in the article mentioned in Note 7.

[10] A copy is set out in the article referred to; those interested will find a form in Chitty, Criminal Law, 2nd Edit., 1826, Vol. II, pp. 67-84.

out of the hundred present being of that mind, etc. Robert Grindell (or Grindle) followed, but his evidence was ambiguous; he did not swear as had been anticipated or as he had sworn in a deposition before Mr. Geoffrey Lynch. The whole case was weak, and Mr. O'Reilly moved for the discharge of the prisoners on the ground that there was no evidence of a conspiracy to levy war against the Queen, etc., as charged; but Mr. Justice Macauley ruled that there was some evidence to go to the jury and the defence proceeded.[11]

O'Reilly followed the modern practice and called his witnesses without opening to the jury. John Shaw swore that Benham did not advise to throw off allegiance or to join Mackenzie; that the whole object of the meeting was to protect the life and property of the settlers in Eramosa, mutual defence, and a meeting was arranged for a week later if Toronto was taken; they were to protect themselves from Mackenzie; there was no talk of rebellion. Joseph Parkinson testified to much the same effect, as did James Smith and George Sunley.

The counsel for the prisoners addressed the jury, and MacNab replied; then the Solicitor-General claimed the right to follow—quite against our modern practice although good in strict law—and had his claim allowed.

The charge was impartial; the jury was told that if the prisoners at the meeting declared in favour of revolt, openly approved of the rebellion and pledged themselves to support it, they would come within the indictment, as it was of common notoriety that the object of such rebellion was to overthrow the Government by force; but that if what was meant or contemplated was self-preservation, mutual protection, reform properly so-called as distinguished from rebellion or revolt, the verdict should be for the prisoners. "The jury retired and in just eight minutes returned into court with a verdict of not guilty."[12]

---

[11] In Mr. Peters' Statement in the *Guelph Weekly Mercury and Advertiser*, August 9, 1906, he says: "The evidence was so much in our favour that we told our Counsel we were willing to submit our case to the jury without examining any of the eight witnesses we had on our behalf." If such were the case, Mr. O'Reilly did not risk that course because he called four witnesses. Mr. Peters is apparently under a misapprehension as to the responsibility for calling these witnesses, for he says: "The crafty Queen's Counsel (Draper and MacNab) would not consent to this arrangement probably expecting to get something out of our witness they could not get out of their own, but after examining three of them they gave it up for a bad job"; this is quite incorrect.

[12] The language of Mr. Peters in the article mentioned in Note 11; he says: "After seeing the political complexion of the petit jury . . . our chance of an impartial trial was very small." In the previous article he said that "the Grand Jury . . . nineteen in number, were all pure, thoroughbred Tories. . . . There were eighty petit jurors summoned, namely fifty-seven Tories to the backbone and twenty-three Reformers."

The conviction of Lount and Matthews, in Toronto, in January, 1838, was believed by the time of the trial of the Eramosans to be about to be followed by their execution; and the country at large did not desire further convictions unless guilt were clearly proved. Moreover, Canadians, while bitter enough partisans at election times, do not usually carry political feeling so far as to desire the shameful death of political opponents.

Mr. Peters adds: "Six of the seven jailbirds are still (1866) living—Clear Grits yet. I do not think any of them has given a Tory vote since."

Of the twenty-one others tried for high treason at this Assizes ten were acquitted and eleven convicted;[13] of the latter class, one died in gaol, one escaped and the statute of March 6, 1838, 1 Vic., c. 10, saved the life of one of the rest.

That statute provided that before arraignment every person charged with treason might petition for pardon; and, if pardoned, the effect would be the same as on an attainder; and the pardon might be on condition of transportation or banishment for life or for a term of years. In all the other cases there were pardons either conditional or otherwise, so that no one was executed.

I here subjoin copies of letters of the time, kindly furnished me by Dr. Janet M. Armstrong, of Cobourg, granddaughter of James Peters and of George Armstrong, brother of William Armstrong. I have also to thank Dr. Armstrong for copies of the *Guelph Mercury and Advertiser* to which I have referred.

"Wednesday, March 28 .... Horatio Hills, Guilty.
Willard Sherman, Not Guilty.

Thursday, March 29........................ Stephen Smith, Guilty.
Nathan Town, Guilty.

Friday, March 30.......................... Charles Walrath, Guilty.
William Lyons, Not Guilty.
Oliver Smith, Not Guilty.

Saturday, March 31........................ Adam Yeigh, Not Guilty.
George Rouse, Not Guilty.
John Leonard Uline, Not Guilty.
Samuel Marlatt, Not Guilty.
Isaac B. Malcolm, Guilty.
Finlay Malcolm, Not Guilty.
Norman Malcolm, Not Guilty.
Peter Malcolm, Guilty.
Ephraim Cook, Guilty.
Elias Snyder, Guilty.

Monday, April 2.......................... William Webb, Guilty.
John Tufford, Guilty.
John Hammill, Guilty.

Tuesday, April 3.......................... Solomon Lossing, J.P., Not Guilty.

Those found guilty were sentenced Wednesday, April 4, and the Court adjourned.

Horatio Hills died in gaol after his sentence had been commuted to banishment for life; Charles Walrath escaped from gaol; Stephen Smith was pardoned on giving security to keep the peace and be of good behaviour for three years; Isaac B. Malcolm is said to have petitioned under 1 Vic., c. 10, and received a pardon on the same terms; Nathan Town who was an unlicensed physician, Peter Malcolm, Elias Snyder, William Webb, John Tufford and John Hammill were treated in the same way as Stephen Smith; Ephraim Cook, a physician, was banished for life; he had received his license to practise only in April, 1831.

See Lindsey's Life of William Lyon Mackenzie, Toronto, 1862, Vol. II. pp. 391, 392, 393. There is an evident error on p. 392, as Nathan Town is said to have been acquitted; Lindsay's "Civil Court" means this Special Oyer and Terminer, and he frequently makes a mistake in the dates.

Endorsed "Mrs. Hannah Peters, Eramosa."

HAMILTON GAOL, Dec. 30th, 1837.

Dear Wife & Children;—
I send these few lines to inform you that I am in good health but troubled with a tickling Cough. I should be very glad to hear that you are all well and as much Reconciled to your present circumstances and separation as myself. I expect you would like to know something of the situation of myself and my companions, who has been lodged in Malone's Hotel (this is the Jailor's name) and methinks the Dear Children are often wishing to know what kind of a place Father is in, and in order to satisfy their innocent curiosity Shall endeavour to give a short account of my present Residence, and the number of our Family, which at present amounts to 45 in this part of the House, containing two rooms each about as large as our shop, these are well lighted and ventilated and 12 feet between the floors. We have also a spacious Hall of 8 or 10 feet wide, by 26 long, the Hall door is made of good oak six inches thick, and the windows well secured with Iron grates, so we have no fear of thieves or Robbers, And to conclude this hasty sketch shall just mention that it is the best House in the Town. We expect ten of our number to remove into another part of the house tomorrow morning. The high Sheriff visits us every day when at home and has certainly shown us much kindness. He has been with us this evening and Intimated that it is probable that a special Commission will be appointed to examine into the nature of the charges said to be against us. We hope that this will be the case for we have no desire to see Toronto at her Majesty's expense; and if we must be under confinement we have no reason to expect better treatment at any other place and should we remove we are afraid that it will be much worse. I forgot to mention that there is a Respectable Phisian or Doctor who comes and offers his services which has been sometimes much needed. Our company consists of one ex-member of Parliament, three Doctors, and five that either is now or has been school masters. We have made some Bylaws which is calculated to promote health, comfort and cleanliness which you will see if there is room in this letter. I wish in this place to acknowledge Mr. Malone's kindness unto us and if ever it should be in my power I should be very ungrateful if I did not make some suitable return.

Dec. 31. The Jailor has favored us last night with the Hamilton Gazette which contains the Speech of the Lieutenant Governor at the opening of the Provincial Parliament and also MacKenzie's Proclamation and as near as I can see without Spectacles the coming week is likely to be the most eventful one that has been known since 1812. And I must confess that there is a gloomy prospect for us as it Respects our examination; for nothing can be done at present owing to the excitement which prevails at this eventful Period. I have heard your William is with you at present. If it true I want him to get 2 new straps for the Harness and unless the leather is very heavy they ought to be double and any business which is necessary to be done from home I want it to be done with the Mare. And if it should happen that I am detained here which is very likely at present I would like him to get John Kennedy or John McKerlie or any of the Neighbours to fetch Wheat or Barley to Dundas but as my note is not

due to Charles until the 1st of February it is best to let the grain remain at home as long as possible hoping that things will be more settled ere that time arrives. However, I do not wish you to be governed altogether by my directions for I have been so long from home and you have never favoured me with a letter so that I am ignorant of how you are getting on at home. You will exercise your own Judgment according to circumstances. I hope all the children are industrious—at least all that is able to work, and if they have any sympathy or love for their Father which I do not doubt in the least, I wish them to render implicit obedience to your commands; hoping you will not abuse your Authority over them I shall now close this letter by wishing each of you a happy New Year. I received supplies yesterday from somewhere, least it seems to me they did not come from you. You need not send anything more until further directions as the mess received heavy supplies at the time. Give my best respects to your Father and Mother and all your Brothers and Sisters & Uncle Peter, to my Mother & to George & Mary Ann, to John. & my sisters, & except the same for yourself and all the children, from your Affectionate Husband,
  James Peters.

It is my wish that you should be careful and not take any Bank notes unless W. Armstrong will take them at his own risk & have nothing to do with that note against Charles Crowther at present. If it is not done already get some straw to put on the Pits in the garden.

 Addressed on outside: "William Hewitt, Esq., Guelph."

             Eramosa, July 10th, 1838.
Dear Sir:
 In compliance with your request I have endeavoured to state some facts on the subject of our conversation. But have purposely left the Congratulatory address to Lord Durham to your superior judgment well knowing your abilities to compose it with a better grace and more formal manner than I am able to do, and have only to mention that no one entertains a higher opinion of His Lordships exalted character than myself. Should you find anything in this humble attempt to throw light on an unpleasant subject you are at liberty to cull it out. If there is nothing it is only my time lost. I regret that the busy time has prevented more attention to the composition of these hasty schetches requesting you to let me have these lines again at some convenient oppertunity, by so doing you will much oblige.
             Yours respectfully,
                James Peters.

 A statement of facts relative to the arrest of James Benham, Hiram Dowlan, John Butchart, Calvin Lyman, James Peters, William Armstrong. and James Parkinson. All inhabitants of the Township of Eramosa, in the District of Gore and Province of Upper Canada. And also short account of their Imprisonment and subsequent treatment previous to being brought to trial for High Treason, together with some facts respecting the manner which Jeffrey Lynch, one of her Majesty's Justices of the Peace, insulted and extracted money from the pockets of the People of 60 or 70 of their Neighbours in the Township aforesaid (the exact amount which Jeffrey Lynched at that time I am not able to state being Boarding and Lodging at Her Majesty's expense in those days).

On the Night of the 13th. or the Morning of the 14th. of December, 1837, John Inglis, Esq., one of Her Majesty's Justices of the Peace, with a body of Armed Men amounting 30 or more, entered our dwelling Houses with fixed Bayonets and Arrested James Benham, Hiram Dowlan, Calvin Lymans, John Butchart, James Peters, William Armstrong and James Parkinson, and took them prisoners to Guelph where the said John Inglis, Esq., promised the Prisoners should have an examination. And he kept his promise with respect to William Armstrong, James Parkinson, Hiram Dowlan and Calvin Lyman, this formal examination took place before His Worship, in presence of Major Young, a leader of an Orange Lodge at Guelph, James Hodgert acting as Clerk on that occasion, said Hodgert also a leading Member of the same lodge, after some delay William Armstrong, Hiram Dowlan, James Parkinson and Calvin Lymans were admitted to Bail and James Benham, John Butchart and James Peters were committed to Gaol without any examination at all. And in my Humble opinion the said John Inglis and Co. Virtually suspended the Habeous Corpus Act in these Arbitrary proceedings 12 days before the House of Assembly met. Benham, Butchart and Peters were taken to Hamilton Gaol, and thrust into the Cells at midnight without either Bed or Blanket, one of the coldest nights ever experienced at that season of the year. They was kept in the Cells until 4 o'clock next day and then removed to the Debtors' Rooms, 3 weeks after James Peters was admitted to Bail in the sum of £250 and two sureties in one hundred pounds each and James Benham and John Butchart were kept 4 Weeks longer although great exertions were made to get them out on Bail, thus it will be seen that James Benham and John Butchart were kept 7 weeks in prison & James Peters 3 also besides 2 weeks each after the Grand Jury found true Bills against them, these three men each was torn from his distracted Wife two of which were left with 9 children each and the other with 5 for an alledged crime of which an Intelligent Jury after eight minutes consultation a part of which time must have been taken up in choosing their Foreman, pronounced them not Guilty.

I shall now proceed to mention one or two of the Causes that in my opinion has had a tendency to involve this Province in this deplorable situation, for if Lord Durham could get at the root of the evil, or find out the cause he would be better able to apply the remedy. It is well known though it was not susceptible of proof at the time, that undue influence was used by the Government to defeat the Reformers when Governor Head dissolved the late House of Assembly because they refused to grant supplies. Sir Francis succeed in his scheme and got such a house as he wanted but in an evil hour this most Intelligent (he said) nay this almost Immaculate House passed a law to violate the British Constitution by holding their seats in case of the demise of the King and for anything we know these same Members may at the coming Session pass another Law for them to keep their seats during their invaluable lives for they had as much right by the Constitution to pass the latter as they had the former, and it does appear to me that this late attempt to overthrow one of the best features of our glorious Constitution has been the direct cause of sundry wicked Persons attempting to overturn it in another way, but mark the difference, those who were the first aggressors are loaded with fat offices while the others are stigmatized as a band of Rebels; it my opinion if the odious Law alluded to had not been passed Rebellion would not have raised its Hydra head in this Province for I am fully of opinion that this detestable act stands at the head of all our Grievances for by this and some other measures the Government party has done more to create disaffection and bring about a Revolution than all the Reformers put together previous to the passing the law alluded to.

The Clergy Reserve Question is another stumbling block in the way of the present House of Assembly for the quibling underhand manner in which they have attempted to dispose of them will forever stand foremost amongst their sins of Commission. When the King and the Imperial Parliament granted these Reserves for the benefit of support of Protestant Clergy they do not so much even as hint that the Church of Rome is considered as having any claim to these valuable lands and their conduct in endeavouring to give a fifth part of them cannot be Justified nor excused.

I have a few observations to make Respecting the Legislative Council but must be very brief having already extended my remarks to an unreasonable length, but so far as I am acquainted with the sentiments of all Constitutional Reformers a reformation of some kind must begin here for so long as it remains as at present constituted we have no reason to hope for a better state of things for the House of Assembly may be composed of the Best men in the Province and pass the most Judicious Laws, yet they have the power and have always had the disposition to reject everything that seems to confer any priviledges on the people. I have something to say Respecting a responsible Executive Council but must defer it for want of Room.

XIII.

MEMOIR OF COLONEL JOEL STONE, A UNITED EMPIRE LOYALIST AND THE FOUNDER OF GANANOQUE.

By Judge Herbert S. McDonald, Brockville.

In June, 1884, at the meeting held at Adolphustown, to celebrate the centennial of the first settlement of Upper Canada by the United Empire Loyalists, one of the speakers intimated that the celebration had been set on foot in order (to use the words of Dr. Ryerson) " to do at least a modicum of justice to the memory of a Canadian Ancestry whose heroic deeds and unswerving Christian patriotism form a patent of nobility, more to be valued by their descendants than the coronets of many a modern nobleman." Concurring entirely in the truth of the tribute to those who may justly be called the forefathers of the great Province of Ontario, it is at once a pleasure and a privilege to be permitted to prepare a memoir of one among them who risked life and sacrificed property for loyalty to his king and country.

It is impossible for us at this remote period of time to enter into the feelings and to appreciate the conduct and action of those who are known as United Empire Loyalists. It has been so much the habit to have the virtue of true patriotism accorded to the American revolutionists and to have the loyalists, under the name of Tories, depicted as men who were false to their country and cruel and cowardly in their actions, that many even of the descendants of the latter have not known the truth of the matter. For this state of things United States writers have been largely responsible, and the thanks of the Canadian people are justly due to the lamented late Reverend Dr. Egerton Ryerson, for having in his work entitled " The Loyalists of America and their Times " done justice to the loyalists and exposed the cruelty and injustice with which they were treated.

Dr. Ryerson says: " From the beginning the Loyalists were deprived of the freedom of the press, freedom of assemblage, and under an espionage universal, sleepless, malignant, subjecting the Loyalists to every species of insult, to arrest and imprisonment at any moment, and to the sacrifice and confiscation of their property."

And again: " The Americans inaugurated their Declaration of Independence by enacting that all adherents to connection with the mother country were rebels and traitors; they followed the recognition of Independence by England by exiling such adherents from their territories. But while this wretched policy depleted the United States of some of their best blood, it laid the foundation of the settlement and institutions of the then almost unknown and wilderness provinces which have since become the widespread, free and prosperous Dominion of Canada."

Joel Stone was born in the Town of Guilford in the County of New Haven, and (then), Province of Connecticut, on the 7th day of August,

1749. A number of the original settlers of Guilford came from England in a ship which sailed from London on the 20th May, 1639, and arrived at New Haven about the 1st July in that year. During the voyage a covenant was entered into which may well be transcribed to these pages:

"June 1st, 1639, WE, whose names are hereunder written intending by God's gracious permission to plant ourselves in New England, and, if it may be, in the southern part of Quinpyack, we do faithfully promise each to, each for ourselves and our families and those belonging to us that we will, the Lord assisting us, sit down and join ourselves together in one entire plantation and be helpful each to the other in any common walk according to every man's ability and as need shall require and we promise not to desert each other on the plantation but with the consent of the rest or the greater part of the company who have entered into this engagement. As to the gathering ourselves together in a Church and the choice of officers and members to be joined together in that way we do refer ourselves until such time as it shall please God to settle us in our plantation.

"In witness Whereof we subscribe our hands this 1st day of June, 1639.

"Robert Kitchell, Francis Bushnell, William Lute, John Jordan, John Hoadly, Richard Guthridge, William Parmaley, John Mephon, Abm. Cruttenden, William Halle, Henry Kingsworth, Thomas Cooke, John Bishop, Brother of Lt. Governor Bishop of New Haven, William Crittenden, Thomas Jones, (Wm. & Jno. Stone, Brothers), William Plane, Jno. Housegrove, William Dudley, Thomas Norton, Francis Chatfield, Thomas Naish, Henry Dowde, Rev'd. Henry Whitfield.

"Of their arrival in Connecticut, of a meeting which was held by the people of New Haven for prayer and thanksgiving for their safe arrival," an account was given in a letter from the Rev. M. Davenport, of New Haven, to Lady Vere, Countess of Oxford.

William Stone, one of the two brothers above named who signed the covenant, died 16th November, 1683. His son William died on the 20th March, 1712, leaving a son Stephen, who was born on the 1st March, 1690, and married on the 9th December, 1711, Elizabeth Leeming, a daughter of one Christopher Leeming who came to East or South Hampton, Long Island, about 1640. Stephen Stone died 24th December, 1753. His son Stephen was born at Guilford, 13th August, 1721, and married for his first wife Rebecca Bishop, daughter of Stephen Bishop, and a descendant of the John Bishop who signed the covenant above mentioned. Of this marriage, Joel Stone, the subject of our memoir, was one of the issue. Stephen Stone survived his first wife (who died in 1769), was married to one Deliverance Chapman and died at Litchfield, Connecticut, in the month of September. He and his family had removed to Litchfield on the 23rd of April, 1751, when Joel was less than two years of age. Of this removal to Litchfield, Joel speaks in a narrative, and says of his father that there "by indefatigable labour and industry he improved a competency in land of which he was proprietor."

Of the early life of Joel Stone we have not any record further than that, in the narrative above referred to, he says that he remained at home with his father, in the improvement of the estate, until he was twenty-one years of age, when he proposed to try his fortune in a line of business more agreeable to his inclinations, and with his father's approbation entered on a branch of the mercantile trade, travelled to several places in North America, and returned in about three months with a considerable property. So great had been his success that he was induced with his father's consent, in 1774, to enter into a partnership with a merchant named Jabez Bacon, of Woodbury, in the County of Litchfield. From a copy of the partnership articles, which has been preserved, it would appear that Jabez Bacon and Joel Stone "joined themselves to be co-partners together, or traders in company, in the business of Merchandising and all things thereto belonging; and, also in buying, selling, vending and retailing of all sorts of goods, wares and commodities whatsoever, which said co-partnership is to continue from this First day of February, 1774, for and during unto the full end of six years from thence next ensuing." The partnership did not expire by effluxion of time, for long before the end of the six years the Revolutionary War had broken out and the Junior partner had found employment of quite a different character from that for which the partnership was formed and carried on. But while the business continued it appears to have flourished for Mr. Stone in his narrative says: "I soon had the happiness to discover myself in the confidence and esteem of my neighbours and the public in general. By dint of an unwearied diligence and a close application to trade I found the number of my friends and customers daily increasing and a fair prospect of long happiness arose to my sanguine mind in one of the most desirable situations beneath the best of laws, and the most excellent government in the Universe."

It is quite unnecessary in a narrative such as this to enter upon the causes or discuss the events which led to the revolt of the colonies and the declaration of their independence as the United States of America. We only have to do with them in so far as they affected the subject of our memoir, and he appears soon to have experienced their effects. He says:

"But alas! the dreadful commotions that commenced about this period quickly involved that once happy country in all the dreadful horrors of an unnatural war, and filling the pleasant land with desolation and blood removed all my fair prospects of future blessings; yet amidst all that anarchy and rage I was fixed in my resolves, rather to forego all I could call my property in the world than flinch from my duty as a subject to the best of sovereigns; sooner to perish in the general calamity than abet in the least degree the enemies of the British Constitution."

Entertaining such sentiments as those above stated and with the public mind in the state in which it then was, it may be readily supposed that his life became a disturbed one.

In the year 1775 being suspected of unfriendliness to the provincial or continental party he was cited to appear before a Committee and was accused of having supplied the people whom they called "Tories" with sundry articles of provisions, and with having supported and assisted the British prisoners confined in Connecticut. It was with much difficulty that he at that time escaped a very severe prosecution at the hand of the emissaries of Congress. His aged father appears to have occupied much the same position as Joel for we are told that he was repeatedly imprisoned, threatened, and harassed "for his steady perseverance in maintaining with all his ability the true liberty of his country and just cause of his rightful Sovereign."

At length, in the year 1776, Joel Stone discovered that it was perfectly impracticable for him any longer to conceal his sentiments. The agents of Congress having peremptorily urged him to declare without further hesitation whether he would immediately take up arms himself against the British Government or procure a substitute, he could no longer avoid giving a positive reply. His resolution not to take the step which was required of him was unalterable, both because he detested to do so, and because what was required of him had been repeatedly deemed an act of rebellion by the public proclamations of General Howe. Having received his reply the leaders of the party to which he was opposed informed him that his conduct would undergo the strictest scrutiny and that he might expect from those in authority and an incensed public the utmost severity to his person. In consequence he determined in his own mind to withdraw as soon as possible from Connecticut and go to New York, designing upon his arrival there to join the British forces and use all his influence in favour of his king. Before he could carry his design into execution a warrant was issued for his apprehension by order of the agents of Congress, and he having become apprised of this, and that men were actually on their way to his house, packed up his books and bills and delivered them to a friend to secrete, and leaving a sister who had lived with him for some time in charge of his household effects, took flight upon horseback, and the night being a dark one had the good fortune to elude those who were searching for him and escaped. The party seeking him was attended by a tumultuous mob who surrounded the premises, and vented their resentment upon his sister. Using language the most opprobrious, they broke every lock in the house and seized all the property they could discover.

Mr. Stone made his way to New York, which was then in the possession of the British forces. When or how he arrived there we cannot tell, but it became his residence for a period of several years. From his own statement it would appear that he took up arms and served the king from the 20th June, 1777, until the evacuation of New York. He first became a volunteer in Governor Wentworth's command, and his service as such appears to have been purely of a gratuitous character, for he received no remuneration, nor indeed did any of the volunteers in that command, until after he had ceased to be attached to it. By a commission or warrant bearing date the 15th day of April, 1778, he was authorized and empowered by Gabriel G. Ludlow, Esquire, Colonel of the third battalion of Brigadier-General Delancey's Brigade to recruit able-bodied men, not less in number than fifty-four (including those recruited by the subalterns in his company) to serve His Majesty in that battalion for "two years or during the present rebellion in North America," under the command of his Excellency, Sir William Howe, or under the commander-in-chief of His Majesty's forces for the time being, and was further authorized and empowered to inform the men that upon their being mustered and approved they should receive five dollars bounty, and the same pay, clothing, provisions, and other necessaries as the British troops then had. Having gone to Huntington, Long Island, to recruit men he was surprised, while asleep, on the 12th May, 1778, by a company of whale-boat men and carried to Fairfield, Connecticut, and there committed to close custody upon a charge of high treason. While in prison he was subjected to abuse, being informed that he should be hanged as a traitor. On the 23rd July, 1778, he escaped from what he calls "that town of horror" and with great difficulty arrived on Long Island again on the 30th of that month.

On the 3rd of August he was seized with a severe fever which nearly proved fatal, and on his recovery from it went to sea for several months, and his health by this means was re-established. He returned to New York and entered into a mercantile business.

By commission dated the second day of February, 1780, he was appointed by James Pattison, Esq.,* Major General of His Majesty's forces, Commandant of New York, etc., etc., etc., to be second lieutenant of Company No. 22 of the City Militia, of which company Willett Taylor had been appointed Captain. On the 9th March, 1780, Mr. Stone received a captain's commission to command a company of militia, and commanded the same until the king's troops left New York, without receiving any pay or compensation whatever.

In reference to his services generally in behalf of his king it may be of interest here to quote a certificate subsequently given by General Lym, who was, we believe, at one time Governor of the State of New York:

"I do certify that Mr. Joel Stone came into the king's lines at New York from the colony of Connecticut early in the American War—was employed in recruiting the provincial corps, and conducted himself as a faithful, loyal subject—therefore particularly recommend him to the consideration of Government."

"Given under my hand in Upper Grosvenor Street, this 23rd of January, 1784."

Nor must we judge only of Mr. Stone's loyalty by the services he rendered to his king but also by the sacrifices which he made. We have already seen that on the night on which he made his escape every lock in his house was broken and all the property which could then be discovered was seized. But his enemies were by no means satisfied with their actions or with having driven him from the colony, and steps were taken to confiscate his estate.

It would appear as regarded personal property, that by the statute law of Connecticut the "select men" of any Township from which any person absented and joined the British army were directed to represent such person and the state of his property to a Justice of the Peace, who then had power to issue a warrant to a constable to seize and hold all the absentee's goods and chattels and make returns to the County Court which was to adjudicate in the matter, and might issue an order to the said constable to sell the property so seized for the use and benefit of the State. By another statute, provision was made for the sale of real estates of such absentees.

Upon the representation of select men of Woodbury in the County of Litchfield, to Daniel Sherman, Esquire, a Justice of the Peace, for the said County, against Joel Stone, showing that he was inimical to the States of America and did sometime in the month of December then last (1776) join the army of the King of Great Britain, and had ever since continued under the protection of the said King's chief commander at or near New York, and that he had an estate in goods and chattels in said Woodbury

*The letters of Gen. James Pattison, while he was commandant in the City of New York, appeared in the volume for 1875, of the New York Historical Society.

which was forfeited by force and effect of the statute law of that State to the State of Connecticut, a warrant was issued by the said Sherman, apparently on the 7th day of January, 1777, to seize and hold all the goods, etc., of the said Joel. At a County Court holden at Litchfield in and for the County of the same name on the fourth Tuesday of March, 1777, it was found that the property in the goods seized was Mr. Stone's and judgment was given that they should be sold for the use of the State and that an execution should be issued according to law, which was done on the 2nd April, 1777. At the same Court, enquiry was made as to the truth of an information of the select men of Washington in Litchfield County against Joel Stone for joining the enemies of the United States and upon the evidence produced judgment was given that his estate was forfeit and an order was made to dispose of the same according to law.

Under the judgment as to personal property and the execution issued thereupon, one Enos Mitchell, a constable, appears to have sold such personal property and according to his return the avails amounted to the sum of £491 6s. 9d. lawful money of the State of Connecticut (viz.), at the rate of twenty-eight shillings for an English guinea or six shillings for a Spanish milled dollar, and he paid the sum so realized to the Treasury of the State.

It would appear that under the judgment of the County Court, proceedings were subsequently taken in the Court of Probate as if Mr. Stone was deceased. Indeed, in an inventory of his estate he is described as "politically deceased."

At a Court of Probate held at Woodbury, June 18, 1779, administration of Joel Stone's estate was granted unto one Daniel W. Brinsmade, sufficient bonds having been given. A commission was granted to certain persons, one of their duties apparently having been to appraise the value of the estate. Under date of the 28th day of June, 1779, Jonathan Fornand and Ebenezer Clark, Jr., stated that they had appraised to the best of their judgment under oath. They appraised at the rate of twenty-eight shillings for a guinea or six shillings for a Spanish milled dollar, or at the rate of silver at 6/8 per or gold in the same proportion, and it would appear that they valued the estate at £359 10s. 4d., of which £354 13s. 0d. was the value of real estate. How they came to deal with personalty (which they did to the extent of an appraised amount of £4 17s. 4d.) we do not know, unless they found some items which had escaped Enos Mitchell in his seizure and sale. In making the valuation of land which had been conveyed to Mr. Stone and his partner, Jabez Bacon, hereinbefore named, one-half was valued. Claims were allowed by the Commissioners against the estate to the amount of £61 7s. 9d. Let it not be supposed that this sum was allowed to creditors of Joel Stone. No; for it is said the greatest part of it was paid as wages to the people who hunted Mr. Stone around the country just before his departure to join the British Army, and as costs incurred by those who proceeded against the estate. But notwithstanding the vigilance and zeal of those who took these proceedings, there was one valuable piece of real estate situated in the Township of Winchester containing about 250 acres in which Mr. Stone had a one-half interest with his partner Bacon, hereinbefore referred to, of which they had no knowledge, as the deed was not registered. Samuel Talcott, Jr., of Hartford, had sold the land to Mr. Stone on 12th September, 1776, for £500, and had received his money. But when afterward discovered, as the forfeiture was of the estate of Joel Stone, it was contended that this piece of land or his interest therein was included in it. According to Mr. Stone's own statement it would appear that previous to the War the firm of Bacon & Stone had a capital of £12,000 Stg. in stock, and that in addition to the value of the property confiscated or forfeited as above mentioned (amounting to about £11,000) his books, bonds, etc., were confiscated, thus adding to the amount of his loss.

The statements as to the mode of procedure required to obtain forfeiture of property of absentees, and as to the particular proceedings had in Mr. Stone's case, may seem somewhat uninteresting, but we believe some persons will find them of interest, and any narrative which failed to furnish a statement of Mr. Stone's losses would be incomplete.

During his residence in New York, Mr. Stone's time appears not to have been so fully occupied by his military and business duties as to prevent his forming social ties and eventually the still closer relations of married life. On the 23d of March, 1780, he was married to Leah Moore, daughter of William Moore, of New York, and May his wife, the officiating clergyman having been the Reverend Charles Inglis, then Rector of Trinity Church, New York, afterward of London, England, and eventually the first Bishop of the Church of England in what is now British North America. Mr. Inglis was appointed to the See of Nova Scotia in or about the year 1787, and the centenary of his appointment or consecration was duly celebrated at Halifax, in 1887. There is in existence an affidavit to which he was one of the deponents, sworn at the Guild Hall, London, 27th February, 1784, before Robert Peckham, Mayor, in which Mr. Inglis deposes that on the 23d day of March, 1780, the said Joel Stone was married by him to Leah Moore. The father of the bride was a mariner by occupation and appears to have been absent from New York at the time of the marriage, for in a letter written by him to Mr. Stone dated at Lisbon, 21st February, 1782, he acknowledges the receipt of a letter dated 26th January, 1781, informing him of the marriage and says: "as it was with the consent of my late consort you have also mine." Further in this old time letter he mentions having heard of the death of his own wife, speaking of which he says: "the greatest shock I ever felt in my life and such a loss as I shall ever have reason to sympathize for with you all who have lost the best of mothers and I the only comfort I had left in this world." He then goes on to say that he had written to Mr. Van Dorn (presumably his agent) and desired him to leave his furniture with Mr. Stone for the use of his daughter till he should hear further from him, and that he should not charge him anything for the first year after they were married, and to allow and pay to him out of the rents of his houses, etc., one hundred pounds per annum till he heard further from him and says: "which is all that can be done in the present circumstances, and rest assured that you will always find in me a real friend and affectionate parent." Further on he mentions that he had heard by letter from Mr. Van Dorn that Leah (Mrs. Stone) has brought her husband a fine son and made him a grandpapa, and that although he does not know the baby's name Mr. Stone must "insinuate" to him that he has a grandpapa who will always love him and his mamma and papa. The references to this letter and the quotations from it may seem somewhat lengthy, but let us remember that it was written over one hundred years ago and that its kindly thoughts and sentiments, perhaps sometimes clothed in language a trifle old fashioned, possess an interest all their own and give evidence of having been the outcome of a gentle heart.

Three children appear to have been born to Mr. Stone and his wife Leah. Of these, the eldest was named William Moore and is the one referred to in his grandfather's letter above mentioned. The date of his birth is uncertain, but it certainly occurred previous to 21st February, 1782. Another son named Lewis was born on 9th April, 1784, and died in infancy or childhood. A daughter named Mary was the third of these children and grew to woman's estate and married as will hereafter appear.

After the evacuation of New York by the British and in or after the month of July, 1783, Joel Stone sailed for England. The primary object of his going appears to have been that he might, upon his wife's behalf, recover a legacy to which she was entitled under the will of her deceased uncle, Commodore John Moore, formerly of Bombay in the East Indies, and at one time in the Honourable Company's service. This John Moore appears to have been in marine service for over 30 years and to have acquired a very large property, including at least three slaves, one boy named Paris and two girls named respectively Mary and Clarinda.

Sometime previous to July, 1780, Mr. Moore had determined to return from India to Europe. At or about that time Senhor Manvel Jose Mochado de Sampago, of Lisbon, had arrived at Bombay in the East Indies and had brought letters of recommendation to some English gentlemen there from some of the English merchants at Lisbon. His object was to purchase in India a ship and to lade it with a cargo fit for the Lisbon market, and he depended on being supplied with the funds for this purpose by the English in India, who being then—as is presumed owing to war between Great Britain and France—deprived of the means of remitting their fortunes by bills on the English in East India, were glad to procure good bills payable in Europe though drawn by foreign merchants.

Senhor Sampago became acquainted with Mr. John Moore, and as the latter was desirous of remitting his fortune to Europe and was the possessor of a ship called the *Virgin Dove* a connection arose between him and the Senhor which resulted in his selling to the latter his ship and advancing to him sundry sums to enable him to purchase a cargo, in return for which it was agreed that the Senhor should draw bills of exchange on some responsible merchant of Lisbon but payable in London. On these terms Mr. John Moore was to advance as far as the sum of 160,000 rupees and the Senhor having occasion for more money applied to other parties and took up in all at Bombay to the amount of 2,041,000 rupees, for which he drew different bills of exchange in favour of the different persons from whom he had received money at Bombay on sundry merchants at Lisbon payable in London at the house of Mayne & Graham, bankers, in Jermyn Street at the rate of two shillings and five pence per rupee.

Mr. Moore had determined to return to Europe and had arranged with Senhor Sampago to take his passage with him on board the ship which he had sold him. His health was then not very good but between that time and the month of July, 1780, it became so much worse that prudence required some provision to be made in case of his death on board of ship before reaching Lisbon.

It had been arranged between him and Senhor Sampago that Mr. William Moore, father-in-law of Mr. Stone, was to have the command of the *Virgin Dove* and he accordingly did command her during a short trip from Bombay down the Malabar Coast and back, but previous to the sailing of the ship to Europe the two brothers had a disagreement which led to the command of the ship being taken from the latter. It was then agreed that Senhor Sampago although totally ignorant of marine affairs should take command and appear both as owner and captain. But inasmuch as in case of a passenger's death the Captain would take charge of his papers and effects unless some arrangement was made to the contrary, and as under this rule Senhor Sampago would, in case of Mr. Moore's death, become possessed of the bill he had himself drawn, and of a mortgage on the ship and cargo granted in case the bills drawn by him should not be accepted or paid, Mr Moore thought it prudent to secure the services of an old acquaintance named Farmer, who was to embark with him in the same ship for Lisbon on his way to England, to represent the interests of his estate in case of his death during the voyage. He did die, and as it would appear before the ship reached the Cape of Good Hope. The Captain was ignorant of sea affairs, the chief officer, a Portuguese, was little better and would have run the ship on rocks the very night before reaching the Cape of Good Hope had not Mr. Farmer perceived that he was wrong and called upon a passenger named William Hardcastle, who had been a chief mate on the *Grafton* (Indiaman), and who totally altered the course of the vessel, and the only remaining officer was a young man who would not pretend to undertake navigating the ship. Mr. John Moore had with great trouble formed a crew of Europeans made up of deserters from the Company's vessels, from the garrison at Bombay, and other runaways, who knowing that the ship had formerly belonged to him and that he governed in everything, looked on him as the real commander of the ship. After his death and previous to the arrival of the ship at the Cape they had expressed great dissatisfaction with the treatment they received from Captain Sampago, who had curtailed them in their supply of liquor. Provisions ran short and many threatened if they met with any other ship on the passage to seize the boats and desert. They were quieted by Mr. Farmer and Mr. Hardcastle who desired them to exercise patience until their arrival at the Cape when all would go well. Mr. Farmer spoke to Sampago who promised to satisfy them by ample supplies at the Cape. Instead of this he went on shore himself and neglected to send off supplies to the ship. The crew grew mutinous and one or two deserted. Sampago went on board to look into matters and becoming angered he struck one or two of the people. Instantly and in his presence they seized the boats, quitted the ship and divided themselves some on shore and some on board the British fleet then lying at the Cape. The boatswain and one or two indifferent hands were left, but the crew was virtually gone and the ship unable to sail until a new crew should be obtained; and to add to the difficulty of the situation, Mr. Hardcastle, who was anxious to reach England as soon as possible, decided to take passage on another ship. Mr. Farmer resolved to take the same course, and would perhaps have done so, had he not reflected on what the consequences might be to the Moore estate (possibly involving a loss to the heirs of above £18,000 Sterling), if he left this ship while in the helpless condition in which it then was.

The causes of risk were various. The principal one was the risk of capture by the French. To avoid this it was material that the ship should be considered to be Portuguese. Already with a view to this the name had been changed from *Virgin Dove* to *Nossa Senhora De Arrabida*, and a pass had been procured from the Governor of Goa. But in some way it had become known at the Cape that the ship had been English and had been bought since the commencement of the war. This was ground enough for the French to seize and detain her, for an edict of the King of France warranted his officers to seize all ships purchased from the English since the war commenced, and had the *Virgin Dove*, otherwise the *Arrabida* been so seized, the matter would have been one of dispute between the Courts of France and Portugal, which might have been long in course of settlement, and meantime the insurers would have declined paying the insurance money on the ground that there being no war between France and Portugal there was not any proper capture but a mere detention of the vessel to be determined by application to the French authorities. At this time Commodore Barber with three English ships of the line and a convoy of twelve Indiamen was returning from India, and unless a crew could be got from them the ship would probably have to remain at the Cape until from among some of the Dutch, Danes or Swedes returning from China to Europe in the following February or March, such crew could be obtained. It was now October and such a long detention meant not only additional risk but also the incurring of great expense in providing for the passengers on the ship, and this expense would have to be met from Mr. Moore's estate, at any rate to some extent, as he had undertaken to convey some, if not all, of these passengers to London. Under these circumstances Mr. Farmer deemed it prudent to secure the services of Mr. Hardcastle as Master, as he was capable of navigating the ship and understood how to procure a crew. Senhor Sampago demurred to being at the expense of paying Mr. Hardcastle, and as a matter of prudence Mr. Farmer deemed it better to pay a portion of it. Mr. Hardcastle was engaged, a crew was obtained, the ship sailed with the English fleet and reached Lisbon in safety. It is quite possible that had this course not been pursued there would have been a heavy loss to the estate of Mr. Moore.

It may be asked why should these particulars be given at such length in a memoir of Joel Stone? The answer is that they are, at this period of over one hundred years after, interesting in themselves as an incident, and that they are intimately connected with one of the matters which caused Mr. Stone to go to England.

He arrived in London on the 23rd day of December, 1783, after a long and tedious passage, during which he was very seasick by turns for eighteen or twenty days. The affairs of the Moore estate were thrown into Chancery by Mr. John Blackburn, one of the executors, and as Mr. Stone had to attend to his wife's interest in it, and had also a claim of his own for losses incurred by his loyal adhesion to the British cause to press upon the Government, his stay in England was probably much longer than he had intended. From the draft of a letter to his wife dated in 1784, we learn that he had private lodgings with Mr. S. Stott, shoe and boot maker, No. 20 Snow Hill, and he informs Mrs. Stone that Mr. and Mrs. Stott present their compliments to her and are often enquiring after her, and

COL. JOEL STONE.
b. in Guilford, Connecticut, Aug. 7, 1749.
d. in Gananoque, Nov. 20, 1833.

the little boy; they often hear him mentioned; that they have a pretty family of children and appear to be wealthy and he believes he shall lodge there until he leaves London which he seems to have hoped might be soon. Also in the same letter he speaks of coming out to some part of America, and says he hopes to settle with his family, presumably for life, as he has not altered his opinion of England since he left New York, although he enjoys the blessings of health.

From a statement made in one of his papers or letters it would appear that his solicitors were Messrs. King, Empy & Spillan, No. 9 Cloak Lane. It might be of interest to know whether such a firm name still exists, for of course the individuals who then composed it must have long since passed away. His agent was Charles Cook, No. 98 Wardour Street, Soho, and in the same document in which he is mentioned, reference is made to W. Graves, No. 10 Symonds Inn, Chancery Lane, a Master in Chancery and member of the House of Commons; W. Scape, Tooks Court, Carristor (query Cursitor) Street; Brassel and Wm. Herne, No. 41 Paternoster Row; Frederick Pegaw, No. 11 Mark Lane; Mr. Lansom, No. 16 London Street; and Wm. Sandell, No. 28 Princess Street.

During 1784 he took steps to bring before the Commissioners appointed by Parliament, his claims for compensation for losses sustained by him owing to the confiscation of his property, and in a memorial dated 9th July, 1784, he asked for an immediate hearing. At this time he had removed from Snow Hill to a house called the Boot in the Foundling Hospital Fields.

In a letter to his wife dated 15th July, 1784, he congratulates her on her safe delivery on the 9th April of a fine boy and repeats his most anxious wishes and endeavours for her health and happiness, and refers to a small trunk containing presents which he is sending to her. From a list subjoined it would appear that of these presents a fan and a pair of shoes are the gift of Miss Louisa Moore, and that he is sending 28 yards of Calico at five shillings the yard, a table cloth, 6 pocket handkerchiefs, 1 India silk handkerchief, 1 pair of shoe buckles, a miniature, and some other articles to his wife, a pair of plated shoe buckles to his elder son, and a coral for the baby boy. He tells her that he presents the miniature picture wishing it fully to supply the place of a ring she unfortunately has lost. It may be remarked that this miniature is still in existence and in the possession of his grandson's widow, herself a lady well on in years, and that from it has been obtained a photograph of wonderful distinctness and clearness (and now reproduced in connection with this article).

At length on the 24th August, 1784, he had a hearing before the Commissioners, and appears to have entertained the idea that he could after that get away to America, for in a letter to his father-in-law, dated 5th September, 1784, he says: " I had my hearing before the Commissioners 24th and 25th August, I had proposed to take my passage in the *Skinner,* Capt. Cummins, to New York, but believe she will sail before I can hear from you, which I wish if possible to do, and to effect some plan for future provision for myself and dear family before I go, which with the assistance of my wife's property hope I shall be able to do." But there seems to have been in the matter of his wife's legacy the proverbial delay in Chancery proceedings, for from a letter written at the New York Coffee House, London, on the

2nd August, 1786 (nearly two years after the date of the letter last named), and addressed to John Blackburn, he speaks of a final settlement having been prevented owing to some mistake which he says he trusts will be rectified during the next term, and announces his expectation of going on board the *Providence* packet then at Gravesend, and bound for Quebec that day with a view of settling himself in that country (presumably meaning Canada).

Previous to this, and in the month of April, 1786, he had been introduced to William Smith, late Chief Justice of New York, and who was going out with Sir Guy Carleton as Chief Justice of Canada, and that gentleman most kindly proposed that Mrs. Stone should join Mrs. Smith, and under her care, and that of Mr. Livingston who was accompanying her, go to Canada where her husband hoped to meet her. This offer Mr. Stone most gratefully accepted.

In a letter to his wife dated the 1st August, 1786, he informs her that he is to go on board the *Providence,* Captain Lithbee, the next day bound for Quebec and Montreal, and that all his effects and clothes are on board, well insured. He informs her of the delay in the Chancery proceedings and refers to her proceeding to Canada at the time Mr. Smith's family go. It is probable that Mrs. Stone went with Mrs. Smith when that lady journeyed to join her husband. As before stated, Mr. Smith was going out to Canada as Chief Justice. In M. M. Bagg's work entitled "The Pioneers of Utica" (at page 650), it is said of him that he adhered to the Crown during the War of Independence, and was afterwards Chief Justice of the Province of Quebec, in the City of which name he died in the latter part of the year 1793.

Before we pass from that part of Mr. Stone's memoir which refers to his visit to England, it may be well to mention in connection with the matter of his claim before the commissioners, that under date of 31st January, 1788, he writes that in the previous October he had received a letter from his agent in London informing him that he was permanently provided for as a military pensioner with the rank of Captain at £40 per annum from the 24th June, 1786.

We presume that he went on board the *Providence* (packet) at Gravesend on the 2nd August, 1786, according to his intentions, and sailed for Quebec, for in a letter or memorial to Governor Wentworth dated at Quebec, 27th October, 1786, he says: "I arrived here the 6th inst. from London, where I have been since the evacuation of New York." What induced Mr. Stone to come to Quebec instead of going to Nova Scotia as he appears at one time to have contemplated, we do not know. It would appear that he was acquainted with some parties who had settled in the latter Province (which, until 1784, included what is now New Brunswick), for we find two letters written to him, apparently with a view of furnishing him with information as to the country. Of these one is from J. Tomlinson, Jr., written from Camp Managonish, River St. John, Nova Scotia, and dated August 18th, 1783, while the other is from Anthony Reece, written from Carleton, St. John, and dated July 25th, 1784.

CAMP MANAGONISH, RIVER ST. JOHN,
NOVA SCOTIA, Aug. 18, 1783.

"Dear Sir: I thank you for your letter of the 27th of July, which I received the 10th instant. The one you mention to have wrote before has not come to hand. I am happy to learn the welfare of you and yours, and much obliged by your kind wishes for mine. So Mrs. Stone is gone to Connecticut to see her new relations. Why did not you attend her and introduce her yourself? Show her that country and all those fine prospects you were obliged to abandon. What less than your fear of further persecution and abuse from the hands of your cruel and relentless countrymen could have prevented you. Nothing I am sure. I have recently heard the cursed spirit of persecution still prevailed. Oh discord! discord! how long wilt thou continue to distract with thy baneful and sooty influence the unworthy descendants of Britain to the utter extinction of all the noble virtues, of justice, and humanity. It is not enough that the din of war should summon up the resentments and clarion forth the fury of man, but must the golden winged messenger of peace be insulted also with the most untimely and revengeful persecution? Surely you will not regret, my friend, but rather rejoice at the prospect of taking leave of an ungrateful country which experience has taught us has long been in a state of total anarchy and void of every principle of justice. Here is an asylum of freedom and safety not only for you, but for all our loyal American friends, and well worthy their acceptance; and were the prospects here a thousand times less than they are, who among the noble sons of honest loyalty would not sooner accept them, than deign to ask or condescend to receive protection (longer than entitled to demand it from the treaty of peace to settle and adjust their affairs), from the hands of men who have so cruelly and unjustly robbed them of their just rights and drove them from all their connexions? I presume no one will ever have cause to envy the boasted freedom of the American States with all their ill-gotten possessions. I am willing for my part they should enjoy that portion of happiness allotted them without becoming a sharer in any part with them, trusting rather to that experienced happy government under which I was born, and have enjoyed with my fellow subjects in general so many unrivalled blessings.

"You ask me to inform you particulars of this country; what part of it will be best for business, etc. I am too little acquainted with the province in general to give particular descriptions of it. I have not been on the east side of the Bay of Fundy, and the most I have seen of the country on this side lies on the River St. John. This river is beautiful and affords a good navigation from 50 to 100 miles up. The country around is extremely pleasant and fertile, and I have no doubt will soon be a well settled part of this province. Accounts from the east side of the bay, which no doubt you have seen as well as I, speak highly of the harbours, soil and advantages there. Indeed everybody, whether from ignorance or an unaccountable attachment to the particular part of the country they happen to have a prospect of settling on (no matter what), conclude themselves more lucky than their neighbours at 50 miles distant from them— a proof of the propriety of the old proverb—every one thinks his own geese swans. Where trade will be best I cannot pretend to say at present. I have no doubt there will be a great run of business at several different ports in this province in a very short time. As I am determined to settle on the River St. John no doubt my wish is it may become the most flourishing part of this country. If I did not think it the best I should not have resolved to have settled on it. (Apply the proverb and welcome.)

I presume, as you ask my information of this country at this period, you can have no idea of leaving New York this year, conscious that you must have in mind that a few weeks (at least) are necessary in this new world to make provision for a cold winter which will soon stagger upon us, and I tremble lest too many of our friends should be overtaken while they are unprovided with necessary shelter. Although everything is pushed forward here with an emulating spirit of industry, everything cannot be accomplished which perhaps will be necessary.

"To convince you we are not deprived of society or all its gay amusements, I must tell you that three evenings ago we had a most agreeable ball at this place. Our music appeared to have the same influence which it used to inspire in our native walk, and the lady appeared as gaily decorated. Why should we attribute as misfortune to leave New York or Connecticut for Nova Scotia or any other country, while we still enjoy and carry along with us the only valuable blessing of life, the society of our friends, the necessary comforts of life, and the blessings of a happy government. For my part I conceive no difference (so the climate is healthy and my friends are with me), whether I were to live in the Antipodes or where I am,

I am, sir,

Your obedient and humble servant,

(Signed) J. TOMLINSON, JR.

"P.S.—My respects to Mrs. Stone and other friends be pleased to communicate.

"Captain Stone:"

"CARLETON, ST. JOHN, July 25, 1784.

"Dear Sir: Your kind letter dated March 19th I received, which gave me great pleasure in hearing of my friend Stone's health, which blessing I hope kind heaven may bestow on you until your hopes and cares are ended. Our little family are well, and as for my boy he is the admiration of the whole place, for a finer child I never beheld, not that it is mine, but because everybody says so. But here I must stop, and according to your wish inform you of St. John. The situation is formed somewhat like New York, for on the east and west side is formed two large towns, that on the eastern side much larger than that on the western side. The town on the east side goes by the name of Parr Town. The amount of buildings is 1,500 and daily increasing. That on the west side by the name of Carleton; the amount of buildings is 370 houses, and are also increasing daily, and these towns are all built since my arrival at the place. The beauty of their situations you can form no idea of, nor is it possible for me to describe it to you. But I hope in a short time that I shall have the pleasure of seeing you in our flourishing town where you will be a better judge of the place.

"The land up the River St. John, in general, is equal to any that ever I saw in all my travels, and the navigation very good for upwards of 85 miles, except just at the entrance of the river a small fall where you cannot go through only once on the flood tide, but after you get through, it is nothing to proceed, as there is no tide after you get 15 miles through the falls. Commerce is just beginning to flourish, as everybody is striving to do something. But upon the whole, in my weak judgment of the place, St. John will be the capital of Nova Scotia, as there is a large back country to support the towns, which in time must make the place rich. And as for fish, in the spring the place abounds with cod, salmon, herring and other fish we catch until July, and then there is no more fish in the harbour that season. So now I have told you as much of St. John as I well know. This will come by a mast ship which makes 19 since last summer. My dear friend, I must beg that you will not neglect writing often to me, for a few lines from you will always be acceptable to your old friend, and you may depend upon hearing from me often. I have now to wish you joy of the birth of your second son, which I heard you have got, and may God prosper you and their healths, together with your dear consort's; that you may all be a blessing to each other, is the sincere wish of, dear sir,

"Your friend and well wisher,

"(Signed) ANTHONY REECE.

" P.S.—Mrs. Reece's kind compliments to you, and she says she hopes if you come to Nova Scotia that St. John will be the place you pitch upon, as she likes to be with her old friends and acquaintances. Nancy wishes you well. She is married to Mr. Cox, and lives 85 miles up the river. Adieu; God bless you.

"(Signed) A. REECE.

Mr. Joel Stone."

We do not know the extent of Mr. Stone's investigations before he decided upon a place of settlement, but in a memorial dated at Quebec, 14th February, 1787, and addressed to Brig.-General Hope, Lieutenant-Governor of Quebec, etc., etc., in Council, he states that he wishes now to fix himself and family in New Johnstown Township No. 2, and asks that an order be granted him to take up and possess the same quantity of his Majesty's ungranted lands as are usually given to the Captains in His Majesty's established regiments, together with the usual quantity of such lands to his wife, Leah, and son William M. Stone, and also for an order for three of His Majesty's batteaux, well manned, to assist in carrying his effects from Montreal to the said Township as soon as the ensuing spring should open. In a letter to General Hope, written in the same month of February, he applies, in addition to an order for the land, for such utensils and provisions as are necessary to effect his settlement at the said Township. He does not appear to have awaited the opening of navigation for from a letter written to his brother-in-law, Lewis Moore, and dated 3d April, 1787, we learn that he arrived at New Johnstown with his family on the 16th March, 1787, in good health.

New Johnstown, now Cornwall, in the County of Stormont, appears to have taken its name either from Sir John Johnson or from Johnstown in the State of New York. In a very old map dated the 1st November, 1786, designated "A plan of part of the new settlements on the north bank of the south-west branch of the St. Lawrence River, commencing near Point au Bodett or Lake St. Francis and extending westerly along the said north bank to the west boundary of Township No. 5 laid down from the latest surveys and observations by Patrick McNiff," and which is said to belong to the Sir John Johnson papers, and to be in the possession of D. B. Maclennan, Esq., Barrister, of Cornwall, the present site of the Town of Cornwall, or of a portion of it, is laid down as Johnstown. It appears to lie between Township lot 6 on the east and 13 on the west, and shows two points named respectively Pt. Mallim and L. Pt. Maliver. At the west side of the Town plot, Patrick McNiff seems to have owned land, and it is believed this now forms a portion of the estate of the late William Mattici.

From the historical atlas of the United Counties of Stormont, Dundas and Glengarry, published by H. Belden & Co., (1879), we learn that at the close of the Revolutionary War, Sir John Johnson's regiment, about 800 strong, was at Isle Aux Noix, a fortified post at the northern extremity of Lake Champlain. The men having determined to settle in Canada, surveyors were sent up the St. Lawrence to survey townships along the river in the present Counties of Stormont and Dundas. The wives and families of the soldiers came from the Mohawk Valley to Whitehall where they were met and conveyed in boats to Isle Aux Noix late in the fall of 1783. After spending the winter in barracks they ascended the St. Lawrence in the summer of 1784 in batteaux and arrived at the present site of Cornwall, where they found a settlement recently formed of loyalists who had rendezvoused at the Isle of Jesus some time before, making their way to their new home in the woods. At Cornwall the loyalists had their farms allotted to them on the lottery principle, i.e., each one would draw from a hat or box a slip of paper on which was marked the number of a lot, and of the lot so drawn he became the owner. Each soldier received a grant of one hundred acres fronting on the river, and two hundred acres at a point within the County in which he located, removed from the stream.

In a letter to his father written from Montreal and dated 3d September, 1787, Joel Stone speaks of the tenure under which land shall be held. He says he had been led to believe before he left London that it would be upon a free socage, but found upon his arrival in Canada that this mode of tenure was powerfully opposed by a majority in the Council, and doubted whether that principal point could be obtained, and says: "at least I consider it a very principal point, having the strongest antipathy against the French tenure of holding lands under seigniory, by which tenure every man is in reality a tenant to his seignior or lord." (More than half a century after these words were written by Mr. Stone the seigniorial tenure in Canada was abolished.) In the same letter he says that every man who can prove himself friendly to the king and Constitution of Great Britain, during the late rebellion, will be able to obtain a grant of at least 100 acres to a single man, 200 acres to each master of a family, 50 acres for his wife and each child, and that much larger quantities are granted to those "who have supported rank or any superior character in life." He further says that as some of his friends and former acquaintances may wish to come to settle from the reports and favourable description he must give, he thought it his duty to endeavour fully to satisfy himself in those principal points before he wrote, and being satisfied, he will briefly assure them he never saw "so valuable a country of land, taking so large a tract together" as is now given away by the king to such persons as before mentioned.

In the same letter he says that he has fixed himself in a Town called Cornwall about 70 miles from Montreal up the river, which place was lately called New Johnstown, and has purchased some land and is endeavouring to complete a dwelling and still house which he is building there, and that he has or is to draw at least eight hundred or a thousand acres of land from Government.

Judging from what he says about having purchased land, and from the contents of a draft letter dated 25th April, 1787, it is more than probable that when Joel Stone arrived at New Johnstown, or Cornwall, all the farm lots had been located.

In the last mentioned letter he says that not having been able to find any lands unlocated nearer, he has laid out and located 500 acres on the River Gananoque, agreeable to a survey to which he refers, but also wishes to take possession of a six-acre lot No. 24 in Township No. 3, which was drawn by Michael and Jacob Dinyer, and which had become vacant by their absenting themselves to settle in Scoharie in the United States, without having made improvements. He appears to have been anxious that his survey of the land at the River Gananoque should not be shown until it was assured that he could by that means secure it.

At one stage of his dealings with, or application for, the Gananoque property, he appears to have been associated with Mr. Daniel Jones, who was, like himself, a United Empire Loyalist, and who previous to leaving the United States, or the country since and now known as such, had resided, at any rate occasionally, at Glens Falls in the State of New York, and owned a part of the great water power there. He was one of a family of Welsh descent and composed of seven brothers and one sister. The latter married an English officer and removed to England. Of the brothers, Jonathan Jones was the eldest. His occupation was that of a millwright, but he became a captain of engineers in the British service, and appears after the close of the Revolutionary War to have removed to Halifax, and to have received half pay during his life. John Jones, the second son, lived for a time near Fort Edward, and was subsequently a captain in the British service, and received half pay until his decease. Thomas Jones was also a captain in the same service and was killed near Oswego during the war. Dunham Jones died previously to the commencement of the Revolution.

Solomon Jones acted as an assistant surgeon in the British army, and after the peace settled in Canada, in the vicinity of what is now the Town of Prescott, and died at the age of sixty-five years. David Jones was a lieutenant in the King's service. He was betrothed to Jane McCrea, who was killed under the most painful circumstances on the 27th July, 1777, at or near Fort Edward. The engagement had been made before the commencement of the Revolutionary War, and supposing that the struggle would not be a lengthy one the lovers concluded to defer their marriage until it was over. But it soon appearing that the war would probably be of long continuance, it was arranged that Lieutenant Jones and Miss McCrea should meet at a house situate between the camps of the two armies, and not far from Fort Edward, and there be united in marriage by a clergyman. In pursuance of this arrangement Miss McCrea left her residence and proceeded alone in the direction of the appointed place of meeting. Scouting parties of the Indians being frequently out, it was feared by Mr. Jones that she might be intercepted by some of these, and thus become alarmed if not injured, and his solicitude for her safety was so great that he procured the services of an intelligent chief in whom he had confidence to keep watch over her, at such a distance as not to create alarm in her mind, and yet near enough to render her assistance in case of need. It so happened that she was discovered by one of the Indian scouting parties who made her a prisoner, but without any intention of doing her personal injury. The friendly chief approached the party for the purpose of affording her protection. A dispute arose amongst the captors as to which of them should have the honour of taking Miss McCrea into the British camp as a prisoner, and an Indian then recently from the North-West in order to settle the quarrel and to gratify his own savage propensity, drew his tomahawk and killed her before the friendly chief could interfere for her protection. He appears also to have taken off her scalp. The tragic and melancholy occurrence created a strong sensation in the British camp, and cast a gloom over the mind of her lover from which he never recovered; and in fact he was never known by the members of his family to smile afterward. After peace was concluded in 1783, he settled not far from Prescott, and lived with his brother Solomon above-mentioned until his death, which occurred suddenly, as was supposed from his having been overheated, but quite possibly from an affection of the heart.*

Of the seven Jones brothers, Daniel appears, with the exception of Dunham, to have been the only one who did not enter the King's service. But this did not secure him from persecution at the hands of the Revolutionary party. He had purchased a large tract of land in the Township of Kingsbury, and having gone down the Hudson River to make payment of a sum of money for part of this land, it was reported by persons hostile to him that he had gone to hold communication with the enemy. He sought safety in flight, and his personal property, which was large, was taken and converted to the use of the American service, and his real estate was subsequently confiscated by the State of New York. He came to Canada and eventually settled in Elizabethtown and within the limits of the present Town of Brockville, where he died in 1820. He had several daughters, and two sons, named respectively David and Daniel, who entered the profession of the law. Daniel was knighted at St. James Palace, London, in 1836, by King William the Fourth, and died soon after. David was for many years Registrar of the County of Leeds and died at his residence in Brockville in June, 1870.

By an instrument dated the 20th April, 1787, signed by Messrs. Jones and Stone, it is stated that they have been viewing and locating lands on the River Gananoque jointly, and have agreed that whatever advantages

*See also Ontario Historical Society, "Papers and Records," Vol. XII, p. 29.

might thereafter arise from the mill places on the said river should be held jointly between them, whether the said mill places might be obtained by the said location of one or the other or both of them. Mr. Stone appears to have forwarded Mr. Jones' application to a Mr. Delaney for recommendation by him, and after that had been obtained, the papers, surveys and letters were to be forwarded to Mr. Isaac Ogden of Quebec to make the application. But a rival applicant appeared in the person of Sir John Johnson, and there appears to have been some delay and also considerable danger that Sir John would carry the day. In a letter from Mr. Stone to Mr. Jones dated at Cornwall, 31st January, 1789, he says he has received a letter from Mr. Ogden, his agent in Quebec, who informs him that Sir John Johnson is determined to have the land they have surveyed at Gananoque, and that Mr. Ogden is apprehensive it will not be in his power to secure it to them. Mr. Stone says that in consequence he will set out the next morning for Quebec, and is determined to prosecute the business, and, in case he is "cast there," is determined still to seek for justice in England. He begs Mr. Jones to write to him at Quebec and let him know what he determines upon, and should he wish to join him in the prosecution he will need to send him more money. That he himself will begin the prosecution with ten guineas, and provided Mr. Jones puts in that sum and from time to time supplies him with cash to the amount of one-half of the expenses that may accrue, he will prosecute the business for their joint benefit, otherwise for himself only, and he asks to be informed of Mr. Jones' decision with all possible speed. It would appear that the latter gentleman for some reason withdrew from the negotiation or application, and we believe that the rival claims to the Gananoque property and water power including much of the present flourishing Town of Gananoque, were settled by a division between the claimants, Mr. Stone obtaining the west side of the river and Sir John Johnson the east, the boundaries running to the centre of the stream.

In a letter dated at Cornwall on the 29th March, 1789, and addressed to Mr. John Wilson, tinman, Montreal, Mr. Stone says the appearance of want in that quarter is every day more alarming, in consequence of which he encloses an order in his favor for £5 Halifax currency drawn by Mr. James Lynch on Messrs. Elliot & Forsyth, merchants of Montreal, and wishes Mr. Wilson to purchase for him four barrels of flour, two barrels of pork, and one-half cwt. of rice, but before doing so to call upon Col. Rankin with his best respects to himself and family, and learn of him if he has purchased any provisions for him, and if so to let that be in part of what he is to purchase for him, and to pay him for the same, and also to pay Captain Brennan five dollars due to him. He leaves the matter of price to Mr. Wilson's discretion, and says if he has an opportunity so that he can possibly send him any part thereof, particularly one barrel of flour, before the ice is out, he will oblige him. He also desires him to retain the remaining part of the money until further orders, but in a postcript asks him to pay 40/ or £3 to Mr. Finley Fisher, the school master, for his little boy's schooling, etc.

In the year 1791 Mr. Stone visited Connecticut and took with him his two children, William and Mary, whom he placed at school in Hartford. His wife Leah appears to have died subsequently to April, 1791, and (as is supposed) in 1793.

In 1800, 1801, or 1802 he appears still to have owned property in Cornwall, and to have been corresponding with one Dr. James Johnson in reference to it.

In or about 1792 or 1793, Mr. Stone appears to have settled in Gananoque. In a letter dated at that place on the 2d February, 1793, in that year, and addressed to His Excellency, Governor Simcoe, he says: "Permit me to inform your Excellency that I recovered my health sometime in November last from a fever I took at the head of Lake Ontario last July, since which I am commissioned to build a schooner of 40 tons burthen on my premises here. She is to sail out of this river and is to be called the *Leeds Trader,* and I expect will sail by the first of July next.

"I have erected a log hut for the convenience of the workmen, and hope in the course of this year to build for my own convenience, and stores for the public, and by that means to have it in my power to make some acknowledgment for the civility I have received, and the obligations I feel myself under to your Excellency."

According to a statement said to have been made in 1854 by one Mrs. Charlotte Jameson, then the oldest inhabitant of Gananoque, Joel Stone was the first white person who ever resided on the peninsula on the west side of the Gananoque River. He was landed from a French batteau and left alone. He raised a white handkerchief on a pole and a man living on an island saw it and sent off two Indians in a canoe to relieve the distressed traveller. They took him over to the island where a Frenchman named Cary, an uncle of Mrs. Jameson, lived alone in a hut. Eventually Mr. Stone and Cary removed to the mainland and the latter kept a house of public entertainment. The only mode of conveyance for travellers was by open boat, and the only bread to be obtained was hard biscuits. For Mr. Stone and for travellers they kept a kind called King's Biscuit, while for others they provided navy biscuit. They kept two cows and exchanged the milk with the batteau men for biscuit, and exchanged the latter again with the Indians for fish, venison, game, and wild fruit. Cary had been formerly a waiter and knew how to cook for and wait upon gentlemen, so that they were tolerably comfortable. One day when they were all absent, the building and all Mr. Stone's effects were burned, and this was the means of breaking up their family arrangements, as Cary took a farm two miles above Gananoque at Jameson's or Sheriff's Point, and lived there with his sister Mrs. Sheriff and his little girl, afterward Mrs. Jameson.

After having been five or six years a widower, Mr. Stone in 1798 made a proposal of marriage to a widow lady named Abigail Dayton, then residing in the Township of Burford in Upper Canada, but who had previously resided at or near New Milford, Connecticut. Her maiden name was Abigail Coggswell, and according to Leavitt's History of Leeds and Grenville, page 126, she was born at Preston, Connecticut, 13th August, 1750. Of her "foremothers" there are preserved the names of Judy Perkins, Hannah Brown, and Sarah Coggswell. A napkin made (woven) by Judy Perkins with her name on it, and now over two hundred years old, is still in existence and in the possession of a great granddaughter of Abigail Coggswell.

Abigail was a daughter of John Coggswell, who in an early day went to Wyoming, on the Susquehanna River, where he purchased a tract of land for which he paid and returned home. Not long after he heard of the rapid settling of North Carolina and "made an adventure" to that part of America and there died. In course of time the news of his death reached his family, and his son, a young man, set out to take possession of the land at or on which his father died. He was accompanied by a friend (a kinsman) and a faithful dog. Time passed on and in the course of a few months the family were joyfully surprised to see their old friend "Lion," the dog, enter the house one summer day just as evening was closing in. They all rushed out expecting to see Lion's master or that he would shortly appear, but alas! he was never more to return, and in far off North Carolina the father and son slept side by side.

A few days after the kinsman who had accompanied young Coggswell returned and related that the poor dog was missed immediately after his master's funeral. Thus it was evident that he had started alone for home, and had successfully accomplished his journey, during which he had had to traverse hundreds of miles. This was in or about the year 1754, when Abigail was only about four years of age. She was brought up in the care of a pious and exemplary grandmother, who trained and disciplined her young mind. At an early age she was impressed with a sense of religious things, but subsequently lost much of those impressions, until some years after her marriage it pleased God effectually to awaken her, and she was subsequently instrumental, under God, in bringing both her first and second husbands to Christ.

Miss Coggswell was married on the 8th April, 1770, to her first husband, Abraham Dayton, whose grandfather and father were also respectively named Abraham. The father married one Abia Bansley by whom he had several children. He was an officer in the British service and as such was upon the Plains of Abraham, near Quebec, under command of General Wolfe.

It would appear from his writings that Abraham Dayton, the husband of Abigail Coggswell, was one of the Society of Friends commonly called Quakers. He is said to have remained loyal to the King during the Revolutionary War. On the thirteenth day of the seventh month (13th July), 1787, and some years after the close of the war, he left New Milford, Connecticut, and set out to explore the western country to fix a settlement for the Friends. He first went to see Peter Miller's land at the head of the Juniata, then crossed the Alleghany near Fort Pitt, but finding no satisfaction returned and arrived at New Milford the eighth day of the ninth month (8th September). In 1788 he appears to have journeyed to Suffield and Granville, and at some time to Harpersfield, and Hudson. He settled at or near Cayuga Lake, and built mills, but subsequently finding things uncomfortable resolved to settle in the King's dominions and removed to Canada, as is supposed between 1790 and 1795 and settled in the Township of Burford, on the Grand River. It is said he was promised by Governor Simcoe a tract of land if he would bring a certain number of settlers to that part of the province. How far this was carried out is not known, but he appears not to have survived long after his settling in Burford, and to have died of consumption. Some little time previous to his death, two men named Fairchild—father and son—(one of whom was a Baptist preacher) happened to come to Mr. Dayton's house. They owned a mill about twenty-five miles away toward Lake Erie. Mrs. Dayton went outside the house to speak with them and asked them to saw four cherry boards for her and put them to season. (These were intended for Mr. Dayton's coffin.) When she re-entered the house her husband asked her what she had been saying to them and she told him. He said he ought to have thought of it himself. After his death two men were sent on horseback to get the boards and brought them, holding one under each arm, and John Eaton, a carpenter, made the coffin.

Shortly before his death, Mr. Dayton said to her " you have been a mother—a wife—a sister—and a friend." She supported him in her arms when he died and folded his arms and closed his eyes. It would appear from an entry in his family bible that he departed this life on 1st March, 1797, at Burford, he being then in the 52d year of his age.

A brother of Mr. Abraham Dayton named Nathan had settled at Gananoque, and in all probability it was from him or some member of his family that Mr. Stone learned of the death of Abraham. He waited until a year and a day had elapsed after that event, and then made an offer of marriage to the widow. The letters which passed between them both before and after marriage, or some of them, have been preserved, and may well form a part of Mr. Stone's memoir; and they are therefore published (not as exact copies in every respect, but virtually so, to all intents and purposes).

LEEDS NEAR KINGSTON,

30th March, 1798.

Madam:

I hope you will have the goodness to excuse this abrupt address to you—and suffer me to assure you that I am actuated by honorable and sincere motives in this proposition of M.— to you, and that from the knowledge I have of your character and situation since you resided in New Milford, I have to beg you will inform me, and in case you are not engaged I shall presume to wait on you in person for the purposes here hinted.

When you resided in New Milford I resided in Judea, a parish of Woodbury and had the pleasure to supply Mr. Dayton with many articles of goods, etc., etc., etc.

I saw Mr. Nathan Dayton and his family a few days past. They are all well and desire to be remembered kindly to you. I have consulted Mr. and Mrs. Dayton on the subject of this letter. They have recommended the proposal and say they hope it may meet your approbation, and have desired me to make use of their names.

I am sincerely,

Your very humble servant,

(Signed) JOEL STONE.

Mrs. Abigail Dayton.

LEEDS AT THE RIVER CADANOGHQUA,

NEAR KINGSTON, 13th April, 1798.

Madam:

Will you have the goodness to excuse whatever may appear impetuous in this second address to you, before I have had time to receive an answer to the first.

I have lived a widower five or six years past and am now determined to marry—provided I can find a person whose age, character, inclinations, etc., promise to add happiness to both. You are the person I have fixed my hopes upon—and pray Madam be kind enough candidly to inform me if you are married or engaged to marry. If not I shall take the liberty to come in person to see you and endeavor to convince you that our lives may be more happy together during the remainder of our time in this transitory world. And be assured that you are the first and only person I have ever (directly or indirectly) made any proposals of this nature to since I have been a widower.

I have two children—one a boy about 17 years (he is with me); the other a girl living with my sister in Connecticut.

I am most sincerely,

Your obedient humble servant,

(Signed) JOEL STONE.

Mrs. Abigail Dayton.

BURFORD, May the 28th, 1798.

Sir:

I received your letter the 22d of this instant, which causes me to write to you to let you know that I am not engaged to anyone, and I know not what to say for I have almost concluded in my own mind not to change my condition, for the world appears to be in a great tumult, and I am now free from any engagement to anyone, therefore I have no one to please but myself. I lost a tender companion, which I do not forget. There is no one that knows the loss of a kind friend but those that experience it. Therefore if you think it proper to form any further acquaintance on the subject by the lines which I have wrote to you, act your own pleasure, etc., etc.

Please to give my kind love to brother Nathan and his family. Tell them that brother Reuben lives with me and is like to be a cripple all his days. My daughter is well. I desire them to write to me the first opportunity.

So I subscribe myself a friend to all sincere, true hearted, and upright souls.

(Signed) ABIGAIL DAYTON

Mr. Joel Stone.

BURFORD, the 15th of June, 1798.

Sir:

I received your letter of the 30th of last March the 20th of May last, which causes me to write to you to let you know my present situation.

I am unfortunately left without a companion in the world and the loss of a kind friend is not easily to be erased out of my mind. I understand you are in the same situation for which I think you can sympathize with me.

I would further inform you that I have received another letter from you the tenth of this instant, and by examining the contents of your applications I have thought it most expedient to answer you on the subject of so weighty and important consequence. I would inform you that at the present I am not engaged to any person and had almost concluded never to change my present situation, but after solemnly contemplating upon the subject I would inform you that if you have a mind to pay me a visit the fore part of this fall I have not any just objection to make, so you can act your pleasure about it. As I have had some acquaintance with you formerly, I have not so much occasion to take up so much time in consideration before I can give an answer.

Please to remember me to my brother Nathan and family. Tell them that at the present we are all well and I am very desirous to see them.

So I have the honour to subscribe myself your, etc.,

(Signed) ABIGAIL DAYTON.

To Mr. Joel Stone, Esq.,
    Leeds, near Kingston.

LEEDS, 25th September, 1798.

Madam:

I duly received your very judicious answer to my two former letters dated at Burford, 15th June last, and assure you I am much disappointed to find myself in duty bound to write again, as I fully expected to have seen you in person before this time. I must inform you that I have been very ill with the Lake fever. Since I received your favor, on finding myself recovering I was fortunate enough to engage a man worthy of the trust to take charge of my raft to Montreal, in order that I might still cross the Lake this season. The person who was to take charge of my raft is now taken very ill, and I am obliged to go to Montreal (as the proceeding of my raft is indispensable).

It is now uncertain whether I shall be able to return soon enough to cross the Lake this season. Provided I can possibly return soon enough you may depend on seeing me this season. If not I shall endeavor to proceed in the winter—but Madam, I cannot wish that my promises and disappointments should stand in the way, provided you should have a good offer from another. I only trust in your good sense, that you will not accept a very crooked stick—until I can have the pleasure to see you.

Your brother Nathan and family are well, and Nathan says he intends to see you this season himself if possible.

I am, Madam, yours sincerely,

(Signed) JOEL STONE.

Mrs. Abigail Dayton.

KINGSTON, 23d May, 1799.

Dear Madam:

I this day arrived in Kingston and have barely time (before the vessel sails) to inform you that it is totally out of my power to be gone from home until the latter end of June next. I did expect the pleasure to receive a line from you, in answer to my letter to you dated the fore part of February last, which I sent in charge of a Mr. Kilborn to be delivered with his own hand.

I am, very sincerely,

(Signed) JOEL STONE.

To the Widow Abigail Dayton.

The exact date of their marriage is not known, but it must have taken place between the date of the letter last above contained and the early part of September in the same year, for in a letter dated at Kingston, 5th September, 1799, and addressed to her as Mrs. Abigail Stone, at River Cadanoughqua, (which must be the same as Gananoque) he says:

My Dear:

I forgot to inform you that Mr. Reuben Sherwood, Surveyor, agreed to survey the land whereon I live, at my request and to be at my house for that purpose on this day. I beg you will order Alexander McDonald and endeavor to get one hand more—Rosback, Gray, Loyd or one of Landon's boys, and Billy to assist him, as he will want three men with him. Roach and Sheriff will work at the chimney, but in case you cannot furnish Mr. Sherwood with three hands otherwise, Roach must go with him, and let the plowing be until I return.

I am your affectionate,

(Signed) JOEL STONE.

Mr. Stone appears to have been engaged in both milling and mercantile business, and also to have engaged in farming, and his wife appears to have been to him a true help-mate. Under date of 7th August, 1800, he writes to her from Montreal:

My Dear:

I expect this will be delivered to you by Mr. Marcus Hulings. He will leave a bill of boards and plank with you such as he will want next spring. I wish him and his father to be attended to if convenience will permit.

I gained health fast for several days past until this time, am not so well. I drank a pint of beer yesterday for the first time since I was in Town. The consequence is I have had an unpleasant night and day, but am getting somewhat easier. Mr. John Gray, Merchant, has returned from Upper Canada. He says that you had recovered your health in some measure, that he did not call on you, but that he was at the red house and in the mill on his way down. God be pleased that your health may be restored, my dear, I hope may be the case.

I yesterday sold four cribs of my boards and I hope soon to sell the whole, but at a very low rate indeed. But boards are not falling now—they are rather gaining, and my health will not as yet permit me to travel. But I hope that may be the case soon, and that I may be able also to settle my business. Also tell Billy to procure timothy seed and clover seed if possible and let that field be well stocked down to grass, whatever is or is not put into it, and tell him to apply to Mr. Nathan Dayton for seed wheat, and let it be well and effectually harrowed, and sowed with wheat and grass seed—all that is not or cannot be sowed with turnips and timothy.

Tell Bean and Holsted by all means to push the mill, cut all the boards and plank they possibly can, and remember that after a storm comes a calm. Let us not fail to be prepared with dishes, when it may rain.

I am, my dear,

Your most affectionate,

(Signed) JOEL STONE.

And under date 6th July, 1801, he also writes to her from Montreal:

My Dear:

I received your letter dated the next day after I left home, 17th June, about three days past, by mere accident. I mark well the contents thereof, approve of what you have done, and must, with pleasure, submit to your own wisdom to do as you think best until I can get home, which I do not intend shall be long; but I have not yet been able to deliver any of my boards and plank. Andrew, William and David will set off to-morrow morning with the boat loaded with the following packages and articles agreeable to the enclosed bills:

One large cask wine, two large trunks, one small trunk, the box or chest, two barrels, two kegs (one best Madeira wine, one cider vinegar), one cask nails, two small bales, one shovel, one spade. Enclosed I send you four keys, one to each of the trunks, and one to the chest. Please to be careful in unpacking the pork barrel. It has a bottle of castor oil and a phial of pikery roped up in the blankets.

In the barrels and in your chest you will find a number of the articles we had on board the raft, two or three axes, etc., and you will find tobacco and snuff (viz.), two lbs. snuff only; also Bohea tea in one of the casks, and Hysen tea in one of the large trunks. The Bohea tea is 6/ per lb. in case you sell any, and the tobacco 3/. Please to put the tobacco in some moist place. The other articles I have marked the price to sell at in the bills in my own hand writing. I need not caution you to sell for cash only, except where we owe and to pay for what we must buy. The large cask of wine may be very good to drink as wine and water, and you may sell it at 5/ per gallon if you can, but I bought it with a view of making vinegar only. I gave 1/0 per gallon for it. The articles in the large trunk where the Hyson tea is are not marked, nor is the bill sent. You will find Turlington's drops in the trunk where the Hyson tea is, which you may sell at 5/ per bottle, but those in the pork barrel, large phials, keep for your own use.

You will set the people at work as you find most necessary until I get home. I must, if possible, bring down another raft this season. Old Mr. Chaple will be up again as soon as he has done visiting his friends.

I am, my dear in great haste, with a very bad pen and ink and my best exertions.

Your most affectionate,

(Signed) JOEL STONE.

Mr. Stone was also at an early day Collector of His Majesty's Customs at Gananoque, and it is more than probable that he was the first one appointed at that place. The duties were not probably very onerous, and William Moore, whose birth in 1781 has been already referred to, and who is called "Billy" in some of his father's letters, appears to have acted as a deputy collector of customs. There was a tariff, of which a copy is subjoined. It was certainly not as extensive a one as is in force now.

By a commission dated the 2nd January, 1809, and given under the hand and seal of His Excellency, Francis Gore, Lieutenant-Governor of Upper Canada, Mr. Stone was appointed a colonel in the second regiment of militia in the County of Leeds, which rank he held during the memorable war of 1812-14, and appears during it to have been in command at Gananoque. In September, 1812, a body of United States soldiery under the command of one Forsyth made an attack upon the place, and one of the soldiers fired a shot into Col. Stone's house with the result of wounding Mrs. Stone in the thigh. So great was her fortitude that she did not mention her wound, probably for fear of alarming the women who were with her, nor did they become aware of it until they saw the blood running from her shoe. Forsyth's raid was an inglorious one, apparently quite worthy of the man, and Col. Wm. F. Coffin in his book on the war of 1812 describes it.

Colonel Stone reported this affair to his superior officer, Colonel Lethbridge, then in command at Prescott, and under date of the 21st September, 1812, that officer wrote him as follows:

"I am extremely concerned at the report you have made in your letter of yesterday of the successful attack made by the American vessels on the port of Gananoque, and though there can be no excuse for the devastations committed by the enemy, yet I cannot help inferring from the tenor of your letter that some omission of necessary vigilance must have occurred, and it is my particular desire that you will distinctly state what number of officers by name—non-commissioned officers— and private men were present at the port when the attack on the part of the enemy (occurred). After my orders to have the flank companies completed to the establishment provided by law, I presume the force at Gananoque must have been considerable, unless your detachment to assist in guarding the batteaux to Kingston was very large indeed. Of the numbers sent on this service you will be pleased to inform me. I hardly know how your losses can be supplied. I regret much to find that the least injury should have been sustained by Mrs. Stone.

"I am in hopes to hear more particulars of this unpleasant affair and that the post can be still held with increased energy.

"In the possibility of your express to Kingston being intercepted I sent from this an express to Col. Vincent by way of the back concessions.

It is not in my power to furnish any succor to your post from hence. The disaster is not without a remedy, and I trust that should any similar attempt be made in future it will end in the disgrace of the assailants. I have as yet received no rolls of the flank companies, agreeable to my circular letter of the 9th inst.

"I have this day sent down an officer on purpose to Montreal to procure the necessary equipment—such as shoes, pantaloons, jackets and watch coats.

I have the honor to be,

Your most obedient servant,

(Signed) R. D. LETHBRIDGE, *Colonel I.F.O.*"

"You will be pleased to send as soon as possible an accurate return of the arms, ammunition, and flints that have been received by the 2d Batt. Leeds Militia from the public."

It would appear that Col. Stone deemed it expedient that a block-house should be built at Gananoque, and under date 19th October, 1812, Mr. Richard Cartwright (grandfather of the late Sir Richard Cartwright), wrote him from Kingston as follows:

Dear Sir:

I wish your block-house had been thought of earlier and mentioned to Colonel Vincent when you were on the spot. He is alarmed at the expense, and indeed I think that the same purpose might be answered at a much cheaper rate. What is there to prevent the men themselves from throwing up a building of round logs that would be equally strong and warm, though it would not look so well? By making it double and filling it in with earth and sod this would be completely effected. The nails and glass would be cheerfully furnished. But in times like these it is expected that the people of the country will do as much as they can for their own protection.

We have obtained an important victory but it has cost us dear. We have lost our heroic Governor, who fell at the head of the 2d flank company of the 49th Regiment in ascending the hill at Queenstown. The invaders to a man have been killed or taken. Major General Wadsworth, many officers and about a thousand men are our prisoners. It is not known how many were killed. The fighting continued near seven hours when the Americans were completely surrounded and called for quarters. Many of them must, of course, have fallen. The General and his aide-de-camp, Lt.-Col. McDonell, are the only officers slain on our side, and their loss spreads a gloom over our triumphs. The militia are said to have behaved well on this trying occasion; and I hope their noble example will have a proper effect in every other part of the Province. This affair took place on the 14th. The Americans landed at Queenstown before daylight, and at some part above the mountain, as it is called, where it was supposed to be impracticable to cross the river, and which was in consequence unguarded.

Yours truly,

(Signed) RICHARD CARTWRIGHT.

After having retained his military command for several years, Colonel Stone tendered his resignation which was accepted and the following general order issued:

ADJUTANT GENERAL'S OFFICE,

YORK, 10th January, 1822.

His Excellency, the Lieutenant-Governor, is pleased to accept the resignation of Colonel Stone of the 2d Regiment of Leeds Militia.

His Excellency upon this occasion is pleased to declare in general orders, the high sense he entertains of the services of Colonel Stone who for a period of forty years has served his King and country with exemplary fidelity, and his regret that advanced age should deprive the Militia of the Province of so good and so zealous an officer.

In transmitting this order Colonel James Fitzgibbon wrote as follows:

Dear Colonel:

Col. Coffin is anxious that you should receive a copy of this order without delay. The post is going out and I cannot find the Colonel to add his signature; I therefore send it without rather than lose the post, and remain dear Colonel,

Truly yours,

(Signed) JAMES FITZGIBBON.

Upon this occasion the militia residing within the Townships of Burgess and Elmsley were formed into a regiment to be styled the third regiment of Leeds Militia, and Captain Jonas Jones (afterward the Honourable Mr. Justice Jonas Jones), was appointed Lieutenant-Colonel thereof, while Captain Charles Jones, (then or afterward the Honourable Charles Jones), was appointed Colonel of the second regiment *vice* Stone resigned.

Mr. Stone was a commissioner of the peace or justice of the peace for many years, and for a time was Chairman of the Court of General Sessions of the Peace for the Johnstown District. He was also one of the commissioners for the District of Johnstown for administering the oath to half pay officers.

In 1812 he was returning officer at an election of a member for the County of Leeds to the Assembly of Upper Canada. Upon this occasion Livius P. Sherwood (afterward the Honourable Mr. Justice Sherwood) was returned, and the indenture of election, which bears date 2nd June, 1812, was executed by Joel Stone, Samuel Simmon, (or Seaman), John Kincaid, John McNeil, Joshua Adams, James Breakenridge, Robert McLean, and Livius P. Sherwood.

In March, 1819, a Land Board was appointed for each of the Districts, and that for the District of Johnstown was composed of Solomon Jones, Chairman, Joel Stone, Charles Jones, Adiel Sherwood and Dr. E. Hubble. The members of the Board were empowered to locate any emigrants or other persons desirous of becoming a settler in the respective District on a lot of 100 acres under such limitations, restrictions and rules as from time to time might be made for the government of said Boards by any order in concert.

It has been already mentioned that Mr. Stone had three children by his first marriage, one of whom died in infancy, while the other two—a son and daughter, attained maturity. This son is the one for whose schooling, as we have already seen, he requested Mr. John Wilson to pay Mr. Finley Fisher, the school-master 40/ or £3, and who was seventeen years of age when his father wrote to Mrs. Dayton in April, 1798. He appears to have acted as a collector of customs in Gananoque, and is said to have died of consumption at that place in 1809.

The daughter, who was named Mary, in the year 1811 married Charles McDonald, who had settled at Gananoque in or about the year 1810. He was the son of one John McDonald and his wife Emily Cameron, both at one time of Blair Athol, Perthshire, Scotland, and who emigrated to America in or about the year 1787, and settled at Athol, Warren County, New York.

Charles McDonald appears to have been an active man of business and built a saw and grist mill, and in 1812 opened at Gananoque a general store for the supply of the inhabitants of the adjacent country with dry goods, groceries, hardware, and crockery, in exchange for the products of the country; these consisting largely of square pine, oak, and elm timber, saw logs and staves with some potash. Pork, beef, hay, oats, and wheat were not produced in sufficient quantities to fully supply the demand for the shanty men engaged in lumbering during the winter.

In 1817, John McDonald, a merchant of Troy, New York (and afterward the Honourable John McDonald of Gananoque), joined his brother Charles, and the well known firm of C. & J. McDonald was formed. Their business rapidly increased until it controlled the greater part of the lumber trade of the Gananoque River, and its tributaries. Money being scarce, the whole of this trade was carried on upon credit, and the books of the firm not only bore the names of almost the entire community, but also recorded the transactions of each with the firm and also with his neighbours.

In 1825 Colin McDonald, another brother became a member of the firm, which was henceforth known as C. & J. McDonald & Co. It may be of interest to state that among others who were at one time in the employ of this firm, were Mr. J. J. C. Abbott, afterward the Honourable J. J. C. Abbott of Montreal, Senator, a distinguished lawyer, Government leader in the Senate, and Premier of Canada, and Mr. John Macdonald, afterward the Honourable John Macdonald, of Toronto, Senator, one of the merchant princes of Canada, and a gentleman who was foremost in all Christian and charitable work.

Charles McDonald died in 1826 and his wife Mary some years subsequently. Of their marriage were born two daughters who died in infancy, and three sons, of whom one is William Stone Macdonald, Esq., of Blinkbonny, Gananoque.

Of Mr. Joel Stone's religious life in his early years we have not much, if any, information, although he is believed to have been a member of the Church of England. The clergymen of that community were, in the early part of this century, few in number in what was then Upper Canada. Indeed, from the Quebec Almanac of 1810 it would appear that at that time in the Province of Upper and Lower Canada there were (including the Bishop of Quebec and the Chaplain to the garrison at Quebec), only some fifteen or sixteen clergymen, of whom there were in Upper Canada, at Kingston, Rev. Dr. Stuart; at York, Rev. Mr. Stuart; at Niagara, Rev. Mr. Addison; at Fredericksburg and Ernest Town, Rev. Mr. Langhorne; at Cornwall, Rev. Mr. (after Bishop) Strachan; and at Sandwich, Rev. Mr. Pollard; while at the same time there were but three clergymen of the Church of Scotland in the two provinces, viz., the Rev. Alexander Spark, D.D., at Quebec, the Rev. Mr. Somerville at Montreal, and the Rev. John Bethune at New Oswegatchie.

The Methodists were among the early pioneers of the country and Mr. Stone's second wife was a member of that communion. Their house was a home and a stopping place for the preachers and ministers, who travelled backward and forward, and it would appear that the Rev. Thomas Whitehead, Elder Ryan, and the Reverend Thaddeus Osgood were among those who visited Joel Stone and his wife. It has been already stated that the latter was the means of bringing her first and second husbands to Christ, and in a letter by her to her daughter, Mrs. Abia Mallory, and dated 20th November, 1818, informs her that the Colonel has joined the Methodists.

The following extracts from letters written by Col. Stone afford some evidence of his spiritual state. Writing to his sister, Hannah Levingworth, on 13th March, 1821, after his return from a journey, he says: "The more I reflect, the more thankful I feel to the Fountain of all Good that my health and strength has been preserved throughout my whole tour, which has afforded me so great consolation, in once more seeing in time three (of my) own dear sisters, one brother, four brothers-in-law, with the greater part of their respective families, also the greater part of the families of my departed sisters. May it be a means of renewing in us all a full determination to persevere in performing the duties and embracing the great privileges allotted to each of us here on earth, in that only way whereby we may justly obtain a hope of a much more joyful meeting in peace before our great and awful judge, there to join with one accord and sing praises to the Lamb that takest away the sins of the world, forevermore."

And in a letter to his brother Leman Stone, dated 15th February, 1823, he says: "Dear brother, it gives us real consolation to have reason (from the tenor of your letter) to hope you are seeking the only way for future bliss, through the Blessed Mediator. May you obtain justification and sanctification through that faith which worketh true repentance into perfect love for our blessed Lord and Saviour, Jesus Christ; and in order that you may free your mind from tradition and prejudice even for or against the Methodist, I beg leave to recommend a small book entitled 'A True and Complete Portraiture of Methodism.' It may cost a dollar, and permit me to beg as a favor you will purchase it and read it carefully once through."

In October or November, 1833, Col. Stone was attacked by a severe cold which, at his then great age, proved to be fatal; and he died at his residence at Gananoque on the 20th November, 1833. His death was a great blow to his wife, and it is said that some of the stern fortitude displayed on a previous occasion appeared to be gone. She survived him nearly ten years, and died at Gananoque, after a short illness, on the 4th day of August, 1843, at the age of nearly 93 years.

Of her it has been written by one who knew her well that "by her death her extensive family connection lost their safe and wise counsellor, the church lost a pillar, and an ornament, the widow and orphan lost a protector, and one that was often a safe depository of their little fortunes, or any valuable papers, the poor lost a warm friend, and heaven received a beautiful spirit, purified by the trials of life."

About four miles from Gananoque, on the front road to Kingston, and near the beautiful River St. Lawrence, is the Willow Bank Cemetery. Within it are interred the mortal remains of Joel Stone and Abigail his wife, and there shall they rest until the Lord Himself shall descend from heaven with a shout, with the voice of the archangel, and with the trump of God, and the dead in Christ shall rise and shall be caught up together with those who shall be Christ's at His coming, in the clouds, to meet the Lord in the air, and so shall ever be with the Lord.

XIV.

PIONEER SCHOOLS OF UPPER CANADA.

By Frank Eames.

The essential function of the common school is the faithful development of character and executive habits in the child. The child of normal birth has executive, reflective and receptive possibilities, in some degree equal. If the two latter are trained, and the former slighted, in the child, one may deem it as a weakling hurled into the maelstrom of life, where it is invariably overwhelmed by disappointments. If a child's receptive powers enable it to reflect, any ultimate good which might accrue from its mental activity is doomed if it cannot execute the thought. Hence the need of the school to develop the child's executive powers.

The first healthy sign of awakening in a new community is evinced when decisive action is taken in behalf of intellectual, moral and spiritual uplift. Crude and humble may have been the edifices erected for the propagation of religion and education, and yet from beneath their roofs and from within their precincts have emerged the youth who have been the hope and pride of the country for more than a hundred years; by their statecraft and oratory Canada has been elevated to a proud position among nations in a brief space; by their deeds of arms in the field she has won not only mere glory and honours, but the respect of all noble and refined races as well as the awe of the most unscrupulous.

The humble roofs of the early Common Schools of Upper Canada sheltered children whose natural will and executive abilities won them positions during their lives, the memory of which will be imperishable so long as the pen of history may trace their lineaments.

This paper is intended to give a more intimate knowledge of those early edifices, affording to the teachers of history a ready reference list, showing when and where, throughout Upper Canada, the first schools were located and organized. Such meagre details of their inception as my opportunities have afforded, are here given to both student and teacher. The annexed data is too much dispersed throughout the county and local histories and archives to give ready information; so that, although there is still a lack of completeness which is perhaps regrettable, yet it is hoped the compilation may prove sufficiently useful to warrant some approval of both the effort and the idea.

In the Canadian Archives Report for 1889, page xxi, 3rd paragraph, we are informed that the Rev. John Stuart was a teacher in Montreal and later became the earliest teacher in Upper Canada. The paragraph, in part, reads as follows: " The earliest teacher in Montreal of whose life there is any definite information was the Rev. John Stuart, afterwards first Anglican clergyman at Cataraqui, now Kingston. He was born in the Province of Virginia, in 1736, according to Hawkins; Sabine says 1740, and was ordained in England, returning in 1770 to Philadelphia, from which place he was sent to the Mohawk Valley as an Indian Missionary."*

"In the following October (1781) he was, however, in Canada, and opened an academy in Montreal for youth, in conjunction with Mr. Christie." (*Ibid.*)

"The warrants show that the Government allowance to him was £50 sterling a year, continued until he left to become chaplain at Cataraqui." (Page xxii.)

"The great desire of Mr. Stuart appears to have been to settle at Cataraqui, and in February, 1784, he wrote twice to Major Mathews, pressing his request. In April, he had engaged a substitute to take charge of his school during the time he proposed to be absent. In July he reported that he had visited Cataraqui, where he obtained a lot within a mile of the barracks, and had spent some time among the Indians. The Society had left to himself the choice of the place of his future residence, but had reduced the salary he had received as missionary to the Mohawks from £70 to £50 for the new station, and he asked if he was to obtain the office of Chaplain at Cataraqui. In 1786, says Sabine, he opened a school at Kingston, which agrees with the indications afforded by the warrants, the last of which, for his salary as schoolmaster in Montreal, is for the six months from the first of November, 1785, to the 30th April, 1786, for £25, equal to £50 a year; the first for his salary "as Minister of the Church of England at Cataraqui" for the six months beginning on the first of May, 1786, and ending on the 31st of October, for £50, being double the salary as schoolmaster. It is unnecessary to follow Mr. Stuart further, as he ceased from this time to have any connection with the work of education in Montreal." (*Ibid.*, p. xxii.)

Dr. J. G. Hodgins, in his valuable history of "Schools and Colleges of Ontario, 1792-1910." (Chap. I, par. 2, page 1, Part I) gives the date of the first school established in Upper Canada as 1785, which refers to the "Select Classical School." But the date of the same event seems to be more correctly given as 1786 in Dr. Hodgins' "Documentary History of Education," Vol. I, p. 30. The Rev. Mr. Stuart's lament in a letter to an old friend in the United States in 1785 is, "The greatest inconvenience I feel here, is there being no school for our boys." (Canniff's "History," p. 330.)

THE LIST OF PIONEER SCHOOLS.

1786.

KINGSTON (Cataraqui). Enough has been set forth to establish the fact that the first school in Upper Canada was taught at Kingston by the Reverend John Stuart, who commenced his work immediately following the first coming of the U. E. Loyalists. A Mr. Donovan taught the Garrison school there at the same time. Ryerson Memorial Volume, by J. G. Hodgins,

*Henry J. Morgan, in his "Sketches of Celebrated Canadians", states that the Rev. John Stuart was born on the 24th Feb., 1740, at Harrisburg, in the State of Pennsylvania. La Rochefoucault (see Ont. Archives Report, 1916, p. 74), also gave Harrisburg as Mr. Stuart's native place.

LL.D., p. 38 (1889). La Rochefoucault mentions in his Travels in Canada, 1795, the school at Kingston, where, he says, the scholars paid one dollar per month. (Canniff, p. 331; and Ryerson Mem. Volume, p. 38; also, Ontario Archives Report, 1916, p. 75.)

FREDERICKSBURG (Bay of Quinte). Mr. Clark, the father of Major Clark of Edwardsburg, Dundas County, was the teacher. (Canniff, p. 330.)

ERNESTTOWN (Bay of Quinte). A Mr. Smith was the teacher. (Ryerson Mem. Volume, p. 38.) Rev. John Langhorn, a Church of England Missionary at Ernesttown and Bath from 1787 to 1812 was also teacher of a school there. (Ryerson Memorial Volume, p. 40. See also Ontario Hist. Society's "Papers and Records," Vol. I, p. 13, for sketch of Rev. Mr. Langhorn, by Thomas W. Casey, and his parish registers.)

1787.

GRAND RIVER. In Colonel Stone's "Life of Joseph Brant," page 398, under the year 1795, referring to the Chief's appreciation of the great value of education, there is the following statement: "In his first negotiations with Gen'l Haldimand after the close of the war, he made provision for the erection of a Church and Schoolhouse." On page 431, under the same year, the following statement appears: "One of his first stipulations with the Commander-in-Chief on the acquisition of his new territory, was for the building of a Church, a Schoolhouse and a Flouring Mill." Again in reference to the Grand River School, on p. 49 of the Canadian Archives Report (1889), from a report on the state of religion in Canada written apparently in 1788, we learn that "There is a Settlement likewise of the Six Nations, at a Village upon the Grand River, 40 miles above Niagara, who stipulated with General Haldimand that Government should build them a Church and furnish them with a Minister and Schoolmaster. Sir John Johnson has already established the latter, and pays him."

1788.

MATILDA (Dundas County). From the "History of Dundas," we learn that Mr. Clark, above referred to as being at the Bay of Quinte, "arrived with his family in Montreal, in the year 1786, and proceeded to the Bay of Quinte. He remained two years at the Bay, employed in teaching. In 1788, he came to Matilda, Dundas County .... A few of the neighbours assisted in the erection of a school house, in which he taught for several years. This was the first school in Dundas County."

ADOLPHUSTOWN. Playter states: "In the year 1788, a pious young man called Lyons, an exhorter in the Methodist Episcopal Church, came to Canada, and engaged in teaching a school in Adolphustown," "upon Hay Bay, or the Fourth Concession." Quoted in "History of the Settlement of Upper Canada," by William Canniff, M.D. (1872), p. 331.

1789.

PORT ROWAN (Norfolk County). A school was taught here by a gentleman called Deacon Trayes, who was also a Baptist Minister.

1791.

FORT MALDEN (Essex County). Gottlob Senseman, a Moravian Church layman, teacher. See Rev. John Morrison's paper in Vol. 12, page 176, Ont. Hist. Soc. "Papers and Records," "David Zeisberger and his Delaware Indians." The Rev. gentleman states (p. 177) that, "He, (Zeisberger) after negotiations with the British Authorities, led his band of Delaware Indians into Canada, in 1791, spending one year on the bank of the Detroit River, where Fort Malden was afterwards built." During this year's residence at the site of the "Warte, or Watch Tower," it is evident that school was taught. From David Zeisberger's Diary, which is published in the above article, there is an entry (p. 187) under date of Saturday, September 10th, 1791: "Mr. Dolson came from the Thames, bringing his two children to put them to our school, of which Bro. Senseman was teacher."

NAPANEE. In Canniff's "History of the Settlement of Upper Canada," page 331, Mr. Robert Clark says, "My boys commenced going to school to Mr. Daniel Allen Atkins on the 18th of January, 1791."

1792.

NEWARK (Niagara). The Rev. Robert Addison taught at Newark in this year. (Ryerson Memorial Volume, p. 38.) Rev. Mr. Addison was the Episcopalian minister at the seat of Government at Newark (Niagara).

BAY OF QUINTE. The Rev. John Stuart, soon after going to Kingston, took steps to secure and place a school teacher among the Mohawks of the Bay of Quinte. According to one statement this role had been filled by the Missionary himself, he having, according to certain stipulations, divided his activities between the Loyalists and the Indians. The Society for the Propagation of the Gospel had arranged and set aside, for the teacher's maintenance, the sum of £30. According to Canniff's "History" (p. 314), the precise time when this school was opened it is impossible to determine, and he adds that the first reference to it is in a letter "written by John Bininger, then living in Adolphustown, to his father, the Rev. Abraham Bininger of Camden, New York." The letter bore date, Sept. 18th, 1792, and states that "Being in Kingston, I heard, as it were accidentally, that the Rev. John Stuart wanted, on behalf of the Society in England, to hire a teacher for the Mohawks up this Bay, accordingly I made an offer of my services." Mr. Stuart accepted the offer, John Bininger giving his employers notice of his desire to make a change; they, however, refused to release him for two months, after which he removed to the Mohawk Village (p. 315). From an old account book the following was taken, referring to John Bininger:—"November the 13th (1792) moved from Adolphustown to the Mohawk Village."—Canniff. p. 315. "Mr. John Bininger ceased to be a teacher to the Mohawks some time in the latter part of 1795 or first part of 1796."—Canniff, p. 317. In 1796 one William Bell was the schoolmaster to the Mohawks of Quinte. (For several letters from the Rev. John Stuart to Mr. Bell regarding the Mohawk school, see Canniff's "History," pages 317-319.)

1793.

MORAVIANTOWN (Township of Zone, Kent County). David Zeisberger's settlement on the River Thames. Rev. John Morrison's paper (previously quoted) (Ont. Hist. Soc., XII, p. 189.) Zeisberger's Diary states: "Dec. 26th, 1792. All the brethren went out to cut, square and split timber into boards for a schoolhouse." The next item but one bears date "Jan. 10th, 1793. Our schoolhouse finished." Oct. 14th: "Our schoolhouse covered with clapboards." David Zeisberger's diary also has the following:—"Towards evening, March 31st (1794), Governor Simcoe arrived with a suite of officers and soldiers and eight Mohawks, by water from Niagara. He at once asked for our schoolhouse as a lodging. It was cold, having snowed through the day. He was much pleased when Bro. Senseman offered his house, where he, together with his officers, then lodged. Two of his officers had been here with him last year. The soldiers lay close by in the schoolhouse, but the Mohawks were divided between two Indian houses." (*Ibid*, p. 192.) In 1796 an item reads, "Feb. 22nd. Our young people who go to school are so set upon it, they make it their chief business and prefer it to everything. Went and cut wood for Brother Senseman at his sugar hut, so he might not be hindered by work from keeping school. Many of them can write a good English hand."

1794.

NEWARK (Niagara). Rev. Mr. Burns opened a school here, he being also the Presbyterian Minister. Ryerson Mem. Vol., p. 38. Mr. Richard Cockrel opened an evening school in Newark in 1796. (Ryerson Mem. Vol., p. 38, also Canniff's "History," p. 331.) From the Ryerson Memorial Volume, p. 38, we also learn of a Mr. James Blayney opening a school at Niagara in 1797.

1796.

ANCASTER. In 1796 or in 1797, Mr. Cockrel opened another school, viz., in Ancaster, having transferred his school at Newark to the Rev. Mr. Arthur. (Ryerson Memorial Volume, p. 38.)

1798.

TORONTO (York). William Cooper taught what appears to have been the first school established here, situated on George Street. Hodgins' Ryerson Memorial Volume, p. 38.

1799.

ADOLPHUSTOWN. Ex-sheriff Henry Ruttan has left us some information regarding the first school of this locality, which he attended when he was seven years of age. (Canniff's "History," p. 331.) Mrs. Cranahan taught the school to which he was sent. She is the first woman teacher of this Province of which there is a record. Teachers at other places near there bore the several names of William Faulkiner, Thomas Morden, Jonathan Clark. He further stated that there was an evening school some five miles away. (Canniff's "History," pages 331, 332.)

ST. CATHARINES. By an Act of the Legislature of Upper Canada, "To provide for the Education and the Support of Orphan Children," an Orphan School was established near St. Catharines. (Ryerson Memorial Volume, p. 39.)

1800.

BROCKVILLE. Adiel Sherwood taught a school near here according to Canniff (p. 275), but whether it was at the old "Tin Cap," or at the Hallock schoolhouse, is not made clear. (See 1811, near Brockville.)

KINGSTON. John Strachan, a name destined to remain prominent as a founder and scholar, left his schoolhouse in Kettle, Scotland, where he was the master, to recommence his career in Kingston, U.C., where he arrived on the last day of the year, 1799. Upon the foundation so well and truly laid by his worthy predecessor, John Stuart, along educational lines, John Strachan expected to establish a college which it had been proposed to erect during the Simcoe regime; the Governor having left for England, the proposed College project had been abandoned, for a time at least. Mr. Strachan thereupon entered into an understanding with the Hon. Richard Cartwright (grandfather of the late Sir Richard) and Mr. Robert Hamilton to open a school in which, beside instructing their sons, he was to be privileged to give tuition to ten others, the fees to be ten pounds sterling from each per annum. John Strachan remained at this post three years, during which time he proceeded to apply himself to the study of Divinity. He was ordained in 1804 and removed to the Mission at Cornwall, where at the request of the parents of his former pupils, he established a private school and later a Grammar School, and from their portals there emerged three men who respectively became the worthy recipients of the honours of their King and country: Sir John Beverley Robinson (Chief Justice of Upper Canada, 1829); Sir J. B. Macaulay (Chief Justice of the Common Pleas), and the Hon. Jonas Jones (a puisne judge). The Rev. John Strachan became the well known Bishop of Toronto in after years. (Rattray's "Scot in British North America," Canniff, Hodgins, Morgan's "Sketches.") When Barnabas Bidwell removed from Bath to Kingston in 1813, he continued his occupation of teaching, and taught at the latter place for twenty years until he died in 1833. (Ryerson Mem. Volume, p. 40.) The Midland District Grammar School at Kingston was incorporated in 1815. (*Ibid*, p. 40.)

1802.

NIAGARA. A Mr. and Mrs. Tyler taught school in the near neighbourhood of this place; the exact site of which I have been unable to learn. (Ryerson Memorial Volume, p. 38.)

TORONTO (York). The Classical School conducted by Dr. Baldwin came into existence at this time. (Hodgins' Ryerson Memorial Volume. p. 38.)

1803.

GRASSY POINT (Bay of Quinte). The first school was taught here by John James. (Canniff's "History," p. 332.)

HIGH SHORE. At this locality (Township of Sophiasburg, Prince Edward County) a school was carried on by a Mr. Salisbury. (*Ibid*, p. 332.)

VITTORIA (Norfolk County). The Rev. Dr. Egerton Ryerson is authority for the statement that a Mr. Mitchell taught a school here in 1803.

KINGSTON. John Strachan opened another school at this place.

1804.

CORNWALL. It was in this year that Dr. Strachan opened the school at this place. (Ryerson Mem. Vol., p. 38.) The Rev. Robert Baldwin was appointed Grammar School Master at Cornwall in 1814, *vice* Rev. John Bethune, resigned. (*Ibid*, p. 40.)

1805.

MYERS' CREEK (Belleville). Rev. Wm. Wright (Presbyterian) opened its first school this year, according to the authority of Dr. Hodgins, following Canniff's "History" (p. 332). (Ryerson Memorial Volume, p. 38.) This gentleman was succeeded by a Mr. Leslie.

SCARBORO. "James Elliot's house was utilized by an Englishman named Mr. Pocock, as a school, in the year 1805; it was the first school in the township and stood on lot 22, concession D, in the extreme north-west corner of the present section 9. The first schoolhouse built in the township was on the Springfield farm, near the line between lots 23 and 24, concession I, and within a few rods of where the Church of St. Andrew's now stands." David Boyle, Scarboro, 1796-1896.

1806.

ERNESTTOWN. In the second concession a Mr. Smith was tutor of a school at this period. (Canniff, p. 332.)

HAY BAY. School was taught in a log house here by a Mr. McDougall. (Canniff, p. 332.)

1807.

MYERS' CREEK (Belleville). James Potter succeeded teacher Leslie, referred to under "1805."

TORONTO (York). Rev. Geo. O'Kill Stewart, D.D., was appointed, by Governor Gore, Headmaster of the Home District Grammar School at York. This school was opened the first Monday in June. It stood in a field north of Adelaide Street, containing about six acres, bounded west by Church Street, east by Jarvis Street. The building was a plain wooden structure about 55 feet long and some 40 feet wide. The appointment was signed by Governor Gore. Hodgins' Ryerson Memorial Volume, p. 39. In 1812, the Rev. John Strachan succeeded the Rev. Geo. O'Kill Stewart, as Headmaster. (Ryerson Memorial Volume, p. 40.)

1810.

ELGIN (Leeds County). Township of South Crosby, County of Leeds. The first schoolhouse was built about 1810 or 1811. "Leeds and Grenville." (Leavitt.)

PRESCOTT. Major Jessup, immediately following his completion of the survey for the townsite, made preparation for a schoolhouse. Leavitt's "History of Leeds and Grenville."

1811.

JOHNSTOWN DISTRICT. Seven miles west of Brockville there dwelt a minister known as the Rev. Mr. Halleck or Hallock (both modes of spelling the name are to be found in the two authorities available) and it was at the home of this gentleman in all probability that the school existed. That it did exist we are informed in Leavitt's "History of the United Counties of Leeds and Grenville." According to a paper by Holly S. Seaman on the missionary labours of the Rev. William Smart, that Rev. gentleman visited at the Hallock School and preached there for twenty-seven consecutive New Year's days and at the old "Tin Cap" schoolhouse the same number of Christmas days. Page 184, Ont. Hist. Soc. "Papers and Records," Vol. 5 (1904).

BROCKVILLE. Sometime prior to 1812 the first settler permitted the use of a room in his house for a school. The gentleman was Wm. Buell, and the teacher's name was Joseph Pyle. Mr. Sylvester succeeded him and an Indian scholar, Paul J. Gill, came next to Sylvester. The Indian had been educated at Dartmouth College. Leavitt's "Leeds and Grenville."

BATH. Barnabas Bidwell in 1811 conducted a Latin School at Bath on the Bay of Quinte until he removed to Kingston in 1813. (Ryerson Mem. Volume, p. 40.)

1815.

GANANOQUE. Information regarding the first school in Gananoque, for which steps were begun in 1815, is singularly complete. The one point not quite clear is, that of two persons making proposals to teach the school, we have no documentary evidence as to which one was accepted as the first teacher. The documentary evidence of its foundation in 1816 has been published, and may be found in Vol. 17, Ont. Hist. Soc. "Papers and Records," in an article entitled "Gananoque's First Public School, 1816," by Frank Eames. Col. Joel Stone reports in 1818: "One good frame building erected and finished for a schoolhouse." This report, I have reason to believe, while made at a meeting called by Gourlay, or proposed by him, never reached that gentleman, and was one of several which he did not receive, other districts having also defaulted.

MIDLAND DISTRICT. Andrew Lorrimer taught a number of scholars in 1816 at a school located ten miles west of Kingston, according to Carter's work on the County of Dundas, which is my authority for the statement.

1817.

SCARBORO. In school section number one, the first schoolhouse was of logs, built on lot 13, 3rd concession, in 1817. The first teacher was a Mr. Edward, whose successors to the number of seventeen are to be found mentioned in David Boyle's "Scarboro, 1796-1896."

BLENHEIM TOWNSHIP. In Oxford County, one authority states, there is but one school.

Burwash's life of "Egerton Ryerson," page 55, has the following statement: "Mr. Gourlay collected statistics of no less than 259 Common Schools already in operation, and these were by no means the whole number in the Province in 1817." From Gourlay's census of 1817, for a period of ten years (1827), the number of schools increased to 340, while the number of scholars is recorded at the latter date to have been from 12,000 to 14,000.

1818.

JOHNSTOWN DISTRICT. In South Crosby there is one schoolhouse, doubtless the one at Elgin, recorded under "1810." (Reported for Robert Gourlay.)

In Kitley Township also there is one schoolhouse reported for the Gourlay Meetings.

1819.

MATILDA TOWNSHIP. Mr. Alex. McFarling, School Section No. 1. This was held at "Flagg's." (Carter's "Dundas.") James Croil, in his "Dundas," which he published in 1861, says on page 141, "The duty of instructing their children seems from the very earliest time of the settlement to have been recognized, and although of necessity a few years elapsed without a schoolhouse, yet from the very first they had their schoolmaster. A good old German, whose name we cannot recall, gratuitously spent his time in going from house to house teaching, two weeks at a time in different neighbourhoods." On page 144, Croil continues, "Before the close of 1792, the settlers in Dundas had erected two churches, and established several schools."

SCARBORO TOWNSHIP. The late David Boyle, in his "History of Scarboro," page 194, states that "Among all the dominies who have exercised sway in this township, Thomas Appleton deserves special notice. He was a Yorkshireman and a Methodist, who came to Upper Canada in 1819, and began to teach school the same year in Scarboro, remaining here for twelve months."

1820.

TORONTO (York). Joseph Spragge, father of Chief Justice Spragge, opened the Central School at York in this year and became its master. A very keen interest was shown by Lieut.-Governor and Lady Sarah Maitland in this school which was founded as a Church of England, or National, school. (Ryerson Memorial Volume, p. 40.)

1822.

BATH. The academy at Bath which had been so ably conducted by Barnabas Bidwell until his removal to Kingston in 1813, was in a prosperous state in 1812, when the war upset and deranged the whole fabric which had been gradually reared after the turmoil of the revolution. Upper Canada was slowly but surely rising from wilderness and emerging into the light of civilization, but soon all was changed and teachers were warriors once more. At the commencement of war the academy classes were broken up and scattered. The academy building was transformed into a barrack and the rattle of accoutrements took the place of the call to prayer and the classes. Unfortunately the end of strife saw no revival of the school's former status until 1822, "when the building was once more transformed and utilized as a place of public worship and a common school."

GRAND RIVER. Stone's "Life of Brant," page 527, under date of 1822, states that, "it was the design of young Brant (this would be John, the son of Chief Joseph) on his return to Canada to resuscitate and extend the schools among his Nation." On page 531 of the same authority also appears the following: "In my next I shall draw on you for the amount appropriated for the building of the Mohawk and Oneida School Houses, as also for the School Master at Davis's Hamlet. As you have not mentioned Laurence David's, I shall continue to draw for his salary as usual, out of the two hundred pounds appropriated by the Corporation in 1822. In my next I will tell you how the Scholars get on."
(A letter from the Mohawk Village, Grand River, U.C., 1828, to James Gibson, Esqr., Treas. of the New England Corporation, London.)

DUNWICH. John Pearce's home became the first pioneer school here, and Thomas Gardiner its first teacher for a term of six months. (Ermatinger's "Talbot Regime.")

1823.

WEST GWILLIMBURY. The Scotch settlers erected a log schoolhouse on lot 8, con. 6, to be also used as a church when occasion required. Lieut.-Gov. Sir Peregrine Maitland once visited this school and addressed the scholars. The first teacher was Mr. William Moffat. (A. F. Hunter's "History of Simcoe County," Vol. I, p. 281.)

SCARBORO. There is some doubt about the exact year and the exact location, so far as the concession number is concerned, of the first school in Section number 5. Local tradition says that the school "was known as the Squaw Village School," (see Boyle's Scarboro, page 187, in the footnote), and although the teacher is not named for this year we have it that "A Mr. Carruthers taught in 1824." This building was erected on the Northwest corner of lot 26. In school section number 9, the first schoolhouse is stated to have stood on lot 18, concession D. ("Scarboro, 1796-1896," page 191.)

1824.

DUNWICH. In the home of John Miles Farlane, scholars were taught the rudiments of education, and it was in this year that a schoolhouse was erected on the farm lands of Mr. Backus, in which at least three of the Ladd family became masters, their Christian names being Alvro, Lemuel and Phural, respectively. (Ermatinger—" Talbot Regime," page 285.)

SCARBORO. The site of one of Scarboro's early schools was on the side road between lots 34 and 35, concession C, and nearly in front of the Thompson home. It was erected about 1824. The first teacher is not now known, but a Mr. Fitzgerald taught in this school in 1826. (See Boyle's "Scarboro," p. 189.)

1825.

ST. THOMAS. The Rev. Alex. McIntosh is presumed to have been the first dominie in a school erected at this time in St. Thomas. He is referred to as having been the probable choice of the Rev. Dr. Stewart. It appears that a few individuals, chiefly farmers, had guaranteed the payment of one hundred pounds sterling per year for three years for the maintenance of a school, and in this year the school was reported to be in operation under the superintendence of a young gentleman from the Lower Province. (See "The Talbot Regime," page 287. Ermatinger, 1904.)

1826.

CREDIT RIVER (Mississauga Indian Mission.) Egerton Ryerson having been appointed to the Credit Indian Mission, took up his work among them in the middle of September, 1826. A quotation from his diary describes his first days among the natives as follows: "In one of these bark-covered and brush-enclosed wigwams, I ate and slept for some weeks, my bed consisting of a plank, a mat, and a blanket also for my covering; yet I was never more comfortable and happy." Again he says: "I feel an inexpressible joy in taking up my abode with them. I must acquire a new language to teach a new people." Ryerson was soon to show his qualification for the task before him by assuming the role of master builder. In less than ten days after his arrival among the Indians, it was resolved to construct a building which should answer the dual purpose of church and school. The Indians, though very poor, responded to the resolve with readiness, and although but two hundred in number they nevertheless subscribed one hundred dollars toward the building in less than one hour. (See Burwash's " Egerton Ryerson," in the Nation Builders Series, page 21.) At the expiration of six weeks the edifice was completed and paid for, thanks to the great enthusiasm of the young missionary, who rode to the Hamilton, Niagara, Yonge Street, and York Circuits until he could secure the sum required. That he found gratification and reward for his efforts seems certain since later he reports in his diary, "I am very certain I never saw the same order and attention in any school before."

GRAPE ISLAND (Mississauga Indian Mission). Grape Island and Huff's Island (or at this date of 1826, "Logrim's") were leased for a period of 999 years for the sum of five shillings. Fifteen Indians signed the indenture, which was dated Belleville, October the 10th, 1826. The above islands comprised some sixty-one acres, and upon Grape Island, the smaller of the two, a village was projected and constructed. The first winter many Indians camped at Grape Island, since the dwellings were not yet up, and these were visited by two itinerants and two interpreters. Jacob Peter, with William Beaver, taught them the Lord's Prayer, also the Ten Commandments. The tribe numbered some 130 persons, ninety of them being adults. From the Kingston band some forty arrived in May that spring. A school and meeting house was erected in July, 1827, 30 feet long by 25 feet in width. William Smith was the first teacher and he instructed thirty scholars in the day school. These grew to fifty for the Sabbath School. (See Canniff's "History of the Settlement of Upper Canada," pp. 325-7.) The Report of the Methodist Episcopal Missionary Society of the United States for 1829 says that "Fifty children are taught in the schools." This would imply at least that another school had been added to the mission. Lorenzo Dow, visiting there in 1829, writes under July 29th regarding the good conduct of the children.

PETERBOROUGH. The pioneer school of Peterborough was called the Union School. It was commenced in 1826 and was a log structure with shingled roof. Tradition has it that the Rev. Samuel Armour taught the pupils. (Poole's "Town and County of Peterborough, 1867.")

1827.

HAMILTON. John Law taught the district school here in 1827. It was at this school the future head of Ontario's Educational activities received a part of his education. (Durand's "Reminiscences.")

RICE LAKE AND MUD LAKE MISSIONS. Burwash, in his life of Egerton Ryerson, states that in 1827 the missionary was appointed to Cobourg Circuit, but that, "the Indian work at the Rice Lake and Mud Lake Missions was an object of his care." We may feel certain that the word "care" covered instruction to children, especially when associated with so energetic a nature as Dr. Ryerson's.

BAY OF QUINTE. Dr. Oronhyateka, in his Address to the National Education Association, in Toronto, 1891, says: "The Government established a school for the Six Nations Indians at Bay Quinte, 1827. (Page 235, Proceedings.)

CROWNHILL. William Crae was the first to teach in a log school erected here about 1827. The structure was erected on lot 10, on the Oro side. (Hunter's "History of Simcoe County," Vol. I, p. 285.)

1828.

LONDON. A Mr. Van Every opened the first school in the new town after its survey and establishment as the capital of the district. This school was maintained in the temporary jail and courthouse. (Ermatinger's "Talbot Regime.")

1830.

SCARBORO. The increase of population led to the erection of an additional schoolhouse. This was constructed of logs, on lot 25, concession 3, and its first teacher was James Little. (Boyle's "Scarboro.")

1832.

WEST GWILLIMBURY. John Garbutt taught the first school on the eighth line of this township, and was succeeded by Eli Hough. (Hunter's "Simcoe," I, p. 282.)

DUNDAS. Benjamin Meade was one of the early teachers of Dundas. His school was in Dumfries, and it was here he first began to teach, while his last school was old Number Eleven in Williamsburg, 1871.

1833.

SCARBORO. The first school to be opened in School Section number seven was located on the Fishery Road. It was an ordinary square building, constructed of plank, built in 1832, and its first teacher was John Wilson, an Englishman from Yorkshire.

LONDON. London had an early private school which was taught by a Mr. Taylor. He was a very poorly educated man, scarce able to master the simple rudiments known as the three "R's," likewise a very unhealthy person. He was assisted by his wife, whom Sheriff Glass has described for us as "a tough, wiry little woman with less education, but more energy" than her husband, with whom she also shared her labours when he was making lath, a business which they combined with teaching. The Sheriff tells us further that, "The schools were opened by the persons themselves as a private enterprise, without government or municipal aid." (Ermatinger's "Talbot Regime," p. 286.)

WOLFE ISLAND. This township is a portion of Frontenac County to-day and lies to the south of the mainland, and at the foot of Lake Ontario. Some twenty-one miles in length and seven in breadth at one point, it constitutes one of the several large islands situated in the headwaters of the St. Lawrence River. Mr. R. M. Spankie, in a paper read in Queen's Convocation Hall on the History of the Island, says, "In 1833, the first school was opened in a house situated at the foot of Lambert's Hill, named after an early resident, about half a mile from the village. It was a log structure, without a floor at first; the only furniture consisted of a few wooden benches without backs, with a particularly high bench for writing on, at which the pupils would stand or kneel as best fitted their size. Ten years later a school was opened for the foot of the Island. Such was the state of travel that parents were known to accompany their children to school in the morning and upon their return homeward to blaze a trail for the youngsters to follow at night."

It is evident from all of the foregoing that the pioneers of Upper Canada were almost unanimous in adopting measures for the education of their children. That a common school education was the just and perfect right of all, had become a settled point in their plans for establishing the institutions of a great and free nation. The government of the country would require men of sound intelligence and executive ability, the exercise of which became the duty of all for the common good.

XV.

GENEALOGICAL TABLES AND THEIR RIGHT USES IN HISTORY.*

BY A. F. HUNTER. M.A.

Fully sixty per cent. of the papers that reach the Ontario Historical Society, as in many similar societies, relate to our grandfathers—who they were, what they told us, or what their times were like. As topics having the genealogical trend, therefore, and all matters pertaining to them, bear such a preponderant interest and importance in the aggregate, it may be profitable to spend some time in examining the general principles that underlie genealogy, glancing at the same time at social systems founded upon them.

The rapid growth of societies, also, in which membership is confined to some line of descent—societies based upon a particular nativity, for example, or the sons or the daughters of some other class whose descent can be circumscribed by genealogical limits—and the spread in recent years of Eugenics and Euthenics, all create a need for some wider diffusion of knowledge of the first principles of genealogy. As a regular subject of pursuit, genealogy has received more attention in various countries than hitherto in Ontario, obviously on account of the youthfulness of this province and the plebeian character of many of its settlers; but as the years pass, this branch of research with us will doubtless gain a larger number of devotees.

The proposed undertaking will necessarily lead us to regard history in its relations with the single individual—history on its biographical side. The personal factor has always been important in history—equally as much as the group. But whether we adopt the greatman directorship of affairs. as followed by older historians, or restrict history to the all-essential factor of social and political institutions and the records of groups, as its proper sphere, thus adopting the limitation that is fast gaining ground especially in modern writers, or use a combination of the two methods, it is unlikely that historians will discard altogether the hero-idea in history for some time, but will maintain a place for it and for the extensive influence of leadership in human affairs.

The first feature that will demand our attention in this investigation will be the construction and use of proper genealogical tables.

I.

Nearly everyone bears in mind the fact that he had four grandparents; very few persons, however, recognize the further fact at all times, without having their attention drawn particularly to it, that everyone also had

---

*A paper forwarded by the author and read at the joint meeting of this Society and the Historical Section of the Ontario Educational Association held in Toronto, April 15th, 1903, with the title " How to Study our Grandfathers."

eight great grandparents, sixteen great great grandparents, and so on, increasing in a twofold ratio with each step backward into the past. The accompanying diagram will help to make this clear. The roots of the

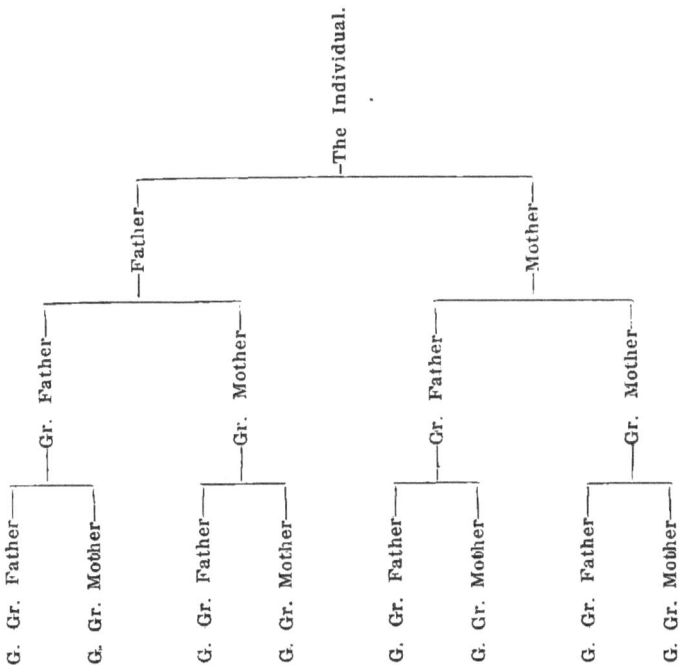

family tree diverge at such a rapid rate that we have to go backward for only about 250 years (allowing, as Herodotus did, three generations in a century) to find that each of us had 256 grandparents. In other words, 256 persons living in the time of Oliver Cromwell and the first effectual attempts at colonizing and settling this new continent, are to be claimed by each of us as our ancestors.

To go still further backward to a date say three thousand years ago, everyone now living can claim as his ancestors of that day, not a single pair, but nearly the whole of the human race living on the earth at the time. The only circumstance that operates against the rapid divergence of the lines of descent is the marriage of cousins or other near relatives, which occasionally happens; but this has the effect of only partly retarding the divergence, and as a rule is only occasional, not operating usually for more than one generation. In such a case the individual descendants might have three pairs of great grandparents instead of four. Preceding lines of descent for the same individual go on diverging, and in no case do the lines converge.

This system of defining one's descent may be called a Natural, or Analytic genealogy. It gives, in fact, the roots of what is more commonly known as the family tree—that part of the tree which is underground in more senses than one—and is too frequently treated in a fallacious way, if treated at all. The system deserves the name Analytic to distinguish it from the Synthetic specimens of genealogy with which we are so familiar, especially those of royalty in school histories. This latter kind, often reduced to a garbled or artificial form, is prepared for the purpose of showing the relationships of the crown-wearers. Other synthetic or eclectic specimens are also to be found in great numbers in the Peerage volumes (Burke, Debrett, Dodd, Lodge, etc.), sometimes in family trees in publications of the Societies for Eugenics and Euthenics, and in genealogies. People have grown so accustomed to these synthetic genealogies that they forget there is a complete analytic family tree for every person. Accordingly, there are two sorts of family tree, the one analytic and proceeding backward as described above; the other synthetic and branching forward, giving (when complete) the record of actual descent of the progeny.

It is a trite saying that we all include our ancestors—it has been explained by scientific men, sung by the poets. The statement that a person had two parents, four grandparents, and so on, is merely an application of numbers to the course of nature, and it is liable to suffer from fallacious treatment, so that caution is necessary to avoid mistakes. Its proper arithmetical treatment always affords some useful knowledge, but errors have to be guarded against.*

The net outcome of this analytic mode of enquiry is to teach us that one person has just about as good ancestry as another person. There is very little real foundation for pride of ancestry. Every pedigree has, in the ultimate analysis, about the same percentage of creditable folks and the same percentage of the opposite kinds, as other pedigrees contain, viz., about half of each. Very idle are boasts, therefore, about superiority of descent, and about being long-descended "from some fine old family." Every one of us is descended from myriads of families, and good citizenship calls for no pride of ancient descent.

Our historical literature is lamentably corrupted with boasts of descent from ancient and illustrious families. The descent of every individual is of equal antiquity with the descent of every other individual. And if some particular pair of one's ancestors was once illustrious, it could have had very little effect upon the descendant of three or four generations later. It is almost needless to cite examples, but the subject is so important that a few may help to emphasize the point. So valuable a writer as Samuel Smiles makes this vague and confused statement in "Self Help," p. 261:

"Warren Hastings' family was ancient and illustrious; but their loyalty in the cause of the Stuarts brought them to poverty, and the family estate, of which they had been lords of the manor for hundreds of years, at length passed from their hands." (Here the family meant is evidently the line of primogeniture.)

---

*Herbert Spencer, in "Facts and Comments," (p. 210), opens one of his chapters with a discussion of this subject under the title of the "converse ancestral tree," and proceeds along lines similar to those which the present writer adopted in this article. His use, however, of the principle is subordinate, as he proceeds from this organic example to inorganic sequences. A. K. Venning also contributed a letter to the "Scientific American" of May 22, 1909, in which he also treated the subject from the analytical point of view.

In another book we are told of "heirs to the polish of a far-reaching ancestry," (Francis Parkman on the French in North America, "Pioneers of France.")

But it is needless to multiply examples. The literature of biography and history is full of negligence in regard to the fundamental principles of descent, and of vague, bombastic talk of "fine old families." We are also told by pedigree-makers how the subject of a particular sketch was related to this or to that illustrious personage, showing the constant and natural ambition of weaker persons to claim alliance with the stronger.

This analytic line of enquiry has much practical use notwithstanding St. Paul's advice to Timothy not to give heed to endless genealogies—a practice so characteristic of Asiatic life. Solomon's proverb of an earlier time seems to be more to the point than St. Paul's admonition, when he says: "the glory of children are their fathers."—Proverbs, xvii, 6. This was almost the reverse of St. Paul's attitude unless the latter was a repudiation of idle boasts, such as we are also now endeavouring to disparage.

If we use the means of enquiry furnished by the analytic tabular form, we can also see how it comes that there is scarcely a full-blood Indian on the east side of the Rocky Mountains to-day. Where the white and red races have lived together or near each other for three centuries, there is not one chance in 250 that any particular Indian can have full-blood, nearly all now having some infusion of white blood. On the Lake Simcoe Reserve, for example (Georgina Island and neighbouring islands), with a population of about 125 persons, only one Ojibway family (now also reduced to one person) claimed purity of descent. In Mexico, the situation has become a real problem, as over 80 per cent. of the people are of mixed Indian blood, about half of this being considered full blood but really having more or less infusion of white blood, and the unsettled characteristics of hybrids are showing themselves very clearly in the political life of that country.

Within the past forty or fifty years the subject of heredity has grown into a distinct science in the hands of Francis Galton, August Weissman, Havelock Ellis and others; more recently the outgrowths of the applied sciences of "Eugenics" and "Euthenics" have been receiving widespread attention; and a more critical spirit now examines all the statements of pedigree-makers.

Passing forward along family trees, instead of backward as we have hitherto been doing, we discover how rapidly families die out. "Burke, in 'Vicissitudes of Families,' points out that of the twenty-five barons selected to enforce the observance of Magna Charta, there is not now in the House of Peers a single male descendant." (Samuel Smiles, "Self-Help," p. 233.) Among the nobility, families are continually running out and fecundity may have been below the average on account of over-nourishment and negotiating many absurd nuptial alliances (as the frequent marriage of near kin) with the view of holding estates or other property in the family. But be this as it may, the families of the present day appear in the long-kept registers to follow families now extinct, which, in turn, followed older ones. If we found the ratio of increase to be rapid in the backward order, the ratio of decrease is almost equally rapid in the forward order. It is from the combination of these two processes that the doctrine of Malthus can perhaps get some further elucidation.

II.

Individuals of most European races and their descendants have the surname or "sire-name" from the line of the father's father backward indefinitely, and it is the indelible mark of the patriarchal system derived from the Oriental nations of old. But quite different was the system of tracing and recording consanguinity amongst American aborigines. With them, the clan system was based upon descent through the mother's family, i.e., by matriarchal descent, or following the female line. The elaborate rules with which the matriarchal system is replete are of great antiquity—almost as ancient as the inflections of language itself, and they date backward for probably many thousands of years. Lewis H. Morgan was one of the first to investigate the matriarchal system in a scientific way for the American aborigines, his investigations having been based upon the system as he found it among the Iroquois tribes of New York State.* It is worthy of note also that the same matriarchal system exists among races in Asia, and it points to earlier contact of Asiatic and American races.

Totem names and tribal names arising from totems, also came into use at an early date in human history.† Throughout Western Europe, many names from animal clans, especially, are found amongst surnames, and these exist concurrently with surnames derived from the more recent patriarchal names and customs, which have been introduced from the Orient. Family surnames of the first kind have persisted for so many generations since their first adoption, that whoever now bears a clan surname has only very remote connection with the clan that originally bore the name. The ancestors of James Wolfe, for example, in every successive generation, became part of a person not a Wolfe, and so, after the passing of some generations became scarcely even a Wolfe at all. The Wolfe blood, in other words, became dilute, like the diluted Indian blood of North America where few pure Indians are left. This is partly the result of the patriarchal custom of women changing their names at marriage, each to that of the husband.

The line of the mother's mother all the way up from the remotest roots of one's family tree as known by records, is more important physiologically than any other line, because the same blood flows in the veins of mother and child. Hence, the great importance of the matriarchal line in genealogy. Champlain observed the priority of the female line among the Hurons in 1615, but was sometimes cynically disposed toward the Indians and their customs, and attributed the importance of the matriarchal rule of descent in reference to possessions passing in the female line to an entirely different cause, viz., female faithlessness, a claim that Francis Parkman, the historian, corroborated. But there can be no doubt or question as to the great physiological importance of the matriarchal system.‡ Improved quality of blood in a person's lineage, whenever there was such, only came by inheritance into the line of the mother's mother followed backward, and accordingly, that line is of great physiological value. But the line of the father's father followed backward, as in European and other

---

*Lewis Henry Morgan—"Laws of Descent of the Iroquois" (1859); "Systems of Consanguinity and Affinity of the Human Family," (1869).
†See Andrew Lang—"Custom and Myth," for a discussion of this subject.
‡Francis Parkman—"Jesuits in North America." (Introduction—A Sketch of the "Native Tribes.")

patriarchal peoples, was merely the naming line, and of no great importance other than socially.

An extensive knowledge of heraldic crests has less practical value for its possessor nowadays than in olden times, but the subject deserves a few passing remarks at this place. Heraldic designs (of beasts, etc.) have a strange interest for most of us, as they are the European relics of totems or tribal marks, which many of our ancestors bore. Although the crests or symbols of clanship had their original source in the matriarchal system, they were readily transferred to the patriarchal system of more modern times in Western Asia and Europe, where the symbols have now come to denote an almost indescribable mixture, or at most, a faded custom. Family coats-of-arms may have had their uses in days when the masses were unlettered, but the blazonry of arms is no longer necessary, except as an aid to decipher the records of the past, and they may be allowed to remain as objects of antiquarian interest belonging only to the earlier social institutions.

III.

Closely allied to the subject of personal relationship is that of using composite terms to denote national mixtures and groups. The hyphenated terms Scoto-Irish, French-Ojibway, etc., have distinct meanings, and denote races or individuals of mixed blood. But it is only to a limited extent that such terms can be used to define nationality. When individuals in this country become much mixed they may be called "Canadians;" but residents of Canada born of Irish parents, for example, would still be Irish, and the term Irish-Canadian would properly designate a person of mixed nationality. The hyphen makes the difference, and in a similar way the French-Canadian, in a proper use of language, is really a person of mixed ancestry.

IV.

The compilation of family history is a part of everyone's private duty. Sir Walter Scott, as the author of "Tales of a Grandfather," has not overdone the duty of preserving his family history. He did what many people regret, when it is too late, they did not do—he noted down and cherished the words of older folks before they departed, and at a later time gave them in print. The histories of other families are perhaps equally interesting, if told with the same degree of eloquence, and even Scott becomes almost wearisome with his reiterated descriptions of his whole ancestry in books written for the general public. Much of his information about earlier times, however, and about things not bearing upon his own family, was derived from ancestral sources; and the example set by this prince of historical novelists shows what can be accomplished by others through persistent efforts.

It is indispensable for every person to know something about his ancestors and their characters for at least three or four generations. This information gives him a better knowledge of himself, and makes him a better-informed citizen. In seeking to learn all we can about our ancestors, it does not follow that we betray any weakness on the point of family descent. Nearly every enquiry is liable to suffer from fallacies creeping into it. But it is no fair objection to the quest of this kind of knowledge to say that the worst pitfall to which the pursuit is exposed—in this case, the pomp of illustrious ancestry which has such a fascinating charm for many people—should furnish an argument against the investigation of one's descent.

While it is thus the duty of every person to learn all he can about his ancestors, it ought not to be for the purpose of pestering friends and neighbours with stories about illustrious forefathers, but for the fulfilment of the duty of self-development. It has been well said by someone that self-development, rather than self-interest, should be the aim of everyone; and therefore, to know what our ancestors have been, will teach us what we ourselves may become. It can, however, be of little general interest to know that in the ancestry of some particular person there were certain other persons, say, the Smiths and the Browns, all fine old families. Most naturalists are agreed that there is more in the race or ancestry, than in the surroundings and nurture, of the individual. Hence, while the biographies of only a few well known persons may arrest our attention generally, the biographies of one's own ancestors should be the particular object of his attention. They may have possessed but few traits to mark them from other men and women of their time, yet their few characteristics are all important to their descendants. All we can learn of them may be merely some dates of their births, marriages, or deaths, as contained in the old registers published by this society and elsewhere. But even this much is some satisfaction.

In the foregoing paper the writer has merely attempted to outline some of the uses of the systematic study of our grandfathers, to show its value as well as its weaknesses, and to gauge the limits of our particular enquiries in this field. It is hoped that, on the practical side, these reflections may be of some use to those engaged in the preparation of family records—and this is a work in which everyone should be engaged to a rational degree.

GEORGE COVENTRY
1793-1870.
From a photograph loaned by A. J. Hewson, Esq., Cobourg.

Ontario Historical Society

PAPERS AND RECORDS

VOL. XIX

TORONTO
PUBLISHED BY THE SOCIETY
1922

CONTENTS.

1. George Coventry—A pioneer contributor to the history of Ontario (1793-1870) 5
2. Public Life and Services of Robert Nichol, a Member of the Legislative Assembly and Quartermaster-General of the Militia of Upper Canada, BRIGADIER-GENERAL E. A. CRUIKSHANK 6
3. Humours and Interests of an Historical Building, MISS JANET CARNOCHAN 82
4. When Jefferson Davis Visited Niagara, A. J. CLARKS 87
5. The Church of England in Augusta Township, THE LATE JOHN DUMBRILLE 90
6. Gleanings from the Blue Church Burying Ground, Augusta Township, F. J. FRENCH, K. C. 91
7. The Historical Position of the Six Nations, ASA R. HILL 103
8. The Diary of Benjamin Lundy Written during his journey through Upper Canada, January, 1832. Intro. and Notes by FRED LANDON, M.A.) .. 110
9. Deep Waterways Movements—Their origin and Progress in Ontario, JAMES MITCHELL 134
10. An Old Provincial Newspaper (1836). HON. WM. RENWICK RIDDELL, LL.D., F.R.S.C. 139
11. Some References to Negroes in Upper Canada, HON. WM. RENWICK RIDDELL, LL.D. F.R.S.C. 144
12. "Was Molly Brant Married?" HON. WM. RENWICK RIDDELL, LL.D., F.R.S.C. 147
13. The Rev. Robert Addison and St. Mark's Church, Niagara, PROF. A. H. YOUNG 158
14. The Rev. Robert Addison—Extracts from the Reports and MS. Journals of the Society for the Propagation of the Gospel in Foreign Parts, (With Notes by PROF. A. H. YOUNG.) 171

I

GEORGE COVENTRY—A PIONEER CONTRIBUTOR TO THE HISTORY OF ONTARIO.

(1793-1870)

Various articles from the pen of George Coventry have appeared in former issues of these "Papers and Records":—he recorded the personal narrative of Capt. T. G. Anderson published in Vol. 6; also three papers in Vol. 7, viz., "Testimonial of Mr. Roger Bates," "Reminiscences of Mrs. White," and "Memoirs of Colonel John Clark." He also wrote "A Concise History of the late Rebellion in Upper Canada, to the Evacuation of Navy Island," which appeared in Vol. 17 (with Notes and a Sketch of Coventry's life by the Honourable William Renwick Riddell, Justice of the Supreme Court of Ontario).

Mr. Coventry's indefatigable zeal for recording is best exhibited in the collection preserved in the Parliamentary Library, Ottawa, known as the "Coventry Papers," and extending to 10,000 folio pages of manuscripts. He lived and worked in a period when it was easier than it is now to obtain further information upon the early times of Upper Canada—before the hand of time had destroyed so many valuable records, or had removed the pioneers. He made good use of his opportunities so he deserves the approbation of historical workers in these later times. In his day the audience or circle interested in the history of Ontario was smaller than now, the facilities for publication were fewer, and accordingly much of his work went unpublished. Nearly every present day worker, however, knows something of his published work, or has met with some traces of his industrious career, about one-half of which in Canada he had spent in the historic Niagara peninsula.

Through the courtesy of Andrew J. Hewson, Esq., of Cobourg, who was an acquaintance of Mr. Coventry, the accompanying portrait now appears.

II

A SKETCH OF THE PUBLIC LIFE AND SERVICES OF ROBERT NICHOL, A MEMBER OF THE LEGISLATIVE ASSEMBLY AND QUARTERMASTER GENERAL OF THE MILITIA OF UPPER CANADA.

BY BRIGADIER-GENERAL E. A. CRUIKSHANK.

During the first twenty years of the last century, probably no man was better known or more prominent in the public life of the Niagara and London Districts of Upper Canada than Robert Nichol. Yet his manifold activities as a pioneer in the rather primitive industrial and commercial enterprises of that time and place, and as a legislator, public official and militia officer, have been so nearly lost sight of that they are barely mentioned in a single short paragraph in Dr. H. J. Morgan's "Celebrated Canadians," published sixty years ago.

In this paper an attempt is made to arrange in narrative form as much information as the writer has been able to discover in authentic documents, respecting the public career of a very able, energetic, and capable man, who rendered no small service to his adopted country.

No record of the date or place of his birth has been found, but it is stated that he was born in Dumfriesshire, Scotland, about the year 1774, and was related by blood or marriage to the Honourable Robert Hamilton, the three Dickson brothers, and Thomas Clark, a notable group of Scotsmen, who took a very active part in the commercial development of the newly organized province of Upper Canada. Nichol's correspondence shows beyond doubt that he had received a good English education, and possessed some knowledge of the French language, which he may have acquired after coming to Canada. His bold, firm, masculine handwriting and the direct and lucid tone of his letters and other documents have a certain value as an index of character.

The date of his arrival in Canada and the causes that induced him to emigrate can only be conjectured.

The first record I have found of his life in Canada, is contained in a certificate over his signature, dated at Amherstburg on January 21, 1798, in which he states that he had been employed by Mr. Askin, a British merchant of Detroit and had transacted all his mercantile business at Amherstburg, since the establishment of the fort at that place. The British garrison was withdrawn from Detroit and removed to Amherstburg, late in June, 1796.

In 1803, Nichol's name appears in militia records as a lieutenant in the Lincoln Artillery company at Niagara.

The records of the Executive Council of the province of Upper Canada show that he was granted four hundred acres of land on February 28, 1798. In a petition, dated March 15, 1806, praying for leave to locate this land under the original grant, he describes himself as a merchant, residing in the township of Bertie in the county of Lincoln, and an extant plan of about the same date, shows that he had a store or warehouse in the little village that had grown up near Fort Erie, which was a port of entry, and where there was a government wharf and landing-place for merchandise. It was a place of considerable trade as the point of transhipment of goods on their way to and from Detroit and Mackinac. Other warehouses, close by, were owned by Robert Hamilton and Thomas Clark, who were magnates in the commercial life of the district. Here there was a tolerably secure anchorage for the small sailing vessels navigating the upper lakes, in the adjacent bay, partly sheltered from the prevailing winds, and directly opposite, at the mouth of Buffalo Creek, was the principal village of the Six Nations still remaining in the United States, where their large councils were generally held.

Nichol's petition was granted and he proceeded to locate his land in the new township of Woodhouse, in the county of Norfolk, then being rapidly settled by immigrants from the United States, attracted by free grants of rich virgin soil.

There is considerable evidence that during the first decade of the nineteenth century, he had acquired some interest as a partner or local agent, in the lucrative fur trade with the Indians of the northwest, carried on by a powerful association of Montreal merchants, who were also mostly Scotsmen. The Scottish merchants of Upper Canada and these merchants of Montreal were closely allied in commercial transactions and exerted a dominating influence with the government of the province. The letters of Justice Thorpe contain spiteful references to the "Shopkeeper Aristocracy" and the "Scotch Pedlars" whom he blamed for the appointment of Thomas Scott as Chief Justice in preference to himself. "There is a chain of them," he wrote, "linked from Halifax to Quebec, Montreal, Kingston, York, Niagara and so on to Detroit."

In the autumn of 1807, the high-handed attack of the British ship Leopard upon the U.S. frigate Chesapeake to enforce a search for deserters was resented by an embargo on trade, followed by the passage of an Act by Congress practically prohibiting all commercial intercourse between the United States and Great Britain and all British possessions. The influence of the Montreal merchants, aided by the British Minister at Washington, secured the introduction of a clause into this Act providing that "it was not to be construed to prevent the exportation by land or inland navigation from the territories of the United States into those of Great Britain of furs and peltries, the property of subjects of Great Britain, and by them purchased from the Indians; or to prevent the importation by land or inland navigation from the territories of Great Britain into those of the United States of merchandise, the property of British subjects and by them imported solely for the use of the Indians aforesaid."

While this bill was still pending in Congress, the merchants of Montreal, trading with the Indians of the Northwest, residing in the territories recognized by treaty as being within the United States, under the name of the Michilimackinac or Southwest Fur Company, had despatched from Lachine a fleet of twenty large bateaux, laden with goods, valued at more than £15,000 sterling, with orders to follow the usual route by the St. Lawrence, and up the lakes to the island of Saint Joseph, the principal depot in Lake Huron, where there was a small British military post and trading station. It would there be joined by the usual staff of agents, who would proceed by the Ottawa river and bring with them final instructions as to its destination, as a confidential agent had been sent some time before, with the approval of the Governor-General, to ascertain through the British Minister, whether it was the intention of the government of the United States to continue in force that part of the treaty of 1794, which gave British subjects the privilege of participating in the fur trade within their territory or to declare it at an end.

These boats pursued their course in their customary manner, coasting along the south shore of Lake Ontario, touching at the port of Oswego, where there was a custom-house, and landing from time to time to cook their meals and rest, without meeting with any molestation, until on May 21, 1808, the first division of five entered the Niagara. While near the middle of the river and between Fort Niagara and Fort George, then both occupied by small garrisons of regular troops, and, it was asserted, nearer the British than the U.S. station, they were hailed and fired upon by soldiers sent out in a boat from the former fort to detain them. Two of them were overtaken and carried by force with their crews as prisoners to the U.S. shore where they were delivered into the custody of John Lees, the collector of customs, by whom this high-handed act had been prompted and authorized. The remaining three boats made their escape to the British side, although repeatedly fired upon while in their national waters, at such close range that the bullets struck the land beyond them. Learning from the prisoners that several other boats were approaching, a boat, manned by armed soldiers, was at once despatched from Fort Niagara to intercept them and succeeded in capturing six others in the open lake. Robert Hamilton and Thomas Dickson, who were at Niagara at the time and were probably partners in the company, crossed the river and made a vigorous protest against this seizure of property, as an unlawful act. The collector attempted to justify it on the ground that these boats had not been regularly reported and entered at some U.S. port, while passing along the coast, alleging that they could not have made the voyage without touching land at some point. On the other hand the claimants stated positively that only on one occasion before had an entry been required of them under similar circumstances and then the point had been decided in their favour. They termed the present charge, preferred against them, a mere subterfuge or quibble put forward to their detriment, for, they said, " the right of Lake Navigation common to both Nations, necessarily implies its being used in a way practicable to the Vessel Navigating, whether *Decked* or *Open;* if the *former,* she must sometimes anchor when the wind is contrary, and if the *latter,* stop on the beach without any infringement of good faith, when there is no purpose of trade or any object of stopping beyond the necessity of waiting for wind, weather, or daylight to resume the voyage."

On the evening of the same day, having been informed that nine other boats were still on the lake and that a boat from Fort Niagara was lying in wait to capture them, Thomas Clark, who was also apparently a partner with, or an agent of the owners, took a boat and in company with some of his friends went down the lake after dark and succeeded in meeting these boats at the Eighteen Mile Creek in New York State and warned them of their danger. They at once took to flight and crossing the lake, made their way to Niagara eventually in safety by the north shore, having been chased for nearly one hundred miles.

Nichol, who was apparently already on terms of some intimacy with Brigadier General Brock, then commanding the troops at Montreal, wrote to him that day, before he was fully aware of the facts, warning him that strong reinforcements of regular troops had been ordered to join the garrisons at Detroit and Mackinac, and that one detachment had already arrived at Presqu' Isle on Lake Erie.

"My reason for being so forward to report this to you," he said, "is that the sudden collection of a large force at the present time in these places might very materially affect our intercourse with the Indian Nations and dispose them to commit hostilities on our distant settlements before we could afford them the necessary protection. While writing, a most unpleasant circumstance has taken place which is I think strong evidence of the hostile intentions of the United States.

"Twenty Boats belonging to the North West and South West Companies —navigating Lake Ontario under the Faith of the Treaty of Amity and Commerce —were this morning fired upon by the American Garrison and Seventeen of the Twenty Captured—the remaining three made their escape to this side. It is unnecessary for me to say more on this subject as I presume correct statements of the facts will be forwarded to the proper authorities.

"I write in great haste the vessel being just on the point of sailing."

The value of the boats and cargoes actually seized was stated as being six thousand pounds, and the total damages claimed by the owners, direct and indirect, arising from the seizure of their property, £26,842.5.6. The owners at Montreal determined to send an agent to support their claims at Washington and the partners or agents at Niagara were also instructed to send a representative familiar with the locality and special circumstances of the seizure. For this important mission they selected Robert Nichol. The person sent from Montreal, a Mr. Michael, of whom little is known, but who was described as "a faithful servant acquainted with route and mode of travelling in the States," carried with him a carefully prepared memorial to be handed to Mr. D. M. Erskine, the British Minister, whom he found at Philadelphia. He was then directed by Erskine to proceed to New York and deliver a letter from him to Mr. Gallatin, the Secretary of the Treasury. Gallatin declared that he would be unable to take any action until he had seen the official report of the person who had made the seizure. This would not be put before him until his return to Washington a few days later. At New York, Michael met Nichol and gave him this information. Nichol then went on to Washington to receive Gallatin's final decision. This appeared to uphold the validity of seizure on the plea that an entry and report to the American custom house should have been made. He announced, however, that the boats and goods would be surrendered on receiving security to abide the judgment of the proper court in the United States. No account of this mission from Nichol has been found.

Soon after his return from Washington, Nichol seems to have taken up his residence on his property near Port Dover, where he built grist and saw mills and a distillery. He prospered in these ventures and in a few years became fairly wealthy and influential in local affairs. He soon identified himself with the government "interest" and of course made friends and gained supporters and at the same time incurred the enmity of others. He became the local agent of Colonel Thomas Talbot, the local landed magnate of the London District, for the disposal of some of his lands in that neighbourhood. He was appointed a Justice of the Peace and a Commissioner of Roads for the expenditure of the public money voted by the Legislature in 1810 for the improvement of the highways in the London District. These appointments were made by the Lieutenant-Governor and the latter eventually brought Nichol some rather disagreeable notoriety.

On December 21, 1811, he was married at Queenston, by the Reverend Robert Addison, to Theresa Wright, the daughter of a surgeon in the British army, and a granddaughter of Hon. Alexander Grant of Amherstburg.

The third session of the fifth Parliament of Upper Canada began on February 1, 1811. Lieutenant-Governor Gore seems to have anticipated considerable contention and display of party animosity for he took occasion to conclude his speech with these significant remarks:

"It is by removing from our minds partiality, prepossession, and prejudice that we can hope either as Legislators or as individuals to be of real benefit to the community.

"Banishing, then, everything from our thoughts that may weaken or divert our attention from the love of our country, let us cordially unite in the enacting of such laws as may best tend to the peace, welfare, and good government of this province."

This sensible advice had apparently little effect in moderating the militant mood of the critics of the administration. One of their first acts was to repeal an act allowing a salary to the Adjutant General, who was also a member of the Legislative Council, passed at the first session of the same parliament. This was soon followed by the adoption of an act to repeal certain laws and ordinances of the late province of Quebec, still in force in Upper Canada.

On March 4, the select committee appointed to examine the accounts of the Road Commissioners for the several districts presented its report, which contained a statement that no report had been received from Robert Nichol of the application of £300, appropriated for the improvement of highways in the District of London for the year 1810, and that the said sum of £300 remained to be accounted for.

A week later Philip Sovereign, member for the county of Norfolk, who was chairman of the select committee on public accounts, reported a series of resolutions, among them being the following:

"Resolved, that it is the opinion of this Committee that the Commissioners of Highways for the London District have abused their Office by the misapplication of the moneys committed to their care, and that Three Hundred Pounds rests in the hands of Mr. R. Nichol, a Commissioner, no part of which appears to have been applied to public uses."

There seems to be little doubt that this resolution was framed merely for the purpose of gratifying personal spite or to gain some petty political advantage by casting discredit upon Nichol's private character.

Feeling that a great injustice had been done him, Nichol hotly resented the censure implied in this resolution and on the 25th of April following, he addressed a letter to the civil Secretary of the Province, transmitting an account of the expenditure of the money granted by the Legislature for the improvement of the highways in the London District for the year 1810 and paid to him in the autumn of that year, accompanied by an explanation why the account had not been rendered before. From his statement, which gave full details of his acts as commissioner, it appeared that he had expected that the two other commissioners, Daniel Springer and Adam Yeigh, who actually resided on the Talbot road, for the improvement of which the grant had been more particularly made, would have drawn the money and superintended its expenditure. Late in the year he was informed that they had done nothing in the matter, and he advised them as the favourable season for doing any work on the road was nearly at an end, to commence operations at once, stating at the same time that his private business was so urgent that he would be unable to give them any assistance in overseeing it. They agreed to do this but stipulated that he should go to York and draw the money. This he had done on October 11, 1810. He then intended to pay the contractors and obtain vouchers but on visiting the road he found that the work had not been completed. Part of the sum was paid over to Yeigh for the work done under his personal supervision and a further sum left with him to be delivered to Springer. A month later he was informed that Springer had been unable to spend all the money left for him within the time limited by the act. He had then called upon the Receiver General and offered to refund to him the unexpended balance, but he had refused to accept it and advised him to retain it and expend it next year, in conformity with the terms of the act. He had not been able to obtain proper vouchers from either Springer or Yeigh until it was too late to have them audited in time for a report to be made to the Assembly at its session. Had he contented himself with this explanation, it would no doubt have been accepted as being entirely satisfactory. But Nichol concluded his letter with the following remarks:

"Throughout the whole of this business I have endeavoured to discharge the duties of a Commissioner in such a manner as to prove that His Excellency's confidence has not been misplaced. Experience has, however, convinced me that no integrity of heart nor rectitude of conduct are a defence against malevolence and detraction; and that actions the most upright and disinterested may be misrepresented when individual characters are to be sacrificed and party purposes to be gained. I have the satisfaction, however, to feel that I have acted right, that there is no foundation for the insinuation against me in the resolution alluded to, and that I have not been benefitted either directly or indirectly by one shilling of the Public money."

In the autumn of that year Lieutenant-Governor Gore was granted leave of absence for twelve months to visit England, and, as the critical state of relations with the United States seemed to warrant the expediency of combining the highest civil and military authority in the same person, Major General Brock was appointed to administer the government.

He had been in command of his regiment in the province for several years and no doubt was personally acquainted with the principal people. For five years past he had been stationed in Lower Canada, but had kept up a correspondence with some of his former friends and may have been informed in this way of the course of political events.

The last session of the fifth Parliament began on February 3, 1812. Brock in his opening speech referred significantly to the menacing language and military preparations of the government of the United States, and remarked with great solemnity: " We wish and hope for peace, but it is nevertheless our duty to prepare for war."

Although the Assembly, as usual, in their reply to the speech, echoed its expressions in a general way and announced their readiness to carry out its recommendations, a majority of the members soon displayed an inclination to give more attention to party quarrels and private spite than to public affairs.

On February 11, a motion was adopted, declaring that William Warren Baldwin, barrister, Master in Chancery, " has been guilty of a false, audacious, and contemptuous libel of this House, by publicly charging this House, in the hearing of several members thereof, with injustice to his father, Robert Baldwin, one of the Commissioners for amending and repairing the Public Highways and roads for the District of Newcastle." It is rather surprising to find that the minority against this motion was composed of only three members, Benajah Mallory and Joseph Willcocks voting with Matthew Elliott.

At the request of the House in an address to the Legislative Council, W. W. Baldwin, was dismissed from his office as clerk of the Legislative Council. An address for his reinstatement was then carried to demonstrate that the House was not actuated by vindictive motives.

On February 18, John Small, the Clerk of the Crown was brought to the bar of the House and examined. A motion was next adopted that he had been guilty of a breach of privilege in issuing from his office a *capias* against the person of Alexander Macdonell, a member of the Assembly, but having made a satisfactory apology, that he be dismissed.

On February 20, Nichol's letter to the Provincial Secretary was read and a motion was at once made that " Robert Nichol has been guilty of a breach of the privileges of this House, by making a false, malicious, and scandalous representation to the person administering the Government, relative to the proceedings of this House, contained in his letter of the 25th of April, 1811, accompanying his road account; and also by words used in the presence of a Member of this House."

The motion was carried by a majority of six on a division, eighteen members voting.

It was immediately followed by a motion "that the Speaker do issue his warrant to the Sergeant at Arms to apprehend Robert Nichol, who has been guilty of a Breach of the Privilege of this House, and that the said Robert Nichol be forthwith brought up to answer for the said contempt."

In the course of the same day, the Speaker, Samuel Street, read the warrant that had been prepared for Nichol's arrest, and, by order of the House signed the same.

On February 26, Stephen Jarvis, the Deputy Sergeant at Arms, made a return to this warrant, stating that he had arrested Nichol. The prisoner was then brought to the Bar of the House and the resolution was read to him. Philip Sovereign and Joseph Willcocks, two members of the House, were called and gave evidence of the disrespectful words used by Nichol, in their hearing, with regard to the House of Assembly. He was then heard in his defence, and it may be safely inferred that he refused to withdraw his statements or to apologize for them. He was ordered to withdraw from the House, and a motion was made that "Mr. Nichol has been guilty of a breach of privilege, in addition to his former offence, in denying that this House have the privilege of committing an offender, who by them has been found guilty of a breach of privilege." A division was taken and the motion carried by a majority of four, twenty-two members voting.

A motion was then made that "Robert Nichol be committed to the common gaol of this district during the pleasure of the House, and that the Speaker do issue his warrant for that purpose." Another division took place, when the motion was carried by a majority of two, twenty-two members voting. The Speaker read his warrant prepared for Nichol's committal, and signed it by order of the House.

The report of the select committee appointed to examine the accounts of the Road Commissioners, was presented on February 28, and supplied a somewhat singular comment on the recent proceedings. The committee reported with respect to the London District that they "had examined the accounts and vouchers of Robert Nichol, Esq., for the appropriation of the year 1810, which are minute in detail and properly attested. The balance of his account, £75.15s.8d., he has paid to Sylvester Tiffany, one of the Commissioners for the year 1811, as appears by Mr. Tiffany's receipt for the same."

On the morning of Saturday, February 29, it was stated that Mr. Nichol had been released from the gaol by a writ of *habeas corpus,* issued by Chief Justice Thomas Scott, who was also Speaker of the Legislative Council. Joseph Willcocks, long noted as a most persistent and violent agitator, eagerly seized the opportunity for launching an attack upon this Judge, against whom he nourished an ancient grudge. He moved that the sheriff of the Home District should be commanded to attend at the Bar of the House immediately. A short adjournment was made until the Sergeant at Arms announced that the sheriff was in attendance. On his appearance the Speaker by order of the House asked the sheriff "whether he had not in custody the body of Robert Nichol, and whether the said Robert Nichol remained still a prisoner by virtue of the order of this House." Mr. Sheriff Beikie then informed the House that "he had received into the Gaol of the Home District the Body of Robert Nichol by virtue of the warrant of the Speaker of the House of Assembly; that the said Robert Nichol had since been brought up by writ of *habeas corpus* before the Hon. Thos. Scott, His Majesty's Chief Justice of this Province, and was by him liberated out of his custody."

He was asked to produce the writ, which he did, and Mr. Willcocks moved that it be read with its endorsement by the Chief Justice, showing that the prisoner had been discharged by his order.

When this had been done, Willcocks moved:

"That the Hon. Thos. Scott, Chief Justice of this Province, has been guilty of a violent breach of the privileges of this House by discharging from the Gaol of this District the body of Robert Nichol, who was committed to prison for having committed a breach of the privileges of this House."

A division was taken, when this motion was carried by a majority of three, twenty-one members voting.

A motion was next passed, directing that a message be sent to the Legislative Council, informing them of the resolution of the Assembly. A committee was appointed to deliver it and a message drafted requesting the Legislative Council "to proceed in that case as the nature of the case requires."

The Journal of the Legislative Council shows that this message was delivered on Monday, March 2, and duly reported to the Council by Chief Justice Scott, himself, to whom it had been delivered as the Speaker.

After the deputation from the Assembly had withdrawn, Scott made an explanation of his conduct in the matter, which was entered in the Journal.

He stated that the Chief Justice was bound by his office to grant a writ of *Habeas Corpus* and to discharge the prisoner if the commitment in the warrant appeared illegal. The warrants issued by the Speaker of the House of Commons in England showed distinctly the particular privilege violated; the judgment of the House upon the charge; the time when that adjudication was made; the order of the House for the specific punishment, and the date of that order. The warrant under which Mr. Nichol was detained being found to be defective in these particulars and appearing in all respects as the personal act of Mr. Street, he was bound to discharge the prisoner.

The Legislative Council then resolved itself into a committee of the whole to consider the message from the Assembly. A resolution was reported and adopted as follows:

"It is considered that this House disclaims any right to interfere with the proceedings of the Chief Justice in the exercise of his judicial functions: but the Honourable the Chief Justice, as Speaker of this House, having thought proper to enter into an explanation of his conduct in the matter stated in the aforesaid resolution, it is ordered that the explanation so given shall be entered upon the Journals of this House and a copy thereof sent to the Commons House of Assembly."

On the same day, March 2, General Brock notified the Speaker of the Assembly that it was his intention to prorogue the Legislature next day. This would undoubtedly be followed by the dissolution of the Assembly and an election which might result in the defeat or voluntary retirement of several of the sitting members. A resolution was adopted without a division ordering an address to be presented to the President, praying him to grant a longer time for the completion of the unfinished business of the session. In reply, General Brock promised to give his decision on the following morning. At the appointed hour a message was received stating that he would consent to postpone the prorogation to afford the House "an opportunity of terminating such public business as may be of importance to the true interests of this Province." A certain significance is apparent in the wording of this reply.

On March 4, Mr. McNabb moved that the clerk be ordered to furnish Mr. Nichol with a certified copy of the resolutions of the committee of the House on his public accounts as a Commissioner of Highways for the London District. The motion was lost. He then moved that the clerk be ordered to furnish Mr. Nichol with a copy of the proceedings of the House relative to his commitment for a breach of privilege. On a division this motion was defeated by a majority of six, twenty-two members voting.

During the course of this day, the Assembly again took up the burning question of its privileges.

Mr. Gough moved, seconded by Mr. Willcocks, "that the Hon. the Legislative Council by their message of the second of March disclaimed any right to interfere with the conduct of the Hon. Thomas Scott, Esquire, Chief Justice of this Province, guilty of a breach of the privilege of this House, which they allege as not to be done as a Member of their House, but in his character as a Judge, notwithstanding they did interfere during the present session and punish an officer of their House upon a complaint of this. It therefore becomes the duty of this House to vindicate its rights and privileges in the manner which shall appear to it best calculated to preserve them.

"Mr. Gough moved, seconded by Mr. Willcocks, that this House do present an humble address to His Royal Highness, the Prince Regent, representing the breach of its privileges by the unconstitutional interference of the Hon. Thomas Scott, Esquire, Chief Justice of this Province, by liberating Robert Nichol, a prisoner committed to the Gaol of the Home District by virtue of a warrant from Samuel Street, Esquire, its Speaker, for a breach of the privileges of this House; and humbly beseech His Royal Highness to adopt such measures to prevent the recurrence of the like as to His wisdom may seem meet."

These two motions were treated as one and carried on a division by a majority of two, in a house of twenty members. A motion to draft the proposed address caused another division but was carried by a majority of three, twenty-one members voting.

The address was then prepared, but a motion to receive it was also opposed. It was carried by a majority of two, twenty-two members voting. A motion to dispense with a rule of the House, requiring that a day's notice should be given for its second and third readings, was next adopted on the same division.

This address, when engrossed, read as follows:

"We, His Majesty's most dutiful and loyal subjects, the Commons of Upper Canada, in Provincial Parliament assembled, entertaining the most exalted sentiments of the superior excellence of the British Constitution and Laws and of the incalculable privileges they impart, humbly beg leave to address Your Royal Highness and represent their sincere conviction of the necessity of preserving pure and untouched those rights, privileges, and immunities, which the people of England and we, as their descendants, have so long possessed and enjoyed. We lament that on any occasion we should be called upon to lay before our Sovereign complaints of an unpleasant nature, but an imperious sense of duty urges us to state to Your Royal Highness that an alarming, dangerous, and unjustifiable violation of the privileges of the Commons of this Province has been lately made by the Honourable Thomas Scott, His Majesty's Chief Justice, inasmuch as he liberated from prison Mr. Robert Nichol, who had been committed by them for a high contempt and breach of their privileges. Such an interference on the part of judicial authority we cannot too much deprecate, impressed as we are with the important results resulting from it to the representative body of the people of this Colony. We therefore humbly pray that Your Royal Highness will be graciously pleased to pursue such measures as in your wisdom may be deemed the most proper and efficient to afford us prompt redress."

A motion that the Speaker should sign this address caused another division, when it was carried by a majority of four, only twenty members voting.

Next day an address to the President was introduced and adopted without opposition praying him to forward the former address to the Prince Regent, in which, however, it was deemed expedient and politic to affirm confidence in a general way in the Chief Justice.

This address was worded as follows:

"May it please Your Honour:—

"We, His Majesty's most dutiful and loyal subjects, the Commons of Upper Canada, in Provincial Parliament assembled, beg leave to address Your Honour for the purpose of expressing our earnest desire that Your Honour would be pleased to transmit with all convenient dispatch to His Royal Highness, the Prince Regent of the United Kingdom of Great Britain and Ireland, the address of the Commons of this Province, representing to His Royal Highness the violation lately made by the Hon. Thomas Scott, Chief Justice, upon their privileges, in liberating from prison the person of Robert Nichol, committed by them for a breach of privilege.

"And we beg leave to assure Your Honour that we have the highest opinion of the integrity and good intentions of the Hon. The Chief Justice, and sincerely lament that he has been, as we apprehend, so badly advised as to interfere with the privileges of the Commons; but that a sense of our duty, and a desire to preserve the Constitution unimpaired, has compelled us to adopt the present method of obtaining redress."

The committee appointed to present this address reported that they had been informed by General Brock that he would not fail to transmit it.

The contingent accounts submitted for payment included several items for expenses incurred in connection with Nichol's arrest, as follows:—

"Fee to Mr. Baldwin, Barrister, for his opinion to the Sergeant at Arms, respecting the mode of executing the Speaker's warrant in the case of Robert Nichol .... £1. 3. 4.

"To be paid Jno. Burk for carrying the Sergeant at Arms with a sleigh to Long Point .... £10. 0. 0.

"To the Sergeant at Arms for his time and expenses in going to arrest Robert Nichol .... £25. 0. 0."

On March 6, the Legislature was prorogued until April 10. The dissolution of the House of Assembly soon followed.

Brock's personal views on the subject of Nichol's arrest and the action of the Chief Justice in directing his discharge from prison were very positively stated in a despatch to Lord Liverpool, dated March 23.

"Your Lordship will likewise receive by this conveyance a second address from the House of Assembly to His Royal Highness, the Prince Regent, commenting upon and praying for redress from the decision of the Honourable Chief Justice Scott, on a point involving, as it is pretended, their privileges.

"This being a question of primary importance, in which the security of the subject is so deeply interested, I considered it my duty to lay the address before His Majesty's Executive Council, with directions to investigate in detail the circumstances that gave rise to this most extraordinary procedure.

"Your Lordship will be pleased to observe by the accompanying Report that every privilege exercised by the British House of Commons is arrogated by this body, and that they refuse to subject their actions to any established force, or submit on any pretence to the interference of the Judicature. Such undefined power in the hands of weak and ignorant men, who suffer themselves to be led by two or three artful demagogues, would be intolerable in the practice.

"Mr. Nichol, a gentleman of strict probity, education, and ardent loyalty, has been too successful in his endeavours to expose in his neighbourhood, the machinations of a licentious faction, to escape their resentment, and the wanton act of oppression committed against his person is a sure proof of what they meditate to prevent public animadversion on their proceedings.

"In detailing the proceedings of the fourth session of the fifth Provincial Parliament, I have considered it my bounden duty to state without reserve to your Lordship my opinion of the character of those who took a lead in the House of Assembly.

"I did not think it politic to appear in any way interested in the decision which took place respecting the Chief Justice.

"It was expected by the leaders of the faction that such was my intention, and they already rejoiced at the prospect, which the least interference on the part of Government would have afforded, of promoting their views at the ensuing general election and the accompanying address to me will shew your Lordship the cordiality with which we separated."

Writing on March 9, to the Governor-General, Brock remarked:

"The inordinate power assumed by the House of Assembly is truly alarming and ought to be resisted, otherwise the most tyrannical system will assuredly be pursued by men who suffer themselves to be led by a desperate faction that stops at nothing to gratify their resentment.

"Mr. Nichol is a gentleman of education, and who, in the district in which he resides, has done essential good in opposing the democratic measures of a Mr. Willcocks and his vile coadjutors. The palpable injustice committed against his person by dragging him at midnight without any previous warning, one hundred miles from his home to the bar of the House, and then committing him to gaol under the most frivolous pretences, has greatly alarmed the most thinking part of the community. Efforts are to be made by several respectable characters to get into the next Assembly, but such is the spirit which unfortunately prevails that I much fear they will be foiled in their attempt. I was inclined to dismiss the House before the members passed such harsh resolutions against the Chief Justice, but his friends recommended that they should be allowed to proceed without interruption."

Reverting to the subject some six weeks later, he said:

"I transmit for Your Excellency's perusal a detailed account of the transactions which led to the unjustifiable censure passed by the House of Assembly upon Chief Justice Scott. It is written by Mr. Nichol himself, and the warmth with which he has expressed himself, his indignation at the wanton exercise of a power yet undefined, as far as regards this Province, is not therefore surprising. I am convinced that whenever the business is brought legally before the judges, they will refuse to sanction the enormous power, under the name of privilege, which the House arrogates to itself. The Executive will in that case be placed in a very awkward predicament. Mr. Nichol, having commenced civil actions against the Speaker and the Sergeant-at-Arms for false imprisonment, will, should he succeed in obtaining damages, bring the question with double force on the *tapis*. The violence and ignorance, which will in all probability, mark the proceedings of the House cannot fail of producing a dissolution. I apply forcibly to the Ministers for instructions, but should they be contrary to the opinion which the judges of the King's Bench have formed of the law, I am led to believe they will not influence the members; therefore, one of two alternatives must be resorted to, either the appointment of more docile judges, or the decision of the question by a British Act of Parliament. I trust for the tranquillity and prosperity of the Province, that the latter may be preferred. I have thus freely, and perhaps with rather too much haste to be sufficiently explicit, stated the difficulties, which, in all likelihood, I shall have to encounter at the next meeting of the Legislature."*

A private letter from Captain James B. Glegg, then an aide-de-camp to General Brock, addressed to Colonel Thomas Talbot, on March 12, 1812, throws some further light on this affair:

---

* Brock to Prevost, April 22, 1812.

"The very communicative temper of our friend Nichol," he said, "will, there is no doubt, ere this arrives, have put you in full possession of the *éclat,* his name, or rather his imprisonment, has created. The Burdett business is a mere farce when compared to it—badinage apart—he has been most infamously treated, and I sincerely hope redress may be obtained for him. He may with truth exclaim, in the words of the celebrated Lord Chatham (affair of Wilkes in 1770), 'that an outrage has been committed, which struck at everything dear and sacred to the liberties of Englishmen.' I can make every allowance for his indignant feelings, tho' I sincerely regret his having made such a personal attack upon Goff and Rogers the day before he left York, as it has produced an address, which subjects his *best friend* to trouble, which ought to have been avoided."

"The General enters warmly into his hard case, and was not to be dictated to by such gentry, nor was he humbugged by the representation of the attack having taken place in the 'Speaker's apartments.' He was aware that it happened at *Jordan's* and declined interfering in the squabbles of a Tavern."

In the same letter he mentioned that Brock had just received a letter from Nichol, written at the head of the lake, stating that "in consequence of efforts made by Willcocks, Mallory, and others to create apprehensions respecting the intended operation of the Militia Bill, the young men of the country appear much alarmed and emigration is already in their contemplation." Glegg's passing comment was that "this must surely be a false alarm or intended merely as an electioneering trick by those notorious Characters."

At the session of the Legislature just ended, the Militia Act had been amended in such a way as to authorize the formation of two flank companies in each regiment, to be called out for training six days in each month, until the men composing them were pronounced "duly instructed in their exercise." Other amendments, particularly desired by Brock, had, however, been defeated, and a Bill intended to enable him under certain circumstances to suspend the *Habeas Corpus* Act, was likewise lost, mainly, he believed, through the sinister influence brought to bear upon members of the Assembly by recent settlers from the United States, who had votes as freeholders. These persons were most numerous in the London District, whither they had been attracted by free grants of land. The loyalty of many was a matter of great doubt.

As soon as the act was amended, Brock took vigorous measures to re-organize the militia of that district, then composed of the three counties of Middlesex, Norfolk and Oxford. The militia of the county of Norfolk hitherto formed in one regiment, was divided and instructions were given for its re-organization into two. Nichol was nominated for the command of the second. His appointment apparently caused some dissatisfaction among other officers, who probably felt that they had been passed over. At the same time he had become a candidate to represent the county in the Legislative Assembly. He was accused of having said that no native American could be a loyal subject, and as perhaps a majority of the men of the new regiment he had been appointed to command, and a great many of the electors, were native Americans, this charge seemed likely to create a strong prejudice against him.

He instantly demanded a Court of Inquiry to investigate the conduct of Lieut. Colonel Joseph Ryerson, who had been appointed to command the First Norfolk Regiment, Captain Abraham Rapelje, and himself, and announced his intention of preferring seven distinct charges against Rapelje, one of them being for circulating this calumnious statement.

In a letter written to Captain Glegg for Brock's information, he said:

"It is a well-known fact that almost ever since the first establishment of a militia in this county, it has been little better than a legalized mob—the officers without respectability, without intelligence, and without authority, and the men without any idea of subordination—Now, Sir, I am desirous of putting an end to such a state of things in my part of the country—My wish is to *Command a Regiment and not to be the Leader of a Mob*. To enable me to reform abuses and to bring both Officers and Men into those habits of regularity and subordination so necessary in all military service, I shall have occasion for all the popularity and Influence over Public Opinion that I possess—and had I ten times more it would not be too much—and therefore I do conceive it to be my bounden duty to resist and punish on the threshold every attempt of my immediate officers to weaken or destroy these."

The result of this application is not recorded, but a few months afterwards harmony was apparently restored with both Ryerson and Rapelje.

A certificate was obtained from Henry Bostwick, a young lawyer just appointed to command the Oxford Regiment, in whose hearing the injurious statement was reported to have been uttered, that it was not true. This certificate was printed in the form of a handbill and circulated among the electors.

Nichol was successful, but I have been unable to ascertain the name of his opponent nor have any further particulars of the contest been found. A considerable change took place in the composition of the House of Assembly. Of the twelve members who had voted for Nichol's commitment and the subsequent motion of censure of the Chief Justice, only four were re-elected, and of these, Joseph Willcocks alone had taken an active part. Among the new members, noted for their active loyalty, Mahlon Burwell, John Chrysler, Ralfe Clench, Thomas Dickson, John Macdonell, acting Attorney-General, Thomas Ridout, Livius P. Sherwood and Timothy Thompson may be named. Of twenty-five members, only seven had occupied seats in the last Assembly.

Early in April, General Brock decided to put in effect that part of the new Militia Act, which authorized the formation and training of flank companies. A circular letter, varied to suit local conditions, signed by himself, was addressed to the commanding officers of twenty-five regiments, instructing them to form two flank companies in each. They were directed to prepare depots in safe and convenient places where their men could be assembled and drilled in squads, for storing the arms after each day of exercise. As far as possible, non-commissioned officers from the regular troops were detailed to assist in giving instruction. A well-thumbed drill-book which had been used by one of these instructors is in the writer's possession.

"I cannot dismiss the subject," Brock thoughtfully remarked in this circular, "without expressing my expectations that your knowledge of the country will enable you to make such arrangements as will give the utmost facility to the important object in view, without subjecting the men to any material inconvenience. Coming generously forward with an offer of their services, they are the more entitled to every consideration.

"Not only the place but likewise the time for assembling the companies or squads will be strictly attended to by you. It is my earnest wish that the little the men have to learn may be acquired by way of a pastime and not looked upon in the light of an irksome restraint. The generality of the inhabitants being already acquainted with the use of the musket, have the less to learn. You may, therefore, under the existing circumstances, limit the parade of the companies to three times in each month.

"A little attention on the part of the men will very soon enable you to reduce even that short term of attendance. The chief object of the flank companies is to have constantly in readiness a force composed of loyal, brave and respectable young men, so far instructed as to enable the Government in case of emergency to engraft such portion of the militia as may be necessary on a stock capable of giving aid in forming them for military service. To your prudence and exertions I confidently look for the attainment of a system so evidently conducive to the safety and tranquillity of the province."

The force thus embodied, consisted of one troop of cavalry and forty-nine companies of infantry, containing one hundred and fifty-two officers, one hundred and sixteen sergeants, one trumpeter, forty-eight drummers, and one thousand six hundred and ninety-five rank and file. The quota required from Nichol's regiment consisted of two companies each to be composed of three officers, two sergeants, one drummer and thirty-five rank and file. It is perhaps worthy of remark that Captain Abraham Rapelje, with whom he had been so recently squabbling, was chosen by him to command one of these companies, and afterwards commanded a company in the battalion of incorporated militia with credit, until the end of the war.

There is no record of Nichol's personal share in the formation of these companies, but it is fair to assume that he acted with his usual energy and promptitude. Early in May, 1812, General Brock made a tour of inspection through the Niagara and part of the London district, lasting about two weeks, for the purpose of ascertaining the progress that had been made, and reported to the Governor-General that the flank companies had been instantly completed with volunteers of the best class of young men.

Nichol, himself, stated that the first intelligence of the actual declaration of war by the United States was communicated to Brock in seven days from Washington through mercantile connections of his own, and that the government despatches, announcing that important event, were not received until fourteen days later. The leading British merchants of Montreal, James McGill, John Richardson, William McGillivray, and others were vitally interested at that time in the fur trade of the North-West. They had lately disposed of a part of this business, which had been carried on in the country bordering on Lake Michigan, under the name of the Michilimackinac or South-west Fur Company, to John Jacob Astor of New York, with whom they were closely allied, but it was still conducted from Montreal with the former staff of agents and servants. It was a matter of the highest importance to them to obtain and utilize the earliest information of hostilities for the protection of their property. They accordingly made secret arrangements to have the report of the proceedings in Congress transmitted by special messengers travelling with the greatest possible speed from Washington to New York, thence to Albany. From the latter place one express was hurried off to Montreal and another to Queenston, where the message was delivered to Thomas Dickson, an agent or partner in the North-West Company, by whom it was communicated to Brock without delay. The value of such early information was very great, and might have been much greater, had not Brock been restricted to the defensive by positive orders, for he declared that he could have swept the opposing forces from the Niagara frontier and the south shore of Lake Ontario, yet at the same time he admitted that this success would only have been temporary.

He sent for Nichol, who seems to have been at Niagara at the time, and offered him the important and responsible office of Quartermaster-General of the Militia. This would involve the entire organization of a new department, charged with all the duties of supply and transport for a considerable body of men suddenly called into service, for whose equipment, subsistence, quarters, and movements, no previous arrangements of any kind had yet been made. Everything must be improvised. Nichol said that at first he refused to accept this appointment on the ground that his private business would be neglected and ruined, if he undertook any kind of permanent employment in the public service, and that he felt himself unable to perform its duties properly from inexperience, although at the same time he was quite willing to do any duty of which he was deemed capable for the limited period of six months, as required by the Militia Act. Brock insisted on his acceptance, saying that Nichol was the only person in the province whom he considered fit for the office, and added that while he was aware that it meant a great personal sacrifice, "the British Government was never backward in rewarding faithful and meritorious services."

His appointment as Quartermaster-General of Militia was accordingly announced in orders on June 27. James Cummings, an energetic young merchant of Chippawa, was soon after appointed his deputy. At that time there was no commissioned officer of the Quartermaster-General's department of the regular troops nearer than York, and Nichol was required to conduct all services of that description for them as well as the militia for nearly a month, when Colonel Christopher Myers, the Deputy Quartermaster-General, arrived from Lower Canada.

A letter from Nichol to Cummings has been preserved, dated at Queenston on the day of his appointment, directing the latter to make arrangements for the conveyance of boats over the Niagara Falls portage.

Another letter, dated at Niagara on July 3, evidently written by Nichol in reply to a demand for supplies from Lieutenant-Colonel Thomas Clark, reveals in a striking manner the poverty of his resources. Clark was informed that none of the articles he wanted could be furnished except *nails*. General Brock had ordered camp-kettles and haversacks to be made by local contracts, and as soon as these were delivered he would be supplied with a due proportion. He must not expect to receive tents and was directed to quarter his men in the neighbouring houses and barns. General Brock, he said, was constantly employed in devising measures to relieve the wants of the militia and make them more comfortable, and the commissariat was busy with the same object. As next day would be the fourth of July, Clark was advised to be more than usually vigilant, as the enemy might attempt to begin their campaign by giving a little additional *éclat* to that day.

A general order was published on July 4, probably at his suggestion, complimenting the militia on their good conduct and admitting that they had been required to endure great privations and hardships, but assuring them that every effort was being made to supply their wants, and adding that under the existing circumstances it was absolutely necessary that every inhabitant should have recourse to his private means to supply himself with blankets and other necessary articles while on duty. Many of them were, indeed, in want of proper clothing, and some were without shoes, which could not be obtained in the province.

Shortly after Colonel Myers's arrival, a chain of beacons was established from lake to lake with stations on the high land at Stamford, Pelham and Queenston Heights, for the rapid transmission of intelligence by a system of signals, which was tolerably effective.

Letters, still extant, from Edward Couche, a Deputy Commissary General, show that he had little difficulty in making satisfactory contracts for the delivery of the most essential articles of food, such as flour and fresh meat, but the distribution of these supplies to several outposts was a task of equal importance, which in the absence of decent roads, required extraordinary exertions.

When Brock went to York to attend the short emergency session of the Legislature which he had convened, and at which his presence was indispensable, the command of the troops was taken over by Myers, and all of the duties of the Quartermaster-General's department were again turned over to Nichol. Cummings was sent to Oxford to collect provisions and hire waggons for the movement of a body of militia, which had been directed to assemble there and march to Amherstburg.

On July 28, Nichol, who was then at York, apparently attending the meeting of the Legislature, was unexpectedly required by Brock to make immediate arrangements for the transport of five hundred men with necessary provisions and baggage, by water from Port Dover to the Detroit frontier. Owing to the limited resources and thinly populated state of the country, this was an undertaking of considerable magnitude. Two small sailing vessels and a number of large row-boats, provided with sails, were impressed with the necessary number of horses and carriages and brought to the point of embarkation at the time appointed, under his personal supervision.

As the Journals of the House of Assembly for that session have disappeared, it is not possible to acertain what part, if any, Nichol took in its proceedings.

On the afternoon of August 7, Brock arrived in the township of Woodhouse and took up his quarters at Nichol's residence, where several other officers had been previously entertained, but moved out to make way for their commander. The schooner *Chippewa* and a number of large undecked boats were in readiness for the transport of the troops, with their baggage and a quantity of ordnance stores, which included one six-pounder field-gun. Another schooner, the *Nancy*, had already sailed from Fort Erie with sixty men of the 41st Regiment. The number of men assembled at Port Dover, mostly militia flank companies from the counties of York, Lincoln, Norfolk and Oxford, was considerably greater than could be embarked and a part of them was left behind in consequence, some of whom were ordered to march by land to Amherstburg. Considerable uncertainty then existed whether the small garrison of that place could hold its position against the much superior force opposed to it, until the reinforcements arrived.

On this journey in open boats "of upwards of two hundred miles along a most difficult and dangerous coast," Nichol stated in his Memorial that he not only had acted as Quartermaster-General but also as "pilot and guide." The embarkation began on Saturday, August 8, and a halt was made for the night near the eastern end of the portage over Long Point at the mouth of a small creek. The conveyance of the boats with the baggage and stores over this primitive carrying-place was not an easy task, and several hours were thus occupied. The flotilla put into the mouth of Kettle Creek, now Port Stanley, for shelter and rest on the following evening. Next morning the wind was fair and strong, gradually increasing during the day to a violent gale with every appearance of a storm so that General Brock gave orders for the boats to run into the bay near Port Talbot, where some of them, not being able to enter the creek, were hauled up on the beach for safety. Heavy rain fell during the night drenching many officers and men who had not been able to find quarters in the buildings of the small settlement at that place. After sailing for some hours next morning the wind changed and the crews were obliged to resort to their oars, until the gale grew so strong that they were forced to land once more near the mouth of a small stream flowing into Lake Erie from the township of Aldborough, since commonly known as Brock's Creek. Here orders were issued to embark again at midnight and prohibiting all boats from going ahead of that conveying the general and his staff, which would display a light. On the following night a halt was made at Point Pelee, a settlement that had already been visited by the enemy's mounted patrols, and outposts were accordingly established a mile in advance of the camp. At 8 o'clock next evening the expedition arrived at Amherstburg and learned that the invaders had returned to Detroit.

Nichol's exertions were then directed to preparations for crossing the river some distance below Detroit and the attack of the enemy's position, which it was expected would be resolutely defended. This movement was largely based on his intimate local knowledge, for he states that he "not only designed the point of disembarkation but actually superintended the landing of the troops," crossing in the first boat himself. In Brock's general order, published on the day of the capitulation, he acknowledged the assistance he had "derived from the zeal and local information of Lieut.-Col. Nichol," and made a similar mention of his services in his official letter.

His next important duty was the embarkation of the prisoners for Cleveland and Fort Erie and the removal of a great quantity of captured stores. To complete this task he remained at Amherstburg and Detroit until the beginning of September, during that time reconnoitering the country on the enemy's side as far as the rapids of the Miami in company with Colonel Procter. He then solicited a few days' leave to attend to his private business, which was readily granted as an armistice had been concluded for an indefinite period, which it was hoped might terminate in a treaty of peace.

On returning to Niagara about the middle of September, Nichol relates that he was ordered by General Brock to make a confidential report on the state of the western command, which he did to the general's satisfaction. This report has not been found. He was then instructed to go to Lower Canada to make extensive purchases of necessary articles for the use of the militia, who were still in great want of many things, and carried with him a despatch for Sir George Prevost, in which Brock said that Nichol was "perfectly qualified from his local knowledge and late return to afford every information of the state of affairs in the Western District." Nichol, himself, states that he was sent "ostensibly to purchase stores and clothing for the militia, but in reality to communicate confidentially to the late Sir George Prevost the very critical situation in which General Brock found himself placed, restrained from acting offensively and expecting to be attacked by an overwhelming force of the enemy at some one point of his very extensive line while the zeal and enthusiasm of the militia were subsiding from the state of inactivity in which they were kept." The tenor of the letter he bore, corroborates this statement.

He was directed to request an advance of £5,000 to the account of the Receiver General for Upper Canada for civil expenditure, being the amount voted at the last session of the Legislature for the support of the militia, and supplied with a letter of credit to that extent from the Receiver General, to enable him to purchase the supplies required. On his arrival at Montreal, about the end of September, he delivered this letter to Prevost, who was there at the time, and no doubt made a verbal report.

In a letter to Brock, dated September 30, Prevost refers to Nichol's mission and made these remarks on the proposal, evidently advanced for the resumption of hostilities by a vigorous offensive:

"Having received information that the revocation of the Orders in Council, the conciliatory disposition shown by His Majesty's Government towards the United States, and the knowledge of the pacific advances made have produced throughout America the best effects upon the public opinion so as to render the war extremely unpopular, I should consider it extremely unfortunate if any temptation or provocation should induce you to abandon those defensive operations suited to the present state of the contest, and which it has become both prudent and politic to persevere in observing."

Brock was killed before this letter was delivered but it no doubt influenced his successor to remain strictly on the defensive.

Nichol returned to Niagara from Kingston on November 7, with two small ships, almost entirely loaded with the stores he had purchased at Montreal, and the distribution of these articles began at once. Greatcoats and other clothing, blankets, and shoes were badly needed. These were issued without charge, while underclothing and stockings were to be paid for by the recipients at their original cost. An order announcing these regulations was published on November 14.

Nichol was at Niagara during the bombardment of the fort and town on November 21, 1812, and his effective assistance on that occasion was acknowledged by Major-General Sheaffe in his official letter.

A week later he took part in the operations at the other end of the line, between Fort Erie and Frenchman's Creek, in which the flank companies of the two regiments of Norfolk militia fought bravely and sustained comparatively severe losses, on the night of November 27/8. Colonel Bisshopp in his despatch stated that the greatest credit was due to Nichol and his own staff-adjutant, Lieut. Barnard, for their exertions.

On November 30, General Sheaffe wrote to Bisshopp, informing him that no more reinforcements could be sent to his assistance, and adding that he considered the force then under his command too small to resist with success the superior numbers opposed to it. He was advised to consult the field-officers of the line and militia, and, if a retreat was decided upon, as he presumed would be the case, to make it as swiftly and quietly as possible. Besides Bisshopp, himself, the council of war, thus assembled, consisted of two regular and four militia officers, of whom Nichol was one. A written opinion was prepared and signed by them all, saying:

"We do not, under existing circumstances, consider retreat at all necessary, nor do we consider it a measure which ought to be looked forward to. We think that our position may be defended and that a small reinforcement would enable us to gain a decided advantage over any force the enemy has in his power to bring against us."

For the adoption of this resolute declaration of confidence in their ability to hold their ground, Nichol asserted that he was mainly responsible and "principally instrumental in preventing the evacuation of Fort Erie and the abandonment of the lines in the neighbourhood at a time when the moral effect of such a measure would have accelerated the ruin of the King's affairs in Upper Canada."

The decision of this council of war was fully justified by subsequent events. The attempt at invasion was soon abandoned and active hostilities ceased for more than three months. On December 12, Nichol wrote a very short letter to Colonel Talbot, enclosing General Smyth's extraordinary proclamation, heralding his contemplated conquest of Upper Canada, and added in a thoroughly downright way his opinion that Couche, the Deputy Commissary General, should be hanged. The exact cause for this explosion of anger is not apparent.

Six days later, he wrote again to Talbot at considerable length in language that shows he was not on cordial terms with his new commanding officer and had but little confidence in him.

"This cursed office," he said, "to which for my sins I have been appointed, engrosses *all* my time, and if I don't soon get leave to resign it, I believe I shall go crazy . . .

"Alas, my dear Colonel, we are no longer commanded by Brock, and our situation is most materially changed for the worse. Confidence seems to have vanished from the land and gloomy despondency has taken its place. I dare not trust myself to write you all. I feel that the field officers of the troops and militia have saved the country for a time, *but their efforts will be unavailing against bad management and despondency in those who are at our head and who ought to be better qualified to fill energetically the high and important positions they hold.* You may, however, depend upon it that those on this line will not relax in their exertions to save the country . . . . I have no longer access to the staff papers."

The Legislature met on the 25th of February, 1813, and was prorogued on March 13, following. Only five acts were passed at this short session, all of them being intended to aid in the defence of the province. The first of these sanctioned the circulation of Army Bills, issued under the authority of the Legislature of Lower Canada as a legal tender in payment of debts, dues, and demands. The scarcity of gold and silver coin made this measure a subject of great importance. The next repealed that part of the militia act providing for the formation of flank companies and authorized the formation of a battalion of Incorporated Militia in each district, to serve during the war. The third prohibited the exportation of grain and other provisions, and restricted the distillation of spirituous liquors from grain. The fourth provided small pensions for officers and other ranks of the militia disabled on service, and annuities for the widows and orphans of those who were killed or died while on active duty. The fifth prohibited the sale of spirituous liquors to Indians. The session concluded with an unanimous vote placing all the unappropriated revenue of the province at the disposal of the President for its defence. As the Journals of this session have also disappeared, no record of Nichol's participation in it has been found.

After Lake Erie was frozen over, considerable apprehension was felt that scouting parties of the enemy might cross the ice and find their way into the province at some unguarded point, and à chain of outposts, mainly composed of detachments from the flank companies of the Lincoln and Norfolk regiments of militia, was established along shore, as far west as the Sugar Loaf.

On March 17, the British batteries near Fort Erie were subjected to a prolonged bombardment, which was naturally supposed to be the prelude to some offensive enterprise. The vigilance of the outposts was accordingly redoubled. On the 19th, while Nichol was on his way to inspect the Norfolk flank companies at Carter's Point, he observed a sleigh on the surface of the lake at some distance and gave the alarm. A mounted party rode off in pursuit. The chase was unsuccessful but the bodies of two men were discovered, who had apparently been frozen to death while attempting to cross.

On the morning of April 29, at half past three o'clock, Nichol wrote in haste from Niagara to Colonel Talbot, stating that an express had arrived about an hour before with the discouraging information that York was in the hands of the enemy and it was supposed that General Sheaffe had been taken prisoner.

"In such a juncture," he said, "it is necessary that every prompt and decisive measure should be adopted to remedy this disaster and to prevent the enemy from profiting to any great degree by this success. You are so much better acquainted with the country than the General (Vincent) himself that everything in your district is left to your own discretion, but it is hoped that the enemy may yet be prevented from penetrating into the country on the side of the head of the lake. It will be necessary that you keep up a regular communication with Ancaster and regulate your movements by the accounts you may receive from there, keeping an eye at the same time upon the lake from whence, however, it is not supposed the enemy can commence operations for some time yet."

The three next weeks were actively occupied in making preparations for resisting another invasion, which was evidently impending at Niagara.

On May 27, Nichol acted as staff-officer to Colonel Myers, who was placed in command of the left division of General Vincent's small force, which in an obstinate but unavailing effort to oppose the landing of the enemy's troops, was overwhelmed by the fire of their ships and lost fully sixty per cent. of its number. Colonel Myers was disabled by four wounds and the command then devolved on Major Ogilvie. The horse, on which Nichol was mounted, was killed beneath him, but he continued to assist Ogilvie in rallying and withdrawing the remnant of his force.

After a junction was formed with the other divisions which had been posted along the river, General Vincent proposed to retire upon Fort Erie, collecting the troops stationed at Queenston, Chippawa, and other posts, and to order General Procter to join him there with the forces from Amherstburg and Detroit. Nichol at once strongly objected, pointing out that all communication would thus be abandoned with the Commander-in-Chief, who was then at Kingston, and a retreat in the direction contemplated would put it out of his power to reinforce or relieve them. Besides this, there were no magazines of supplies at Fort Erie, and the resources of the adjacent country were very scanty. "That in fact he would go into a *trou de loup*, from which no talent or bravery could extricate him, and that the effect of this movement would be to compromise the safety of the whole division as well as the whole of the province above Kingston." He advised a retirement on

Burlington Heights and assured Vincent that he could conduct it by a safe route, although the principal roads leading in that direction were already occupied by the enemy. His views were supported by Lieut.-Colonel Harvey, Vincent's chief staff-officer, and by Captain Milnes, an aide-de-camp to Sir George Prevost, then with the division on special duty, and were adopted. At St. David's the head of the retreating column was turned westward on the Mountain Road. This meant the sacrifice of the guns in position, the barracks, and some ordnance stores, and perhaps the loss of some men at the more distant stations. Messengers rode swiftly away and the beacons blazed that night all over the peninsula, warning and calling in the scattered detachments from the forts and outposts along the upper Niagara and shore of Lake Erie. By nine o'clock a fighting force of fourteen hundred men, with its field artillery and indispensable baggage, weary but undaunted, halted for the night at Beaver Dam having gained a march of twelve miles on the enemy and misled him as to the direction of its retreat.

Before morning, some of the outlying detachments came up and the movement was resumed next day, the advanced guard marching as far as the crossing of the Forty Mile Creek while the main body halted at Henry's house on the crest of the escarpment, overlooking the plain below. On the following day the entire force, including the garrison of Fort Erie and its dependencies, was concentrated near Grimsby, where an order was issued, placing Nichol in charge of the train of waggons, conveying the baggage. As the roads were then rendered nearly impassable by a tremendous downpour of rain, which lasted most of the night and thoroughly drenched everybody, a halt was made at that place until the morning of May 31, which was utilized for the impressment of more waggons and horses. The march was then continued to a strong, commanding position on Burlington Heights, from which the outposts overlooked all probable ways of approach, as far as the eye could see. It was presumed that pursuit would be attempted by the transportation of troops in ships or boats to some landing-place at or near the head of the lake, which could be watched from suitable points of observation.

"By this movement," to use Nichol's own words, "the Centre Division was placed in a strong and eligible position, its supplies were secured, and its communications with the right and left were completely re-established."

On the morning of June 6, after the night attack on the pursuing force at Stoney Creek had been carried out, General Vincent, who had accompanied the attacking column, and become separated from it in the darkness, did not return to the camp at Burlington Heights for several hours and was believed to have either been killed or taken prisoner. The full effect of recent action was not yet known. Colonel Bisshopp, who had been left in charge of the remaining force, was at a loss how to act and called a conference of officers to consider the situation. Captain Robert McDouall, an aide-de-camp to Sir George Prevost, was present, and produced a letter from him, authorizing a further retreat to Kingston if circumstances seemed to render it necessary. Nichol was again consulted and promptly remarked that since Captain McDouall had held this letter in his possession for several days without making its contents known, it could only be considered as containing discretionary instructions, and advised that another conference of the field and staff officers should be held to decide the question. General Vincent, having soon afterwards returned, ordered that this should be done, when it was determined to hold the position until further orders were received. Within forty-eight hours the British squadron arrived with a small reinforcement, which enabled Vincent to advance in pursuit of the retreating enemy and eventually invest his position at Niagara.

For several days thereafter, Nichol was actively employed in collecting abandoned stores and making returns of these and the prisoners taken. Communication was reopened with General Procter, who requested that all supplies for his division and the squadron on Lake Erie, should be sent overland by waggons from Burlington Bay to the Grand River, and shipped in small boats to Long Point, where they would be taken on board the vessels on the lake and conveyed to Amherstburg. The movement of stores by this circuitous route was unavoidably slow and laborious, but the loss of the Niagara line of communication made its adoption the next best alternative. Some of the more ponderous articles could not be handled over it at all. Heavy guns for the armament of a new ship under construction for Lake Erie were landed at Burlington and went no farther. Still large quantities of the most necessary supplies were successfully forwarded.

For four months during the summer of 1813, owing to the disablement of Colonel Myers by his wounds, Nichol was compelled to take sole charge of the Quartermaster-General's department with the Centre Division of the army in Upper Canada, which at one time numbered more than three thousand regular troops, besides considerable bodies of militia and Indians, and taxed his energies and the limited resources of the adjacent country to the utmost. Assistant Quartermaster-Generals for the militia, had, however, been then appointed for the other districts.

On July 10, Nichol received confidential instructions to accompany picked detachments of the 41st regiment and militia to Fort Erie, whence they were to be transported across the river to Black Rock for the purpose of destroying the enemy's naval station and magazines. Arrangements were then to be made to convey these troops up Lake Erie to Long Point, where they were to be joined by more troops, embark in the squadron, cross the lake and make an attack on the enemy's naval base at Erie in Pennsylvania. The raid upon Black Rock was successful, but the heavy loss sustained in re-embarking, caused the remainder of the plan to be abandoned.

When the loss of the Lake Erie squadron became known, on September 16, at the headquarters of the Centre Division, then at the Four Mile Creek, Nichol was at once instructed to go to the London District and embody a force of militia to establish a new line of communication from Burlington to Oxford on the Thames, and thence by boats to Chatham for the transport of supplies to the British force at Amherstburg. This route was opened and maintained until Procter's disastrous defeat made its further operation unnecessary. Nichol was then ordered to disband this force and rejoin the headquarters of the division which had again retired to Burlington Heights.

Early in November, General Vincent informed Nichol of his intention to retire toward Kingston as he considered his force inadequate to oppose the superior numbers of the enemy, and instructed him to make the preliminary arrangements for beginning this movement. The sick and a portion of the baggage had already been sent on to York. It would become necessary to destroy the surplus stores and dismantle the fortifications at Burlington.*

The outlook was indeed gloomy enough but Nichol was still undismayed and courageously opposed the proposal to retreat with much vigour. He said that he "remonstrated against the measure, stated a variety of reasons against it, amongst others the impossibility of transporting in the then state of the roads the guns and baggage to Kingston, which must therefore be abandoned or destroyed, the want of subsistence on the route, the possibility of the enemy, then uncontrolled masters of the lake, occupying a position by which the small columns in which the division must march would fall into their hands in succession; the actual situation of Kingston at the time, threatened with a siege and with only seven days' flour in the stores; the situation of the Niagara District when deserted by the King's troops, abandoned to the ravages of the enemy, exposed to the fury of the Indians, who seeing themselves abandoned after all our protestations, would in all probability purchase peace of the enemy by the massacre of the population."

The question was referred for further consideration to a council composed of Major-General Procter and four senior officers of the regular army, who reported in favour of retaining their ground. This decision was fully justified by the course of events, which enabled the division to take a bold offensive, resulting in the recovery of the whole Niagara peninsula and the capture of all the enemy's positions on the opposite bank of the river within the next two months.

A raiding party from Buffalo, composed mainly of refugees from the London District, joined by a few disaffected inhabitants and ruffians, who had terrorized the country, stealing horses and cattle belonging to Nichol and others in the vicinity of Port Dover, plundering houses, and carrying off the loyalists as prisoners, was routed at Nanticoke Creek by a small party of the Norfolk militia, led by Lieut.-Colonel Henry Bostwick. Nichol stated that seven thousand barrels of provisions were thus saved from destruction by which the troops were enabled to maintain their position at Burlington until further supplies were received. Several of the traitors taken at this time were tried by a special commission, convicted of treason, and executed at Burlington in July following.

A foraging party, composed of a dozen men of the Norfolk militia and a few provincial dragoons under Lieut. Henry Medcalf, which was despatched a few weeks later from Port Dover in search of a number of cattle reported to be running wild in the woods near Rondeau, learning that the enemy had established an advanced post at McCrea's house near Chatham, boldly determined to attack it. Being joined by a few volunteers from the Middlesex and Kent regiments,

---

* "Colonel Nichol," Procter wrote, "is fully qualified to direct the transport in question."

Medcalf advanced swiftly, surrounded the house, and succeeded in taking the whole of the enemy's outpost, making more prisoners than he had men. These small successes did much to revive the spirits of the militia in the districts most menaced with invasion.

In November, 1813, Lieutenant-General Sir Gordon Drummond was appointed to command the troops in Upper Canada, and administer the civil affairs of the province. Major-General Phineas Riall was sent to relieve General Vincent in command of his division. Both of these officers had lately arrived from Europe and were not fully conversant with the military situation in that province.

Colonel Myers, who was still suffering from the severe wounds he had received at Niagara, wrote to Nichol from Montreal on November 25:

"I have mentioned you to Gen. Riall in the way you deserve, & will do the same to Gen. Drummond if I can see him; he is at Chateauguay and may perhaps cross the River for U.C. without coming here."

Shortly after the conclusion of his short but very successful winter campaign, Drummond received orders from Prevost to report upon the feasibility of an expedition to recover Detroit and destroy the enemy's squadron on Lake Erie, which had been laid up for the winter. He was also directed to make the necessary arrangements for moving a small body of troops to the relief of the garrison of Mackinac by way of Lakes Simcoe and Huron with a sufficient supply of provisions to last several months. Several small gunboats were to be built at Penetanguishene for service on this expedition. On both these subjects, he consulted with Sir James Yeo and Colonel Nichol, who was summoned to Kingston for that special purpose, as Drummond remarked that his local knowledge rendered him competent to give the most correct information.

On January 21, 1814, Nichol was directed to proceed at once to General Riall's headquarters, where he was to obtain and transmit the most reliable intelligence on the following points:

"1. The quantity of Provisions of every Species that may be obtained in the Districts of Niagara and London, the time in which it can be brought to the different Depots and in what proportions to each.

"2. The facility of establishing Depots at different points on the route to Amherstburg, the time required for that purpose, and the facility of carrying them forward if required.

"3. To Communicate with the Commissariat on the providing of Depots of Biscuits, Spirits, etc., etc., contiguous to line of operations in the Western District.

"4. To ascertain the state of the roads generally and the possibility of moving by the Lake on the Bordage from Port Talbot to Amherstburg.

"5. To procure and transmit Correct returns of the Forage of each description that may be obtained on the route to Amherstburg. The returns of the resources of the above mentioned Districts to be collected from the Captains of Militia through their Lieut.-Colonels."

The project was, however, soon dropped as on February 3, Colonel Foster, Drummond's Military Secretary wrote from Kingston to Nichol advising him of this.

"The weather has been so unusually mild," he said, "that little hopes can be entertained of the Ice upon the Lake being sufficiently safe for the intended purpose, independent of the Season being too far advanced to commence the Movement of Troops, part of whom would have a March of not less than 450 Miles before their arrival at the Scene of Action."

He added that Drummond would leave that place in a few days for York, where Nichol was expected to meet him.

The general return of the resources of the nine regimental divisions of the London and Niagara Districts and the west riding of the Home District was completed before the end of February. The comprehensive character of this statement may be understood from the fact that it showed the quantity of flour, wheat, rye, oats, corn, barley and peas, the number of fat cattle, cattle to fatten, working oxen, cows, young cattle, sheep, hogs, horses, tons of hay, sleighs, pungs, waggons, carts, and acres of wheat, barley and rye sown in each regimental division. It is perhaps worthy of remark that the entire number of fat cattle was only thirty-six and of cattle to fatten 361, while only three acres of barley had been sown. The preparation of these returns could only have been effected by a house to house canvass.

The Legislature met at York on February 15. In his address Sir Gordon Drummond referred briefly to the defeat of the invasion of Lower Canada, the destruction of the town of Niagara, and the subsequent capture of Fort Niagara and the devastation of the U. S. frontier in retaliation. The recent successes of the allied armies in Spain and Germany were mentioned.

The importance of a well organized militia required their most serious consideration, he said, as the measure adopted at the last session of incorporating battalions of militia for permanent service had not succeeded. He advised the embodiment of detachments of the militia from the different regiments, not greater than one-third of their actual strength, for a period of not more than one year, as the only method by which they could be clothed and armed in uniformity with the regular troops and become efficient.

During the last campaign military operations had been greatly impeded by the neglected state of the public roads. It was essential that one great road through the province should be put in a condition for the easy transportation of military supplies.

The advisability of calling upon those persons who had abstained from military service from religious scruples to contribute more liberally in money for the defence of the country was suggested. He remarked that the fact that two members of the Assembly had actually joined the enemy was more a matter of regret than surprise, as their malignant influence at the last session had been the cause of the rejection of the request made by the Executive for a modification of the *habeas corpus* act. The punishment of such traitors by the confiscation of their estates, and, as they might evade the necessary personal service of writs for a legal conviction, the passage of an act of attainder was recommended. The Prince Regent had announced his wish that the proceeds of all forfeitures in such cases should be applied for the relief of sufferers from the war in the province. An act to continue the restriction upon the distillation of spirits from grain was necessary.

The state of the province was not cheering. The enemy was in military occupation of the frontier of the Western District and his raiding parties often advanced into the other unprotected settlements, where they caused alarm, destroyed property, plundered the inhabitants, and carried off noted loyalists as prisoners of war. Their other attempts at invasion had, indeed, failed but preparations for their renewal on a more formidable scale were already evident. A large part of the Niagara District had been laid waste, many farms were abandoned and uncultivated. More than three hundred heads of families had fled to the enemy. Two members of the Assembly, Joseph Willcocks and Abraham Markle, and Benajah Mallory, a former member, had accepted commissions from the Government of the U. S. and had succeeded in recruiting a small body of men, whom they called "Canadian Volunteers." These men had an intimate knowledge of the country, its public affairs and resources. Several officers of the militia, whose loyalty had not been suspected, had since joined them. They could give, and in fact did give, the enemy the most important and accurate information respecting those parts of the province that he intended to invade.

The Journals of the Assembly for this session show that Nichol took a leading part in all its proceedings. He was at once named a member of the special committee of five appointed to draft a reply to General Drummond's speech and read this to the House for its adoption. On February 17, he gave notice of his intention to introduce bills to extend and amend the act prohibiting the distillation and exportation of grain, for increasing the duties on shop and tavern licenses, for licensing hawkers and pedlars, for granting salaries to sheriffs, and for continuing the agreement with Lower Canada respecting the collection of custom duties. All of these were eventually passed.

On February 19, he moved that the House should go into a Committee of the Whole to consider the state of the province. When the roll was called it was ascertained that eighteen members were present, one was absent sick, four were prisoners of war, and two had deserted to the enemy. A motion was then made by Mr. Nichol, seconded by Mr. Mears: "sufficient evidence having been offered to this House of the traitorous and disloyal desertion of Joseph Willcocks, one of its members, to the enemy, and of his having actually borne arms against His Majesty's Government, that this House, entertaining the utmost abhorrence of his infamous conduct, which has rendered him incapable of sitting or voting in this House, do declare his seat vacant, and that he shall no longer be considered a member thereof."

It was carried unanimously as was another for the expulsion of Abraham Markle in nearly identical terms, moved immediately afterwards by Nichol, seconded by Lieut.-Colonel Burwell.

On February 21, Nichol introduced the government bill to amend the militia laws and gave notice of a bill to authorize the suspension of the *habeas corpus* act in certain cases. Next day he introduced the latter bill and gave notice of one to ascertain the eligibility of persons to be returned as members of the House of Assembly. On February 24, he challenged a division and voted alone against the acceptance of the report of a committee respecting a bridge over the Grand River, which had not been completed according to contract.

Two days later the circumstances of his arrest were recalled by a petition from Stephen Jarvis, the deputy Sergeant-at-Arms, asking the House to refund to him the sum of ten guineas, he had paid a lawyer for defending him in a suit brought against him by Nichol for false imprisonment. This claim was allowed by the Committee on Public Accounts, of which Nichol himself was chairman.

There was a division on the bill to suspend the *habeas corpus* act, which was entitled " An Act to empower His Majesty for a limited time to secure and detain such persons as His Majesty shall suspect of a treasonable adherence to the Enemy," and a solitary member, Mr. Wilson, voted against its passage.

Acts to amend the Act of Attainder, for the punishment of High Treason, and for the punishment of traitors and conspirators had already been passed by the Legislative Council and were sent down for the concurrence of the Assembly. Nichol at once took charge of the Attainder Bill and moved its second reading. He next introduced a bill to "restrain and prohibit the issue of small notes and to authorize the Governor, Lieutenant-Governor, or person administering the Government to issue a limited number of Army or Government Bills for the convenience of change."

The bill for the punishment of High Treason passed its second reading and went to the committee of the whole, where it was amended. The committee asked leave to sit again in three months, when Nichol moved that a sitting be held next day, but found only four supporters and his motion was lost by a majority of five.

On the afternoon of the same day, March 2, he gave notice of his intention to introduce a bill " to indemnify all such persons as may have acted under any proclamation or general order for subsisting His Majesty's Forces, or for the safety of the Province from disaffected persons, sanctioned by the Commander of the Forces." This was opening a burning question as there was much dissatisfaction in the three eastern districts over the operation of a recent order by Major-General de Rottenburg for the impressment of provisions and forage for the use of the troops, and suits for damages were threatened against several officers. Nichol was probably dissuaded from pressing this measure as he took no further action.

On the third reading of the High Treason Bill he moved that the amendment thereto be read that day three months but his motion was lost on a division by a majority of two.

On March 8, he introduced a bill to appropriate the whole of the unexpended revenue for the defence of the province, which received its first and second reading and was reported by the committee of the whole on the same day without amendment and finally passed on the next.

He also introduced a bill for the appropriation of a considerable sum for the improvement of the public highways which met with no opposition.

Two divisions occurred on the Militia Bill, in both of which he voted with the majority, and it was finally carried by a single vote.

He was named as chairman of a committee to draft an address praying that efforts should be made to accomplish an exchange or obtain the release of officers and men of the militia who were prisoners of war in the United States, many of whom had been taken from their homes.

On March 12, he moved, seconded by Lieut-Colonel Burwell, that a sword, valued at one hundred guineas should be presented to Colonel John Murray, "as a memorial of the high sense which this House entertains of his brilliant and important services on the Niagara Frontier, and of the zeal, talent, and gallantry displayed by him at the capture by assault of Fort Niagara in the United States on the 19th December, 1813." This resolution was adopted unanimously.

He then moved, seconded by Lieut.-Colonel Thomas Dickson, that "a sword, valued at fifty guineas, should be presented to Captain James Kerby of the Incorporated Militia, as a memorial of the high sense they entertain of the very important services which he rendered in crossing the troops to the territory of the United States, and of the gallantry displayed by him at the capture by assault of Fort Niagara on the 19th December, 1813." This motion was likewise carried unanimously.

Later in the course of the same day he moved, seconded by Mr. Beikie, that one hundred pounds should be voted to the Reverend Robert Addison, Chaplain of the House of Assembly, "in consideration of the great care and attention shown by him in relieving the wants and distresses of the wounded soldiery at Fort George, and the inhabitants of that neighbourhood, who suffered from the destruction of their property by the enemy." This motion passed unanimously.

On March 14, as Chairman of the Select Committee on Public Accounts he presented a report, on which was based a special address to the President, with reference to the payment of money to the enemy out of the provincial funds "to prevent the town of York from being burnt," and the amount due from Lower Canada for custom duties on merchandise imported at Coteau du Lac, according to the agreement between the provinces.

On that day too, he moved, seconded by Mr. Pattinson, that the sum of one hundred pounds should be paid to the Reverend Richard Pollard for services rendered the Province. This motion was carried.

As the member first named on a committee appointed to draft an address to the Prince Regent, he presented a draft of an address, which was adopted, and for the preparation of which, he was no doubt chiefly responsible.

The two main paragraphs may be fittingly quoted here:

"When it is considered, may it please your Royal Highness, that the whole male population of Upper Canada able to bear arms does not exceed ten thousand men, and it is scattered over a frontier of at least eight hundred miles in extent, when it is considered that nearly one-half of these were embodied for the whole of the first, and a very considerable proportion for the greatest part of the last campaign, and that they composed the principal part of the force which successively captured the fort of Michilimackinac and the army of General Hull; which carried by assault the batteries at Ogdensburg, which fought and gained the battles of Queenston, River Raisin, and Fort Meigs, and which repulsed the enemy under

General Smyth near Fort Erie; when it is known that in the disastrous affair near Fort George on the Twenty-seventh of May last, they were warmly engaged with the enemy, and actually suffered as severely as His Majesty's regular Forces, when it is known that the greatest part of the transportation and provisioning of the Forces in Upper Canada fell upon them and in such parts as have been visited by the enemy, their properties have been plundered and destroyed, and themselves as prisoners carried away, when it is known that the whole efforts of the enemy during the two last campaigns have been directed towards the subjugation of Upper Canada and that it is yet unsubdued, we think, may it please Your Royal Highness, it will be admitted that the Militia of the Province have faithfully performed their duty; that their services have very largely contributed to the security of this portion of His Majesty's dominions, and that it was the duty of the representative of our Sovereign to have laid before Your Royal Highness a faithful account of our services and our sufferings.

"It cannot have been represented to Your Royal Highness. Nevertheless such is the fact that many of our Militiamen have fallen by the sword of the enemy; many have been disabled, and a large proportion of them have died from diseases contracted while in the field, and from being destitute of every comfort our population has decreased. Our properties have been destroyed, and hundreds are reduced to beggary and want without even the consolation of knowing that their exertions, their fidelity, and their sufferings have been represented to their Government and their Country, for the maintenance of whose rights they have made such sacrifices and such exertions, and to whose favourable notice they look forward as their greatest reward."

He then moved, seconded by Captain Isaac Swayze, that "to commemorate the great and brilliant services of the late Major-General Sir Isaac Brock, Knight of the Bath, while he administered the Government of this Province, and in defence of which he devoted his valuable life, the sum of five hundred pounds be appropriated for the purpose of erecting a monument on the heights of Queenstown near to the spot where he fell." This motion was carried without dissent.

Before prorogation, General Drummond gave the royal assent to nineteen acts, of which not less than thirteen were distinctly related to the defence of the province and the successful prosecution of the war. In his closing speech he particularly referred to the act for the temporary suspension of the *habeas corpus* act as one that " must eminently conduce to the welfare and prosperity of the Province." " The act making more liberal provision for the improvement of the public roads," he said, " would prove to be one of primary importance," while that appropriating so large a part of the public revenue for " the defence and security of the Colony " showed their " earnest determination to promote the public service."

An anonymous writer, who was evidently well informed, and may have been a member of the Assembly himself, in reviewing the proceedings of this session two years afterwards, made use of the following language:—

" The resources of the Midland, Johnstown, and Eastern Districts were lost or not properly called forth from the miserable arrangements of the Commissariat which was the occasion of difficulties of the most serious nature. To correct these faults General de Rottenburg was induced to issue an order respecting provisions, a measure warranted perhaps in these districts by necessity, but a necessity arising from the misconduct of the Commissary's Department. Many things happened during the recess not pleasing to individual feelings and particularly under this order shameful outrages were committed. For these and other grievances the session of 1814 was expected to be stormy, but the friends of the country were agreeably disappointed, private and even general distress was forgotten amidst the pressure of the times, and the members of Assembly with a greatness of mind that has seldom been surpassed, buried private subjects of complaint in oblivion and applied themselves with alacrity to the preparation of new measures of defence.

"The militia laws were modified anew to meet the increasing needs of the Province and measures were taken to facilitate the transportation of troops and stores in an expeditious manner to their different destinations. Money was also granted to render the internal communications more easy by repairing the highways, building bridges, and opening new roads. It having been found that many traitors were concealed in the country by whom a communication was kept up with the enemy, and that in the absence of the most reputable part of the community during the war, they were not so easily discovered and convicted by the ordinary course of law, an act was passed for a limited period empowering His Majesty to secure and detain such persons as were suspected of treason and adhering to the enemy. The object was rather to prevent future evil than to punish them for the past, and such a law was evidently necessary as the disaffected in some parts of the country, under the conviction that we must be conquered, began to be troublesome and in two districts they had broken out into open rebellion. The parliament by another bill declared all those aliens, who had voluntarily withdrawn themselves to the enemy since the commencement of the war and vested their real estate in the Crown. After passing these salutary laws, and one regulating the trial for treason, by which security and protection were given to good citizens, the parliament proceeded to increase and improve the revenue and was then prorogued."

Little time was lost in bringing into operation the act for the detention of suspected persons. On March 24, notice was published of the appointment of commissioners in all the districts of the province to carry it into effect. Seven commissioners were appointed for the District of London, of whom Nichol was one.

With reference to the legislation of the session, General Drummond remarked in a letter to Lord Bathurst, dated March 20:

"Those acts from which such effect may be more immediately expected to result as tending to strengthen the arm of the Executive Government and to suppress or keep in awe that spirit of sedition and disaffection, (promoted, no doubt, by the agents of the enemy), which, I regret to say, prevails in some parts of the country, are:—That authorizing the suspension of the Habeas Corpus: that for the more effective trial and punishment of treason and treasonable practices: and that declaring certain persons therein described aliens and vesting their estates in His Majesty.

"That there are many whom it will be found necessary to detain in custody under the provisions of the former, there is too much reason to apprehend, and not a few will experience the effects of the two latter.

"Having said so much with respect to the disaffected spirit evinced by some, it is at the same time but justice to say that the greater portion of the inhabitants are well disposed, and many have on various occasions manifested their loyalty and devotion to the service by their actions in the field. Those chiefly who have shewn the opposite disposition, it is satisfactory to know, are such as have from time to time crept into the Province from the neighbouring States and settled on lands which they purchased from individuals. This practice will, I trust, be effectually guarded against in future.

"The appropriation of a considerable portion of the revenue for the improvement of the public roads, which are at present in many places impassable for troops, artillery, or carriages of any kind, must contribute highly to the promotion and welfare of the service."

While the Legislature was sitting, the enemy in small parties made several raids into the Western and London Districts from Detroit and Amherstburg. In one of these they captured a militia guard near Delaware, and advancing as far as Oxford, made several officers prisoners at their homes, among them being Lieut.-Colonel Francois Baby, a deputy Quartermaster-General. Their deliberate object was apparently to disorganize the militia by carrying away their officers and other noted loyalists and terrorize the remainder. A small settlement at Point aux Pins on Lake Erie was totally destroyed, and they announced their intention of laying waste the whole of the settlements on the Talbot Road and at Port Talbot. A small force sent in pursuit of another raiding party, although it saved the settlements from destruction at that time, was repulsed with severe loss in an attack upon a fortified position in the Long Woods.

A reorganization of the Quartermaster-General's Department took place, and several officers were attached for special service to supervise the improvement and maintenance of the highways and other similar duties. These were all men of local influence who possessed special qualifications.

Nichol's first task was the preparation of careful and comprehensive general instructions for the guidance of the officers of his staff in the performance of their duties which included the collection of intelligence, the supply of competent guides, and reports of operations. (See Appendix).

By March 21, Drummond had again shifted his headquarters to Kingston with the express purpose of keeping in the closest touch with the naval commander and expediting the movement of troops and stores westward, which in the spring of the year could only be accomplished by water, as the roads became impassable as soon as a thaw set in. This step was taken on the advice of the Governor-General, who, about a week later, moved his own headquarters from Quebec to Montreal, thus greatly shortening the distance between them.

Reliable secret intelligence from the United States stated that great quantities of all kinds of naval and military supplies and provisions were being transported towards Sackett's Harbour and the Niagara frontier, indicating that formidable preparations were being made to gain the superiority on Lake Ontario and renew the invasion of Upper Canada.

On April 22, a U. S. sutler, named Constant Bacon, who had fled into Canada near Niagara, as he declared, to escape the demands of his creditors, was sent to York under guard by General Riall, who suspected that he was a spy.

He was carefully interrogated by Nichol, who obtained from him a very circumstantial and apparently truthful statement, not only respecting the numbers and dispositions of the enemy's forces on that frontier, but also with reference to several small depots of provisions being formed by them at the mouth of Genesee River, Irondequoit Bay, Sodus, Pulteneyville, and Oswego. This information seemed to be of such importance that it was at once despatched to General Drummond by a special messenger. In forwarding it Nichol remarked:

"I was always of opinion that the Enemy's Troops on the Niagara Frontier must be supplied on the opening of Navigation by Water, and that they would form Depots in different places along the South Shore of Lake Ontario, to be transported by water under the protection of their Fleet so soon as it should put to Sea.

"To destroy these is an object, as I conceive, fully within our power, and which if effected must have the happiest effects on the subsequent operations of the campaign, and with the greatest deference I beg leave to propose it. Great quantities of provisions of which we are much in want may be brought off and what we cannot bring away can be easily destroyed. To succeed in this business, however, no time should be lost for if the American Fleet gets out, unless we should defeat them in a decisive action the attempt should not be made. I am only waiting for a Bateau to go to Kingston, when, if you see fit to undertake the business, I will be happy to give every assistance. Bacon says the Enemy intend attacking us on this side, which I think very probable, but I firmly believe their principal object will be Burlington and that a joint attack from both Lakes will be made upon it. A blow of this kind, which if well arranged must succeed, would ruin us, and I fear unless Long Point is soon occupied in force it will be attempted and carried into effect."

A letter from Drummond's secretary in reply, stated that the General considered this information highly important and hoped it might be of great advantage. An attack upon Sackett's Harbour had been planned for some time but had been deferred as a land-force of not less than four thousand men had been deemed necessary and could not be assembled to carry it out. Drummond then believed that a successful expedition against Oswego, which might be accomplished with a much smaller number, would have important results. Prevost doubted the accuracy of a part of Bacon's statement, but did not oppose this proposal. Oswego was attacked with only partial success as some of the stores had been removed. Afterwards the British squadron cruised westward along the coast looking into all the harbours where magazines were being formed. That at Pulteneyville was surrendered but the contents of the others had been removed. The general result of these operations and the subsequent blockade of Sackett's Harbour was the delay of the appearance of the enemy's squadron upon the lake for almost three months, and in this way to upset their entire plan of campaign.

A considerable force of United States regular troops, intended for the invasion of Upper Canada, had arrived at Buffalo early in the year and another body of about a thousand men that had been assembled at Erie for the protection of their naval base at that port during the winter was ordered to join it. As it had been reported that Port Dover on the opposite shore was occupied only by a small outpost, Captain Sinclair, the U.S. naval commander on Lake Erie, proposed a raid upon that place, for the purpose, he said, "of destroying a considerable quantity of flour deposited in five or six large manufacturing mills, standing within the compass of as many miles and guarded by only a company, and distant forty or fifty miles from any military post. These mills supply all the upper part of the Province with breadstuff."

Several noted refugees from Canada were accordingly sent from Buffalo to Erie to act as guides on this expedition. Among the number was Abraham Markle, lately expelled from the Assembly on a motion by Nichol. He had been arrested in the summer of 1813 on suspicion and sent as a prisoner to Lower Canada, but released for want of evidence and permitted to return to his home near Ancaster. He seized the first opportunity to join the enemy at Niagara and was given a commission as captain in the battalion Willcocks was trying to raise. No doubt he eagerly welcomed the prospect of taking revenge upon his political antagonists.

About nine hundred soldiers, two-thirds of them being volunteer militia from Pennsylvania, with a party of marines in charge of three field-guns, were embarked in six armed vessels of light draught. On the evening of May 14, this squadron entered the bay near Port Dover and landed a part of the troops on board at the mouth of Patterson's Creek, just as darkness was setting in.

Nichol had removed his family to Montreal for safety during the previous autumn, when a retreat to Kingston had been contemplated. His mills were being managed by an agent, Mathias Steel. A small party of the Nineteenth Light Dragoons had arrived at Dover a few days before and taken quarters in Nichol's house and the adjacent buildings. Some apprehension of an attack had been felt, as appears from Nichol's letter of April 22, and a detachment of militia had been employed in removing several thousand barrels of flour. A very small quantity still remained.

Colonel Talbot, who was present, decided that opposition would be hopeless and ordered the dragoons to retire to Sovereign's Mills, where there was a ferry across the Grand River. A few shots were, however, fired by a party of the militia, early next morning, at some of the enemy, who were burning a storehouse near the lakeshore. The invaders advanced and took possession of the village, which they found deserted by everybody except a few women and children. In spite of their entreaties, not only the mills, but every dwelling and other building were remorselessly burned, apparently at the instigation of the vindictive refugees, after being plundered of their most valuable contents.

Part of the force then marched several miles up the lake to the mills owned by Lieut.-Colonel Joseph Ryerson, which they destroyed with all the neighbouring houses, " notwithstanding the cries and shrieks of the women and children."

Finch's Mills, still further up the bay, were burned next. Only one house, in which a woman was lying too sick to be removed, was spared between Patterson's Creek and Turkey Point, the furthest limit of their advance. They also shot all the horses, cattle, hogs, and other domestic animals they could find, leaving their bodies to rot where they fell. Altogether twenty dwelling-houses, three flour-mills, three saw-mills, three distilleries, twelve barns, and a number of other buildings were burned. Before leaving the place, they were heard to make threats that Port Talbot would be next destroyed, which in fact, was accomplished only six days later by a party from Detroit.

Nichol was the principal loser by this incursion. He estimated the extent of his losses at the following amounts in Quebec currency:

A flour-mill with 2 pairs of stones and a saw-mill	£2,500.
A distillery with three large stills and apparatus complete	1,250.
Three dwelling-houses with stores for merchandise, &c., attached	1,250.
A large new frame barn and outhouses with stabling for seventy horses	500.
A large flour store fitted up as a barrack	500.
A variety of merchandise, household furniture, cattle, hogs, &c. destroyed which could not be removed	500.

Making a total loss of £6,200, equal in sterling to £5,500 or, in our present currency, more than $27,000.

This, he said, " was nearly the whole fruit of twenty-two years' assiduous application to business, and almost the only resource from whence my family was supported."

He was at Kingston when this occurred and was first informed of this crushing calamity by General Drummond himself, who had received an official report from Colonel Talbot on May 21.

Captain Sinclair, of the United States Navy, who had planned this expedition, did not accompany it and was greatly displeased to learn that so much private property had been destroyed, with the approval of the officer in command.

"I am sorry to learn," he wrote on May 19, to the Secretary of the Navy, " that several private houses were also destroyed, which was so contrary to my wish and of the idea I have of our true policy to those people that I used every argument against it before his departure, and was under the impression that he accorded with me most fully. He has explained to me that he was urged to do so by people favourable to our cause on that side, who pointed out those persons as old revolutionary Tories, who had been very active not only in oppressing our friends in Canada, but in aiding all in their powers the burning and plundering of Buffalo. However much such characters may deserve our vengeance. I do not think it correct that our judgments should be passed upon them from their merely being designated by a partisan officer or citizen, who may, and no doubt are, in many instances, biast by individual motives."

A flag of truce was at once sent by General Riall to General Scott at Buffalo, to inquire whether this destruction of private property had been authorized by his orders or by his government. A few days later, Major Jones, an officer of General Brown's staff, appeared at the British outposts, with a request from him that a lady within his lines should be permitted to join her husband in Canada. He was met by Major J. B. Glegg, who had been instructed by General Riall to ask whether any reply was brought by him to his former letter. Major Jones had none but explained that no disrespect was intended as the letter in question had been forwarded to Washington and a Court of Inquiry was then sitting at Buffalo to investigate the matter.

"Major Jones also observed," Riall reported, "that he believed the circumstances attending that expedition were much exaggerated for that he understood from officers present that nothing but mills, in some degree public property, had been destroyed. When Major Glegg assured him that almost every house at Dover had been destroyed, he replied that he and all the officers in their service lamented the occurrence of such a circumstance as they hoped that an end had been put to such mode of warfare, that it was incumbent on them more than on us to refrain from it as we had it in our power to retaliate upon their coast in a tenfold degree to anything they could do to us."*

The Court of Inquiry, of which General Winfield Scott was president, held that Colonel Campbell, the officer in command of the expedition, was justified in burning the flour-mills and distilleries, according to the laws and usages of war, but that he had erred in burning the dwelling and other houses. No further action was taken in consequence of this opinion, as Campbell was mortally wounded at the battle of Chippawa, about two weeks later.

On June 20, however, Sir George Prevost wrote to Sir Alexander Cochrane, commanding the British fleet operating on the Atlantic coast of the United States, requesting him to retaliate, which soon after the receipt of this letter, he was in a position to do on the city of Washington itself.

Although the exact date cannot be stated, Nichol had removed his office from York to Kingston about the end of April and certainly remained there until about the end of June, 1814.

Drummond proposed to call out a fourteenth part of the militia, mainly as working parties for the improvement of the roads and fortifications and the performance of garrison duties. A commissioner was appointed in each district to supervise the expenditure of the money voted by the legislature. Among the number were Colonel Talbot for the London District and the Reverend John Strachan for the Home District.

Finding that one fourteenth of the militia enrolled in the regiments in the immediate vicinity of York would not be a sufficient number for the service required, Drummond ordered a draft to be made of one-third of the privates from the counties of York and Durham, with one subaltern and one sergeant from each regiment, and attached for duty to the battalion of Incorporated Militia for three months. This made a body of four officers and three hundred and fifty-four

* Drummond to Prevost, Kingston, June 26, 1814.

other ranks. Orders were given for them to be armed, accoutred, and clothed with uniform jackets and trousers. Extant correspondence shows that the provision of clothing for even that small body was a matter of considerable difficulty. Sixteen men from the 41st Regiment were detailed as tailors, and Nichol was directed to purchase blue cloth for facings. The poverty of his stores is exposed in a letter from him addressed to Lieut.-Colonel Robinson, commanding the Incorporated Militia.

"Cloth for the facings," he said, "has been ordered but it has not arrived. When it does it shall be forwarded. We have neither canteens, haversacks, nor forage caps for you but they have been asked & in the mean time the Genl. desires me to say that he will authorize the Commissary to pay for the stuff if it can be had & the men can get them made up themselves."

General Drummond had then been asked by Sir George Prevost to make proposals for building ships of war to regain command of Lakes Erie and Huron. Drummond referred the question to Nichol who made a report, dated May 22, of which two signed drafts, differing considerably in the wording, have been preserved. He advised that operations for that year should be confined to the collection of materials to begin building as soon as navigation closed. Turkey Point on Lake Erie was the only place where a naval yard could be formed and quickly fortified so as to make it secure from any attack. The finest ship-timber could be found near by and all necessary stores could be transported to that place from Burlington with greater facility than to any other point on the lake.

"I speak with certainty," he wrote, "as to the ease with which every species of stores may be transported from Burlington to Turkey Point during the summer, Guns and Anchors, and Cables excepted, and even these may be transported but nothing of that kind, excepting the guns required for the works, before the winter at which time every species of equipment may be taken forward with the greatest ease."

He had already made a survey of the harbour and its entrance in the spring of 1812, and given a chart of it to General Brock. He had then found the depth of water on the bar nowhere less than eighteen feet, but the lake was very high. Fifteen feet, he said, could always be reckoned on. At the "deep hole" where the yard ought to be placed, a large ship could be launched at once into seven fathoms of water and the bank was so steep that a first-rate vessel could lie afloat with her broadside touching the land. Captain Barclay had caused a survey to be made the previous summer and was much pleased with the result.

"In the Bason," he added, "there is room & water for the whole Royal Navy sheltered from every wind."

He suggested that officers of the Royal Engineers and the Navy should make a joint survey of the harbour and its neighbourhood to plan the necessary defensive works, and if their report was favourable, immediate measures should be commenced for their construction. When these were completed the transportation of the necessary naval stores should be begun. He recommended the construction of two large and two small frigates and several gunboats.

The establishment of another naval yard was also recommended at Penetanguishene for Lake Huron, near which place plenty of ship-timber could be obtained and there were many excellent sites for saw and grist mills, but a road twenty-four miles in length must first be opened, north of Lake Simcoe.

In forwarding this report Drummond remarked with reference to its author: "This officer being possessed of much local information, I considered him the most capable of affording under existing circumstances the best opinion."

A sketch of the site proposed for the dockyard at Turkey Point was afterwards forwarded and Drummond recommended that Nichol's project should be adopted as soon as the naval superiority on Lake Ontario was recovered.

The formidable invasion of the Niagara Peninsula, which took place in July, and the temporary loss of the command of the lake delayed this until late in the fall when little could be accomplished before the winter set in.

Soon after the battle of Chippawa, a levy *en masse* was ordered of the militia of the London, Niagara and Home Districts. On July 19, Drummond left Kingston for York to take personal command of the troops engaged in the field. On his arrival at York, he was presented with a petition by Thomas Ridout, the member of the Assembly for the east riding of the county of York, on behalf of his constituents, stating that "unless there be a sufficient number of hands left at home to secure the approaching harvest, (which promises to be very abundant in this vicinity), the supplies for H. M. Commissariat established at this place and the necessaries of life for the inhabitants will be extinguished and the farms become a scene of desolation." He added that only a small part of the grass had been or would be made into hay that season for want of hands.

On July 15, General Riall had reported from the Twenty Mile Creek "the loyal and patriotic conduct of the militia of the London District, who have marched hither in numbers." Two days later he stated that a considerable body of militia had been assembled and "it would be a great pity if the reinforcements that had been ordered up should not arrive in time to take advantage of their assistance." "Their hay being now receiving injury," he added, "and their corn ripening fast, they will not be induced, I fear, to remain long. They are all fine serviceable men, few or none coming under the description you wish should be sent home."

Another small brigade of militia was assembled at Burlington Heights, and advanced to Forty Mile Creek. About July 20, information was received of the advance of another raiding party, one-third of whom were mounted men, from Detroit into the Talbot settlement, where it had done great damage to the grain and threatened other parts of that district, which had hitherto escaped injury. The Oxford regiment of militia was accordingly detached with some Indians to oppose it.

The mobilization of such a comparatively large portion of the population must have taxed the efforts of the Commissariat and the Quartermaster-General's department to the utmost. Nichol's movements in July cannot be traced. His actual presence with the Right Division is not mentioned until August 2, when Lieut.-Colonel Harvey, in giving instructions to Major-General Conran for the passage of a force across the Niagara river for an attack upon the enemy's batteries at Black Rock, remarked that "Lt. Col. Nichol, Quartermaster General of Militia, will accompany Lt. Col. Tucker, who will not fail to derive the greatest benefit from his valuable local knowledge and his zeal and ability."

This enterprise was unsuccessful, although the landing was not opposed. The troops, being then suddenly surprised by rifle-fire, were seized by a panic and fell into great confusion. They were unable to cross a deep, unfordable creek, over which the bridge had been destroyed and the attempt was finally abandoned with considerable loss.

In making approaches to the enemy's batteries and intrenchments at Fort Erie, the covering and working parties were much annoyed and suffered considerable loss from the distant fire of three schooners, armed with long range guns, anchored in the bay above the fort. Nichol, being very familiar with the country from his former residence there, suggested that boats could be carried across from the river to the lake by a little known but very practicable natural road along the limestone ridge from near the mouth of Miller's Creek to the bay east of Point Abino. This was accomplished very secretly under his personal supervision. A gig and five large bateaux were conveyed over this route, a distance of about eight miles, a good part of the way on the shoulders of the men employed, and successfully launched in Lake Erie after dark. The attack was made on the night of August 12 / 13. Two of the schooners were captured and the third driven up the lake.

In the assault delivered on the night of August 14 / 15, Nichol conducted the column that advanced by the road through the forest in rear of the fort, and was mentioned in despatches.

The disastrous failure of this attack protracted the siege much beyond the time expected, and the wants of the beseiging force soon became "at once so alarmingly great and urgent" for provisions, ammunition and stores of every kind that Drummond was obliged to address a letter to Sir James Yeo, stating that "nothing but the assistance of the whole of H. M. Squadron on Lake Ontario" could enable him to continue his operations or maintain his position.

On August 19 he gave the following orders to Nichol.

"The public service requiring that extraordinary exertions should be used to obtain a supply of Flour from the Inhabitants of this and the Neighbouring Districts you are hereby required and authorized to Call on the Commanding Officers of the different Militia Corps to carry into Effect such Measures as you may find it expedient to Adopt for that purpose."

On August 24, General Drummond wrote to Sir George Prevost:

"I have employed Lt. Cols. Nichol and Dickson in going through the country to endeavor by their personal influence and exertions and the messages with which they are charged from me to induce the farmers to thresh out their grain earlier than usual, to enable me to hold out until our wants can be relieved by the squadron. I hope their efforts will be successful, but Your Excellency must be aware that this is at best but a precarious dependence."

Nichol, himself, relates in his memorial to Earl Bathurst, dated September 24, 1817:

"That while lying before Fort Erie he was on the 19th of August, 1814, sent for by Lieut. General Sir Gordon Drummond and informed that the Deputy Commissary General (Turquand) had just reported to him that he had only ten day's flour for the whole force on the Niagara and knew not where to get a supply until the arrival of Sir James Yeo, who was not expected before the middle of October. Your Memorialist told the Lieut. General that if he would give him full powers he would ensure a supply. The Lieut. General assented. Your Memorialist by his desire wrote the authority which he required, which was signed by the Lieut. General and in less than fourteen days all fears of want were removed and the King's Magazines were amply supplied by the local knowledge and exertions of Your Memorialist."

Sir Gordon Drummond, who was then living in retirement at Bath, made the following statement at Colonel Nichol's request in support of his memorial.

"It is but justice in me to bear the most ample testimony to the zeal and exertions of Lt. Colonel Nichol during the period he served under my command, viz., from the commencement of the Winter, 1813 to the conclusion of the War, throughout which period his services were conspicuously useful in carrying on the operations in which we were engaged in Upper Canada.

"Independent of the distinguished conduct and services performed by him in a military capacity, his active services in assisting the Commissariat in collecting provisions and transport at a time when the Army was labouring under the most alarming difficulties were highly serviceable."

In the autumn of 1814, Lieut.-Colonel George Macdonell and Captain Reuben Sherwood had directed General Drummond's attention to the subject of opening and improving the water communication by the Rideau river between Kingston and Montreal as an alternative route in time of war, in case the navigation of the St. Lawrence became interrupted. Their reports were submitted to Nichol for an opinion. His report, which was dated at Kingston on January 7, 1815, was unfavorable, although he stated that he had not examined the routes proposed, as the other officers had done.

"I feel I am hazarding much," he wrote, "by expressing my decided disapprobation of the whole plan, and my Conviction *that in the present uninhabited state of a great part of the route, it is quite impracticable with any, however large, outlay of Money to make it an available route of Communication.*"

Two routes had been suggested in these reports. In the one especially proposed by Captain Sherwood, he remarked that it was not certain that at all seasons of the year the channel would be sufficient to take loaded boats and there were ten carrying-places, which he enumerated, having a total length of eleven miles, where boats must be unloaded and transported with their cargoes by land-carriage to points where the water again became navigable. Assuming that navigation would begin on May 1 and close on October 31, with a daily passage of sixteen boats and estimating that two yokes of oxen or two teams of horses would be needed for each boat and six yokes or teams for its cargo, and adding one third of the number for unforeseen contingencies, one hundred and seventy yokes of oxen or teams of horses would be required at each portage. Multiplying this by ten, seventeen hundred yokes of oxen or teams of horses must be constantly employed. Admitting that the animals and their drivers could be obtained from the settled parts of the country, forage could not possibly be supplied. The same objections applied to the route by Irish Creek, proposed by Lieut.-Colonel Macdonell. He recommended, however, that Captain Sherwood should be employed to open the roads at the different portages and that one or two boats might be seen over the route at the end of the following July as an experiment. The conclusion of peace prevented anything more being done for some years on this proposed route.

Late in October, 1814, a raiding force from Detroit, composed of seven hundred mounted rangers and volunteers from Kentucky and Ohio, and seventy Indians, under the command of General Duncan McArthur, advanced with the intention of destroying the flour mills on the Grand River and near the head of Lake Ontario, and then, if possible, forming a junction with the U. S. army at or near Fort Erie. For the purpose of concealing the real object of the expedition, the troops employed marched westward along the shore of Lake St. Clair, and boats were sent in the same direction, ostensibly for the attack of the Saginaw Indians, which were used to ferry the men and horses, first across St. Clair river and then across Bear Creek. By this means the march was conducted with so much secrecy and quickness that McArthur's arrival at the Moravian village was absolutely unexpected, although Drummond had been warned a few days before that a raid was projected. About the same time, a small scouting or raiding party landed at the mouth of the Grand River, probably to divert attention in that direction and almost immediately re-embarked.

McArthur continued his advance along the right bank of the Thames and arrived at Oxford unheralded. Two of the inhabitants made their escape and gave the alarm at Burford. Their houses and barns with their contents were at once ruthlessly destroyed by the invaders, who were undisciplined and extraordinarily vindictive.

Lieut.-Colonel Bostwick hastily assembled some men of the Oxford regiment of militia and retired to Malcolm's Mills, where he summoned the men of the two Norfolk regiments to his assistance.

On November 5, McArthur advanced with his whole force to Burford intending as he stated in his report, to cross the Grand River and move upon Burlington, but he found that stream much swollen by recent rains and entirely unfordable. He then marched against the force being collected at Malcolm's Mills and dispersed it with little difficulty. Five mills were destroyed and the country along his line of march plundered unmercifully as the invaders lived entirely upon the inhabitants. On November 7, learning that a small regular force was rapidly approaching and that Fort Erie had been evacuated by its U. S. garrison, McArthur retired in great haste by the Talbot Road. Many of his horses had become disabled and were left behind, but others were stolen to replace them.

"The avowed object of the enemy," Major P. L. Chambers wrote to Major-General de Watteville, "was to destroy all the mills in the country, (so as to prevent our advancing this winter to Amherstburg), which I happily defeated by the rapidity of my advance. I did not give them time to complete the work of destruction, three mills being left. Had we not arrived in time the whole of this valuable settlement must have fallen a prey to famine this winter. At present not a single barrel of flour is to be purchased in the district. The enemy have plundered the inhabitants most disgracefully and stolen every horse they could find."

The misery caused by this raid enormously increased the feeling of bitterness already excited by former depredations and provoked a demand for retaliation.

Sir George Prevost promptly instructed General Drummond that, "As it appears from Lt. Colonel Smelt's report that the enemy have marked their route by the destruction of all the mills that have fallen in their way, I am called upon to meet and chastise this ravaging system by every means of retaliation, and have therefore to desire that you will direct the troops under your command no longer to abstain, as hitherto directed, from burning the mills in the enemy's country but on the contrary to set them in flames wherever they may be able to approach them."

Steps were at once taken for the fortification of Turkey Point and the establishment of a dock-yard as recommended by Nichol. A small force of all arms was detached as a garrison with officers of the engineers and navy to superintend the work.

As the Journals of the House of Assembly for the session held in 1815, have been lost, little definite information as to its proceedings is available. The anonymous writer already quoted contents himself with the following brief statement:

"Entertaining no hope or desire for peace the parliament met on the 1st day of February, 1815, and in full conviction of a long continuance of the war, the great part of the session was spent in making laws to suppress secret and open enemies and in preparing for a fresh campaign. Just as all the measures for these important purposes were completed, intelligence of the peace arrived, which rendered them unnecessary. This news was received in gloomy silence. All were desirous of one campaign more and few could restrain their indignation. The parliament remained a few days in session after peace was announced and made some excellent laws for a period of tranquillity before their prorogation."

The sum of six thousand pounds was voted to provide six months' pay as a gratuity to the officers and men of the battalion of Incorporated Militia and the Incorporated Militia Artillery and for the purchase of a sword, valued at one hundred guineas, to be presented to Lieut.-Colonel William Robinson, the commanding officer of that battalion.

An act was passed appropriating twenty thousand pounds for the repair of roads already laid out, for opening new roads, and building bridges, of which three thousand pounds were to be expended in the Western District and two thousand five hundred pounds in each of the other districts. The amount allotted for each road and bridge was carefully specified.

On March 10, 1815, a general order was published, announcing that the General Staff, the battalion of Incorporated Militia and all other units of the incorporated and embodied militia would be permitted to return to their homes on the 24th of that month, after which all their pay and allowances would cease, except that the Incorporated Militia would be granted a month's pay as a travelling allowance to enable them to reach their former places of residence.

As a result of this order, Nichol remarked that he "was thrown upon the world with business lost, his fortune ruined & the means he had *possessed* of supporting his Family on the restoration of peace destroyed in consequence of having been found by the Enemy in possession of the King's troops."

Having been assured by Sir George Prevost that he had written on the subject of his loss of property, Nichol had already submitted a claim for an indemnity to the Secretary of State, in which he stated that "it must in a great degree be ascribed to its being occupied by His Majesty's Forces and to the zeal and activity which he had uniformly shown, not only in providing supplies for His Majesty's Troops and in his personal exertions for the defence of the Country, but also in bringing out and leading the Militia and in punishing Traitors and disaffected persons—all of which rendered him personally obnoxious to the Enemies of His Majesty's Government."

He had not the means of rebuilding his mills or of resuming his former business and the high cost of labour and general state of trade did not warrant an attempt to do this with borrowed capital. While he had not only lost his business but the greater part of his property, other more fortunate merchants had been greatly benefitted by the war.

"Had he remained in business as others did," his brother remarked after his death, "the war, instead of being detrimental, would have been highly for his interest owing to the great circulation of money and high price of goods occasioned by the expenditure of the Troops and the expenses attending the movements of the Army and the supply at enormous expense of the Commissariat. Many merchants in Canada were enriched by the War and many made fortunes during that period, who must otherwise have remained in poverty and obscurity. The war itself though in some cases injurious to individuals was a benefit to the Country at large, but in Col. Nichol's case he was precluded from commercial transactions not only by the etiquette of Military *duty* but also from the impossibility, had the two professions been compatible, of attending to business. In general he was at the headquarters of the Army and there his time was wholly engrossed."

His annual profit from his mercantile transactions before the war, as shown by his books, amounted to £750.

Many changes in the administration occurred during the year. The recall of Sir George Prevost caused the transfer of Sir Gordon Drummond to Lower Canada. He was succeeded in Upper Canada by Sir George Murray, who had been Quartermaster-General in Wellington's Army in Spain. He is said to have been highly popular but Napoleon's return from Elba caused his recall to resume his military functions. Major-General Frederick Robinson took his place for a few months until Lieutenant-Governor Gore arrived from England and resumed the administration of civil affairs, after an absence of four years.

"The return of Governor Gore," said a friendly writer, "was associated with many pleasing recollections. His government had been chiefly known to the Province by acts of justice of the most pleasing condescension and benevolence.

"The voice of congratulation and joy at his resuming the reins of Government burst from every part of Upper Canada. It was a spontaneous tribute of applause, flowing from former experience, the most precious reward that could be offered to a generous mind and the most delightful compensation that could have been given for the labours and anxieties attending his exalted station."

The Assembly met for its fifth and last session on February 6, 1816. In his opening speech, Gore declared that "the gallant defence of this Colony by its own Militia, supported during the early period of the war by a very small portion of His Majesty's Regular Forces, has acquired for it a high distinction for loyalty and bravery. The obstinate contention with succeeding armies of invaders, and their ultimate discomfiture, has not failed to attract the notice of the world and given to this Province an importance in public opinion which it becomes us to maintain."

Referring to measures for its future defence, he said:

"The Militia code has undergone many changes, but still requires your serious attention to give the best possible effect to that force, should it again be called into action. Experience shows that the most disposable and therefore the best form into which it can be molded, so as to serve with a regular force, is that of independent companies, upon the principles on which the flank companies were formed in the year 1812."

He added that the district schools, already established, required further aid, and recommended the establishment of schools in each township, and a Provincial Seminary for higher education, for which large grants of land had been set apart. The extent of the revenue arising from custom duties collected at Quebec also required investigation and readjustment.

A special committee, with Nichol as chairman, was appointed to draft a reply. The address, prepared by it, was adopted without dissent. Nichol introduced bills to provide for the appointment of a provincial aide-de-camp to the Lieutenant-Governor, to amend the militia act, to alter the time for holding courts of quarter-sessions in certain districts, to amend the act for the payment of members, to appropriate a sum of money for procuring accurate information on the state of water communication between Lake Erie and Lower Canada, to impose additional duties on the importation of articles of the growth, produce, and manufacture of the United States, for ascertaining the population of the Province, to amend the laws for collecting the revenue, to provide for the appointment of a provincial agent to reside in England, and to appropriate a sum of money to provide a library for the use of the legislature. He served as chairman of committees on inland navigation, on the appointment of a provincial agent, on the revision of the militia laws, on the redivision of the province into judicial districts, on the amendment of the alien act, and on finance and public accounts.

The anonymous writer, already several times quoted, remarks with respect to the legislation of this session:

"The Parliament proceeded with alacrity to business and passed many useful laws both of a public and private nature. Of these I shall select two as principally claiming your present notice. It had been found that the law, conferring pensions on those disabled by the war and the widows and orphans of the slain, was too narrow in its principles. This law was now so framed as to take in many individuals, dead or disabled from sickness contracted in His Majesty's Service, who had been excluded from the former act. The second is the Common School Bill, which includes a system simple and efficacious and which will, in a few years, have a most sensible effect in the character of this Province.

"To inform the common people is to make them better subjects, both to God and man. It promotes morality and religion, ameliorates the condition of mankind, and benefits posterity.

"Many acts of great utility have been passed and some of a local nature highly beneficial to individuals. The greatest unanimity prevailed between the different branches of the Legislature, and, after passing a bill appropriating £21,000 for repairing and opening the highways, they were adjourned on the first day of April. In appreciating the character of this Parliament, it is to be recollected that they acted through a period of uncommon difficulty which they met uniformly with energy, wisdom, and ability. Opposed at once by secret and open enemies, their fortitude and patriotism never relaxed. Their difficulties were greatly increased by the encouragement which had been given to Americans on the first distribution of land by which the country had in it characters, always doubtful and always dangerous. Far from contributing in time of need any additional force in defending the Province, several of these citizens forsook their allegiance on the first favourable opportunity, and not only retired into the territories of the enemy, but returned with his armies and wreaked their ruthless vengeance upon the loyal inhabitants. The conduct of these traitors has had one good effect. It has blasted forever the perfidious policy which introduced them without discrimination into the Province and justified the precautions taken by Governor Gore in respect to the American settlers during his former administration."

Two new counties, named Halton and Wentworth, were formed of townships taken from the large counties of Lincoln and York, and erected into the new judicial district of Gore.

The Assembly was soon afterward dissolved and an election was held at which Nichol was again returned as the member for the county of Norfolk.

By a commission, dated May 24. 1816. he was appointed a member of the permanent board on militia pensions for the district of London.

Finding that his name had been inadvertently omitted from the list of senior officers to whom gold medals were awarded for the capture of Detroit, Nichol presented a memorial on the subject. In forwarding this, Gore remarked:

"I can be no judge of his Military Merit during my absence from the Colony, but I can speak to his general Talents, zeal, and ability in the Legislature, and am assured by competent Judges that the same Qualifications were conspicuous in the field and in the conduct of the Important Department of Quarter Master General of Militia entrusted to him by Major General Brock after a long and intimate personal acquaintance."

Nichol's claim was allowed and a medal awarded him.

The first session of the seventh provincial parliament of Upper Canada began on February 4, 1817. Several new members made their first appearance in the Assembly, the most notable being Philip Van Koughnet, Jonas Jones and Peter Robinson. Allan McLean was unanimously re-elected Speaker on a motion by Nichol.

In his speech, the Lieutenant-Governor referred to the great economic distress, existing in Great Britain since the conclusion of peace, and suggested that the Legislature should make every effort in its power to lighten the burdens of the mother country. He particularly commended the improvement of the St. Lawrence river below Prescott to its attention. As usual Nichol was named as chairman of a committee to draft a reply, which was presented next day and adopted without dissent.

A message from the Lieutenant-Governor then drew attention to the fact that no provision had been made in the act forming the two new counties for their representation in the Assembly and advised the immediate passage of a bill for that purpose, stating explicitly that he did not consider himself at liberty to sanction any further legislation until "there was a full representation of the Commons."

Nichol introduced a bill for that purpose, which was passed through all its stages the same day.

He also introduced a bill to amend the militia pensions act, and was appointed chairman of a committee to frame regulations for the legislative library.

On February 8, the Lieutenant-Governor gave his assent to the act providing for the representation of the counties of Halton and Wentworth and announced in a special message that he would take steps to expedite the election of members, but, as according to law, twelve days must elapse before a return could be made, he advised that the Assembly should adjourn for that period. An adjournment was accordingly made until February 20.

On February 25, James Durand, as member for the county of Wentworth, and Moses Gamble, as member for the county of Halton, were introduced and took their seats. Nichol instantly gave notice that he would move that the House do go into committee of the whole to consider the publication in the *Spectator* newspaper, printed at St. Davids, dated February 14, of a letter purporting to be "an Address from James Durand, Esq., to the independent electors of the county of Wentworth, grossly reflecting on the conduct of the late House of Assembly and of persons who are now members of this House."

Nichol's motion was opposed but was carried on a division by a vote of seventeen to four.

On the same day a petition was presented against the return of Moses Gamble by Henry John Boulton, the defeated candidate.

On March 1, Mr. Durand's printed address was read and entered in full in the Journals of the Assembly.

He had been elected after the expulsion of Abraham Markle to represent the fifth riding of the county of Lincoln in the former Assembly, and sat in the fourth and fifth sessions. Durand's military record was good, as he had commanded a flank company of militia with credit in the campaign of 1812, and was mentioned in despatches for his conduct at the battle of Queenston. His electoral district, however, contained many disaffected or apathetic residents, whom he deemed it politic to placate. The offending document was a lengthy review of his actions in the Assembly and in other public capacities.

"It will be remembered," he said, "by you all that the time I became your representative was a boisterous time, the *Habeas Corpus* Act was suspended. Martial law was conditionally proclaimed, the troubles of war were upon our country, we were without a Civil Governor, and Military men, changing every few months, were at the head of the Administration. You all know well the situation of those times and how the Military domineered over the community, and you also know what little satisfaction you could have obtained when applying to the Magistracy for the protection of the law; the *Habeas Corpus* Act being suspended seems to close the lips of most people; and the instances were rare of any man who would presume to dispute the mandates of commanding officers. Your political vessel, freighted with your laws and liberties, was blown about to and fro at the will of the military storm, and your seamen and pilots (the Magistrates) had abandoned her to the merciless tempest . . . It was then, my friends, when the troubled seas ran high, that I offered my little barque to you to tow her into port; 'twas then I launched my pinnace from the shore to use my humble efforts for you, when no larger barge would show its head: and how I succeeded I shall proceed to give an account. It must be still lively in your recollection that General Vincent threatened to burn the houses over the heads of those militiamen who did not obey his calls, nor can it escape your memory the horrible manifesto of even a Colonel commanding a regiment, who, setting aside all regard for the laws, declared that the habitations of those men who did not turn out when ordered by him should be given to the Western warriors, the Indians, and themselves and families sent destitute across the river. Still more recent was the conduct of Colonel James of the thirty-seventh Regiment, stationed at Burlington, the last of the war, who placed military guards on all the various roads, with orders to stop all sleighs having provisions on board, and in consequence the farmers' grists and the travellers' bags of oats were equally precipitated into the military depots, though perhaps a large hungry family were waiting the good man's return from mill, to be fed. This was the period that I entered upon my duty as a Legislator, and, mindful of the solemn pledge I had made my constituents, instantly proceeded to call for an inquiry into the state of the Province, for the purpose of searching into the various abuses that had been committed upon the inhabitants. In my speech I boldly attributed the evils to the unconstitutional measure of declaring Martial Law, I adverted to the conduct of those persons who were employed in the Commissariat and other departments who availed themselves of this declaration to tread down the people, and demanded to know the President's authority for this illegal assumption on his part, and called upon the House to pass a high vote of censure upon the man who would dare to violate the laws of the land. I enumerated the various acts of aggression, such as stopping and pressing of travellers and teams and others in all places, and at all hours of the night, forcing the inhabitants from their homes, and in a manner turning their families out of doors, &c., &c. I remarked upon the shameful state of York Gaol, and of the people who lay there in military custody without Magistrates' commitment, and at length closed my address to the House by moving resolutions which I shall ever rejoice to think were carried by the virtue of the feelings of the members, against the utmost efforts of the advocate of Martial Law, to the great chagrin of the then President, Sir Gordon Drummond."

After citing the text of the resolutions adopted and the President's reply, he continued:

"The Renewal of the suspension of the *Habeas Corpus* Act was amongst the first things at heart with the President at this time. Than this a more baneful Act to the vital liberties of the subject could not have been proposed. I rose from my seat to state my objections to this fatal bill, the very name of which is odious. The suspension of an Act which stands first as the bulwark of freedom. The whole House at this time seemed agitated by the prospects before them according to their various feelings. The tide of temptation at this crisis ran high, the terrors of the bill were on one hand, good contracts were every day and every way on foot on the other; and of course the man who opposed the President's will was forever shut out. This consideration I found to work strong upon men's minds. Faithful, however, to my charge, I stood almost alone in opposition to it . . . "

These seem to have been the statements most resented by Nichol and a majority of the members as a reflection upon their integrity.

The committee of the whole on the question of privilege reported that "the Publication in the *Spectator* of the fourteenth instant, purporting to be the Address of James Durand, Esquire, to the Independent Electors of the County of Wentworth, is a false, scandalous, and malicious libel; and that by scandalously reflecting on the conduct of the Lieutenant Governor and the late Parliament of this Province, as well as individual members thereof, it is a high breach of the privileges of this House." This report was adopted on a division by a majority of six, twenty-two members voting.

On a motion by Nichol, Richard Cockrell, printer of the *Spectator* was ordered to attend at the bar of the House.

On March 3, a motion by Nichol was adopted by a majority of two, declaring that Moses Gamble was not a *bona fide* subject and ought not to have been returned as the member for Halton.

On March 4, Nichol seconded by Burwell moved "that James Durand, Esq., a Member of this House, having been proved to be the author of a false, malicious, and scandalous libel, reflecting seriously on the conduct of His Excellency the Lieutenant Governor, the former House of Assembly, and of individuals, who are now Members of this House, be committed to the Common Gaol of the Home District during the present Session."

Mr. McNabb moved, seconded by Mr. Howard, in amendment that Mr. Durand be forthwith called to the bar of the House to make an apology, but the amendment was lost on a division by a majority of three and the original motion carried on the same vote reversed.

Mr. Nichol then moved, seconded by Mr. Jones that the Speaker do issue his warrant for the commitment of James Durand to the Common Gaol of the Home District during the session, and the motion was carried by a majority of four.

The warrant was accordingly prepared and signed the same day. On March 6, the Speaker reported that the Sergeant at Arms had informed him that James Durand was not to be found in town after a most diligent search and he had in consequence not been able to execute the warrant.

Mr. Nichol, seconded by Mr. Jones, moved that "James Durand, Esq., a Member of this House, having, after he had been heard in his defence, been convicted of the publishing of a false, scandalous, and malicious libel, was ordered to be committed to the Gaol of the Home District for the said offence, and having withdrawn himself without leave from the judgment of the House is thereby guilty of a high contempt of its authority, and of a flagrant breach of the privileges of this House." This motion was apparently carried without dissent.

On March 7, Nichol moved, seconded by Fraser, that Durand be expelled and declared incapable of being re-elected to serve in that parliament, but an amendment, striking out the words declaring him ineligible for re-election, was carried by a majority of one vote on a division.

Nichol's conduct in this matter seems singularly intolerant and inconsistent with his previous record.

He was as active as usual during the remainder of the session, which was not fruitful in useful legislation. He promoted the appointment of a Clerk of the Crown in Chancery and introduced and promoted bills for the relief of Moses Gamble, for imposing additional duties on stills, and for granting gratuities to Alexander McDonell, Ann Bostwick, and Cecile Cadet, sufferers by the late war.

On April 7, the Lieutenant-Governor prorogued the two Houses with the following laconic speech:

"The Session of the Provincial Legislature having been protracted by an unusual interruption of business at its commencement, your longer absence from your respective avocations must be too great a sacrifice for the objects which may remain to occupy your attention.

"I have therefore come to permit you to return to your homes and close the Session."

James Durand was re-elected to represent the County of Wentworth, and took an active part in the proceedings of the subsequent sessions of that Assembly.

Nichol had been obliged to mortgage his remaining real estate to obtain money to pay his debts and support his family as his income was insufficient to meet his ordinary expenses. In the summer of 1817, he determined to press his claims for compensation for his losses and some suitable reward for his services. With this object he went to Quebec and presented a memorial to Sir John Coape Sherbrooke, who had succeeded Sir George Prevost as Governor-General. In this, he stated that he had relinquished a lucrative mercantile business for the purpose of undertaking the "arduous and responsible office of Quartermaster-General of Militia" in which he had served until the end of the war.

"That from the nature of the Service in Upper Canada," he said, "and from the great difficulty of procuring intelligent and faithful Guides together with the very limited Staff in the Upper Province, during the first campaigns, Your Memorialist was from the necessity of the case employed on many important and Confidential Services purely Military, and had at different periods the Sole Charge of the Quarter Master General's Department of an entire Division of the Army, more particularly on the Expedition against Detroit, on the retreat from Fort George, and on other Services . . . .

"That your Memorialist from the undivided attention given to his public duties, and from the destruction of his property by the Enemy had been reduced from a state of Comparative affluence to great Straights, Wherefore your Memorialist most respectfully Solicits your Excellency in consideration of His Military Services with the King's Troops and great losses and Sacrifices during the War to recommend him to the Consideration of His Majesty's Government for some Military allowance to enable him to support His Family."

The statements of the memorial were supported by a number of documents and extracts to substantiate their accuracy.

As none of the General Officers, under whom Nichol had served, were then in Canada, Sherbrooke referred his petition to Colonel Christopher Myers, the Deputy Quartermaster-General, and Lieut.-Colonel John Harvey, the Deputy Adjutant General, both of whom had served in Upper Canada, at the head of their respective departments during the greater part of the war, for a report how far his statements were correct.

Colonel Myers reported: "In general I can freely assert that Lt.-Col. Nichol's services and abilities were highly beneficial to the cause in which the King's Troops were engaged in Upper Canada during the War, that his attention to his Publick duty engrossed the whole of his time for that period, and that to the best of my belief he suffered severely in his pecuniary concerns from his devotion to Military duty, and from the destruction of his Property by the Enemy in the Predatory Warfare carried on by the Americans in Upper Canada."

Harvey affirmed that Nichol's statement of his military services was correct. "His local knowledge, intelligence, and zeal," he added, "pointed him out to the selection of the Commanding General on many occasions . . . .

"At different Periods during both Campaigns when the Commissariat was labouring under the most serious difficulties in collecting Provisions and Transport, Lt.-Col. Nichol's influence and active exertions were had recourse to and were highly serviceable. In short, throughout the whole of the war, (of two out of the three Campaigns I speak from my own knowledge), Lt. Colonel Nichol has been conspicuous for his active, zealous & useful services with the King's troops & extremely forward in every Situation of danger connected with the Service in which he was employed under the orders of the Commanding General."

Both of these reports were dated at Quebec on July 3, 1817.

In another testimonial, also endorsed by Harvey, which is not dated, and may have been written previously, Myers stated:

"That the zeal and intelligence of Lieutenant Colonel Nichol were of the greatest use in the concentration of the Several Detachments on the Frontier and in taking up the Position at Burlington Heights. That the Services of Lieut. Colonel Nichol in the Quarter Master General's Department for that Division for the greatest part of the subsequent operations of the Campaign were highly meritorious & beneficial. That at his own desire he was employed after the loss of our Flotilla on Lake Erie in the London District, where his exertions and influence kept on foot a respectable Militia Force for the preservation of Communication between the Right and Centre Divisions."

The answers returned to his enquiries and the evidence of other authentic documents was so satisfactory that on July 15, 1817, Sherbrooke wrote to Lord Bathurst, transmitting Nichol's memorial and other papers supporting it, and saying, "I cannot in justice refuse to forward his Memorial, and to recommend the prayer of it to the favorable consideration of His Majesty's Government."

Nichol must have sailed for England immediately afterwards for on September 18, General Sir Henry Torrens, the Military Secretary at the Horse Guards, wrote to Hon. Henry Goulburn by the direction of the Commander-in-Chief, referring to him a letter and memorial from Nichol, dated on the fifth of that month, to be laid before Lord Bathurst, and adding that His Royal Highness, the Duke of York, was "induced by the active zeal and important services of that officer" to recommend his claim for favorable consideration.

On September 24, Nichol wrote a long letter to Mr. Goulburn, enclosing two memorials, from one of which, stating his services during the war, many quotations have already been made, and the other referring to the great delay in compensating him for his losses. Three documents, illustrating these memorials, were likewise transmitted.

In his letter Nichol said:

"The absence of many distinguished Military Friends, who would have been listened to, and who could have personally explained to His Lordship my Military services and pretensions, has necessarily compelled me to go much more into detail and thereby to occupy much more of His Lordship's time than I would otherwise have presumed to do—the same reason has compelled me to become an Egotist—but I think the testimonials of Character and services heretofore transmitted by His Excellency Sir John Coape Sherbrooke, will establish the Credit due to my assertions, the whole of which, however, I have it in my power to prove.

"It is not my wish to draw Comparisons between my own services and those of others who have experienced the Bounty of His Majesty's Government, I may, however, I hope, be permitted to State that during the late War in Canada, I have been personally engaged with the Enemy in Canada & *in the United States* upwards of thirty times.

"That I have seen more and a greater variety of trying service than *the Voltigeurs who have received half pay*. That I have seen more and done more than Colonel Norton who has got *Army Rank and a Pension*. That my services have been more important and useful than Mr. Dickson's, who has got an order for land and a pension, and that I have sacrificed more to my public duty and lost more by the War than all of them put together.

"In addition to my Military & Militia Services, my Exertions in the House of Assembly of the Province during the War & since the Peace—I appeal to the Journals in the Colonial Office for a confirmation of what I assert—have been highly useful and important. During the War every strong measure for the Security of the Government and defence of the Country was brought forward and carried through by me. It was by my measures and exertions that the Revenues were increased and liberal appropriations towards useful publick purposes were made—the permanent grant of £2,500 per annum was brought forward and carried through by me.

"From that Fund Ministers have been enabled to Pension the late Chief Justice Scott for his past services to the amount of £800 per annum. From that fund the present Chief Justice Powell has received, (as Speaker of the Legislative Council), in addition to his very handsome salary as Chief Justice, the sum of £400 per annum. From that fund Ministers, if inclined & they think me deserving, have it in their power to provide for me. My case is a hard one and my situation unique. I am the only Militia Officer of Upper Canada, who was on permanent duty throughout the War. The present Adjutant General is a Half pay Officer and was an inhabitant of Lower Canada. He came to Upper Canada in Sept. 1812, as Regular Aide de Camp to Major General Sheaffe. He became afterwards

Provincial Aide de Camp to Major General de Rottenburgh, was appointed by Lt. General Drummond first Depy. Adj. General and after the Peace on his going to Lower Canada—Adjutant General by which he now enjoys £365 per annum for his very Meritorious Services.

"He gave up no business to take upon himself Military Office. He lost no property from the ravages of the Enemy, for he had none in the Country to lose. While I have been subjected to both these Misfortunes.

"I have thus detailed to you all that I conceive necessary for a full understanding of my case. Extreme bad health, the consequence of a Constitution ruined in the Service, has prevented my paying that attention, has prevented the drawing up the Memorials & Statements with method, which under other circumstances I should have been happy to give."

In his memorial respecting compensation for his losses, Nichol made the following statement:

"That early in the year 1814, it having been determined by the Officer Commanding His Majesty's Forces in Upper Canada to establish a Cavalry Post and Commissariat in the London District of that Province, the Commanding Officer of Cavalry and an officer of the Quarter Master General's Department, both of them now in England and stationed in the County of Essex, were ordered by Major General Riall, then commanding the Right Division of the Army, to select a proper place for those purposes, who after due examination made choice of the Dwelling and other houses of your Memorialist, which were immediately appropriated to the above mentioned purposes.

"That Your Memorialist, although at the time on duty and stationed at the headquarters of Lieutenant General Sir Gordon Drummond, was never consulted on the Subject, nor was any arrangement made with him for the payment of rent or for any other emolument for the use of his property, nor has your Memorialist ever received any compensation for the possession of the same by His Majesty's Forces.

"That the first information Your Memorialist had of his property having been so occupied, was a communication, on or about the 21st May, 1814, from Lt. General Sir Gordon Drummond, stating your Memorialist's loss, and that the Enemy had landed in great force, compelling the Detachment of the 19th Light Dragoons to retire and their destroying every building which had been occupied for any public purpose as well as some private ones which were contiguous.

"That the Mills and other property of your Memorialist, destroyed at this place had been erected by your Memorialist at great expence and were the only means he possessed of re-establishing his business and supporting his Family on the restoration of Peace.

"That it is now nearly four years since your Memorialist was, by the Act of the King's General, deprived of his property, his sole means of subsistence and of the Fund from which he hoped to pay a debt by which he was burdened in consequence of other very heavy losses from the Capture of property by the Enemy. part of it before the declaration of War, and for which he has never been able to obtain any Compensation.

"That your Memorialist has been obliged to mortgage the whole of his little remaining property to secure his Creditors and has already paid them interest to the amount of Twelve Hundred Pounds. Whilst your Memorialist is perfectly prepared to prove to your Lordship's satisfaction—by which, as it is still going on, the whole amount of your Memorialist's claim will soon be swallowed up, leaving the principal unliquidated to *consummate the ruin* of your Memorialist and his family.

"Wherefore your Memorialist hopes That as his property was taken from him by the Act of the Agent of the Government—was found in their possession by the Enemy, and in consequence thereof, was considered public property, and as such destroyed, and as your Memorialist has by this Act been prevented on the restoration of Peace from returning to his usual Avocations, by which he would have been enabled to satisfy all just claims upon him and to support his family—Your Lordship will be pleased on a due consideration of all the circumstances of his case to recommend him to the proper office for full compensation for all his losses as well as for the time which has elapsed since the property was taken out of your Memorialist's possession."

In his letter to Mr. Goulburn, Nichol stated that he was going into the country for a few days to regain his health and strength. Action upon his claims was greatly delayed and his stay in England was prolonged in consequence, as he had evidently determined to remain there until a decision was given. Late in October, 1817, an order was made for striking medals for the capture of Detroit, awarded to himself, Colonel Mathew Elliott, and Lieut.-Colonel John Macdonell.

On November 2, 1817, at his solicitation, Sir Gordon Drummond addressed a strong letter on his behalf to Lord Bathurst. Still no decision was reached and Nichol was again obliged to borrow money from an acquaintance, Mr. C. H. Turner of Rook's Nest near Godstone in Surrey, and as security gave a mortgage on some lands in Canada, possessed by his wife in her own right before marriage. Finally a pension of £200 per annum was granted him as a reward for his services, but the Commissioners of the Treasury declined to recommend to Parliament any grant of money to indemnify him for losses sustained by the casualties of war, which they held should be compensated by the Provincial Legislature from a fund formed by the sales of forfeited estates.

His absence in England prevented him from attending two sessions of the Assembly held in February and March, and in October and November, 1818.

The fourth session of the seventh provincial parliament met on June 7, 1819.

The attention of the Legislature was directed in the Lieutenant-Governor's speech, to the amendment of the laws respecting the assessment of real estate and the improvement of the roads.

"The growth of the Province in population and wealth," Sir Peregrine Maitland remarked, "justifies a reasonable expectation that the measures adopted to encourage it will receive your fullest support. And I must suggest for your consideration the expediency of affording the new settler, unavoidably situated more remote from the great lakes and rivers, an easy approach to market."

Nichol, as usual, was made chairman of the committee appointed to draft a reply. The address prepared was adopted without objection.

Nichol then moved the House into committee of the whole to prepare an address on the death of the Queen.

He introduced and promoted bills to repeal the act respecting sedition, to amend the highway act, to amend the assessment, to amend the militia act, to repeal the jurisdiction act, to enable the magistrates of districts to build gaols and court-houses, to incorporate the Bank of Upper Canada, to impose additional duties on stills, to amend the act for imposing duties on imports from the United States, for the relief of John Wagstaff of Niagara, and to provide for the administration of justice and the support of the civil government. He was appointed chairman of the select committee on public accounts, and presented his usual careful detailed financial statement, in which he estimated a deficiency of £16,600 to be provided for. "The delinquency of several Public Accountants in retaining large balances in their hands, to the great detriment of the Public service," was commented upon.

"In examining the estimate of sums requisite to carry on the current service of the year," the report said, "Your Committee were forcibly struck with the very large sum required for the payment of Militia Pensions, and do not hesitate to state, for the information of Your Honourable House, their opinion that most shameful impositions have been practised in recommending individuals to be placed on the Pension List. This is a subject of such serious magnitude that Your Committee should feel that they had neglected their duty did they not recommend some measure by which the Provincial Treasury will be relieved from the heavy drain it would otherwise experience for that service."

The recommendation was accordingly made that payment of arrears should be suspended to enable the subject to be investigated "and some efficient measures adopted for checking the frauds that there is too much reason to fear have been practised."

Correspondence was entered on the Journals between William Halton, the Provincial Agent in London, and late secretary to Lieut.-Governor Gore, with the Hon. Henry Goulburn, respecting the payment of losses to individuals by the late war and invasion of the Province. Mr. Halton stated that the Commissioners appointed in January, 1816, to investigate the amount of these losses had made their report in the following July, and that the sufferers had received no relief whatever. This, he said, had caused great dissatisfaction in the Province.

He added: "I am aware of the order given respecting the sale of the forfeited estates, but many years may elapse before proper purchasers can be found; and were they actually found, several persons long resident in Upper Canada, and, as I believe, very capable of forming the estimate, have represented to me that they will not probably produce one-sixth part of the losses stated to have been sustained; for by a Provincial Statute the estates are subject to the debts of the proprietors who fled the country; and various heavy charges must accrue for Commissioners, Sheriffs, and others to prevent fraud and superintend the sales.

"There is one local circumstance I must submit to you which is mentioned in several of my letters from Upper Canada, and which cannot fail to operate on the minds of the inhabitants of that Province, that those subjects of the United States who sustained losses during the war, whose houses are in several parts within view of the Upper Canadians, and with whom they have continual intercourse, have long ago received remuneration from their Government."

No reply was received for almost five months, when Mr. Goulburn asked for further information, and Halton referred him to the detailed report of the Commissioners, transmitted to Lord Bathurst in July, 1816.

Nichol moved that an address should be presented to the Lieutenant-Governor praying for an account of the revenue received from the Clergy Reserves and its disposition, and was appointed chairman of a committee to draft it.

He also moved that an address should be presented on the subject of the payment of pensions to wounded militia officers, and was appointed chairman of a committee to draft it.

He was appointed chairman of a committee to consider the petition of Colonel Joel Stone, respecting his account of the expenditure of militia fines received by him, which reported that the petitioner "had made considerable disbursements, apparently from the Militia Fines, to enable him to carry on the public service; and though they feel themselves compelled to notice and animadvert on the extremely irregular, injudicious, and very reprehensible conduct of the Petitioner in the exercise of his authority," recommended that a bill should be introduced to indemnify him.

Upon the third reading of a bill to increase the representation of the Commons in the House of Assembly, Nichol moved the following resolution as a rider to the act:

"That whenever an University shall be established in this Province it shall and may be lawful for the Governor, Lieutenant-Governor, or person administering the Government of this Province for the time being, to declare by proclamation or otherwise, the Tract of land appendant to such University, and whereupon the same is situated, to be a Town or Township, by such name as to him shall seem meet, and such Town or Township, so constituted, shall be represented by one member. Provided always, nevertheless, that no person shall be permitted to vote at any such Election for a member to represent the said Town or Township, who besides the qualifications now by law required, shall not also be entitled to vote in the Convocation of the said University."

A division was taken and this motion was lost, only three members, besides Nichol, supporting it.

On July 4, James Durand proposed a resolution declaring a letter signed by Robert Gourlay, published in the Niagara *Spectator* of July 1, to contain matter of a libellous character and of a treasonable nature, and that an address should be presented to the Lieutenant-Governor praying him to direct the Attorney-General to prosecute the Editor of the paper and other persons concerned. A debate took place, which was adjourned.

Next day on the resumption of the debate, Nichol moved, seconded by Mr. Jones, "that the letter printed in the Niagara *Spectator* of the 1st instant, signed by Robert Gourlay, is a most scandalous, malicious, and traitorous libel, tending to disturb the peace of the Province, and excite insurrection against the Government." This resolution was carried without dissent.

Nichol then moved, seconded by Jones, "that an humble Address be presented to His Excellency the Lieutenant-Governor, praying him to direct His Majesty's Attorney General of this Province to publicly prosecute the author, printer, and publishers of the letter printed in the Niagara *Spectator* of the 1st instant, signed Robert Gourlay." This motion was also carried without opposition.

Nichol was appointed chairman of a committee to draft this address, which was duly presented and adopted without dissent.

A supplementary report of the select committee on public accounts was presented by Nichol, stating that although a large amount had been received during the year on account of arrears of duties due the Province, there were still large sums due, and praying that measures should be taken to obtain payment of the balance by appointing commissioners for that purpose.

Most of the bills promoted by Nichol at this session were passed and the Legislature was prorogued on July 12. In his speech the Lieutenant-Governor expressed his satisfaction "at the benefits you have conferred on His Majesty's people, by adopting a principle in your Assessment Bill and your amendment of the Road Law which subjects all the granted and leased land in the Province to an equal Duty. . . . .

"You have consulted with laudable feeling the very respectable character of the Militia Service in enabling me to afford to any of its members an opportunity of obtaining in time of peace, but properly at his own request, the verdict of a Court Martial, and you have at the same time relieved me of the unpleasant necessity of having on every occasion to decide by the light of evidence unguarded by the sanctity of an oath."

A letter printed in the Upper Canada *Herald* of Kingston on March 16, 1819, throws some light on Nichol's former attitude on the agitation for measures of reform advocated by Robert Gourlay.

"To shew how little foundation there is for the assertion that there were no grievances complained of in this Province until Mr. Gourlay pointed them out and persuaded people to complain, please to insert the following Resolutions, moved by Mr. Nichol, in the Provincial Assembly in 1817; the three first of which were adopted, but before the House came to the conclusion upon the others, the Parliament was prorogued.

Historicus.

"Resolved,

"That an Act was passed in the 13th year of George the 2nd, for naturalizing such foreign Protestants and others therein mentioned, as were then, or should thereafter be settled. 'An Act for encouraging new settlers in His Majesty's Colonies in America.'

"Resolved,

"That an Act was passed in the 30th year of His Majesty's reign entitled 'An Act for encouraging new settlers in His Majesty's Colonies in America.'

"Resolved,

"That the said Acts were enacted for the express purpose of facilitating and encouraging the settlements in His Majesty's American Dominions.

"Resolved,

"That the said Acts are still in force, and that the subjects of the United States may lawfully come into and settle in this Province, hold lands, and be entitled to all the privileges and immunities of natural born subjects therein, on complying with the several formalities required by the said acts and the existing laws of this Province.

"Resolved,

"That the Province contains immense tracts of uncultivated land of the very best quality, which, if occupied by an industrious population, would, in a short time, furnish ample supplies of provisions and lumber for His Majesty's West India Colonies, increase the carrying trade of our mother country, and add considerably to the general wealth and prosperity of the British Empire.

"Resolved,

"That, at the present moment from the discouragement given to settlers from the United States, very many respectable and valuable settlers have been prevented from emigrating to this Province.

"Resolved,

"That an humble address be presented to His Excellency the Lieutenant Governor, stating the injury that has been sustained by the Province and the check given to its population and prosperity, by preventing emigrants from the United States from taking oaths of allegiance to His Majesty, and Praying that he will direct any orders that may have been made, prohibiting the admission of persons from the United States to take the oath of allegiance to be rescinded.

"Resolved,

"That the large tracts of Crown and Clergy Reserves throughout the Province are insurmountable obstacles to the forming a well connected settlement, which is an object of no small importance in a country where the opening and keeping roads in repair is attended with great expense and labour; but, in a political point of view, the measure is still more objectionable, from its holding out great inducements to future wars with the United States by affording the means of partially indemnifying themselves, or rewarding their followers in the event of conquest.

"Resolved,

"That the sale of the Crown Reserves, instead of leaving them (as at present) would relieve the Province from a heavy charge now brought against its revenue, and would relieve the mother country from all charges for the civil establishment and introduce into the Province a respectable population, which would add to its wealth and resources.

"Resolved,

"That the reservation of one-seventh of the lands in this Province, for the support of the Protestant Clergy, is an appropriation beyond all precedent lavish; that from the sale of these, churches might be erected and endowed, without any charge to the mother country; and that to obtain so desirable a measure, a respectful representation be made to the Imperial Parliament, recommending that of the lands, now appropriated as Clergy Reserves   be sold and applied as above stated, and that in future there should be the   instead of the one-seventh part in each Township reserved."

The only record on the Journals of the Assembly that seems to refer to these resolutions, shows that on Friday, March 21, 1817, Mr. Nichol gave notice that he would, on Monday next, move that "this House do resolve itself into a Committee of the Whole to take into consideration the state of the Province."

On Saturday, April 5, Mr. Nichol, seconded by Mr. Fraser, moved the order of the day, for the House to go into Committee on the state of the Province, which was carried. Mr. Cameron took the Chair.

"Mr. Speaker resumed the Chair to receive the Niagara Roads Commissioners' Accounts, delivered at the Bar of the House by Samuel Peters Jarvis, Esq.

"The House again went into Committee on the state of the Province, Mr. Cameron in the Chair.

"The Speaker resumed the Chair. Mr. Cameron reported two resolutions, and asked leave to sit again on Monday. Mr. Clench, seconded by Mr. Van Koughnet, moved that the Report of the two Resolutions be not now received." On a division this motion was lost, seven members voting for and thirteen against it. It was ordered that the report be adopted and leave granted.

On Monday, April 7, the Legislature was prorogued without the transaction of further business.

The seventh Provincial Parliament was convened for a fifth session on February 21, 1820.

In his speech on opening the session, Sir Peregrine Maitland said:

"I feel the most sincere pleasure in communicating to you that the timely interposition of the Legislature, the just administration of the Law of the land, and, perhaps more than all, the prevailing good sense and good principles of the great majority of the people, have dissipated those appearances of disturbance and discontent, which were beginning to defame us abroad, and which, unless happily checked, would have soon been fatal to an increasing prosperity. Assured that there exists no reason at present for desiring more than the ordinary safeguards of the Constitution, I am fully disposed, should you deem such a measure expedient, to acquiesce in a repeal of the Act passed in the last session, for preventing seditious meetings, freely confiding in the prompt energy of the Legislature, and the steady loyalty of the great mass of His Majesty's subjects to meet any further occasion.

"The judgment I have been enabled to form of the situation and interest of this Colony leads me to appreciate highly your provisions for the amendment of the Road Laws, and for the more equal and general assessment of property. The Acts may admit of improvement, and like all other measures tending to introduce a change of system, will be found, no doubt, when they shall be brought into operation, to require alteration in the detail, but the session in which you introduced, and have, I trust, for ever bequeathed to your country, the principle of an unexempting and impartial assessment, will form hereafter an honoured era in the annals of her Legislation."

Referring to the public accounts and estimates, he remarked that "the revenue has been insufficient to meet the accumulating charge for Militia Pensions, imposed upon it by law, I fear more extensively benevolent in their provisions than our means could justify."

The session was short, lasting only until March 7.

Nichol introduced bills to amend the assessment act, to enable the magistrates of the London District to borrow money to complete a gaol and court-house, for the compensation of commissioners, to validate certain marriages, and to prohibit killing deer at certain seasons. He moved for an inquiry into the administration of the post-office department of the province by a committee of the whole. This was proceeded with and William Allan, the Postmaster, having been ordered to attend at the Bar of the House, was examined by Mr. Nichol. After hearing his evidence a committee was appointed to draft an address on the subject, of which Nichol was chairman. This stated that it had been satisfactorily proved that the rates of postage charged in Upper Canada for several years past, had exceeded the charges authorized by law, and prayed for the interference of the Ministry with the Postmaster-General in Great Britain to prevent the continuance of so serious an evil.

Nichol moved for the production of documents connected with the claims of sundry inhabitants of the Province for compensation for losses sustained by them in the war with the United States, for returns of the revenue of the Province, for returns of the officers employed in the several departments and their emoluments, and for copies of the inquests held respecting forfeited estates.

He was chairman of the committees appointed to draft addresses on forfeited estates, on the civil expenditure, and of the special committee on finance. The latter committee reported that "owing to the unexpectedly short period allowed them for the examination of the accounts submitted to them, (a circumstance beyond their control), and the necessity of obtaining further important expenditure, they were unable to make a detailed report.

"Your committee," the report stated, "cannot avoid observing that the only branch of the public service, which appears to be in arrears, is the provision for the payment of Pensions to Wounded Militiamen, and to the Widows and Children of Militiamen, who may have been killed or who have died in the service. Your Committee are of opinion that this evil has increased, is increasing, and ought to be diminished, and that if sufficient time had been allowed them to make the necessary investigation with the receipt and expenditure of the Public Revenue of the Province, they would have been furnished with data which would have enabled them to report to Your Honourable House that in their opinion means might be devised without adding materially to the public burthens, viz., by a well digested system of economy and retrenchment, to meet effectually every present as well as future exigency of the public service.

"Your Committee are entirely without information respecting the intercourse between Lower Canada and this Province, they are aware that large sums are and have long been due from that Province to this, and regret that Your Honourable House have been furnished with no information on that subject, and that so little effect has been produced by the repeated representations respecting it made in former reports to Your Honourable House."

They reported that several commanding officers of militia had neglected to pay over the balances of militia fines in their hands.

This report plainly censured the administration of the civil government, and Maitland expressed his displeasure by saying in his speech on prorogation:

"My expectation on the subject of the Pension Laws has not been fulfilled, and those public creditors must remain unprovided for until recurrence can be held to another Parliament. The improvidence which has created this charge, so disproportionate to our means, is not to be accounted for by any defalcation of the revenue, nor by any increased demand for any other public services. Had your judicious corrections of the Common School Bill been followed by a just and liberal modification of the Pension Laws, the apparent deficiency would have been reduced nearly within the actual revenue to be expected for the last half-year, and I should have been enabled to gratify my own feelings and the public expenditure by a regular discharge of all just claims."

At the ensuing general election, Nichol was again returned to represent the county of Norfolk in conjunction with Francis Leigh Walsh. The membership of the House of Assembly had been increased to thirty-eight. John Beverley Robinson was elected for the town of York, and Christopher Alexander Hagerman for the town of Kingston.

In conjunction with Thomas Clark and Robert Grant, acting as agents for "a numerous body of claimants for losses sustained in the late war with the United States," Nichol prepared a strong appeal to Earl Bathurst, dated at Niagara Falls on December 1, 1820.

"We feel no desire to remark," they said, "upon the want of preparation in Upper Canada to resist the Enemy, at the time the Americans declared war, being convinced that it is sufficient to state to your Lordship that such was the case, neither are we inclined to urge, with a view of strengthening this application, the zealous and efficient services of the inhabitants in its defence. We, however, request your Lordship's attention to the circumstance that from the want of preparation and actual poverty of the King's Magazines at the time, the private properties of individuals were taken possession of and were, without hesitation and without compensation to the proprietors, applied to the public service, by which they, (the owners), were not only deprived of the use of them, but were exposed from the reverses of fortune experienced by His Majesty's Arms, to the risk, (too fatally realized), of their capture or destruction, and to all the difficulties and embarrassments attending their endeavours to re-establish their affairs, Many of them at an advanced period of life, destitute of Capital, or overwhelmed with debt.

"We humbly submit for your Lordship's consideration that the War was altogether a National one, that it was not occasioned by any misconduct of the Colonists, neither had they any voice in its management. Individual Colonists, therefore, we with deference suggest to your Lordship, ought not to be permitted to sustain exclusively the loss.

"If Upper Canada, my Lord, was defended, if Lower Canada was protected against invasion, if, by the determined resistance made to the Enemy, and the successful termination of the War in Upper Canada, the Maritime Rights of Great Britain were effectually maintained, and, if in the attainment of these great national objects, the private properties of individuals were taken or sacrificed for the public service, destroyed either by Accident or by order whilst in the occupancy of the King's troops or by the Enemy, whilst the proprietors were zealously engaged in the performance of the duties required by their Allegiance—We are of opinion, may it please your Lordship, that those individuals whose properties were thus sacrificed, whether from want of due protection or from having been taken for the public service, have an indubitable claim, not on the Provincial Legislature, but on the Imperial Parliament, for relief."

They asserted that the sum received from the sale of forfeited estates, after various deductions for legal charges had been made, was so small as scarcely to merit notice.

The claims were classified by them in the following manner:—

1st. Direct demands against the Government for supplies.

2nd. Destruction of property by His Majesty's Generals' orders to prevent it being useful to the Enemy.

3rd. Destruction of property by the Enemy from its having been occupied or used for Military purposes.

4th. Destruction of property by accident while in possession of the King's troops.

5th. Destruction of property by the Enemy to prevent its being made use of in defence of the Province.

6th. Destruction of property from irregularities of the Soldiery and of the Indians acting with them.

Seven years had then elapsed since the end of the war and many of the claimants were in the greatest distress and actually dependent upon the lenity of their creditors, which from the general state of depression in the commercial world they could hardly expect to be extended to them much longer.

"Should this appeal . . . produce no effect," they declared, "the complete ruin of the sufferers is inevitable, and their families."

John Galt, the author, was employed to act as their representative in London, and pressed their case with great energy and persistence. He finally proposed that compensation should be made by raising a sum of one hundred thousand pounds or more, half to be charged to the Imperial Government, and half to the province. This plan was adopted and in 1823, the Lieutenant-Governor was directed to distribute the sum of £57,412.10/, provided by the British Treasury, without waiting for the provincial legislature to vote an equal amount.

He had already received instructions to pay certain claims and reported that this had encouraged the presentation of others through Mr. Nichol, and he had consented to transmit some documents in explanation of cases already under consideration. This had induced Nichol to urge his own claims, which were quite distinct from the others and he had informed him that the papers presented by him in their support would be forwarded without any recommendation. Maitland then advised the appointment of commissioners to investigate claims for damages arising from incursions by the enemy.

The eighth provincial parliament was convened for its first session on January 31, 1821. The Lieutenant-Governor announced that he did not think fit to declare the causes for which it was summoned until a Speaker of the Assembly had been elected.

A motion was made that Nichol should be chosen, which was lost. Alexander Macdonell of Glengarry, and Allan Maclean, the late Speaker, were successively proposed and defeated. Then Nichol nominated Livius P. Sherwood, who was elected.

The speech of the Lieutenant-Governor was read by the Speaker on February 2. It stated that the wealth and power of the province had been unusually advanced by "the late emigration from the Parent State" and referred to the "numerous advantages that would attend on the improvement of our land and water communications, thereby rendering access easy to a country that offers to capital and skill a wide field for agricultural improvement, and ample materials for many purposes of commercial enterprise." Forty townships had been surveyed in the last two years and "in a great measure bestowed on conditions of actual settlement." This had been accomplished without making any demand on the provincial treasury for expenses through the system adopted.

A large amount of arrears was due for militia pensions as no adequate provision had been made for their payment by the last parliament.

Mention was made of the depression in value of the chief products of the province but nothing was said respecting the recent imposition of duties upon colonial timber imported into Great Britain.

The usual motion was made to refer the speech to a committee to draft a reply, to which Nichol moved an amendment to take it into consideration by the whole House next day. His motion was carried. After some debate the Attorney-General moved a short resolution merely affirming the sincere disposition of the Assembly "to concur with the other branches of the Legislature in all measures that may tend to the public good and of their entire confidence in the desire of His Excellency to promote the interests of the province." Nichol moved the adjournment of the debate until the following Monday but his motion was lost and a committee was appointed to draft a reply of which he was not a member.

He asked leave to introduce bills to "secure the independence of the Commons House of Assembly," to repeal the act for repressing sedition, and to repeal the assessment acts and substitute others. He also gave notice of motion for the production of correspondence respecting duties on timber exported from the province into Great Britain. He was elected a member of a special committee appointed to "take into consideration the internal resources of the Province in its agriculture and exports, and the practicability and means of enlarging the same."

On February 5, Nichol moved for returns of the population of the province. Next day he opposed and moved the three month's hoist for a bill, introduced by the Attorney-General, for the more certain prevention of illegal marriages. His name was added to the committee on militia pensions from which it had been omitted. His motion for information on timber duties was adopted with an amendment asking for copies of any other communications on subjects connected with the interests of the province. He was made chairman of a committee to draft an address on the subject of a donation made by the Duke of Richmond for opening new roads from Richmond to Perth. His name appears in the public accounts submitted, as collector of customs at Port Dover, for which he had received half the amount collected, being for the year 1820 the sum of £61. 2. 9, and also as collector of tonnage duty at the same place.

Much of the time of the Assembly was occupied in hearing the evidence on two petitions presented against the return of members.

On March 2, Nichol moved, seconded by Colonel Burwell that a resolution passed in the third session of the seventh provincial parliament on Tuesday, the twentieth day of October, 1818, "that no known Member of the meetings of persons styling themselves delegates from the different districts of this Province, shall be allowed within the bar of this House" together with all the proceedings thereon, should be expunged from the Journals, and this motion was carried without a division.

His bill to repeal the sedition act had passed but had not received the concurrence of the Legislative Council and on his motion a committee was appointed to inspect the Journals of the other chamber and report its proceedings on that bill, and by a special motion he was added to the committee.

A resolution proposed by him, declaring "that location tickets granted under the authority of the Lieutenant Governor and Council of this Province do not confer such a freehold qualification as to entitle the locatee or locatees thereof to vote for the return of a member or members to represent any District, Circle, County, or Town within this Province," was carried on a division by a vote of twenty-five to ten, the Attorney-General voting in the negative.

His bill for "the better securing the independency of the Commons House of Assembly" passed but was amended by the Legislative Council and on his motion a conference was requested on the subject and a committee appointed to prepare reasons to induce the other house to recede from their amendments.

On March 14, Nichol moved the appointment of a select committee to examine into and to state the annual income and expenditure of the province from the 1st day of January, 1793, to the 31st December, 1820, both days inclusive; also to investigate and inquire into the emoluments annexed to the several offices of the Provincial Government, or paid from the Provincial Funds during that period, and to report their opinion, whether any and what reduction may be practicable or deemed expedient to make in the emoluments of such offices respectively.

On March 17, he moved for information "respecting the appointment of Commissioners on the part of Lower Canada to adjust and stipulate for paying over the Drawbacks due to this Province on goods imported from the 1st July, 1819, to the 31st December, 1820; also of the arrears of former years and such other information respecting such duties and arrears as might be in the possession of the Executive."

As chairman of a committee to inquire into the duties of the Adjutant-General of Militia, Nichol reported in favour of an additional salary but declined to suggest the amount.

He prepared a long and evidently very careful report for the select committee on Internal Resources, which is an historical document of very considerable economic importance. The committee had not been able to obtain any very correct information as to the quantity of exports. In masts, spars, pine and oak lumber it was presumed to have been considerable; but the exportation of flour was relatively small, having never exceeded thirty thousand barrels in a year. The exportation of furs and peltries had greatly declined.

Their value was fluctuating and affected by many causes and circumstances.

"The staples of this Province," the report said, "from the long and desolating wars occasioned by the French Revolution, and failure of harvests in Great Britain, and her occasional differences with the Northern Powers of Europe, together with the restrictive policy of the American Cabinet, naturally became in great demand, and were in consequence thereof raised to a value which in time of profound peace they could not be expected to maintain. At that time, the numerous fleets and armies which were kept up by the contending powers, drew from agriculture a large portion of its labour, which being taken from a productive to a destructive employment, increased the demand for provisions, while it limited the means of raising them, and this foreign demand was increased by blights, by the ravages of the contending forces, and the destruction of property incidental to a state of active warfare, which occasioned a steady demand for every article which the Province could supply.

"On the return of peace, and resumption of domestic habits by a large portion of the armed population, the demand for our staple articles decreased, and consequently they fell in price. Another cause of the depression in the value of our staple articles may be found in the deteriorated quality of the article sent to market. For instance Upper Canada flour, which, when it first found its way to Montreal, was greatly esteemed, and much in demand, is latterly, (from the greater attention paid to the manufacturing and packing of that article in the United States, from the damage the flour of Upper Canada very frequently sustains from its exposure to heat and moisture, and from the negligent manner in which it is transported to Montreal), so little sought after in Lower Canada and other markets, that it can with difficulty be sold, when that of the United States is brought into competition with it.

"Your committee, therefore, can have no doubt as to the fact of a very material depression having taken place in the value of our commodities, and have reason to believe that they are not worth so much by one-half, as they were before the commencement of the late American War."

The price of flour manufactured in Upper Canada was affected by the regulation requiring its re-inspection in Lower Canada.

"Large sums," the report stated, "are also annually levied on the trade of Upper Canada, under Acts imposing duties for improving the navigation of the Saint Lawrence, which duties, while they add to the embarrassments of our export trade, give it no additional safety or accommodation, a great part of the money raised from them remaining at this time in the hands of the Receiver General of Lower Canada unexpended."

The effect of the Corn Laws, the duties on timber and rum, and the heavy charges for transportation were commented upon.

The measures recommended were:

"1st. A revision of the Inspection Laws, and prohibiting the exportation of any flour from the Province, until it has been inspected and branded Upper Canada, fine, superfine, or as the case may be.

"2nd. An application to the Imperial Parliament claiming their interference to protect the staples of Upper Canada against any Acts of our Sister Provinces which might otherwise affect the same.

"Also a modification of her corn laws, in such manner as to admit at all times the bread stuffs of this Province into the British markets, subjecting them only to duties when below a certain average. Also the reduction of the sterling duty on rum imported from other British Colonies to the same rate, as is by law imposed on that article coming from the West Indies and Bermuda, and that she will continue her protection to the Canada lumber trade. But the great and indeed the only efficient measure by which, in the opinion of your committee, a permanent relief can be afforded to the commerce of Upper Canada, 'and the safe, easy, expeditious, and economical exportation of our staples to the markets to which we have access can be secured,' is the improvement of our inland navigation.

"This is a measure, which in the opinion of your committee, claims the earliest and most profound attention of your Honorable House. It is a measure deeply involving the national interests as well as the commercial prosperity of the Province, and one, which if entertained by your Honorable House, should in the opinion of your committee be undertaken on an extensive scale, a scale commensurate with the increasing power and rapidly accumulating commercial resources of the Province.

"That it is perfectly practicable to connect the lakes Erie and Ontario with Montreal by canals of sufficient depth to enable vessels of burthen to sail without unloading directly to that port cannot be doubted. The successful enterprise of our jealous neighbours sanctions your committee in forming this opinion, and is an example which ought to excite us to similar exertions.

"We ought not to allow ourselves to be deterred by the magnitude of the undertaking from undertaking at all. Difficulties there are no doubt, but they are not insuperable, and will be found to be comparatively insignificant when encountered by perseverance and determination."

It was admitted that the Province was without funds to carry on a work of this kind on the most moderate scale, but the Imperial Parliament might be induced to give " such facilities and encouragement to this stupendous undertaking as would insure its success."

The estimates of the American Canal Commissioners, with respect to the Erie Canal, were referred to as furnishing data to go upon.

The opinion was expressed that " a work of this description should not be upon an exposed frontier, but should be, wherever circumstances admit of it, inland. Could it be completed on a scale which would enable the Government to bring the smaller sized vessels of war right into the lakes it would prove in the opinion of your committee the best barrier against the future hostile attempts of the United States that could be formed. Military protection and commercial facility would thus be united, and the Province of Upper Canada, instead of being as it is at this particular time a dead weight upon the Government and commerce of Great Britain, would be one of her most flourishing colonies."

The passage of a bill appointing commissioners was recommended.

"First.—To devise and adopt such measures as shall be requisite to facilitate and effect a communication by canals and locks between the lakes Erie and Ontario, and lake Ontario and Montreal.

"Second.—To examine and explore the country for the purpose of determining the most eligible routes for the contemplated canals; to cause surveys and levels to be taken, and maps filed, books and draughts to be made, and to adopt and recommend proper plans for the construction and formation of the said canals, and of the locks, dams, embankments, tunnels, and aqueducts, and to cause all necessary plans, models, and draughts to be executed.

"Third.—To calculate and estimate the expense of the above operation.

"Fourth.—To devise ways and means for carrying the above purpose into effect."

With respect to the last head of inquiry—" Whether any, and if any, what nature of encouragement it is expedient to give to the manufactures of salt and iron for home consumption," the committee reported:

"That it is deemed sound policy in every country to protect domestic manufactures, provided it can be done without making too great a sacrifice of other objects.

"Domestic manufactures give a value to our raw materials, and serve to retain within the Province Capital, of which it must be deprived for the payment of similar articles when imported.

"Your committee, however, are not prepared to recommend a system of bounties as the Provincial Revenue at this time is not adequate to pay them, even if it were deemed advisable to do so. They are of opinion that the manufacture of the necessary articles of salt and iron should be encouraged by every practicable means. But that until the Public Revenues of the Province are freed from their present embarrassment the only measure which it will be prudent to adopt is to impose heavy duties on similar articles when imported from the United States."

This report was referred to a committee of the whole.

On April 10 a series of resolutions embodying the recommendations contained in it were adopted.

Two days later Nichol introduced a bill to provide for the appointment of commissioners "to explore and survey the internal communications of this Province, to prepare plans and estimates for the improvement of the inland navigation, and to report their opinion as to the most eligible and practicable routes for effecting the same; also to devise ways and means for completing the said canals." It was read a second time and reported by the committee of the whole on the same day and read a third time on April 13. It was passed by the Legislative Council without amendment.

On April 4, Nichol introduced resolutions relative to the appointment of a Provincial Agent, imputing neglect of duty to Mr. Halton in respect to the question of the imposition of duties upon Canadian timber imported into Great Britain, by which the opportunity of remonstrating against this measure had been lost. These resolutions were adopted by a vote of twenty-eight to three, the Attorney-General again voting with the minority. A bill was then introduced repealing the act for his appointment which was passed by a majority of twenty, only five members voting against it.

The Legislative Council requested a conference on the subject, and a committee was accordingly appointed to confer, with Nichol as chairman. The committee from the Legislative Council stated that as a preliminary to the passage of the bill they required that the offensive expression towards the Agent should be expunged, because everything personal to him should be the subject of a joint address and secondly that they should satisfy the Council that a resident Agent in England was no longer necessary and if so to make provision for the present incumbent. The committee of the Assembly replied that they were not authorized to discuss those points. The committee was then empowered to confer freely with the committee of the Council and a second conference was held. Nichol reported that:

"After much discussion, in which it was contended on the part of the Legislative Council, that their House would not pass the bill with the reflection against the Provincial Agent, as it was irrelevant to it, the Conferees of your Honorable House said they did not think there could be any Parliamentary objection to the Upper House expunging the objectionable clause, though they were not authorized to assent to their so doing, but they could not recognize the principle that the Upper House should interfere with any money clauses, either by the introduction of a provision for the agent or in any other way." The bill was thrown out by the Council.

Nichol introduced and carried a bill to repeal the Civil List Appropriation Act, which likewise failed to pass the Council, who stated in a conference, by their Managers, that it "appeared to be modelled on information which that House did not possess, and which they had been directed to request might be communicated for the information of their House."

The Assembly declined to communicate any information on the subject and the bill was accordingly lost.

Nichol was also appointed as chairman of committees to confer with the Managers for the Legislative Council, on the bill to amend the registration act, on the act to regulate trade with the United States, and to prepare a joint address on claims for losses in the late war. The address thus framed stated that the proceeds of sales of forfeited estates would probably amount to less than fifteen thousand pounds, and prayed that the claims for compensation should be laid before the Imperial Parliament "with such recommendation as Your Majesty may be graciously pleased to give," and concluded with the remark "that the war in which this Province suffered was professedly waged by a jealous enemy, with the hope (providentially disappointed), of establishing certain principles of national policy affecting the whole Empire in the defence of which your Majesty's Province of Upper Canada will ever aspire to partake with sentiments of proud devotion to the interests of the parent state."

A resolution was passed without opposition praying the Lieutenant-Governor to appoint Nichol one of the Commissioners to confer with Commissioners appointed on the part of Lower Canada upon the subject of intercourse between the two provinces, or if the Commissioners were already appointed, to add him to the Commission.

On the 13th of April, Nichol moved an address to the King respecting commercial intercourse with Great Britain, making the following representations:

"1st. That the principal staples of Upper Canada, and the only articles with which her merchants, or people can pay for the goods, wares and merchandise imported, (exclusively from Great Britain), for their consumption are her bread stuffs and the timber from her forests.

"2nd. That these articles being various and of great bulk the transportation of them from the interior is attended with great risk, labour, and expense, and the exportation of them from Quebec to Great Britain and other countries to which they are permitted to be sent, (being confined to British shipping), gives employment to a considerable number of her seamen.

"3rd. That during the last season, several cargoes of wheat and flour were exported from the port of Quebec to His Majesty's European Dominions at a time when the ports of the United Kingdom were open, but previous to their arrival the ports had been shut, by which these cargoes were subjected to be bonded for exportation, and future shipments may experience the same fate.

"4th. That flour being a perishable commodity, and one that cannot for a long period be kept in a sound state, the owners may become subject to the total loss of their property with the heavy charges incurred for transportation and commissions superadded.

"5th. That His Majesty's faithful subjects have been apprised of an intention of His Majesty's Ministers to bring under the consideration of Parliament during the present session, the levying of certain additional duties on Canadian timber or of lessening those already imposed on the same article, when imported from foreign ports.

"6th. That should either of these intentions be carried into effect, it will complete the ruin of the Canadian timber trade, and reduce a great portion of His Majesty's subjects in this Province to great distress.

"7th. To implore His Majesty to take the distressed situation of this colony into His Royal consideration and to be graciously pleased to recommend to the Parliament of the United Kingdom to concur with His Majesty in enacting laws by which the corn and bread stuffs of His Majesty's colonies of Upper and Lower Canada shall and may be admitted into Great Britain for Home consumption, subject only to the payment of duty when the price is less than the average fixed by law and also to continue the restrictive duties on foreign timber, by which measure only can the trade of this Province be saved from the ruin with which it is menaced and the Province instead of continuing a heavy burthen to its parent state, become one of the most valuable and important, as it has ever been one of the most dutiful and loyal colonies of His Majesty's United Kingdom." This motion was seconded by the Attorney-General, and carried without dissent. The address was accordingly prepared and adopted.

During this session Nichol had figured as an advocate of liberal and progressive measures, as a champion of economy, and generally as the chief critic of the administration and the leader of an adverse majority. It is scarcely probable that this had strengthened his influence with the government.

The session had continued much longer than usual and had not been fruitful in beneficial legislation owing to the constant and unyielding opposition of the Legislative Council on many bills which prevented them from passing.

The displeasure of the Lieutenant-Governor was thinly veiled in his closing speech, by the polite sarcasm of his remarks.

"The public business no longer demanding your attention," he said, "it gives me great satisfaction to close this long session of Parliament in order that you may be at liberty to attend to your private affairs, which must at this advanced season require in a particular manner your superintendence.

"I cannot allow you to separate without expressing to you the satisfaction I have felt on observing the temper, diligence and regard for the interests of the Province by which your proceedings have been governed.

"The variety and importance of the matters which have been under deliberation and your attention to subjects of public moment, afford satisfactory proofs that your time has not been misemployed.

"I have no doubt that your provisions for incorporating a Provincial Bank, and for establishing an uniform currency throughout the Province will prove beneficial to the commercial and general interests. The Bill for appointing Commissioners to ascertain and report on the improvements which can be effected in the internal navigation may be considered as the commencement of an important undertaking eminently calculated to advance the prosperity and greatness of Upper Canada."

Addressing the Assembly, he said:

"I thank you on behalf of His Majesty for the supplies you have granted in aid of the civil list, which you must be convinced are not more than the exigencies of the public service compelled me to require.

"The appropriation you have made to assist in opening the road from the Ottawa through Richmond and Perth to Kingston, though small in amount, will be regarded as a sufficient proof of your desire to add to the liberal appropriation made by His Excellency the Commander of the Forces for that object, when it is remembered that it is almost the only grant you have been enabled to make for any public purpose."

Nichol's financial position had not greatly improved. During the years immediately succeeding the war, and before obtaining his pension, he had been gradually involved in debt and had mortgaged one piece after another of his remaining lands for the support of his family. The Commissioners appointed to revise claims for losses had awarded him the sum of £4,202. 10/, or rather less than two-thirds of the valuation set by him on the property destroyed, and of this, only thirty-five per cent. was paid, nine years after the date of its destruction.

He was appointed Judge of the Surrogate Court for the District of Niagara, and took up his residence in the township of Stamford. The interest on his debts had become a burden too heavy for him to carry and he conveyed the whole of his remaining real estate to his principal creditors, Messrs. Clark and Street, and the Reverend Robert Addison, leaving still a balance due to both as well as to other persons, which the amount still to be received under the award for losses would not nearly satisfy.

The writer has not succeeded in obtaining much information respecting the last three years of his life, during which he was doubtless as active as ever in several public capacities.

The end came with tragic suddenness. In the night of May 3, 1824, when driving alone, at a late hour, in a blinding snow-storm, from Niagara, where he had been performing the duties of his office in the Surrogate Court, he missed his way and with his horse and waggon, was precipitated over the cliff near Queenston, and literally dashed to pieces.

When his affairs were investigated, it was found that his personal estate did not exceed a value of £400, and the greater part of his property was sold to satisfy an execution, leaving his widow with a family of four young children almost destitute, and many debts still unpaid.

APPENDIX.

General Instructions for the Officers of the Quarter Master General of Militia Staff.

Lieut. Col. Nichol rests assured that the Officers attached to the Staff of the Quarter Master General of Militia, stimulated by a due sense of the honour conferred upon them by his Honour the President in selecting them for the important duties of the department will exert themselves to obtain the approbation of his Honour as well as of their Country by a strict, regular, and conscientious discharge of the duties assigned them respecting,

"1st. Their primary duty will be to provide for the comfort and accommodation of the Militia Forces whether in quarters or in the Field, to see that they are provided with every article of equipment authorized to be issued to them—to report also without delay every deficiency, and when the good of the service may require—to recommend such additions as may be thought necessary for the consideration of His Honour the President.

"2nd. They will regularly at least once a month, and oftener if it be practicable, inspect the Militia Quarters within their respective Districts, and Report specially to the Head of the Department the state in which they may be. They will be particularly careful to report the state in which they may find the Barrack Furniture, which may have been issued, to note all deficiencies and to make prompt enquiry into the causes thereof, that immediate and efficacious measures may be adopted for preventing a recurrence of the same.

"3rd. Whenever they may receive orders to provide for the quartering at any point, or moving any body of Militia in any direction, immediate and prompt attention must be given to this Duty, an estimate of the probable expenses to be incurred must be prepared, which, when sanctioned by the Commanding Officer at the Post, will be an authority for advancing the amount to the Officer commanding the Corps or detachment to be moved, for which he must give a receipt and must regularly account at the place of his destination. The receipt will be transmitted to the senior officer in the department in the district to which the removal may take place, if to a different District, who is to be charged in his Public account with the same, and who is to see the account of disbursements regularly settled. And at the same time a route, accompanied by the order for Marching must be furnished to the Officer Commanding the detachment to enable him on his arrival to claim his account. Great attention will be requisite to prevent the number of carriages required for any detachment exceeding the established allowance.

"4th. They will receive into their charge all Militia Stores whether cloathing, Barrack Stores or Camp Equipage, are to issue the same to the different bodies of Militia in such manner and in such proportion as may be directed by the authority of His Honour the President, on all such occasions regular vouchers must be taken for the delivery and an Abstract of the same must be made up monthly in triplicate, which, accompanied by the authority and receipts must be transmitted to the Office of the Quarter Master General of Militia.

"5th. They are to make themselves perfectly acquainted with the Topography of the Country in which they may be stationed, including the nature and direction of the roads, both Public and Private, Rivers, Rivulets, Ravines, and Eminences, also the resources of the same with respect to Provisions of every kind and the means of transport that they may thereby the more easily not only provide for the marching and stationing the Militia Forces but also be materially assisting and aiding to the Quarter Master General's Staff of His Majesty's regular Forces.

"6th. They are to keep a correct record of all transactions and occurrences in the department under their command with a Letter Book and a District and General Order Book in which all Letters and Orders are to be regularly inserted, these Books are to have an index of reference and to remain permanently in the Office and to be handed over in the event of removal, promotion, or death of the officer to his successor for his information and guidance.

"7th. Regular Reports of every occurrence of moment must be transmitted to the head of the department with whom the Deputy and assistant will regularly correspond.

"8th. On all occasions when the Militia are in the Field and serving, whether alone or in conjunction with His Majesty's regular Forces, it is the Duty of the Officers of the department to give the Officer Commanding, whether of the Line or the Militia, detailed information respecting the country in which he may be acting, to supply him on his requisition with intelligent guides, to trace out the routes and Encampments, and to provide for the marching, Quartering, and stationing the Forces within the same.

"In advancing against the Enemy they are to be with the advance guard to reconnoitre his position, to lead the column of attack and by their intelligence, zeal, energy, and activity to offord material assistance in conducting the operations of the Divisions to which they may be respectively attached.

"9th. Having been engaged with the Enemy a correct and detailed report of the operations that may have taken place, with a sketch and description of the ground must be transmitted without delay to the Office of the Qr. Mr. General of Militia.

"10th. Regular accounts of the disbursements of all Monies expended by the department must be transmitted to the Office of the Qr. Mr. General of Militia in Triplicate and an abstract of the same made up to the 24th of each month.

"11th. All requisitions for clothing, necessaries or Barrack and Field allowance, are to be signed by the Officer requiring and countersigned by the Commanding Officer of the Garrison or Post before any Issue of these articles can take place.

"12th. When the relief of any detachments of Militia is ordered or when they may be ordered to be disembodied an officer of the department will attend to receive and Deliver over the Quarters, and it is his particular Duty to see all delapidations of Stores or Quarters are paid for or made good by the detachment relieved or disembodied.

"The Barrack Furniture is on no account to be removed from the Post to which it is attached without express authority from the General Officer commanding.

(Signed)   Rob. Nichol, Lt. Col. Q. M. Genl. Militia.

III

HUMOURS AND INTERESTS OF AN HISTORICAL BUILDING

By Miss Janet Carnochan.

This may not be solid history but may be called history in a lighter vein, yet even thus some items of real history may be found therein. Many articles in the Historical Building at Niagara have an interesting story connected with them. Many have been given with a wrong name, sometimes quite absurd. With some a joke lingers, with others a pathetic interest.

Visitors vary as much as the articles, many intelligently seeking information and often giving it, others only coming from curiosity to see our "curios," wondering when told that we have no "curios" but that the articles must have some historical value. Here are buttons of the 70th Surrey and thereby hangs a tale. When sending out circulars to those interested in the history of the town and vicinity, I determined to write to the Colonels of every British regiment which had fought or done duty here, asking a contribution for the building fund, we intending to place a tablet to all the regiments on service here. These regiments were scattered, some in India, Egypt, Scotland, Malta, England, Ireland, etc. Five colonels replied, amongst them the colonel of the 70th Surrey in India, stating that he did not think that his regiment had ever been in Canada, but as their records were incomplete he would be pleased to have any information. I replied that in St. Mark's register there are references to births, deaths, marriages of the 70th Surrey, and in the Michigan historical publications there is reference to a traveller visiting Niagara in 1819, and going into the home of Paymaster Scott of the 70th Surrey, on the River Road, who was the brother of Sir Walter Scott, and it was commonly believed among the officers that he was the author of the Waverley Novels instead of Sir Walter. I had known that this brother James had been in Canada, but not that he was stationed in Niagara. The colonel sent a cheque for ten dollars and on my sending thanks and enclosing a button of the 70th Surrey he wrote thanking me and saying that when he reached England he would have it placed on his watch chain. A button which had lain in the ground for perhaps ninety years thus bringing up memories of the Great Magician, and Wizard of the North.

A large key attracts attention and I have to tell its story. The key of the powder magazine of Fort Mississauga, thus stamped, when the British troops were removed about 1860, was picked up by a Niagara boy who afterwards went to the United States, married, settled and, hearing of our building and its articles, sent the key by post from Wisconsin, having possessed it for fifty years.

I do not mind telling a story against myself. When asked about a sword from the United States, near the key, by Dr. Mott, of Buffalo, I said I do not generally say anything to citizens of the United States about this sword, it is that given up to General Murray and handed by him to Lt. Servos when Fort Niagara was captured by the British after the burning of Niagara in December 1813. Dr. Mott replied "Oh, never mind, do you know the story of the little girl from the United States in London who, when shown some bullets or cannon-balls from Bunker's Hill, replied, 'Oh, well, you have the bullets, but we have the hill'." The story is almost too good to be true, the inference for me being, "You have the sword, but *we* have the Fort." Opposite the sword, however, giving the other side of the question, is the scarlet coat, in splendid preservation, of Fort Major Campbell, who was with Cornwallis at the surrender of Yorktown in 1781; it was always called by the family, the "Cornwallis coat."

Many articles have been given with a wrong description, as a piece used to fasten a door from driving back was called "petrified rattlesnakes," found on the shore at Queenston, the giver asserting that formerly you could see the snakes' heads, and certainly the appearance was like snakes twisted and contorted; but an archæological friend gave the scientific name as *Arthrophycus Hernani*, a fucoid often found along the escarpment south of Lake Ontario, it being really petrified sea-weeds, lying on the mud, the water drip, dripping till it formed the limestone.

A saddle given as one of the war of 1812, was soon found to be what was called the McClellan saddle of the civil war, 1861-4. A large weight in the neighbourhood was always said to have been captured from Fort Niagara in 1813, but stamped quite plainly "Geo. 4th," and as George 4th did not reign till 1820, it could not be truly represented as of 1813. But I do not believe any statement to throw doubt on what had so often been told could have any effect. I did not dare to correct the mistake.

Some amusing things have occurred in connection with the contribution box, which was a compromise with our good friend John Ross Robertson, who wanted us to have a fee at the door. I resisted this, saying that as long as I was able and willing to give my services for the benefit of young Canadians, I wished entrance to be free. Someone suggested the contribution box, and as nothing is said to attract attention to it, many do not see it, while others are generous. But one day a young visitor from the United States whose people were staying at the Queen's Hotel was very much interested, and said he would go back and bring them, and the whole family came bearing all the appearance of wealth and luxury; on leaving, the leader of the party said "I have left a contribution in the box." I had the curiosity on their leaving the room, to open the box and found the magnificent sum of four single cents! This box is opened every day on closing the room and the amount entered, and as no one else had been in that day, this was the offering of the whole party. On another occasion an old gentleman attempted to place in my hand a ten cent piece, and frequently visitors try to place money in my hand. I simply say "We do not do that here." Others think I am paid for my services which is very exasperating. The contents of the box vary from copper to silver, bills, even gold, and sometimes there will be no result from a whole roomful, sometimes a generous amount from a few. A statement of the amount contributed during the year appears in the yearly report. At first the card attached said, "Contributions for the Deficit," as at the opening of the building in 1907 there was a sum owing of $300. Another joke at my expense was when Mr. Grey asked how much is the deficit? I replied, "Oh, it is all paid." He quickly and reasonably replied: "Well, what do you have that on for?" This has been replaced by "Contributions for the maintenance fund."

The work on the whole is very interesting; it is a great pleasure to meet those who really appreciate the varied contents of the cases. The book of documents is very valuable, and the case of Niagara printing from 1794, and that of rare Canadian books is highly appreciated by students of Canadian literature as there are some books of which it would be difficult to find a duplicate. On showing a copy of the *Upper Canada Gazette or American Oracle*, printed in Niagara in 1794, to Col. Neilson then visiting the camp, on seeing the name Louis Roy as printer, he wrote in the visitor's book: "My grandfather John Neilson of Quebec, sent his best printer Louis Roy to print that paper." This same paper gave the missing link to a young member in proving his right to belong to the United Empire Loyalists. From our documents many have been able to verify statements of their ancestry. From old newspapers printed in Niagara, anxious inquirers for information have to their surprise gained the long looked-for date of birth, death or marriage.

A large tattered flag is the cause of some amusement to me. Many ask, "Is that a flag of 1812?" It is a large, blue, silk flag with the Union Jack in one corner. I answer, "Well, it has stamped on it, or painted, "2nd Lincoln Geo. IV." I then say, "Do you think it is of 1812?" Of all who have been asked that question only two replied, "No, Geo. IV did not reign till 1820." It is to me also a mystery as the Union Jack is on red ground, this is on blue, and denotes a marine flag; but why should the 2nd Lincoln have a marine flag. There were five regiments of militia in Lincoln County. Can the explanation be that there being marine flags to spare the Lincoln Militia simply painted their name on the flag?

Promises, it is said, are made to be broken; but at least three incidents show the contrary, and the promises made have had their fulfillment even after some years had elapsed. A panel of the coach of Governor Simcoe was brought in a satchel from St. George, and the donor said, "I promised you this two years ago, I remember your showing me through the building." In like manner a bird amulet with other Indian relics was brought by a corporal in the Training Camp, saying, "My friend promised you this but was not able to come himself." The third promise kept relates to a chart from a temple in Pekin, and has a story. A sergeant in the camp here brought me the chart and other Chinese articles saying: "I taught the drill to a Canadian lad some years ago. He became a British officer in the Relief of the Legations in the Boxer Rebellion.

This chart is loot from a temple in Pekin, which he brought me as a present." The sergeant kept the Chinese articles for some years and then brought them to the Historical room. I was always anxious to know the meaning of the Chinese inscription, and meeting a Chinese scholar, a professor at the China Inland Mission, I obtained a translation showing that the chart was placed in the temple by the Wong family, and gave the genealogy of nine generations, male and female. The date he could not decipher but promised to send it. A year and a half had elapsed when to my surprise and pleasure a postal card arrived from Shanghai saying that the date was 1815. Thus were three promises fulfilled.

Here is the Record Book of the first library of Upper Canada, formed here in Niagara in 1800; the book was found in a remarkable way where it had been lying for fifty years or more, no one seeming to know that there was such a book or such a library. Does it not say much for our early pioneers, that this was one of their first acts to give generously for good literature, history, biography, travel, poetry, reviews, one thousand well-bound books? Do their names not deserve mention, especially that of the founder, Andrew Heron, who acted often as secretary, treasurer, librarian, generally without fee or reward?

In another case the first novel published in Upper Canada "St. Ursula's Convent," published in Kingston, 1824, a sensational story of a young girl of seventeen; also the first poem "Wonders of the West," printed in York, 1825; also a translation of the Gospel of St. Mark by Chief Brant in 1787, one page in Indian and the other in English. In another case a copy of the farewell of Samuel Lount to his friends before his execution which has been looked upon as a judicial murder.

And there have been adventures, some of which may be told. Why have some modern locks, instead of being the simple old-fashioned lock, all sorts of combinations? Push one spot the door will open from the outside, push another and the reverse occurs. One evening at a meeting of the Historical Society when preparing to depart it was found that the door refused to open. What to do? The lower windows were all barred. The prospect of remaining all night was not inviting. The thought occurred to me there is a strong Mexican lasso which may be fastened to the railing upstairs and if anyone is adventurous enough to descend from an open window, the door can be opened from the outside. Thereupon our dear W. J. Wright, M.A., the Principal of the High School, descended, not like St. Paul in a basket, but hand-over-hand, clinging to the lasso, and we were liberated. Alas, he is with us no more but gave his life for his country and us at Hill 70. Another adventure brings up the name of a beloved Professor who this time was the victim. Professor Ellis, of Toronto University, who spent a summer in Niagara during the late war, often visited the Historical Room, and on one of these occasions at the regular time of closing, not knowing that the Professor was strolling around the gallery, I locked the door and went home. Now I might have gone for a walk of an hour or two, but fortunately sat down to read the paper in my house next door. when I was startled by a boy saying, "There is a man in the Historical Room and he wants to get out!" On narrating this at our picnic shortly after in the presence of the

Professor, I said, "The lower windows were all barred;" he said rather sadly, "I soon found that out." I believe the story was told often by the Professor and provoked much merriment at the idea of a grave, learned and honored professor being interned as an historical specimen. And I was once shut up myself till I could call a boy passing to open the door. But the lock has been simplified since.

Nothing has been said of the interest of meeting intelligent people from many lands who enter their names in the visitor's book, military, literary, boys and girls eager to know, British, citizens of the United States, Polish, French, Canadian; oh, what variety of faces and persons! It is a real pleasure when interest is shown, but not otherwise. Many documents have been rescued from destruction, many secretaries' books otherwise consigned to the junk heap. Nothing has been said of the work connected with the building; there is no janitor, no salary paid. There are many large scrap books. At the opening of the building in 1907, Mrs. E. J. Thompson, of Toronto, gave much assistance in making scrap books, a large book of original documents filled, others with family, church, town records; also many of the cases were arranged by her care and taste. Since then I little thought when I began a scrap book in 1914 of the war that number fifteen would be reached, 1914 to 1919; also a book of noted Canadians, another of historical places in the vicinity, others of Centenaries, Canadian and United States. The walls are quite covered with portraits, landscapes, documents framed, the frames given by members all at very little expense; and we hope that the contents of the building will form an enduring record of the early history of Canada for many present and future students. While some of the Historical Societies have had a building given them or have a room in a library this is the only Historical building erected for the purpose, the money raised by the Society now in its twenty-sixth year.

IV.

WHEN JEFFERSON DAVIS VISITED NIAGARA

By A. J. Clark.

History has been forced to record some strange reversals. Few of these can equal the change of events which made Canada, so long the terminal of the "underground railway," by which Southern States negro slaves reached freedom, become, at a later date, the temporary asylum of Jefferson Davis, the exiled ex-President of the defeated Confederacy.

Thankfully had the unlettered slave often breathed out his joy at finding himself under the Union Jack. Equally grateful was the eloquent testimony borne by the cultured Southern statesman to the reality of British freedom, as enjoyed by him during one of the most trying periods of his life.

Following his two years imprisonment at Fortress Monroe, in Virginia, Jefferson Davis was released on bail on the 13th of May, 1867, and craving escape not only from his military prison, but also from the territory of the Republic, he came north via New York to Montreal. His sojourn in the latter city was very brief as his real objective was Niagara, where he might enjoy for a short season the society and hospitality of his friend the Hon. James M. Mason. The latter, a former United States Senator, had been appointed Confederate States Commissioner to England. His removal, on the high-seas, from the Royal British Mail Packet "Trent" (together with his diplomatic companion Mr. Slidell) by Capt. Wilkes of the "San Jacinto" of the United States Navy, produced what is familiarly known as the "Trent Affair;" with its narrowly averted serious consequences. *

Promptly released on the demand of Britain, Mr. Mason later came to Canada and lived for a considerable time in Toronto. He subsequently removed to Niagara and established himself in the cosy little residence, still standing—and which our members may have the privilege of visiting during the present meeting. Here he entertained among others, General Jubal Early, one of the foremost in the Confederacy's remarkable galaxy of commanders. In fact, for a time, the Confederate headquarters in Canada might not inappropriately be said to have been located at Niagara. General Early, it may be added, lived for two years in Toronto and Drummondville, following his escape from the South by way of Mexico.

---

* The Royal Mail Steam Packet Company resumes its trans-Atlantic service during the present summer season (1921) after a lapse of half a century.

Among the refugees living in Canada at this same period was Colonel Helm, who had been Confederate agent at Havana. He made the trip from Toronto to Montreal to greet Mr. Davis and accompanied him back to the former city. So little ostentation marked the return trip that it was not known that they were on the up-bound steamer until an hour or two before her arrival. Colonel Denison** in some way learned the news and quickly passed the word around as much as possible among his acquaintances, urging them to come to the wharf to extend a welcome. As a result, when the steamer docked at about 10.30 a.m., several thousand persons filled the old Yonge Street landing-place. Col. Denison and a few intimate friends mounted a nearby pile of coal and led the cheering as Davis and Helm appeared at the rail. Quickly realizing the former's emaciation and weakness, the result of his imprisonment, the crowd's greeting grew more sympathetic and finally swelled its first spontaneous cheers into an enthusiastic welcome.

Col. Helm took his distinguished friend home for lunch; the other guests being Mr. Mason, General Early, Col. Denison and Capt. Winder, of Baltimore. The same little party, with the exception of the host, left by the 2 p.m. boat, the "Rothesay Castle," for the trip across Lake Ontario. Consequently, during the afternoon of Thursday, May 30th, 1867, Niagara received into her midst a man whose life history is made up of a strange mixture of justly-placed admiration, of ill-informed censure and of not a small proportion of romance.

As the little party was walking up from the Niagara wharf Mr. Davis noticed the large Stars and Stripes flying over Fort Niagara on the opposite side of the river and pointing to it said to Mr. Mason—"Look there, Mason, there is the gridiron we have been fried on." Jocular though the words may seem at this far-removed date they doubtless had a burning undertone when they were uttered.

During his brief stay in Niagara, for he returned to Toronto on the 3rd of June and left again for Montreal on the 5th, Mr. Davis was deeply touched by the cordiality of his reception by the citizens of the little community. Serenaded by an out-pouring of the townspeople, headed by their local band, he expressed his thanks in the following words:

"Gentlemen, I thank you sincerely for the honour you have this evening shown to me; it shows that true British manhood to which misfortune is always attractive. May peace and prosperity be forever the blessing of Canada, for she has been the asylum for many of my friends, as she is now an asylum to myself. I hope that Canada may forever remain a part of the British Empire, and may God bless you all, and the British flag never cease to wave over you."

That the memory of the events which marked his short visit to Canada was treasured by Jefferson Davis is proven by a conversation which he had with General Robert E. Lee some months later. To General Lee he stated that he had been hooted at and jeered in the stations throughout the Northern States on his way up to Canada but that when he reached Toronto he was received with the greatest

---

** Col. Geo. T. Denison, (until recently the Senior Police Magistrate of Toronto) was always an unconcealed friend of the Confederate agents and refugees and on many occasions proved his friendship and interest in very practical ways.

enthusiasm. For the first time since his capture two years before, he averred, he drew a full breath feeling that he was breathing free air. "He said," declared General Lee, in recounting the conversation, "that he instantly felt better and told me earnestly that he believed it saved his life." There can be no doubt but that his memories of Niagara were equally pleasant.

After his final liberation at Richmond on Christmas Day, 1868,*** Davis spent but a brief time in the former Confederate capital city before returning to Canada where he remained until the summer of 1869, when he sailed for England. Once again he visited Canada in June, 1881, and returned to his Mississippi home by way of Toronto in order to spend a day with Col. Denison. To the latter—Col. Geo. T. Denison of Toronto—the writer makes grateful acknowledgments for his personal confirmation of many of the facts recorded in this paper, and also for data secured from his work "Soldiering in Canada" in which a most entertaining chapter is devoted to reminiscences of Confederate officers and agents during their visits to our Dominion.

In conclusion and not as a part of this paper the writer asks to be pardoned for introducing a personal note when he states that his interest in the subject of the present sketch was enhanced by a period of residence in Richmond, Virginia, the one-time capital of the Confederacy. There he had opportunity to become familiar with many of the places intimately connected with both the official and private life of Jefferson Davis and there also he witnessed the imposing military funeral and great gathering of ex-Confederates which marked his final interment in the Arlington of the South—Hollywood Cemetery, where thirteen thousand of the Confederacy's "soldier dead" also sleep their last sleep.

*** "Lost Cause," Pollard.

V.

SHORT SKETCH OF THE HISTORY OF THE CHURCH OF ENGLAND IN THE TOWNSHIP OF AUGUSTA, COUNTY OF GRENVILLE.

BY THE LATE JOHN DUMBRILLE.

The first church in this parish was erected about the year 1809, near the centre of the front part of the township of Augusta and was called the Blue Church from the color it was painted. Services were occasionally held in this Church until the year 1813. It was afterwards burned down and the present small one built for the use of funeral services.

In 1813 the Rev. John Bethune, afterwards Dean of Montreal, was placed in charge of the mission of Augusta. He continued at his post until 1819 when he exchanged with the Rev. John Leeds, at that time rector of Montreal. Mr. Leeds continued in Augusta until 1821 when he took charge of the mission of Elizabethtown and Brockville, and was succeeded in Augusta by the Rev. Robt. Blakey (who was sent out to Canada by the Society for the Propagation of the Gospel) and was afterwards appointed rector of the parish of Augusta.

In 1820, St. John's Church, Prescott, was opened for divine service, and in 1826, St. James' Church, Maitland, was erected, and opened for divine service in 1827. The first Church wardens of St. James' Church were George Longley and Dunham Jones.

Mr. Blakey was assisted in the latter part of his life, 1st, by Rev. T. Leach, 2nd, by Rev. T. A. Parnell, and 3rd, by Rev. E. W. Beaven. Mr. Blakey died in 1858 and was succeeded by the Rev. Richard Lewis, M.A., now rural dean.

In 1862 Mr. Lewis was assisted by the Rev. James Bogert, and in the same year Mr. Lewis retired from the charge of Prescott and took up his residence in Maitland, where he still lives, (1888) and is assisted by the Rev. G. S. Anderson.

In 1886 Christ's Church was erected by subscription at Lord's Mills in this parish, under the perseverance and supervision of Rev. R. Lewis, and now on the 22nd day of August, 1888, the corner stone of St. George's Church is laid by His Honor Judge James Reynolds of Brockville, P.D.D.G.M. of A.F. & A.M., Grand Lodge of Canada.

This church is to be built by subscription under the praiseworthy exertions of the curate, Rev. Geo. S. Anderson, and the land on which it stands was kindly given by Mrs. Shepherd, widow of the late Thomas Shepherd.

Previous to the erection of the church at Lord's Mills, divine service was held at the school house there, and at the Temperance Hall, near the site of this church.

(Mr. J. Dumbrille, the writer of the foregoing sketch, was Church Warden of St. James' Church, Maitland.)

Maitland, Aug. 22, '88.

VI.

GLEANINGS FROM THE BLUE CHURCH BURYING GROUND, AUGUSTA TOWNSHIP.

BY F. J. FRENCH, K.C.

This historic spot is part of Lot No. 15, in the First Concession of the Township of Augusta, County of Grenville, being now composed (as enlarged by the addition of the new Church of England portion), of all that part of the east quarter lying along the Nine Mile Road from the Grand Trunk Railway lands to the King's Highway, on which the well-known church edifice stands. Originally the site on which the Blue Church is situated was part of a village plot laid out by the Government, and called the Village of "Augusta," prior to the year 1800. And before that date many years there are evidences on the spot of burials having taken place in the old part of the burying ground. One old tombstone I unearthed was dated 1780.

In 1806 a patent of part of the above mentioned village plot, being a part of Lot No. 14, was granted to Livius P. Sherwood, a name well known locally The Rev. Robert Blakey obtained in 1832 parts of Lots 14 and 15, and also certain of the village lots in 1844.

In 1853 there was a patent granted of ten acres of Lot 15, to the Rev. Robert Blakey, Justus S. Merwin and Alpheus Jones, in trust for the Church of England. The southerly part of this ten acres was recently enclosed with, and added to, the old Blue Church Burial Ground, and the title to the whole plot has also recently been vested in the Synod of Ontario.

The present church is the third edifice on the ground; the first, having stood a little back of the present site, was larger in size and was burned many years ago.

The following is a list of burials copied from the tombstones in 1899, with numerous additions since made to the list, but it is unavoidable that there may be many unintentional omissions:—

Christopher plot. (Southeast corner at junction of Nine Mile Road and King's Highway.) (The head of this large family was sexton of the church and burial ground, and held the position at the time of his death.)

Capt. Oliver D. Shaver, d. March 10th, 1870, age 69.

Macneil Clarke, M.P.P., d. 29 February, 1872. (Removed to new part where a monument has since been erected by his brother, J. B. Clarke, K.C.)

Rev. Andrew H. Melville, a native of Glasgow, Scotland, d. March 2nd, 1875, age 74 years.

Annabella Hutton, his wife, d. May 22, 1867, age 62 years.

John H. Melville, teacher, b. April 18, 1828, d. Apr. 19, 1888.

George Harding, b. at Bristol, Eng., Sept. 17, 1818, d. Mar. 20, 1870.
> Louisa, his wife, b. at Padstow, Cornwall, Eng., Sept. 26, 1814, d. at Prescott, June 7, 1884.

Ellen Johnston, daughter of Rev. W. J., and Eliza Sargent, d. Dec. 1865.
Freeman Daniels, d. February 13, 1889.
> Margaret, his wife, d. April 26, 1869.

William Brown, d. February 18, 1882, age 49 years.
Lucy Ann, wife of Dr. Easton, age 40 years.
> Frank, son of Dr. Easton and his second wife (a Miss Henderson) d. July 20, 1872.
> (A monument to John Easton, M.D., has since been erected by his son, W. T. Easton.)

Arthur Edward, son of H. and E. Daniels, d. June 7, 1877.
Thomas Weir, d. Feb. 18, 1874, age 50 years.
> James Weir, a native of Greenland, near Strabane, Co. Tyrone, Ireland, d. Aug. 7, 1875, age 49 years.

Gerrard Irvine, d. April 30, 1880, age 88 years.
> Ann, his wife, native of Ireland, d. Sept. 21, 1897, age 91 years.

John Smades, d. Sept. 15, 1883, age 60 years.
William Ryder, April 12, 1871, age 67 years. (A veteran under Wellington).
> Wm. Gerald, March 5, 1886, age 63 years.

William Mitchell, d. April 5, 1864, age 49 years.
Elizabeth Smith, d. March 13, 1888, age 74 years.
James Irwin, d. Dec. 26, 1893, age 67 years.
> (Mayor of Prescott at various times).

Mary Hall, wife of Nesfield Ward, d. Dec. 21, 1887, age 64 years
> John Ward, d. May 22, 1850, age 53 years 10 months.
> His wife, d. 1861, age 58 years.
> Alfred, d. Dec. 13, 1881, age 46 years.

W. G. Brunning, d. Feb. 4, 1894. age 54 years.
> Eliza Cox, wife of Wm. Brunning, d. Dec. 25, 1872, age 59 years. A native of Devonshire, England.

Isaac Stone, d. April 28, 1876, age 38 years.
> And three children.

Amos Heath, d. Sept. 17, 1859, age 48 years.
True Love Butler, Esq., d. Aug. 9, 1834, aged 51 years.
> (Prominent in public affairs in his day).

William Twomley, d. Sept. 4, 1867, age 25 years.
George Walsh, d. March 17, 1861, age 61 years.
John Millar, Esq., Agent Com. Bank, Native of Forfarshire, d. at Prescott, May 16, 1860, age 60 years.
Alfred Hooker, d. Aug. 30, 1880, age 81 years.
> Elvira Warner, his wife, d. Aug. 27, 1882, age 78 years.

John Francis, d. Dec. 5, 1895, age 66 years.
> Elizabeth Prosser, his wife, d. Aug. 18, 1895, age 69 years.

Henry Langley, b. Aug. 20, 1808, d. Nov. 14, 1875.
Harriett Rhodes, wife of Patrick Miller, d. 1862.
S. B. Merrill's plot. His 1st wife, d. Dec. 2, 1862.
    Harriett, a daughter.
    Mrs. Ward.
    A daughter.
    (Mr. Merrill was late Collector of Excise, Prescott, and for many years proprietor of the Prescott Telegraph. He is also buried here).
Frederick A. Smades, b. Oct. 23, 1808, d. Oct. 25, 1872.
    Elizabeth Hill, his wife, b. April 21, 1819, d. March 25, 1886.
    Three infant children.
    Thomas Christopher, d. Oct. 16, 1872, age 43 years, 9 months.
Sarah Bishop, wife of Samuel Easter, d. July 18, 1886, age 42 years.
William Guernsey, d. Sept. 6, 1874, age 56 years 10 months, 3 days.
    Heltchey Knapp, his wife, d. March 5 ,1885, age 63 years.
Ellis, wife of Luke Chappelow, d. Feb. 21, 1847, age 60 years. A native of Flamborough, England.
Elizabeth Heck, wife of James Heck, d. Dec. 3, 1873, age 73 years 7 months.
Lois, wife of Rev. Samuel Heck, d. Dec. 31, 1842, age 63 years, 2 months, 18 days.
Rev. Samuel Heck, who laboured in his missionary vineyard for upwards of 38 years. Departed this life in the triumph of faith, on the 18th August, 1844, aged 70 years and 21 days.
In memory of Paul Heck, b. 1730, d. 1792.
Barbara, wife of Paul Heck, b. 1734, d. August 17, 1804.
    (The founder of Methodism in America. A new monument has since been erected as follows),

BARBARA HECK.

Born 1734.   . . .   Died August 17, 1804.

Barbara Heck put her brave soul against the rugged possibilities of the future, and, under God, brought into existence American and Canadian Methodism, and between these her memory will ever form a most hallowed link.

In memory of one who laid foundations others have built upon.

(This monument was erected by public subscription from all bodies disposed to give throughout the United States and Canada, and cost about $3,000. The base stone, of granite, is, (in feet,) 12 x 9; the second stone, 10 x 7, and the third stone, which is nicely ornamented by sculptures, is 9 x 6. The height is about twenty feet. The whole of the Heck plot has been consigned by the Trustees of the Church of England to the Methodist body, which takes care of that portion of the ground, and their enterprise is an incentive to the better care of the other portions of this historic burying ground. This monument fronts immediately on the Ontario public highway, facing the St. Lawrence River, and is visited by hundreds of pilgrims every year. Rev. W. H. Withrow's life of Barbara Heck contains most of the particulars of her life that have been preserved.)

Frances, wife of Jacob Heck, d. Apr. 10, 1844, age 73 years.
Jacob Heck, d. Sept. 24, 1847, age 78 years.
Catherine Heck, d. Nov. 8, 1880, age 78 years, 9 months.
Sophia Heck, d. June 15, 1851, age 53 years.
Frances E. Heck, d. Sept. 13, 1878, in the 75th year of her age.
Ann Heck, d. Dec. 14, 1855, age 59 years.
Margaret Stevenson, d. April 29, 1856.
Jessie, daughter of Andrew and J. Wilson, d. March 21, 1880, in her 23rd year.
    Andrew Wilson, d. Sept. 18, 1893, age 86 years, 3 months, 7 days.
Thomas Guy, d. April 14, 1881, age 76 years.
    Sarah, his wife, d. Oct. 29, 1894, age 92 years.
Annie, daughter of George and Hester Miller, d. May, 1892, age 24 years.
    Adeline, daughter of George and Hester Miller, d. June 12, 1874, age 18 yrs.
    Hester, wife of Capt. George Miller, b. Feb. 25, 1833, d. Sept. 17, 1873.
    William George, son of Captain George Miller, b. June 20, 1861, Drowned on the 7th July, 1870.
Margaret, wife of James Montgomery, d. March 7, 1879, age 83 years, 4 months.
John Robinson, from Gliburn, Westmoreland, Eng., d. Sept. 25, 1828, age 21 years.
Samuel P. Toms, d. July 15, 1854, age 82 years.
Samuel Humberstone, d. January, 1823, upwards of 70 years.
    Mary, his wife, d. August, 1828, at the advanced age of 90 years.
The wife of Edward Shewell, d. August 17, 1884, in the 46th year of her age.
    (Mrs. Shewell's remains have since been transferred to the new part of the cemetery).
Jacob Easter, d. November 18, 1875, age 59 years, 6 months.
    Elizabeth, his wife.
Eva Sybill, daughter of A. N. Striker, b. at Picton, Dec. 12, 1852, d. at Prescott, April 25, 1872.
Anson N. Striker, b. March 21, 1829, d. in Prescott, March 23, 1874.
    (Collector of Excise at Prescott).
Frances N., wife of H. Murray, d. April 8, 1878, age 71 years. A native of Wexford, Ireland.
H. Murray, d. Sept. 26, 1882, age 71 years, 5 months. A native of Ballintemple Falls, Co. Carlow, Ireland.
Thomas Keys, d. Aug. 24, 1881, age 71 years. A native of Co. Fermanagh, Ireland.
J Hurlburt, d. April 29, 1844, age 22 years.
    Rev. Sylvester Hurlburt, d. March 8, 1877, age 77 years. (Rev. Sylvester Hurlburt was a well-known Methodist preacher in various parts of Upper Canada. Four other brothers in the Hurlburt family were also in the Methodist ministry . . . Asahel, Erastus, Jesse, Thomas—a missionary to the Ojibway Indians).
    Margaret, his wife, d. June 13, 1873, age 70 years.
    H. B. Hurlburt, d. April 29, 1865, age 41 years.
    T. D. Hurlburt, d. Sept. 8, 1877, age 32 years.

GLEANINGS FROM THE BLUE CHURCH BURYING GROUND

Sylvester, son of George W. and Charlotte Hurlburt, d. May 15, 1871, age 1 year.
G. A. Hurlburt, d. April 22, 1862, age 41 years.
Georgiana E., daughter of J. and A. Hurlburt, d. May 1, 1862, age 12 years.
Rebecca Hurlburt, d. Feb. 5, 1890, age 87 years.
Heman Hurlburt, d. Nov. 24, 1853, age 81 years.
    Hannah, his wife, d. March 23, 1857, age 77 years.
John Bass, son of Joseph C. Bass, d. Feb. 6, 1813, age 4 years, 4 months, 6 days.
    Hannah Bass, wife of James Martin, d. May 3, 1806, age 30 years, 1 month, 11 days.
Sophia Mary, daughter of Justus S. and Anna J. Jones, d. Sept. 2, 1840, age 10 months, 1 day.
Jonathan Jones, Esquire, who died April 20, 1816, age 28 years.
Here also lies interred the remains of his wife, Sophia Sherwood, who departed this life, Oct. 4, 1813, age 22 years.
John Stewart, Esquire, d. May 23, 1829, age 52 years.
Sophia Elizabeth, infant daughter of Alpheus and Frances Jones, b. Jan. 1, d. Sept. 5, 1829, age 8 months, 5 days.
Henry Alpheus, son of above parents, d. Sept. 11, 1827, age 5 years, 4 months 8 days.
Emma, daughter of above parents, d. Feb. 25, 1828, age 1 month, 25 days.
Peter G. Snider, d. July 27, 1878, age 73 years.
Samuel D. Labar, d. August 8, 1871 age 45 years.
    Martha E., his wife, daughter of P. G. and A Snider, d. May 4, 1865, in the 23rd year of her age.
John S. Hartley, d. March 2, 1852, age 75 years.
Edward O. Snider, d. May 18, 1879, age 25 years.
John Sanders, d. April 25, 1827, age 87 years.
    Elizabeth, his wife, d. Feb. 19, 1827, age 85 years.
William Quartus, d. Jan. 16, 1877, age 88 years.
    Jane, his wife, d. March 19, 1868, age 76 years.
Thomas Cooper, d. Oct. 4, 1853, age 25 years.
Samuel Cooper, d. Nov. 20, 1854, age 18 years.
William Cooper, d. Jan. 5, 1871, age 70 years. A native of Kent, Ireland.
Sophia M. Henderson, widow of Robert Weir, jr., d. Oct. 18, 1874, age 66 years.
Mary Tunicliffe Henderson, widow of Aaron Philip Hart, d. Sept. 13, 1874, age 63 years.
William H. Sharp, d. Nov. 18, 1873, age 53 years.
    Mary Sophia, infant daughter of Anne Hawley and W. H. Sharp, d. 1857, age 1 year, 2 months.
William H. Sharp, d. June 11, 1875, age 23 years.
Solomon Henderson, d. Dec. 4, 1883, age 77 years.
    John Henderson, d. Sept. 27, 1852, age 29 years, 11 months, 29 days.
    Ann Hawley, wife of Dr. Rufus C. Henderson, d. July 24, 1865, in her 79th year.
Dr. R. C. Henderson, d. April 5, 1847, in the 69th year of his age.

Dr. Solomon Jones, who died Sept. 22, 1832, in the 66th year of his age.
> His wife, Mary Tunicliffe, who departed this life, April 23, 1820, in the 65th year of her age.
> (Dr. Solomon Jones was the member for Leeds and Frontenac in the second Legislature of Upper Canada, 1796-1800. For some particulars of his life, see "The Second Legislature of Upper Canada," by C. C. James, Trans. Roy. Soc. Can., second series, 1903-4, Vol. IX, p. 150).

Charlotte Coursolles, wife of Eph. Jones, Esquire, d. Sept. 28, 1805, age 60 years.
> Requiescat in pace.

Alpheus Jones, nephew of Eph. Jones. Obit. April 17, 1793, age 28 years,
> Requiescat in pace.

In memory of Eph. Jones of Augusta. Born, April 27, 1750. Departed this life, Jan. 24, 1812.
> (Ephraim Jones was the member for Grenville in the first Legislature of Upper Canada, 1792-96. For some particulars of his life and family of four sons and four daughters, see "The First Legislators of Upper Canada," by C. C. James, Trans. Roy. Soc. Can., second series, 1902-3. Vol. VIII, p. 102).

Dunham Jones, son of Dr. Solomon and Mary Jones, d. Sept. 16, 1876, age 83 years.

Lucy, wife of Dunham Jones, daughter of Andrew and Peggy Hurd, d. March 17, 1868, age 71 years, 10 months, 3 days.

Jonathan Cornelius Jones, M.D., son of Dunham and Lucy Jones, d. in Mankato, Minnesota, Dec. 4, 1872, age 31 years, 2 months, 18 days.

Frances Ann, wife of Andrew, d. Dec. 28, 1880, age 39 years, 15 days.

Mary Ann, wife of William Jones, M.D., d. Jan. 15, 1889, age 51 years, 30 days.
> (Dr. Wm. J. Jones has since died and is buried here).

Alanson Hurd, son of Andrew and Peggy Hurd, d. Aug. 25, 1876, age 68 years, 11 months.

Harriett Theresa, wife of Alanson Hurd, d. Jan. 11, 1863, age 61 years.

Davis Hurd, d. August 10, 1864, age 34 years, 9 months.

Harvey H. Hurd, d. June 14, 1864, age 29 years, 11 months.
> Inez, daughter of Harvey and Catherine Hurd, d. Sept. 26, 1863, age 10 months, 15 days.

Andrew Hurd, d. March 21, 1842, age, 71 years, 5 months, 14 days.
> Also, Peggy, his wife, d. Nov. 10, 1858, age 82 years.

Alonzo Hurd, son of Andrew and Peggy Hurd, d. August 23, 1838, age 30 years, 24 days.

Sereus, son of Andrew and Peggy Hurd, d. Feb. 18, 1825, age 19 years, 6 months, 18 days.

Maria, daughter of Andrew and Peggy Hurd, d. Dec. 2, 1822, in the 21st year of her age.

Widow Annah Hurd, wife of Phineas Hurd, d. Dec. 21, 1822, in the 87th year of her age.

Israel Foote Jones, Esq., d. April 4, 1844, age 38 years.
> On the left lies Philenia, his daughter, who d. July 28, 1843.

Israel Jones, jr., d. April 3, 1811, age 34 years.

Jonas, infant son of Alpheus and Frances Jones, d. Sept. 12, 1822, age 11 months, 1 day.
Sophia Eliza, infant daughter of above parents, d. July 28, 1825, age 10 months, 4 days.
Frances, wife of Alpheus Jones, Esq., d. May 1st, age 40 years.
(In the Jones and Hurd plot lie buried also the remains of Lieutenant David Jones, the hero of the Jane McCrea massacre by the Indians during the Revolutionary War—an event that played an important part in the war—but there is no stone to mark his resting place. See "The First Legislators of Upper Canada" by C. C. James, in Trans. Roy. Soc. Can., second series, 1902-3, Vol. VIII, p. 103. Also, "The U. E. Loyalists of the old Johnstown District" by Judge H. S. McDonald, in Papers and Records of the Ont. Historical Society, Vol. XII, p. 29, and in "Memoir of Col. Joel Stone" by the same author, in Papers and Records of the Ontario Historical Society, Vol. XVIII, p. 75).
Amos Wright, d. July 18, 1796, in the 36th year of his age.
Nicholas W. Wheeler, d. January 9, 1834, age 32 years, 2 months, 22 days.
Eliza, wife of Samuel Thomas of Maitland, and daughter of the late David Breakenridge, Esquire, of Augusta, d. June 21, 1836, age 30 years.
Bertha, daughter of James and Mary Coates, d. June 15, 1890, age 22 years.
Mary E. Wells, wife of J. E. Coates, d. Jan. 7, 1879, age 41 years.
John Wells, d. February 25, 1889, age 76 years.
Hannah, wife of John Wells, d. January 1, 1879, age 61 years.
Louisa Wells, wife of James B. Millar, d. April 20, 1875, age 35 years.
Richard Kirkby, d. Dec. 26, 1867, age 67 years.
Mary Briggs, wife of Richard Kirkby, d. May 16, 1868, age 77 years.
. . . . Briggs, d. Nov. 27, 1877, age 71 years.
Elizabeth Briggs, wife of Wright Place, d. March 17, 1867, age 67 years, 4 months, 6 days.
Elizabeth, wife of John Briggs, d. Feb, 23, 1862, age 90 years.
John Briggs, who emigrated from Belleau, South Lincolnshire, Eng., 1827, d. January 14, 1843, age 72 years.
Lucy, wife of Henry Sharpe. d. Aug. 27, 1873, age 47 years, 3 mos.
Mary Ann, wife of Frederick Brunning and daughter of Henry and Lucy Sharpe. d. Nov. 20, 1867, age 19 years.
Capt. J. S. Millar. d. June 29, 1897, age 65 years.
Mary Lucy, wife of John S. Millar. d. Dec. 23, 1881, age 40 years.
Their babe. d. Aug. 17, 1864, age 1 year.
Smith, wife of the late Edward Millar. b. Sept. 17, 1801, at Lydd, Co. Kent, Eng., d. June 22, 1883.
Edward Miller. d. Feb. 16, 1859, age 48 years. A native of Co. Kent, Eng.
Capt. William Miller. d. Sept. 5, 1893, age 86 years.
Kate Law, wife of William Miller. d. Dec. 16, 1859, in her 53rd year. A native of Shaddockhurst, near Ashford, Co. Kent, Eng.
John, son of Kate Miller. d. April 27, 1897, age 45 years.
Elizabeth. d. Oct. 31, 1847.

William. d. Sept. 6, 1847.
Ann. d. Sept. 30, 1847.
Three children of William and Kate Miller.
Ellen, daughter of Hugh and Maria Young. d. Oct. 19, 1864, age 4 yrs., 5 mos.
Malcolm, son of Hugh and Maria Young. d. June 24, 1879, age 28 years.
Christie A., wife of James Ruide. d. April 19, 1880, age 36 years.
John, son of H. and M. Young. d. March 15, 1882, age 29 years.
Mary, daughter of Hugh and Maria Young. d. June 24 1873, age 24 years.
Hugh Young. d. July 19, 1878, age 66 years, 2 months, 8 days.
Thomas Mullin. d. August 29, 1887, age 22 years.
William J. Mullin. d. Dec. 15, 1891, age 34 years.

(The Gainfort plot is also in this vicinity, where are buried the late Dr. Thomas Gainfort, a native of Wexford, Ireland, a brother and three sisters, and their old body-servant, James F. Taylor. All their property was bequeathed to the Church of England.)

Mary Findlay, wife of E. Mundle. d. June 1, 1899, in her 65th year.
Emma Luella Mundle, wife of George M. Scott. d. Dec. 18, 1897, in her 31st year.
James Findlay. d. Nov. 20, 1890, age 63 years.
Elizabeth, daughter of Robert and Jane Findlay. d. July 26, 1861, age 30 years.
Jane Dow, wife of Robert Findlay. d. Oct. 18, 1857, age 67 years.
Robert Findlay. d. Nov. 18, 1846, in the 53rd year of his age.
Elijah B. Smades. d. Feb. 17, 1876, age 78 years.
   Helen, his wife. d. Dec. 29, 1859, age 50 years, 5 months, 10 days.
Margaret Shiels, wife of George Bowyer. d. Oct. 24, 1883, age 60 years, 2 months.
William Shiels. d. Nov. 10, 1840, age 55 years.
   Elizabeth Montgomery, his wife. d. May 16, 1838, age 40 years.
Hugh William Shiels. d. July 9, 1876, age 47 years, 6 months.
Sarah Mary, wife of Abraham Easter. d. Dec. 24, 1876, age 27 years.
Jane M., wife of John Moore. d. June 24, 1863, age 22 years.
Sarah M., wife of Archibald Moore. d. June 6, 1861, age 47 years.
Archibald Moore. d. August 18, 1887, age 67 years.
Maria, wife of James Peterson. d. April 16, 1883, age 39 years, 10 mos.
Benjamin French. d. January 4, 1899, age 80 years.

(A grandson of Jeremiah French who was the member for Stormont in the first Legislature of Upper Canada, 1792-6. Mrs. French has since died, and is buried beside her husband. She was a daughter of Col. Henry Burritt, who was in Lundy's Lane and other battles in the war of 1812-14.)

Justus Sherwood Merwin. d. at Prescott, April 27, 1863, age 78 years.
   (He was one of the first trustees of this burial ground).
Dolly Merwin. d. Dec. 31, 1884, age 91 years.
Harriet, daughter of Rev. J. W. Burke. b. June 23 1861. d. May 29, 1872.
   (Rev. Mr. Burke was rector here, and afterward rector at Belleville, where he died).
John Wilson, School Master. A native of Yorkshire, England. d. Dec. 8, 1846, age 56 years.

(Mr. Wilson was the first teacher in the first school opened in School Section No. 7, Township of Scarboro, Ont., built in 1832, and located on the Fishery Road. See the "History of Scarboro," p. 188.)

Augus Grant. a native of Elginshire, Scotland. b. March 10, 1838, d. August, 1896.

(Mrs. Grant, who was Miss Gertrude Feilde, now also lies here).

William Baitson. d. July 9, 1882, age 28 years.

Hannah, daughter of Thomas and Mary Baitson. d. Jan. 10, 1884, age 34 years.

Elizabeth, wife of William Roginson. d. Sept. 7, 1830, in the 27th year of her age.

Mary, wife of Robert Baitson. d. April 16, 1828, age 27 years.

Hannah, wife of Henry Baitson. d. Aug 24, 1824, in the 28th year of her age.

Catharine, wife of Henry Baitson. d. Nov. 5, 1828, age 33 years.

Elizabeth, widow of Henry Myers, late of Hull, England. d. 1830, in the 35th year of her age.

Joseph Merrington. d. Sept. 10, 1855, age 34 years.

Elizabeth Myers, wife of Joseph Merrington. d. June 25, 1891, age 68 years.

Mary E., daughter of Joseph Merrington and wife, d. Nov. 2, 1877, age 32 years.

William Henry, only son of above parents. d. Dec. 29, 1879, age 36 years.

Josephine, daughter of above parents. d. May 3, 1881, age 24 years.

Fulford B. Feilde, Assistant Commissary General, H. M. S. 1799-1885.

(Col. Feilde was a veteran of Waterloo, was sent to Canada in Dec., 1830, as Commissary General of the Forces, and while stationed at Penetanguishene married as his first wife a daughter of Capt. James Wickens. A sketch of his life, with portrait, appears in "Old Penetanguishene; Sketches of its Pioneer, Naval and Military Days," by A. C. Osborne, in Pioneer Papers of the Simcoe County Pioneer and Historical Society, No. 6, p. 123. While stationed at Prescott he married as his second wife, Catharine, daughter of the Rev. Robert Blakey, rector and on retiring after forty years service he settled in Prescott. His widow died June 15, 1915).

James Frederick Feilde, 1838-1886. Interred at Winnipeg, Man.

Fulford. 1848-1881. Interred at Fort McLeod, North-West Territory.

Bertha, wife of Alfred N. Suckling. 1851-1882. Interred at Brigus, Newfoundland.

Sophia, daughter of James Feilde and Jane de Cazalet. 1803-1873.

Robert. 1855-1887.

Harry, son of Alfred and Bertha Suckling. 1880-1882.

Lottie, daughter of Charlotte and Edmond Feilde. 1883-1884.

Charles Edward, son of William and Caroline Skinner. d. at Gananoque, Nov. 28, 1870, age 2 years, 10 months.

Mary E. Blakey, wife of Rufus C. Henderson. d. Feb. 7. 1884, age 56 years.

Mary Ann, wife of the late John Blakey. d. at Prescott, Jan. 5, 1867, in her 59th year.

John Blakey, eldest son of the Rev. Robert Blakey. d. March 12, 1861, in the 48th year of his age.

Ann, wife of James Coates of Wensleydale, Yorkshire, England. d. July 11, 1849, age 85 years.
Ann, wife of Rev. Robert Blakey. d. Oct. 5, 1877, age 85 years.
Rev. Robert Blakey, Rector of Prescott, some time Curate of Erlesfield, Yorkshire, England, for thirty-six years Missionary in this Township. Departed to his rest in Christ on the 24th day of March, 1858, in the 68th year of his age and 41st of his ministry.
Eleanor, daughter of Robert and Ann Blakey. d. Mar. 20, 1833, age 16 years.
Two children of the Rev. Robert and Ann Blakey—
    Clara. d. April 19, 1837, age 6 months.
    William Henry. d. Jan. 17, 1841, age 8 years, 9 months.
Justina Feilde, daughter of Assistant Commissary Feilde. d. Sept. 26, 1847, age 10 months, 12 days.
Mrs. John Cazalet Feilde, relict of James Feilde, Esq., of the County Herts. d. June 12, 1848, in the 88th year of her age.
Robert son of the Rev. Robert Blakey. d. Jan. 19, 1871, age 42 years.
James, the second son of the Rev. Robert Blakey. d. Feb. 24, 1878, age 63 years.
Thomas W. Luard, Esq., late Barrack Master of Prescott. d. April 4, 1853, age 56 years, after many years of military and civil service under the British Crown.
Georgina Eliza Maria, child of Allan and Frances Ann Daniell. d. Feb. 7, 1845.
Clarence, son of Calvin and Hannah A. Dame. b. Dec. 20, 1852, d. Jan. 4, 1859.
Thomas Stevenson, son of Calvin and Hannah A. Dame. b. August 25, 1860, d. Oct. 31, 1869.
William H. Humpries. d. March 23, 1864 age 23 years.
John Humpries. d. June 19, 1888, age 77 years.
N. Humpries. d. March 21, 1891, age 79 years.
John. d April 23, 1889, age 83 years.
George. d. Feb. 5, 1899, age 86 years.
Wilson Briggs. b. May 2, 1803, d. Oct. 15, 1880.
H . . . Briggs. b. June 23, 1811, d. Aug. 13, 1896.
Amable Mackenzie, wife of Neil Dunbar. d. April 7, 1854, age 37 years.
Wente. Mackenzie, wife of James Gunn. d. Aug. 8, 1854, in the 33rd year of her age.
James Gunn. d. January 16, 1845, age 33 years.
Daniel Mackenzie. d. May 4, 1832, age 63 years.
Mary, daughter of J. S. and Elizabeth Lynch. ' d. Nov. 7, 1859, age 14 mos.
Sarah Louisa, daughter of Willard and Z. B. Myles. d. May 13, 1856, age 2 years, 26 days.
Sarah Bottom, wife of Willard J. Miles. d. Nov. 10. 1845, in the 38th year of her age.
William H. Myles. d. Jan. 15, 1864, age 26 years, 7 months.
Ruth, wife of Andy Pearson. d. Oct. 4, 1840, age 25 years.
Elijah Bottom. d. Aug. 6, 1825, age 68 years.
    Molly, his wife. d. Nov. 18, 1852, age 81 years.

GLEANINGS FROM THE BLUE CHURCH BURYING GROUND 101

George McClenaghan, a native of Belfast, Ireland. d. April 16, 1832, age 42 years.
 Also four children who died in their infancy.
William Wells. d. Oct. 10, 1842, age 75 years.
Sarah, relict of William Wells. d. May 15, 1860, age 85 years.
 Mary, third daughter of William and Sarah Wells. d. June 20, 1877, age 72 years.
Samuel T. Sayer. d. April 2, 1882, in his 56th year.
Hugh Murray. d. June 12, 1880, age 42 years.
L. H. Daniels. 1832-1921.
 His wife, Jerusha Young. 1847-1909.
Alexander Dempsey. 1837-1913.
 Nancy Patterson. 1831-1917.
Mary Patterson, wife of John Grant. d. Aug. 12, 1893, age 33 yrs., 9 mos.
Delmer, son of J. and M. Grant. d. Aug. 13, 1889, age 1 year, 3 months.
Russell, son of J. and M. Grant. d. Aug. 22, 1893, age 10 days.
Mary, wife of James Patterson. d. April 16, 1883, age 39 years.
James Patterson. d. Dec. 5, 1917, age 76 years.
 Nancy, daughter of J. and M. Patterson. d. Mar. 20, 1859, age 9 years.
Nancy Moore, wife of Abraham Easter. d. Jan. 9, 1906, age 65 years.
Samuel Moore. d. May 16, 1920, age 64 years.
James Moore. 1845-1919.
 His wife, Mary. 1852-1920.
Sanda S. Smades. 1852-1915.
Robert Rickey. 1819-1892.
 Eliza, his wife. 1827-1907.
Christopher Dalgliesh. d. May 12, 1896, age 61 years.
James Cooper. 1828-1909.
 His wife, Jane E. Read. 1840-1915.
William Quartus. d. Jan. 16, 1877, age 88 years.
Genevieve Ada Horwood. Nov., 1870-Sept., 1896.
 Baby son of E. L. and M. F. Horwood. August, 1898.
 Ellen Mary Horwood. April, 1844-Jan., 1912.
 Clarence G. H. Horwood. May. 1867-October, 1912.
 Harry Horwood. February, 1838-May, 1917.
Calvin Dame. 1828-1885.
 His wife, Hannah A. Johnson. 1829-1895.
Thomas R. Wells. 1861-1915.
 William Brock, his son, and for his king and country, somewhere in France, Jan. 11, 1916, age 22 years.
 Reade Chandler Wells. 1898-1920.
Sarah Ann Ives. 1805-1870.
 Robert G. Ives. 1836-1871.
 Caroline E. D. Weeden, his wife. 1839-1877.

Hon. William Henry Brouse, A.M., M.D., Senator. b. 15 June, 1824. d. 23 August, 1881

His wife, Fanny Amelia Brouse. d. Oct. 24, 1919, age 81 years.

(The Hon. Mr. Brouse was a descendant of one of the first U. E. Loyalists that settled on the banks of the St. Lawrence River. He was reeve and mayor of Prescott, and was first returned to Parliament for South Grenville at the general election, 1872; he was re-elected at the general election, 1874, and was called to the Senate, 1878. His wife was Frances A., eldest daughter of Alpheus Jones of Prescott.)

Alpheus Jones. b. 1794. d. 1863.

Also his wife, Mary L. Dickinson. b. 1817, d. 1882.

VII.

THE HISTORICAL POSITION OF THE SIX NATIONS.

By Asa R. Hill, Secretary, Six Nations Council.

The confederation of the Iroquois known in history as the Five Nations, comprising the Mohawk, Seneca, Onondaga, Oneida and Cayuga, after the admission of the Tuscarora in 1722, became known as the Six Nations. Their name for themselves as a political body was Ongwanonsionni, 'we are of the extended lodge.' The date of the formation of this confederation (probably not the first, but the last of a series of attempts to unite the several tribes in a federal union) was not earlier than about the year 1570, occasioned by wars with Algonquian and Huron tribes.

The confederacy of the Iroquoian tribes, when first known to Europeans, was composed of the Five Nations, and occupied the territory extending from the east watershed of Lake Champlain to the west watershed of Genesee River, and from the Adirondacks southward to the territory of the Conestoga. After the coming of the Dutch, from whom they procured firearms, the confederated Iroquois immediately began to make their united power felt; they were able to extend their conquests over all the neighboring tribes until their dominion was acknowledged from Ottawa River to the Tennessee, and from the Kennebec to Illinois River and Lake Michigan. Their westward advance was checked by the Chippewa; the Cherokee and the Catawba proved an effectual barrier in the south, while in the north they were hampered by the operation of the French in Canada. Champlain on one of his early expeditions joined a party of the Canadian Indians against the Iroquois. This made them bitter enemies of the French, whom they afterward opposed at every step to the close of the French regime in Canada in 1763, while they were firm allies of the English.

Of all American Indians, the Six Nations have best preserved their traditions. From the earliest European arrival they have occupied a peculiar historical position. Whatever uncertainty and doubt surrounds most North American Indians is removed from the Six Nations. Their system of government was so complete and unique and so well fitted to the people that from the earliest times they have been constantly written about. Their confederacy, tribal and individual characteristics, and personal strength of will, together with their great courage and prowess, account for their success in war and the methods which brought comfort in peace. Their friendship was cultivated and their alliance sought for by each European race with whom they came in contact. The story of their alliance with Great Britain is one that no matter how and when told can never lose its interest.

For two and a half centuries they have been steadfast in their alliance with the English. Historians and officers have been pleased to record that it was the power of their strong arms that saved Canada for the British Empire when another nation contested for the Dominion. The Six Nations are an old but diminished power, yet from the time of their earliest contact Great Britain has recognized their rights and sovereignty. She considered them as nations competent to maintain the relations of peace and war and govern themselves in their own way, with a distinct country of their own, with boundaries well defined. It was in 1664, for political reasons, the British entered into a treaty of close friendship and alliance, for the same reasons often renewed and still prevailing. It might well be pointed out that on September 24th, of that year, the first treaty of alliance was entered into between the English and the Five Nations and ratified. I will not give it in full, but it provided:

2. That if any English, Dutch or Indian (under the protection of the English) do any wrong, injury or violence to any of the said princes or their subjects in any sort whatever if they complain to the Governor at New York, or to the Officer in Chief at Albany, if the person so offending can be discovered, that person shall receive condign punishment and all due satisfaction shall be given, and like shall be done for all other English plantations.

3. That if any Indian belonging to any of the Sachims aforesaid do any wrong, injury or damage to the English, Dutch, or Indians under the protection of the English, if complaint be made to the Sachims and the person be discovered who did the injury, then the person so offending shall be punished and all just satisfaction shall be given to any of His Majesty's subjects in any colony or plantation in America.

There were other articles; the English agreed that "they would not assist the three nations of the Ondiakes, Pimakooks, and Petampekookes, who murdered one of the princes of the Maques when he brought ransoms and presents to them upon a Treaty of Peace. That the English do make peace for the Indian princes with the nations down the river. That they may have free trade as formerly. That if they be beaten by the nations above mentioned, they may receive accommodation (help) from the English."

In considering its terms, there are features which cannot fail to impress one, both parties being treated on terms of equality and perfect independence. There was a mutual recognition of sovereignty, each acknowledging the natural and primordial rights of the other party. Political status was on each side conceded. Each covenanted for the members of its own community. The power to govern, to punish, to be responsible for the actions of the individuals forming the respective governments, was assumed and acknowledged by each. It might be pointed out that to this day, the same people who made that treaty, still preserve the same traditions, assert the same rights of self government, proclaim themselves not subjects but still the faithful allies of the British crown.

Again in June 13th, 1717, at a conference in Albany, the terms of the alliance were clearly and definitely stated by Governor Hunter as follows :

"We are met at this place by order of the King of Great Britain, my master, In the same public and solemn manner, I here in his name and by his command renew the ancient covenants with the Five Nations, promising on his part that all the known conditions of the said covenant shall be duly and punctually observed, so long as you shall honestly and faithfully perform what has been in all times hitherto promised and performed on yours. And, to prevent all mistakes on this head, I must remind you of what has ever been meant and understood by you as well as us, by the covenant chain, that is that on the one hand the subjects of His Majesty, on this Continent, should not only refrain from all acts of hostility or anything tending that way towards you, but readily assist you when attacked by others, or enable you by such methods as were in their power to repel force by force, or defend yourselves, and on the other hand, you were on your part to live in the strictest friendship with all his Majesty's subjects, and in case they should be attacked by any enemy whatever, to afford them the readiest and most effective assistance in your power." (N.Y. Colonial Documents, Vol. 5, p. 484).

In 1728, Governor Montgomerie assured the Six Nations :
"You need fear no enemies while you are true to your alliance with him— the King. (N.Y. Col. Doc., 5, p. 861).

In 1739, the Lords of Trade address the Lords of the Privy Council:—
"We shall observe to your Lordships that these Six Nations . . . . . are the most powerful and warlike of the ancient Natives of that part of America, that they have always been faithful allies to the British settlements in those parts. We may add that these Six Nations are looked upon to be a great support of the British Empire in those parts. (N.Y. Col. Doc. 6, p. 157)

In 1744, Governor Clinton wrote the Duke of Newcastle:—
"I have had an interview with the Five Nations of Indians, and have renewed a Treaty of Peace and alliance with them." (N.Y. Col. Doc. 6, p. 259)

In 1748, the Governor of Canada wrote Governor Clinton:—
"That neither the Treaty of Utrecht, nor any other similar one can make the Iroquois subjects of Great Britain. They claim to be free, as they have declared an infinite number of times, and as their conduct and yours towards them proves, inasmuch as for one hundred and fifty years they have concluded peace and made war independent of you, and often in opposition to you, without your ever having attempted to force them to obey you. The Plenipotentiaries of Utrecht could not then legitimately subject them to you. The English are too well read in the law of Nations not to appreciate this truth. (N. Y. Col. Doc. 6. p. 496).

In 1749, Sir Wiliam Johnson wrote Governor Clinton:
"Your Excellency is Plenipotentiary with the Indians, who, though called subjects, are a foreign people, and are to be treated with as immediately from the King, by His Majesty's Governor." (N.Y. Col. Doc. 6, p. 541).

The nature of the Alliance between the Six Nations and the Crown, was the same as between the Crown and other Powers,—

Proceedings of Council, April 19th, 1757, "Brethren—let all nations of Indians know that the Great King of England, my master, is their friend; that he desires all nations of Indians may unite together, be as one body and one blood. He offers them his alliance and protection, which all Princes and peoples over the Great Lakes are proud and glad of." (N.Y. Col. Doc. 7, p. 248).

Sir William Johnson writes the Earl of Shelburne, September 22nd, 1767:

"They (the Six Nations) called themselves a free people who had independent lands, which were their ancient possessions, that the French by ceding Canada, according to the words of the Treaty, granted what was not in their power to give; their outposts and distant possessions being only held by them, not by conquest, but by favour; that if they admitted our rights to the posts we conquered, the country was still theirs, and in fact it is most certain that the French never spoke to them in any other style, as sensible of the consequences it might have with regard to their interests." (N.Y. Col. Doc. 7, p. 958.)

From time to time the terms of alliance were renewed but never varied in substance. In the year 1768, a line of demarcation was established between the lands of the Six Nations and the lands of the King and their full independence acknowledged by the Treaty of Fort Stanwix, on the 5th of November. The position of the Six Nations at this period of their history was regarded as a distinct political community, capable of making treaties or compacts to which the law of England did not extend. The relation of sovereign and subject did not exist. The Six Nations owed the King no allegiance, and in this regard he owed them no protection, but the protection that existed rested upon treaties and not allegiance. The relations, therefore, between the Six Nations and the British, from the earliest times, were determined by treaties, which in the true legal sense of the term could only be entered into by independent sovereignties.

The Crown never attempted to interfere with the national affairs of the Six Nations. They were treated as free and independent nations, governed by their own tribal laws and usages, under their own chiefs, and competent to act in a national and representative character, and exercise self-government; and while residing within their own territories owning no allegiance to the municipal laws of the whites. In order to justify this long established position of the Six Nations one need only turn to the light of the historical evidence for proof.

It is a fact that should not be forgotten by anyone considering the position of these people that neither the Province of New York in its colonial days, nor the Imperial Parliament of Great Britain, ever passed either Act of Assembly or Parliament, by which it was sought to regulate, govern or interfere with the affairs of the Six Nations, and that the first Act of Parliament which ever did so, was that passed by Canada in 1859. It was reserved by the then Governor-

General for Her Majesty's special consideration, and received the Royal assent only on the assurance of the Governor-General in his despatch transmitting a draft of the same to England that it made "no changes whatever in the rights of the Indian tribes."

The Royal Instructions for the management of Indian Affairs of July 10th, 1764, imposed no restraints on the Indians, but only on the whites, and provided the methods by which business with the Indian tribes was to be regulated. Strictly speaking, the original status, rights and privileges of the Six Nations have never been abolished nor abandoned but are retained by them at the present time and historically differentiate them from all other Indians of Canada.

When rebellion broke out in America, the King called on his allies for assistance, and promised, if given, he would "protect them and preserve them in all their rights." Lord Dartmouth on July 5th, 1775, wrote Colonel Guy Johnson, who had succeeded as Superintendent of the Six Nations after the death of the great Sir William Johnson,—

"The present state of affairs in His Majesty's Colonies in which an unnatural rebellion has broken out, that threatens to overturn the Constitution, precludes all immediate consideration in the domestic concerns of the Indians under your protection; nor is it to be expected that any measure which the King may think fit to take, for redressing the injuries they complain of respecting their lands, can, in the present moment, be attended with any effect. It will be proper, however, that you should assure them, in the strongest terms, of His Majesty's firm resolution to protect them and preserve them in all their rights; and it is more than ever necessary that you should exert the utmost vigilance to discover, whether any artifices are used to engage them in the support of the rebellious proceedings of His Majesty's subjects, to counteract such treachery, and to keep them in such a state of affection and attachment to the King, as that His Majesty may rely on their assistance in any case in which it may be necessary to require it." (N.Y. Col. Doc. 8, p. 592.)

On the 24th July, 1775, Dartmouth again wrote Guy Johnston as follows:—

"I have already in my letter to you of the 5th instant hinted that the time might possibly come when the King, relying upon the attachment of his faithful allies, the Six Nations of Indians, might be under the necessity of calling upon them for their aid and assistance in the present state of America. The unnatural rebellion now raging there calls for every effort to suppress it, and the intelligence His Majesty has received of the rebels having excited the Indians to take a part, and of their having actually engaged a body of them in arms to support their rebellion, justifies the resolution His Majesty has taken of requiring the assistance of his faithful adherents, the Six Nations. It is, therefore, His Majesty's pleasure, that you do lose no time in taking such steps as may induce them to take up the hatchet against His Majesty's rebellious subjects in America and to engage them in His Majesty's service." (N.Y. Col. Doc. 8, p. 596.)

The bulk of the Six Nations took sides with the English, but, before joining their forces with the British troops, officers of the British Crown promised them in the name of the King that the Six Nations should not lose anything even should the American colonies win the impending war; and the chiefs of the Six Nations placed implicit faith in these promises.

But when Great Britain had lost the war and the Crown's ministers had "forgotten" their loyal allies of the Six Nations in the terms of the treaty of peace with the American Government the chiefs of the Six Nations in the language of one of them, "were struck with astonishment at hearing we were forgot in the treaty." (Brant). In the treaty of November, 1783, ending the war of the American Revolution, Great Britain made no stipulation in behalf of her Indian allies, notwithstanding "their constancy, their valour," the readiness with which they had spilt their blood, and the distinguished services" of Captain Brant; the loyal Six Nations were not even mentioned in the terms of the treaty, although the ancient country of the Six Nations was included within the boundary surrendered to the American Government. This Royal ingratitude was the more marked because when the Mohawks first abandoned their valley to embark in the cause of Great Britain, Sir Guy Carleton had given a pledge that as soon as the war ended, their country, if lost or devastated, would be fully restored at the expense of the Crown. This pledge was confirmed in 1779 by Governor Haldimand, the Captain-General and Commander-in-Chief in Canada, pledging himself "under hand and seal, as far as in him lay, to its faithful execution."

The loyal Captain Brant could not believe that the King's ministers had made these promises and pledges of reparation and indemnification in case of loss to be broken at will, and so he tirelessly set about having them fulfilled as amply as possible. He made three visits to Governor Haldimand in Quebec before he was satisfied that he had formally secured in fee suitable lands through a formal grant by Sir Frederick Haldimand, in the name of the Crown, of a tract of land upon the banks of the river Ouse, commonly called Grand River, running into Lake Erie, of six miles breadth from each side of the river, beginning at Lake Erie, and extending in that proportion to the head of the river; which the Mohawks and others of the Six Nations who had either lost their possessions in the war, or wished to retire from them to the British, with their posterity, were to enjoy for ever. Of this tract John Norton's Memorial to Lord Camden says: "this tract, though much smaller than that which they had been obliged to forsake within the United States, amply satisfied these loyal Indians, who preferred living under the protection of His Britannic Majesty, (ready to fight under his standard again, if occasion should require) to a more extensive country."

The claim of the Mohawks and their allies, the Six Nations, for indemnification for losses sustained by them "from depredations committed on their lands by the Americans during the late war" was answered by Lord Sydney, His Majesty's Secretary for the Colonial Department, in a communication dated at Whitehall, 6th April, 1786, as follows:

"The King has had under his royal consideration the two letters which you delivered to me on the 4th of January last, - - - - the first of them representing the claims of the Mohawks for losses sustained by them and other tribes of Indians, from the depredations committed on their lands by the Americans during the late war. - - - - Were the right of individuals to compensation for losses sustained by the depredations of an enemy to be admitted, no country, however opulent it might be, could support itself under such a burden (burthen), especially when the contest happens to have taken an unfavourable turn. His Majesty, upon this ground, conceives that, consistently with every principle of justice, he might withhold his royal concurrence to the liquidation of these demands; but His Majesty, in consideration of the zealous and hearty exertions of his Indian allies in the support of his cause, - - - - has been graciously pleased to consent that the losses already certified by his Superintendent-General shall be made good; that a favourable attention shall be shown to the claims of others who have pursued the same system of conduct."

It is thus seen that the lands now held by the Six Nations on Grand River were granted primarily as a partial compensation for actual losses of lands and other property. It, moreover, appears that the King regarded the Six Nations as his allies, as the language of Lord Sydney to Captain Brant, quoted above, clearly shows. The language is diplomatic, but neither the occasion nor the effect of these communications need be enlarged upon.

The question of the relations of the Six Nations to the Crown, since their settlement on the Grand River in 1784, has proved that the sons of their fathers, the warriors whose ancestors promised never to forsake the old alliance with the British King, have never forgotten the force of the obligation, but have been ever foremost in asserting it.

Time and time again as opportunity, force of circumstances, emergency, or what you may call it, arose, the Six Nations always spontaneously, arose to the occasion. In 1812, on many a bloody field, at Queenston Heights, where fell the gallant Brock, at Lundy's Lane, at Chrystler's Farm and Chateauguay, yes, and Chippawa Creek, and how many others I cannot tell, there, lined up with the Red coats, we find their red brethren ever eager and in the forefront of the fray.

In the late great war, in the awful scenes on Flanders fields, the Six Nations showed their interest. They gave themselves as they had done before for the cause, they gave their money, they contributed to Patriotic Funds.

The Six Nations claim the exercise of their ancient right of self-government, and allege the faith and honour of the Crown is pledged for this object.

VIII.

THE DIARY OF BENJAMIN LUNDY WRITTEN DURING HIS JOURNEY THROUGH UPPER CANADA JANUARY, 1832.

Edited with notes and an introduction
BY FRED LANDON, M.A., PUBLIC LIBRARIAN, LONDON.

The diary of Benjamin Lundy on his trip through the western part of Upper Canada in January, 1832, was written down with a definite purpose, namely, that of presenting to the colored people of the United States a statement of the conditions of life in the British provinces that might guide them in seeking a home where their freedom would not be threatened and where their children might grow up without the shadow of possible slavery hanging over them. Though Lundy's trip was made in the winter season his observations with regard to timber, character of the soil and the general possibilities of the country along agricultural lines are remarkably accurate, and incidentally he throws some interesting sidelights on the social life and manners of the day.

Benjamin Lundy, one of the pioneer abolitionists in the United States, was born at Hardwick, Sussex county, N. J., in 1789, his parents being members of the Society of Friends. When nineteen years old he removed to Wheeling, Va., where his attention was first drawn to the evils of slavery. He subsequently settled in St. Clairsville, Va., where in 1815 he founded an anti-slavery society known as "The Union Humanitarian Society." The first meeting was held at his home and consisted of six persons. In a few months it had grown to nearly five hundred persons, including some of the most eminent people in the state. In 1816, he issued a small circular signed "Philo Justicia," in which were set forth his ideas with regard to a campaign against slavery. Greeley, in his "American Conflict," speaks of this little circular as "containing the germ of the entire anti-slavery movement."

The first number of his paper, "The Genius of Universal Emancipation," appeared in January, 1821, and was printed at Mount Pleasant, Ohio. The next seven numbers were printed at Steubenville, Ohio, Lundy going to and fro on foot carrying his printed papers on his back. In a few months the subscription list was quite large and Lundy decided to use a press at Jonesborough, Tenn.

There, for the first time, he undertook the printer's art and did the mechanical, as well as the editorial work. Three years later, in 1824, his paper having obtained a considerable circulation and being the only anti-slavery paper published in the country, he decided to transfer its publication to one of the Atlantic states and settled on Baltimore. The first number was issued at Baltimore in October, 1824, being No. 1 of Vol. 4. Until 1825 it had been a monthly, but was then changed to a weekly and continued to be published at Baltimore until 1830. From that date until 1834 Washington was the nominal place of publication, it being a monthly again, but as a matter of fact it was printed and published wherever Lundy happened to be. He would write out his copy, set it up himself in some printing shop, buy paper and print it, and then send it through the mails to the subscribers. The issues from which the diary in Canada are taken show Washington and Baltimore as the place of publication but may have been printed, and were probably printed, elsewhere in the United States. After 1834 Philadelphia became the place of publication until 1836, when the last issue appeared.

Files of this curious paper are exceedingly rare. The New York Public Library has it complete for several years and less complete for other years. The Library of Congress has but a few odd numbers. It is possible that there may be partial sets in other large libraries of the United States.

Lundy died at Lowell, La Salle county, Illinois, on August 22nd, 1839, and was buried on the banks of Clear Creek, Putnam county, Ill., where his grave may be seen to-day with this simple inscription :

"Benjamin Lundy,
Died August 22, 1839,
Age, 50 years, 7 months, 18 days."

Von Holst, the historian, says of Lundy that he was "the immediate precursor, and in a certain sense the founder of abolitionism," and adds the tribute "that the nineteenth century can scarcely point to another instance in which the commandment of Christ to 'leave all things and follow Him' was so literally fulfilled."

John G. Whittier, in a letter dated Amesbury, Mass., March, 1874, said of Lundy : "Nor is that pioneer of freedom, Benjamin Lundy, to be forgotten. It was his lot to struggle for years almost alone, a solitary voice crying in the wilderness; poor, unaided, yet never despairing, traversing the island of Haiti, wasting with disease in New Orleans, hunted by Texan banditti, wandering on foot among the mountains of East Tennessee and along the Ozark Hills, beaten down and trampled on by Baltimore slave dealers; yet amidst all, faithful to his one great purpose, the emancipation of the slaves and the protection of the free people of color. To him we owe under Providence the enlistment of William Lloyd Garrison in the service which he has so nobly performed."

One further tribute might be recorded, that of Garrison himself, who writing in March, 1874, said : "I trust that the memory and labors of Benjamin Lundy will be especially remembered and honored at this reunion gathering. To him I owe my connection with the cause of emancipation, as he was the first to call my attention to it, and by his pressing invitation to me to join him at printing and editing the "Genius of Universal Emancipation" at Baltimore, he shaped my destiny for the remainder of my life."

First Section, published in "The Genius of Universal Emancipation" for March, 1832.

WILBERFORCE SETTLEMENT.

The editor of The Genius of Universal Emancipation recently visited this interesting settlement of colored people, in the province of Upper Canada. The sole object in doing so was to obtain correct information respecting the situation, climate, soil, the present prospects of the settlers, etc., etc., with the view of publishing an accurate statement thereof, as extensively as possible, for the benefit of that oppressed and persecuted race in the United States. A very minute journal was kept in passing through the province, from Queenston, via the head of Lake Ontario and the aforesaid settlement to Detroit, in order to bear in mind whatever might be observed, worthy of a place in the account thus to be published. This journal will shortly be inserted at length in the Genius of Universal Emancipation. At present our views must be confined to the state of things connected with the actual condition and prospects of the Wilberforce Settlement.

We have heretofore noticed sundry statements, which originated in other papers, relative to the progress of this colony of colored exiles, who have thus sought a refuge from the demon-spirit of persecution in these States, as did the pilgrim fathers of American Colonization, when a similar spirit raged and trampled down the sacred rights of man in the rotten empires of Europe. But much that we were enabled to gather in that way was uncertain and contradictory; of course, little dependence could be placed upon it. We can now vouch for the correctness of what we lay before our readers.

The Wilberforce Settlement[1] is situated on the river Au Sable, in the District of London, Upper Canada. It commences twelve miles from the village of London (London Court House) and extends north-westerly along the road leading to Goderich on Lake Huron, upward of four miles. The last mentioned place is

---
[1] For an account of the Wilberforce Refugee Settlement, see Landon, History of the Wilberforce Refugee Colony in Middlesex County, Transactions of the London and Middlesex Historical Society, part IX, 1918.

about twenty-five or thirty miles from the Au Sable where the road crosses it, north of which the colored people have made but one opening. The distance from York, U.C., to the settlement, by way of London, is 148 miles—from Queenston, or Niagara Falls, by the head of Lake Ontario, and London, about the same distance—from Buffalo (proceeding up Lake Erie to Port Talbot, at the mouth of Kettle Creek) perhaps little more than 100 miles, 37 miles only of which is travelled by land—from Sandwich, opposite Detroit, by London, 123 miles.

No place perhaps in the northern or north-western part of America presents a stronger and richer soil, or a country more beautifully situated for agricultural pursuits than this. It is covered with a heavy growth of timber, consisting of oak, hickory, sugar maple, beech, ash, poplar, bass, etc., etc., with some cherry and walnut; and along the streams may be seen a portion of elm and sycamore. The land, in general, is gently rolling, though very much diversified. Along the streams it is considerably uneven; yet there are no hills of magnitude; and between the water-courses in some places it is quite level. There are some fine springs and the water is clear and excellent. The soil appears generally to be a dark loam, intermixed with more or less clay and gravel; but there is very little sand; and the whole is deeply clothed with a black vegetable mould, which renders it extremely fertile. All kinds of grain, etc., produced north of the Carolinas succeed well here. The ground is entirely clear of stone on the surface, but there are quarries (mostly of limestone) in the elevations, particularly along the streams.

Markets for the produce of this part of the country will be convenient, as it is but a short distance either to Lake Erie, on the south, or Lake Huron, on the north—and the navigable waters of The Thames approach within a few miles of London, the seat of government for the district of the same name. Manufacturing may also be extensively carried on, the various streams with which the country abounds affording excellent facilities for the application of water power.

On a reference to the map it will be perceived that the Wilberforce Settlement is very nearly in the same latitude with Albany, in the State of New York. But the climate is much more mild than at that place, as there are no mountainous elevations to increase the rigors of winter as there are about the middle of New York and Pennsylvania. An account of the state of the weather was kept at Wilberforce, through the month of December, which is annexed to this article; and it will be seen that the severity of the cold was not greater than it is frequently known to be much farther to the south. At no time during the present winter has the snow fallen as deep in this part of Canada as it has south of Lake Erie; and it has been observed by old settlers that it seldom or never does.

It will be recollected that the Wilberforce Settlement was commenced by a few colored persons from Cincinnati, Ohio, who were induced to seek an asylum there from the storm of persecution that appeared to be gathering in that section of country and directing its force towards them.² The business was badly managed at first. The persons who acted as agents contracted for more land than they could pay for according to agreement. A new bargain was then made, and another failure to comply with the terms succeeded. Confidence in their ability to prosecute the business successfully was impaired. At length, a smaller quantity of land has been secured to the company and individuals have made purchases on their own account. A number of very respectable and intelligent men have taken up their residence there. Some of these are in good easy circumstances—a few even wealthy—and it is believed that everything will go on well hereafter.

The members of the Settlement have entered into an Association for mutual assistance, etc. They have appointed a Board of Managers, of which Austin Steward,³ formerly of Rochester, New York, is the President. The Rev. Benjamin Paul, late of New York City, is their treasurer; and the funds that may be collected in the way of donation, etc., will be applied to the purchase of land, and necessaries, for the settlement and comfort of those who may be induced by persecution, etc., to remove thither from the United States while destitute of the means to support themselves or their families. An agent has been commissioned to proceed to England with the view of interesting the British Government and people in the promotion of the desired object; and the friends of the maltreated African descendants may now look for the accomplishment of something there worthy of an intelligent people and the high importance of the occasion. Full confidence may be placed in those at present selected to manage the public concerns of the settlement; and the true friends of the oppressed could scarcely render a more acceptable service to the cause of philanthropy than by assisting, with pecuniary and other means, the persecuted colored man in obtaining a residence there. Under the liberal provisions of the government regulations, as now interpreted and administered, *all are free and equal.* Every citizen, without distinction of color or caste, is entitled to all the privileges and immunities that the most favoured individual can claim. And there is no danger of an alteration in this state of things while the European influence exists in the councils of the province as it now does and will, doubtless, continue to do.

There are, at this time, thirty-two families residing in the settlement, which average about five individuals to each. (It is stated by the settlers that upwards

---

² To the diary as it appears in The Genius of Universal Emancipation the following qualifying note is inserted at this point:

"In justice to the great mass of the citizens of Ohio it must be stated that, notwithstanding the political and moral fanaticism of a few misguided and highly prejudiced creatures, who had found their way into offices of "brief authority," altho they made as much noise (a momentary noise) as the thundering artillery of the heathen Jove; and while a few of their intended victims of their terrible wrath were frightened into exile, not one has been actually forced to go out of the state. Whatever their representations may hereafter do to prevent others coming in from the south there is too much humanity in the citizens generally to drive out, against his will, a single well-behaved colored man who is now there. The slavite 'fanatics,' it is hoped comprise a lean minority in the great States of Ohio."

³ Austin Steward's rather unhappy experiences in the Wilberforce Settlement are recorded in his book "Twenty Years a Slave and Forty Years a Freeman." (Rochester, 1857.)

of 2,000 persons have visited and intended to establish themselves at that place, most of whom were necessitated to go to other parts of the province where they could obtain employment, not being able to support themselves while they could clear the land, plant, etc.). Four or five of the families now there arrived about twenty months since—the rest at later periods, and some few of them quite recently. Twenty-five families have purchased land and the most of them have erected tolerably comfortable houses and cleared a few acres of ground. They have purchased nearly 2,000 acres in the whole, 200 of which are cleared and about 60 sown with wheat. The settlers have cut a wide road through seven miles and a quarter of very thickly and heavily timbered land for the Canada Company[4] —the price for which was placed to their credit in the purchase of their several lots. It should also be remarked that in clearing they leave no trees deadened and standing, as it is customary with many in new settlements; but cut all off, though the labor is great. They have about 100 head of cattle and swine, and a few horses. Oxen are mostly used with them for hauling, ploughing, etc. They have a good substantial sawmill erected on a branch of the Au Sable, within the precincts of their settlement, and, of course, they will hence have no difficulty in procuring lumber for building. (Their dwellings are as yet constructed of logs—some of them hewed and a few have well-shingled roofs.) There are one grist mill and two other sawmills within eight or nine miles of the settlement and one grist mill is partly built within five or six miles of them. Several small stores are located also near by; and a tailor, shoemaker and blacksmith reside among them. They have two good schools for the education of their children, one of which is under the charge of Thomas J. Paul, son of the Rev. B. Paul, a youth of fine promise. Such are the excellent regulations, and so high is the reputation of this school that a number of respectable white people send their children to it in preference to others that are conducted by white teachers. In the summer season a daughter of the same gentleman, a quite accomplished and amiable young woman, also teaches a school for girls. A Sabbath School is likewise kept up in the warm season, under the direction of Austin Steward. Two regular meetings for religious worship are established among them, for the Baptist and the Methodist denominations. A Temperance Society has also been organized, the members of which have pledged themselves to exert their influence in discouraging both the vending and use of all kinds of ardent spirits. The settlers generally are sober, industrious and thrifty. In their houses things mostly appear clean, neat and comfortable.

Between the village of London and this settlement the country is pretty thickly inhabited;[5] and within a few miles to the southwest of it there are a considerable number of white people, mostly Europeans and their immediate descendants born in Canada. Emigrants from the United States are beginning to settle about London and to the south of that place. Twenty-five or thirty miles to the north-west, and about the same distance to the north-east, there are likewise

---

[4] The Canada Company was founded in London, Eng., in 1824, by John Galt as a colonizing scheme. A large tract of land was purchased in what is now Western Ontario, and large numbers of settlers were brought in.

[5] What is now the township of London, in Middlesex County.

settlements, most of those composing which are said to be English, Irish, Scotch, Welsh, etc. These Europeans are, in general, very friendly to the colored people. While the "Yankees", (as they denominate all emigrants from these States) are still actuated by their abominable prejudice against the colored race, the Irish, etc., are often heard to say they prefer the people of color as neighbors and citizens to them. The natives, or Canadians (born in the country) appear likewise quite as friendly to the colored population as to the "Yankees". It is believed these observations will also very generally hold good throughout the Canadas.

The Canada Company, from which the settlers at Wilberforce have purchased their land, is about to make a good road through the whole distance from London to Lake Huron. It is now in part finished to this settlement; and a great number of laborers will find employment there the ensuing summer. Some of the settlers will also want assistance in improving their lands; and good, industrious working colored men may do well by proceeding thither early next spring, if they have only the means of getting there. Some apprehension is felt that the price of land will be raised when the aforesaid road shall be completed; but even should this be the case emigrants will, no doubt, be able to procure enough on favorable terms, near by, if prepared to make prompt payment. Many poor white settlers, in the neighborhood of Willberforce, offer to sell their improvements, upon reasonable terms, in order to go further towards the frontier where they may get more land; and colored persons, who are somewhat forehanded, will find it very advantageous to purchase these improvements. They may be had at from $2.50 to $5.00 per acre including buildings, etc. Unimproved land has heretofore sold at $1.50 per acre.

We learn that there are several other settlements of colored people in various parts of Upper Canada, among which may be enumerated the following: one at Lake Simcoe, in the north-eastern part of the Province; one at Woolwich, on or near Grand River, north of Brantford and thirty or forty miles from the head of Lake Ontario; one at Chatham Creek, near the River Thames, about 65 miles below London, and 55 or 60 above Sandwich, opposite Detroit, and another near Malden, 18 miles south of Sandwich, a little distance from the mouth of Detroit River and opposite Brownstown, at the mouth of Huron River. This last is said to be composed of three or four hundred persons; and there is a ferry from Brownstown to Malden, where many of the emigrants cross when the river is not obstructed by ice.

But the settlement at Wilberforce will be, by far, the most important, as there are men of known intelligence and public spirit there who will give it a consequence that probably will not, at least very soon, be attached to the others. It will indeed, be viewed by the colored people as a nucleus for an extensive emigration from the northern and middle parts of the union especially from Virginia and several contiguous states. Many will go there and obtain information there that will induce them to settle in other places when the price of land shall rise and more new settlements be opened. They will thus scatter over the province, some one way and some another; but many will stop here, as at a central point, which first shall have attracted their attention, and where they will find intelligent friends and brethren.*

Through the early part of January, 1832, the mercury ranged at about one degree below freezing point, with the wind south-west for a number of days. About the middle of the month the weather was mild and it thawed considerably.

Second Section, Published in the "Genius Of Universal Emancipation" for April, 1832.

TOUR IN UPPER CANADA

In the last number of the Genius of Universal Emancipation we inserted a statement of the proceedings of the colored emigrants at the Wilberforce settlement, in the province of Upper Canada. The writer, having travelled through that province from Queenston to Detroit, and made many inquiries and observations, thinks it advisable to publish the result thereof, for the information of such as are now turning their eyes towards that region as a place of refuge for the persecuted colored people of these States. As the tour was performed in the winter, however, there was no opportunity to judge of the quality of the soil (except in a few instances) but by the timber, shrubbery, etc., which could be seen above the snow. To supply the deficiency in personal observation, minute inquiry

---

* The following table, exhibiting the state of the weather at Wilberforce, from the 3rd to the 25th of December last (the coldest part of the season) was politely furnished by Austin Steward, one, among the few of the most intelligent and worthy colored men in America. The thermometer was placed the whole time in the open air:—
State of the Weather at Wilberforce, U. C., December 3-25, 1831.

Date.	Below Freezing.	Below Zero.	Wind.
3	12		Southerly
4	30		"
5		2	"
6		22	"
7	14		S.W.
8	15		"
9	20		"
10	22		"
11	16		South
12	18		S. W.
13	15		North
14	16		South
15	19		West
16	20		South
17	26		West
18	27		South
19	26		West
20	10		South
21	20		North
22	20		East
23	6		South
24	10		"
25	6		"

was very frequently made and it is believed that this together with a pretty general knowledge of the various growth that may be expected on light or heavy soils, has furnished the means of forming correct opinions, and drawing tolerably accurate conclusions upon the particular point here adverted to. As much brevity has been used in the narration as would be consistent with a clear view of matters and things connected with the purpose of the tour; though upon some occasions the reader may, at first, think that more prolixity has been indulged in than was absolutely necessary.

The notes of this tour commenced at Queenston, where the author arrived at the date first mentioned therein. We insert them as follows:

Queenston, U. C., January, 13th, 1832.

Having taken lodgings at Lewiston, N. Y., last evening I crossed the river to Queenston immediately after breakfast this morning. The weather had been severely cold for several weeks past and much ice was collected on the margin of the river. We had some difficulty in getting into the ferry boat but at length found ourselves safe on the Canada shore. I had scarcely put my trunk down at the stage office door when a man of quite an ordinary appearance stepped up to it and giving it a jerk on one side abruptly said in a tone of authority, "Open that". I understood him—he was the Customs House officer— and it was his business to see that travellers do not smuggle goods into the province under the appellation of "baggage" to defraud the revenue. Although I had nothing to sell except a few incomplete volumes or files of my periodical work, this expounder of the revenue laws (he was a deputy) exacted about seven dollars for duties and fees on a few books and pamphlets with a little writing paper. I was afterwards told that the demand was illegal; but I had not then leisure to contest it.

It is known, to the intelligent reader, that Queenston is situated on the west bank of the Niagara River, about seven miles below the celebrated falls, at the foot of what is called "the mountain" which extends from the head of Lake Ontario, in Upper Canada, far east and parallel with the southern shore of the said lake. This "mountain" is nothing more than the old bank or margin of the lake; and there can be no doubt that the great falls were once at the verge of this elevation, near the place where the village of Queenston now stands. In process of time, however, the water has cut away the earth and rock for the space of seven miles and it is still progressing—slowly but steadily—towards the outlet of Lake Erie. The village of Queenston is tolerably well situated, and appears to be in a rather improving condition. There are a number of mercantile stores, some mechanics' shops and taverns, and a few public buildings; but there does not seem to be any very extensive business carried on there. Some of the buildings are of brick and stone, but a large proportion consist of wood. Before taking leave of the place it should be mentioned that the heights, back of Queenston, were the scene of an engagement between the United States and British armies, in the time of the last war; and that it was here the celebrated General Brock lost his life. His monument is erected near the spot where he fell, in a very conspicuous position, from the top of which there is a grand view of the upper part of Lake Ontario and the circumjacent country for a great distance around.

About the middle of the day I got all things arranged and took the stage for Hamilton. There being a sufficiency of snow the stage-box was placed on runners and we travelled on finely. The weather was moderate and being desirous to note every thing of importance as we passed along, I took a stand with the driver, on the front of the vehicle.

Proceeding along, near the foot of the "mountain," in a westerly direction, we have, on our right hand, a beautiful level and exceedingly fertile country, partly clothed with a thick forest and partly chequered with fine farms, and on our left a stupendous ridge, of almost 300 feet perpendicular height, faced, in places, with a wall of limestone rock, on the summit of which straggling pines, scrubby oaks and dwarf cedars occasionally appear. (The traveller who has crossed the "American Bottom" above Kaskaskia, in Illinois, has seen a good sample of this ridge, in the old bank of the Mississippi.) About three miles from Queenston is situated the little village of St. David's. There are a few neat houses here but not much business seems to be doing. Five miles further on we come to Ten Mile Creek. Here are a few scattering houses giving the place the appearance of a village. It is, however, of little consequence. From thence the distance is three miles to St. Catharines where something more like business appears to be going on. We see nothing there, however, worthy of particular notice. The next place of note is Hamilton, situated near the head of Lake Ontario and 48 miles west of Queenston. We arrived here about half past eight o'clock in the evening and took lodgings at a tolerably passable tavern, which is kept as a stage house.

The country through which we passed to-day exhibited a sameness of appearance the whole distance. The fine and level alluvion, on our right, alternately presented heavy dense forests and numerous fields and improvements. The whole is clear of stone, as I was told, on the surface. The timber on this tract consists of oak, hickory, sugar maple, beech, ash, elm, bass, etc., etc., indicating a strong, rich soil. The appearance of the inhabitants, their style of building, improving farms and general mode of living is much like what we meet with in the western parts of New York. A large proportion of them have, indeed, emigrated from the United States. Some English, Scotch and Irish are to be found among them. The white emigrants from the United States are all termed "Yankees." The productions of the soil are about the same here as in New York, New Jersey, Pennsylvania, etc. The country being thickly settled game is scarce. Fish are plenty in the lakes and streams. The water is pure and wholesome. Land sells too high in this section for the poorer class of emigrants. The wealthy may find advantageous locations for the investment of capital.

January 14th.

At daylight this morning I took a walk out to visit the town. Hamilton is, truly, a beautifully situated village. It is laid off on a kind of secondary elevation, a short distance from the foot of the "mountain," so often before alluded to. The plat of the town is delightful. There are some handsome buildings in the place, though not many for public uses. They have a neat Court House and

Jail, several pretty good inns, about a dozen mercantile stores, a fair proportion of mechanics' shops, etc., etc. Two weekly newspapers are also issued. My stay was short and I did not learn what encouragement is given to the arts and sciences; what attention paid to the education of youth; or what regulations exist relative to the duties of religion. The stage roads from Queenston and York to Detroit here come together. The place is about equidistant from the two first mentioned. The stage runs daily in the summer and tri-weekly in the winter, as far west as Brantford, and the mail is carried through to Detroit three times a week. The country around here is said to be thickly settled and many of the inhabitants wealthy. Situated near the lake the advantages of commerce are great; and both town and country must improve.

Between 8 and 9 o'clock in the morning our stage driver notified the passengers that he was "ready to go." All of them huddled into the comfortable enclosure but myself. I again took a standing place with our Jehu, from whence I could "see what was to be seen" as we traversed the "King's dominions." We now take the road towards Detroit, bearing a little more to the south of west than before. The weather is tolerably good for the season. The snow is not as deep as to the eastward. We soon find ourselves rising the "mountain," and here we leave the beautiful alluvial country bordering the lake. The road is good, up the hill, though the ascent is steep. The view of Burlington Bay and the head of Lake Ontario, together with the vast extent of country adjacent as we rise this proud eminence is grand and sublime. On reaching the top of the hill we have before us a different kind of a country from that we have just left. We have no "mountain" to descend but are presented with fine level and beautifully rolling land, though the soil is, evidently, of a lighter cast. There is a good deal of pine timber, mingled with the oak, etc. Proceeding about seven miles we come to the village of Ancaster. In future time it will probably be more noted for classical reference than anything else—some little matter having occured here during the late war that history recognizes.[7] It is an insignificant place and little note was taken of it. The land about here is somewhat hilly, and lightly timbered—soil rather inferior, no doubt. We now pass through a country considerably diversified as relates to soil and settlement. In some places the pine timber is very plenty; in others the general varieties of oak, etc., etc., prevail. Some particular sections are well watered and fertile and some are sandy and barren. There are numerous fine farms on the road.

After a few hours ride we come to the thriving village of Brantford. This place is situated 25 miles west of Hamilton. It takes its name from Brant's Ford, across Grand River, immediately in the neighborhood of the town. Here is a large settlement of the Mohawk Indians. They are quite a civilized people. They have a village, about two miles to the east of this place where there is a meeting for worship at which an Episcopal clergyman regularly officiates. It is called the "Mohawk Parsonage." This place is the residence of the celebrated Brant family, one of whom was, a short time since, returned as a member of the Pro-

---

[7] It was at Ancaster, on Oct. 17, 1813 that General Procter mustered all that had escaped from the fight at Moraviantown, numbering, all told, 246 officers and men.

vincial Parliament. It appeared, however, that a few illegal votes were given for him, and his seat was denied him. But I heard several white persons remark that if he offers again as a candidate he will, no doubt, be fairly elected. He is a full-blooded Indian, well-educated, and, as the white people say, "very much of the gentleman." Until now I saw very few of the African race in Canada. A considerable number of them reside in Brantford, there appears to be a good deal also of mixture of American, European and African blood (but especially the two first) in this section of country. As the stage would not leave Brantford before the morning of the 16th, and being myself a little unwell, I was detained at a public house. The accommodation was good.

January 15th.

This being the first day of the week, the places of business are closed and all is still and quiet. On our arrival yesterday many Indians were in town and a few of them stayed about the taverns pretty late in the evening. Some of them, as well as the blacks and whites, drank quite freely; and I heard this morning that a fracas occurred in our landlord's bar-room among the heterogenous assemblage there. Having retired early I knew nothing of it. The blame was thrown upon the "negroes" by the bar-keeper, who was a "Yankee" of "high pressure" prejudice, but it did not amount to much; and to-day very few Indians or blacks are to be seen in the public places.

By the way, it may not be amiss to observe that the white emigrants from the United States retain all the prejudices here that they formerly held against the colored people in their native country. And the latter, being admitted to equal privileges with them under this government, are accused of being "saucy." Perhaps there is some ground for the charge, for when we reflect that the colored people are now released from the shackles of degradation, and yet, frequently provoked by the taunts and gibes and supercilious treatment of the "Yankees" we need not wonder at their indulging their resentment, sometimes too far and even behaving with impropriety. But when the whites themselves clear their skirts of the guilt of being "saucy" in their deportment towards the blacks I apprehend that we shall hear little more of this kind of complaint. Indeed, if our good Republicans choose to leave their "free" government where they can tyrannize over the colored man with impunity and take up their abode among Monarchists, where all are "free and equal" they would act wisely to assume fewer airs, and submit cheerfully, like good "liege subjects" to the regulations adopted by the government of their choice.

The village of Brantford is quite a neat and stirring little place. It has an Episcopal church and one or more schools. It is situated on the bank of the river, which is here a stream of some importance though not navigable for large vessels. There is a handsome bridge erected over it, opposite the town. A grist-mill, running four pair of stones, is located within its limits and several saw-mills are in operation nearby. There are about a dozen mercantile stores (several of which, however, are very small), a considerable number of mechanics' shops that make a good appearance and two pretty good taverns in the village. They talk of cutting a canal from this place to intersect the Welland Canal between Lakes Erie and Ontario. The *tout ensemble* of the country around is handsome, but from the appearance of the timber, etc., I am inclined to think the soil on the uplands is very light. The river bottoms are, no doubt, more fertile. The settlements on either side of the road, for some distance, are extensive and quite dense. The inhabitants, beyond the Indian reservation, are a mixture of Europeans and Americans. A settlement of colored people is located a few miles to the north of this place, which goes by the name of Woolwich. There is said to be a considerable number of emigrants from the United States there and they are represented as doing well.

January 16th.

The stage set out pretty early this morning for London C.H.[8] in the direction of Detroit. The weather had been mild for a day or so but was now cold and frosty. The snow was so light that the sleighing was very poor. We crossed the river on the bridge before mentioned and went some distance up along its western bank. Then, rising the hill, we took leave of it and entered a level, thinly-timbered tract of country through which we passed several miles without meeting with a single house. The timber here consists solely of scrub oak. Scarcely a bush of any other kind is to be seen, and the land is probably a good deal sterile. The high lands, near the river on either side, exhibit a rather dwarfish growth of timber, of various species. Very little pine is met with in its vicinity. Oak, hickory, etc., predominate. There is also some hazel to be seen in places. Although the general appearance is unfavorable to the idea of a fertile country, I was told that the land, for the most part, produces well. I noticed some stacks of very fine timothy hay, by the road side, and the corn stalks were large in some of the fields that we passed by. About five or six miles west of Brantford the land is evidently of a better quality. It becomes more rolling, better watered and the timber is diversified. A little white pine is mixed with it. Proceeding fifteen or twenty miles further still we entered a very rich tract of country, and I learn that it extends a considerable distance in every direction. Oak, hickory, beech, ash, sugar tree, bass, elm, etc., etc., are the prevailing kinds of timber. There is a little poplar, walnut, and cherry, and also some elder and sumach (but no pine) in this particular section. The land lies exceedingly well, and the soil is unquestionably strong. The society of Friends have a settlement at a place called Norwich, a little to the south of our road and about twenty-five miles from Brantford. The country through which we now pass is newly and thinly settled, and the roads are bad.

At a distance of 30 miles from the last mentioned place we come to a tavern and stage house.[9] Here the country has been long settled. We see fine farms and comfortable dwellings as we pass along, and the land lies well for cultivation. It is also said to be of a good quality. We are now near the head waters of the river Thames, the principal branch of which flows within a mile of the stage house

[8] Court House.
[9] At Beachville.

just adverted to. The character of the inhabitants is much the same in this part of Canada as further to the eastward, and their general mode of living is likewise very similar. Five miles from the aforesaid stage house we cross a fine stream called Ingersoll's Creek. It falls into the Thames a mile or more north of our road. This place has the appearance of a small village. They have a fine gristmill, a saw-mill, a store, and sundry mechanics' shops, and I should suppose that a good deal of business is done there. Passing on, somewhat further, we have a view of the Thames. It may here be called a good large mill stream. Its banks are bold and dry and its waters are clear and transparent. Its course is somewhat serpentine, yet our road henceforth keeps near it, occasionally for a great distance. Although the river is too small to navigate to much advantage thus far, I was informed that logs are frequently rafted down in the spring season. For a few miles back we passed through a high, rolling section of country. The timber is of various kinds among which a small proportion is white pine. We here see what is very uncommon—pine, beech, hickory, oak, ash, etc., all mingled together. The inhabitants say the land is rich and produces handsomely. A short distance further westward our road leads us into a dense forest, exclusively of white pine. For miles, there is scarcely a stick of any other description in view. The mind of man can hardly imagine a more interesting wilderness scene than is here presented to the eye of the tourist. The road very gradually descends as it extends southwestward. The regular and elegant wall of trees on either hand whose spiral tops reach (seemingly) to the heavens, their beautiful evergreen hue, the deep impervious shade beneath their small and straight, yet intertwining branches, all, viewed together, appears at once pleasing, sublime and solemn. Some of the trees are very large and in no other place have I seen a forest so compact, such a vast quantity of timber on any particular space of ground. After proceeding five or six miles over a tract of country in which stumps are by far more numerous than corn hills should be, we lose the pine timber again and find ourselves in a rich country of beautiful rolling land, well settled and handsomely cultivated. We several times pass within sight of the river which gradually increases in size as we proceed towards its mouth but it is not yet navigable for vessels of burden. At about 7 o'clock in the evening we arrived at the stage house of Hiram Martin, three miles south of London C. H. and 60 miles from Brantford. For a great part of the distance the snow was light (except in the woods) and the roads were rough. The body of a curtained coach had been placed on sleigh-runners for the accommodation of our stage passengers, but for my own part I rode the whole day on the outside, standing all the while on my feet. The weather was mild in the latter part of the day and the snow melted considerably.

> Third Section, Published in the "Genius of Universal Emancipation," May, 1832.
> *Tour in Upper Canada (Continued)*

January 17th.

I took an early breakfast this morning and after making some little arrangements relative to my baggage set out on foot for the village of London. I had to go back the way we came the day before one and a half miles. Here the road turns at right angles and leads directly north-west about two miles to the forks of the river Thames, immediately above which the village is situated. I reached that place about 8 o'clock a.m., crossing a handsome bridge over the main branch of the Thames. Being desirous to proceed to the Wilberforce settlement before night, which my information led me to suppose was about 16 miles further to the northwest, and as the weather was mild, the snow melting and the walking unusually laborious I made very little stay in London. A description of the place will be given hereafter. I saw several colored people in the village and when they learned my object in visiting that part of the country one of them kindly volunteered to accompany me to Wilberforce. We crossed the northern branch of the river, (over which there is also a fine bridge) a short distance from its junction with the main stream, and travelled four or five miles through a country greatly diversified by hill and dale, presenting a rich soil and fine timber, also good plantations and healthy looking inhabitants. We passed numerous water courses on some of which mills were erected. At length the land became more level, yet it was somewhat rolling and well timbered. Not a stick of pine, hemlock or cedar is here to be seen (except a few white pines a little north of London) but the prevailing growth is sugar tree, bass, hickory, elm, oak, and beech, with a little poplar, cherry, walnut, etc. In some places we also see the wild plum, thorn, elder, sumach, and other shrubbery common to the richest soil. Several kinds of burrs and some thistles occasionally attract our attention. There are very few vines of any description. No rock or stone are to be found except in quarries below the surface. The snow here was about 20 inches deep in the woods but in the fields and openings it was little more than half that depth as the weather had long been fair and moderate and the sun had dissolved it considerably where it could act upon it. The farms adjoining the road were mostly new, though a few of them had been opened several years past. The population, I understand, consists principally of Europeans and their descendants. Their style of living and improvement is very much like that of the inhabitants of the western frontiers of the United States. The roads in this part of Canada are all laid out with great precision, crossing each other at right angles and stated equal distance as regular as the streets of a city. When the land shall be generally cleared and the settlements compact the country will exhibit a beautiful appearance. We found but one tavern in travelling twelve miles, but there were several little establishments where cakes, apples, cider and a few goods of various descriptions were offered for sale. At about half past two o'clock in the afternoon we reached the dwelling of Elder Benjamin Paul, thirteen miles from London. This gentleman is the regular minister of the Baptist church in the Wilberforce settlement. We had passed three or four houses within about a mile belonging to the members of the settlement and I intended going three miles further to the house of Austin Steward but Elder Paul insisted upon my tarrying with him until the next morning when he proposed to accompany me to the other parts of the settlement. The snow had been soft through the day and the travelling was a little fatiguing, consequently the invitation was cheerfully accepted, on this account as well as that of the politeness, hospitality and interesting sociability of himself and family.

January 18th.

The morning is warm and foggy. A light wind soon rises, however, and the sky becomes clear. At about 9 o'clock I went to the upper or northern part of the settlement, accompanied by Elder Paul, and found our friend Austin Steward with his hands in the mud, plastering, or "daubing" (as the backwoodsmen call it) a new log house. The gentleman is said to be wealthy, but he is not ashamed to work. The reader will bear in mind that the weather here is now so mild as to admit of the performance of this kind of business, at this season of the year. After visiting a few of the settlers, etc., Elder Paul took his leave of us and I engaged lodgings with A. Steward.

January 19th.

I never saw a more beautiful winter morning than this. The sky was clear and serene and the weather was merely cold enough to freeze a little. I did not suppose that one in fifty of the people of the United States could form anything like an adequate idea of it. We had always heard this spoken of as the region of storms and impassable snows and almost perpetual congelation—but instead thereof we are presented with as mild, beautiful, healthful, agreeable weather, near the middle of January as could be reasonably expected in Maryland, Virginia, or even North Carolina at the same season of the year. The wind was southwardly but the weather continued clear through the day. After transacting some business the remainder of the day was spent in visiting the settlers.

January 20th.

The weather still continues moderate and clear. I had a view this morning (for the first time) of a pair of "snow shoes." Three men had arrived in the settlement late last night, from the town of Goderich on Lake Huron, thirty miles to the north-west of this place. They had performed about 24 miles of this journey on those mis-shapen, unweildy travelling vehicles, above named. A brief description of them will be diverting to many a reader. They are used nowhere but in very high latitudes, or in new countries, where the snow falls too deep to wade through without difficulty. The "snow shoe" is made of wood and raw deer skin. A long stick, like a hoop-pole, is dressed four square and bent somewhat in the shape of a diamond; two pieces of the same thickness are placed across—the one a little before and the other behind the middle—and strongly tied with strings; over the whole is woven a sort of close net-work, with narrow strips of thin raw hide, presenting the appearance of a coarse wooden sieve. The shoe when thus finished, is nearly three feet long and twelve or fifteen inches wide. When used it is laid flat on the snow, and the foot strapped to the cross bars; and covering such an extent of surface it bears up the wearer as he walks along with it. Travelling in this way is severe, and frequently sore work. The poor fellows, above mentioned, had their feet sadly blistered.

After visiting the remainder of the settlers at Wilberforce, and attending a public meeting of nearly all the adult males to-day, I took leave of them and went four miles back towards the village of London. When night approached I stopped at the house of an Irish gentleman, where I was agreeably entertained.

He was very friendly to the colored people, and warmly expressed his approbation of the object of my tour through Canada. A colored man named Williams with whom I had been acquainted in Baltimore resides with him and is treated precisely as though he were white.

January 21st.

We have a clear and cold morning. My kind host insisted on my taking breakfast with him, and also proffered his aid in conveying me several miles on my road with his sleigh for all of which he made no charge. I could not brook this, and after thanking him for his kindness, with difficulty prevailed on him to accept a small sum in the way of compensation. Such hospitality is not always met with among strangers. The name of this gentleman is Henry O'Neal. He was one of the earliest settlers in this particular section of the country, has a good farm, and appears to be in easy circumstances. One of the finest springs of water that I have ever seen rises near his dwelling. The stream issuing from it turns a mill, a short distance from its source. My kind entertainer took me in his sleigh about ten miles towards London and I reached the village a little before 11 o'clock in the morning.

It has been observed in another part of the journal that London is the seat of justice for London District, in Upper Canada. It is situated on a high bluff, immediately above the confluence of the two principal branches of the River Thames, as aforesaid; the site is commanding and beautiful, and the town is rapidly improving. The public buildings are not yet numerous, but they have a large and elegant Court House, built of brick and rough cast, which is finished; also two houses for public worship, now building, both of good size. There are three hotels in the place, one of which, particularly, is very commodious. A good deal of business appears to be doing. They have six general mercantile stores; one apothecary; one grocery; one watchmaker; one gunsmith; one tanner and currier; one cooper; three tailors; three saddlers and harness makers; two wagon-makers; one house and sign painter; four shoemakers; two blacksmiths; one cabinet-maker; two joiners; one sash-maker; one chair-maker; a number of carpenters, brick-layers, masons, etc. Of the professions there are two physicians and two lawyers resident there. A weekly newspaper is issued. They have three religious congregations and several schools. Some of the private dwellings are neat and elegant. There are several compact blocks of buildings, and many new houses erecting. The whole number, at present, may be estimated at about 130 —of which I counted upwards of fifty unfinished outside. More than half of the others also had a new appearance. Nearly the whole are frame wooden buildings; many of them two stories high and some neatly painted. A considerable number of the inhabitants of this place are emigrants from the United States. Among them, I learn, there are about 25 or 30 colored people. A glance at its geographical position—the beauty and fertility of the country around it—the advantages of water power applicable to milling and manufacturing in its neighborhood (where several mills are now in operation)—its contiguity to the navigable waters of the lakes, Erie, St. Clair and Huron, etc., are sufficient to convince the intelligent observer that London must, ere long, become a place of wealth and importance. It is situated but about twenty miles from Port Talbot, on Lake Erie; and there is a good road the whole distance. Heavy articles of produce, lumber, etc., may be taken down the Thames; and, indeed, with the aid of a few canals, or short railroads, it will be an easy matter for the citizens of this place to extend and facilitate their commercial intercourse in almost every direction.

Having noted whatever I conceived to be the most important, as far as my limited time would permit, I left the interesting village of London and proceeded to the stage house of Hiram Martin in the evening, with the view of resuming my journey towards Detroit. As the stage would not go on before morning, and having too much baggage to carry on foot, I engaged lodgings there.

January 22nd.

At about 3 o'clock in the morning, our stage officer had his riding vehicle in readiness. The accommodation was not exactly what a New York belle or a Philadelphia dandy would look for. We had a crazy old coach box, fastened to as crazy a pair of sleigh runners; and trunks, boxes and bars of iron were stowed in promiscuously with women and children. But our Jehu was a real Yankee—said he was up to anything in the way of trade—and on he went. I had (as usual) taken a seat beside the driver, where I had the opportunity to see what was to be seen as we passed along. The night was not dark as the moon shone brightly. The weather was quite cold, but the snow was nearly gone in many places, and we had disagreeable riding. The land was rolling, in some places well timbered, and in others cleared for farms. We crossed a number of handsome streams from which I infer that the country about here is well watered. Some time before day, we reached the village of Tiffanyville, or Delaware. Here is a pretty good tavern and some mills. The place is intended for a village but is scarcely entitled to the name as yet. It is situated on the bank of the Thames, ten or twelve miles below London, where there is a considerable fall in the water. Our landlord—a fat western New-Yorker—expressed the opinion that the water power at this place was nearly equal in value to that at Rochester. In this, however, he must have been mistaken. There is an elegant bridge over the river at this place. We now crossed to the right bank, or north side, and passed through a fine rich country, bordering the river, or within a short distance of it. Five miles further on there is a little pine timber; we soon lose sight of this, however, and meet with a general variety of oak, sugar tree, hickory, beech, etc. Daylight now presents us with a fairer view of the landscape; and in some few places the snow is so far gone that the dark rich soil is to be seen. The country is thickly settled, with Europeans and natives of both Canada and the United States. A few colored people are to be seen, but their number is small. At length we reached Griffith's stage house, 8 miles from Tiffanyville. Here we stopped for breakfast and to change horses.

It may not be amiss to mention that among our passengers this morning was an English lady with her two small children, who had recently arrived at New York, and was now going, without any other attendant, to meet her husband at Detroit—he having come over and established himself in business there some months before. Perhaps there are not many American ladies that would fancy such an undertaking. She appeared very genteel and respectable and all took an interest in her situation. She did not complain of a want of attention on the part of any one.

When our breakfast was over the stage went on again. It had been relieved of a portion of its freight, and also a few of the passengers. But we had in lieu thereof other sources of vexation. They had given us a dull span of horses and the ground was bare in many places. For my own part I got along well—I did not grieve at all—as these circumstances gave me numerous opportunities to indulge my pedestrian propensities. It must be confessed, however, that the idea of having paid for a ride, and still being almost necessitated to walk, was calculated to occasion a few ill-natured reflections which required a little philosophical consideration to repress. The soil exhibited a great variety as we passed along to-day. In some places the land lies low, and occasionally it appears a little swampy; in others there are more elevated ridges where the soil is rather light and sandy. The former is clothed with heavy timber among which is to be seen ash, beech, etc., intermingled with white pine; the latter presents a more thin growth, principally of oak and hickory, with a portion of chestnut. Our next stopping place is Ward's stage house, 17 miles from Griffith's. Here we changed horses, made a tolerable bargain of it, and went on somewhat better. We now soon came to an Indian reservation, and went six miles without a half a dozen houses on the road. This tract belongs to the Moravian tribe. In the central part of it, on the same side of the river that our road is located, was the site of the old Moravian town, destroyed by the U. S. troops during the last war. This act has been justly condemned, even by warriors, as the Moravians were a peaceful people, and it is believed took no part whatever in the contest. We passed over the ground where their town formerly stood. The view of its remaining vestiges brought to mind many circumstances relative to the unjust treatment of the native Americans by the avaricious adventurers from Europe and their descendants. (But I have not leisure to dwell upon this subject now). The Indians have, since the destruction of their town, as aforesaid, built another on the opposite side of the river which is in view of the ruins of the first. It makes a very handsome appearance as we pass along. It is laid out in a beautiful level plain on the southern bank of the river, and the land, for several miles above and below is fenced in for farming. There are about 70 houses in the place, mostly frame and log, with shingled roofs. Some of them are two stories high, and their village makes, upon the whole, quite as decent a show as any of ours of similar size. The number of inhabitants, I learn, is nearly 300. They have two white missionaries, or preachers, of the Moravian sect, from Bethlehem, in Pennsylvania, and also a white schoolmaster. I did not understand that they had more than one school among them. Their church, or meeting house, is large, and has a high steeple. Not having been in the town myself I did not learn much about the business done in it, and can say nothing about that without too great liability to err. I suppose, however, from the information I obtained, the greater part of the inhabitants are agriculturists. And, it is said, they have wheat, corn, stock, etc., in abundance. Their land is very fertile along the river bottoms; but that more elevated (though it lies handsomely) appears rather sandy and must consequently be of somewhat an inferior quality. Passing through this reservation we came to fine farms; and after travelling a few miles arrived at Howard's Bridge, 20 miles from Ward's Tavern, a little before dark. Here we crossed to the south side of the Thames again. There is a store kept at this place by an Englishman, who was once engaged in the inland trade between St. Louis and the northern parts of Mexico. A tavern and stage house is also kept here, and we took lodgings for the night. In the course of the evening I was agreeably entertained by a conversation with the young merchant just alluded to. He had called to see the English lady, before mentioned, but she had retired early, and he did not obtain an interview with her. The country has long been settled about here, and some valuable improvements have been made. The river is not large but of sufficient depth to float vessels of considerable burthen.

January 23rd.

The stage passengers were called up again before day; and we got on our way at about half past four o'clock. Our "stage" now assumed the shape of an uncovered sleigh. We proceeded along the bank of the Thames for the greater part of the time, until we came to McGregor's Mill, 10 miles from Howard's Bridge. There is a store and postoffice kept here. The mill is large and does a good deal of business. The morning was cold and we had permission to sit by a fire in a kitchen, a short time, while the mail was assorted. The owner of the establishment (if I mistake not) is a Scotchman. He is wealthy and had a number of hired house servants. Among the rest I observed an aged French Creole. He was kind and communicative; and from the manner in which he appeared to be employed I should judge that he was as fairly entitled to the appellative "Lord of the Kitchen," as the proprietor was to that of "Lord of the Manor." After a few minutes delay we hurried into the "stage sleigh" and went on to the little village of Chatham. It was now daylight and we stopped again for a few minutes. There is a store, and also a tavern and stage house, kept in this place, and I was told that the country was thickly settled around. I had previously been informed that a considerable settlement of colored people is located here; but I had not leisure to stop long and did not learn anything very particular about it. The country through which we passed this morning varies but little in appearance from that last noted. I learn that there are many French and Creole inhabitants in these parts. The major portion of the population is composed of these and Europeans. But few "Yankees" are to be found here. A very fine mill-stream flows through this place, called Chatham Creek. Its bottoms are wide and exceedingly fertile. From Chatham we went five miles and stopped for breakfast at the house of L. Goss. A pretty good tavern is kept by this gentleman on the banks of the Thames. Here our horses were changed and the snow was so far gone that we left our road and took the river. The ice was sufficiently strong and we proceeded at a rapid rate. Never was there a better "railroad" put in order for travelling. On the way we passed several sloops and schooners, some bound up the river and bound down—and to use a landsman's phrase there was no doubt that they were all "bound" fast. We had little opportunity of viewing the country as we passed along—our present road being regularly excavated some fifteen or twenty feet—but I learn that it still continues well timbered and fertile. The whole distance bordering the river exhibits a dense population, consisting of a mixture of French creoles and Europeans with a few Americans from the U. S., as above mentioned. Some African descendants are likewise scattered through their settlements. As we proceed down the river the banks are lower and the country around is more flat and somewhat marshy. After travelling in this way about sixteen miles we come to the estuary of the Thames, and went seven miles southwardly on Lake St. Clair. We kept along near the shore for the greater part of the time though we occasionally bore off nearly a mile from it. The lake was frozen over almost as far as the eye could reach, and the ice was firm where we went on it. But the wind was strong, the ice smooth and our sleigh was frequently blown nearly half way around so that we had, if not a perilous, a rather disagreeable ride of it. Our Jehu was an old Yankee pioneer; he had weathered many a storm in "these here parts" when the country "was new" and he "knowed there was no danger." I did not doubt the truth of his statement but I thought the English lady, with all her courage, could hardly believe him. She did not express any alarm, yet she looked more serious and paid more close attention to her children than usual while the sleigh and horses were both galloping sideways. Having thus travelled or skated 23 miles, on the river and lake, we found ourselves opposite a point where the stage road comes to the bank, and a stage house is erected. Here we had to "go ashore" and change horses. A tolerably passable tavern is kept at this place by a creole of the name of Reoum. The land is flat and swampy for a considerable distance from the lake, (a small strip only along its margin, in many places, is susceptible of cultivation) consequently the settlements are few in number. Nearly the whole population in this part of the country, bordering the river and lake are French creoles and colored persons. The latter are not even comparatively numerous. We now were necessitated to adopt a different mode of travelling. The ice was said to be sufficiently strong about 17 miles further on our way, but below that the lake was open; and as there was no stage house near the place where we must leave the ice, and the ground in many parts of the country being entirely bare, we took a stage wagon and proceeded along the margin of the lake. It should be observed that immediately on the shores of this lake, as well as those of our western lakes generally, considerable embankments are raised by the action of the waves, consisting principally of pebble stones and fine sand, though in many places a great deal of drift wood is deposited, with the other washings of those inland oceans. And as the constant flowing of the streams deepens the channels of their various outlets, the waters gradually recede and widen these embankments. The land thus formed or elevated affords not only the means of locating pretty good roads, but in many places extensive farms, though the soil is of a very inferior quality. We now progressed rather slowly. Our stage wagon (a coach I should call it, for although it was old, tottering and ragged, it was once as new and spruce a stage coach as we need wish to see) was driven by a pair of steeds whose sinews, one would think, were made of whalebone, and whose hides were completely lash-proof. Our driver had the worst of the business, but he had more philosophy about him than fell to the lot of everyone and he managed his travelling machine quite adroitly. I had another "fine chance" to walk, and being fond of it did not let a murmur escape me, though a little grumbling was heard among the other passengers. We got along, upon the whole, tolerably well and after travelling 18 miles with our spiritless donkies we halted at another creole tavern, kept as a sort of stage house and exchanged them for a pretty good span of horses. It was then nearly night and we had yet twelve miles to go before taking lodgings. The road follows the lake shore and bank of Detroit River the whole distance. The sky was clear and of course the evening was not very dark. As we passed on, the land became more rolling and the farms more numerous. I was informed that the inhabitants were still mostly creoles. A few Europeans and Yankees have settled down among them. There were also a small number of colored people in different places but no regular settlement of them in this particular section of the country. When we came to the foot of the lake, or near it, we passed a place where the water had previously overflowed the bank for a considerable distance. It was now frozen solid and presented us with a road, almost equal to a "Macadamized" turnpike. Unluckily, our old stage played us a trick that caused a little detention. While going at a good gait on this beautiful highway, one of the fore wheels broke loose and ran off, tilting the venerable coach much more aslant than was desirable to any of our company. Jehu reined up the horses as soon as he could and several of us scampered after the eloping wheel. It was well that this happened on the ice as the axle-tree slid along until the carriage was stopped without injury. Having repaired damages we proceeded on our way and soon came to more rolling land again. We now took leave of the lake and following the bank of the river we reached the ferry opposite Detroit at about eight o'clock in the evening. For the last few miles we had an excellent road and the country is well settled. The banks of the river are high, the land lies well, and I was told that the soil is of a good quality and produces abundantly when properly cultivated. We took lodgings at a tavern kept by a gentleman of the name of House, who likewise keeps a stage office and a ferry. All were gratified in finding comfortable quarters after performing a journey of 69 miles through the inclement weather and over the kind of road that we had to encounter to-day.

January 24th.

Although the weather had been mild and consequently the river at this place had been clear of ice for a number of days, it was now very cold and somewhat stormy. The ice was running early this morning, and fearing the river would soon close again by which means I might be too long detained, I determined on crossing it before visiting some other settlements on the Canadian side, as I had previously intended. The village of Sandwich is situated about two miles below this ferry and is said to be a place of considerable business. There is also a large settlement of colored people, about 18 or 20 miles lower still, near the village of Malden or Amherstburg at the junction of Detroit River and Lake Erie. I was desirous to see both of these places and to investigate particularly the condition of the latter. I was informed that there are upwards of 300 colored settlers there—nearly or quite all from the United States—and that they are in the general way, doing well. The land in that section of the country is represented as being rather flat, and somewhat swampy, but in the main it is said to be very rich and productive. We made preparations to cross the river in the early part of the forenoon, and though the ice rendered it somewhat difficult, we succeeded and landed safely in Detroit. In a few hours afterwards the ice covered the whole surface of the river and completely interdicted all communication with the other shore. I must not omit to mention that among the number of those who crossed, thus opportunely, were the English lady and her children who had travelled with us the last two days. She found her husband, as she expected, and they were mutually gratified to meet each other in good health and spirits.

Having now finished my tour through this part of Upper Canada and accomplished the object of it as far as the season of the year, the mode of travelling and the time I could devote to it would permit, I shall close my diary with a few general observations.

The reader of this journal has been informed that my sole motive in performing the tour was to investigate the state of things generally in that part of the country as far as my very limited means would allow with the view of publishing the result thereof for the benefit of such colored persons in the United States as may wish to remove thither. I had intended visiting the seat of government for that province and making some inquiries of their statesmen and politicians, but found it impracticable as the time could not be spared. Neither had I leisure to make acquaintance with those exercising the local authority or to examine public works of any description where I went. The view I have taken is indeed extremely superficial, yet, I hope the investigation will not be without its use. I have carefully noted the appearance of the country through which I passed. The general character of its inhabitants has been delineated by comparison with those of our states, from which a pretty correct idea may be formed thereof. The geographical position of several colored settlements has been stated and that at Wilberforce particularly and minutely described. And the peculiar advantages of that part of the country—its fine climate, variety of agricultural productions, convenience of markets, etc., have been adverted to. It remains for me to say that from every investigation I have been able to make and all the information I could obtain by frequent conversation and inquiry among many intelligent persons, both those who were friendly and those who were inimical to our colored people, that the country in question will be very suitable for them, particularly those north of the Carolinas, if they choose to locate themselves therein. The same rights and privileges will be guaranteed to them as to other British subjects and many of the white inhabitants of this republic have voluntarily exchanged their citizenship here for the immunities they may there enjoy. I would not urge, I would not ask a single free man to go, who is not so disposed. My business is to give him information. If he can profit by it I shall rejoice, if he neglects to pay attention to it he does but exercise a perfect right which it would be highly improper for me to question him about. Believing, however, that there are many among the persecuted colored people south of the Delaware who are extremely desirous to change their situation, and would be glad of such information as I have here collected, I shall be amply rewarded for the hardship and expense of my cold and toilsome journey, if I can be successful in laying it, generally, before them.

IX.

DEEP WATERWAYS MOVEMENTS.
THEIR ORIGIN AND PROGRESS IN ONTARIO.

By James Mitchell.

One of the marvels of this Canada of ours, not sufficiently appreciated because so familiar, is the great Waterway of river and lake which forms its southern boundary for 2,500 miles from Belle Isle on the Atlantic to the head of navigation on the Upper Lake. On no other continent of this planet is there such a wonderful stretch of navigable water, and it is probably equally true that on no other continent is there such a volume of water-borne traffic carried each year. This traffic has developed gradually from the time when fleets of birch canoes skimmed the great rivers and lakes, on through such craft as "batteaux" and "Durham boats," samples of which would now be viewed with curiosity if found in a museum, and later, when steam navigation began its race with the schooners and larger vessels of the white-winged couriers of commerce. And now from the eastern end of the mighty St. Lawrence to the great commercial centres at the head of navigation on both sides of the international boundary, each season witnesses an ever-growing number of commerce carriers with capacity such as could not have been even imagined a century ago. With the increase in the size and number of these, has come the need of enlarging the canals and riverways which form the connecting links, and improving the ports and channels along the entire route. Besides such work undertaken by Governments, there have been not a few efforts on the part of marine and commercial interests to push on more rapidly, and on a larger scale, improvements which would meet still greater developments for years to come; and it is the purpose of this brief summary to outline such of these as have gained a place in public attention, leaving to Government reports anything other than a mere mention of the state-directed public works of this character. A U. S. authority on this subject of waterways paid this tribute to Canadian enterprise as long ago as 1896:

"In Canada there is a far better general understanding of the problems of transportation, competition and foreign trade and commerce (than in the United States) learned and inherited from the mother country. In the way of providing an unbroken water outlet to the sea, 2,400 miles from Port Arthur to Belle Isle, and the only real transcontinental railway in America, the whole costing above $275,000,000, the efforts and achievements of this handful of 4,800,000 people have been wonderful."

1. THE WELLAND CANAL,

begun in 1820 as a private venture amid the scoffings and doubts of the public opinion of those days, has grown to a public work carried on by the Canadian Government, till now it is being prepared to accommodate even ocean-going vessels of all but the largest class. It is, of course, a vital link for the needs of our lake commerce, and if the proposed Great Lakes and Atlantic Waterway is to be assured, it can only be with a Welland link enlarged to the greatest capacity.

2. As far back as 1845 we have mention made of,

THE GEORGIAN BAY SHIP CANAL,

which proposed the improvement of the Ottawa and French Rivers to make a short route from the St. Lawrence to the Georgian Bay and Lake Huron, a distance of 430 miles. In 1860 a report of a Government survey was made, and in 1894 a charter was granted to a proposed company, which has been amended and extended several times, but actual work of construction has not yet been begun. In 1908 an extensive Government report of surveys and estimates was published, but the Government still declares it impossible to undertake the construction of the work under existing conditions. Representations in support of the project have been submitted to the International Joint Commission and we may expect their report will contain a review or summary of the arguments on its behalf.

3. Another project which arose over 70 years ago was,

THE HURON AND ONTARIO SHIP CANAL,

of which Dr. Scadding makes this mention in his "Toronto of Old," published in 1873: He is speaking of Mr. Rowland Burr, an emigrant from Pennsylvania, in 1803, who "had a strong desire to initiate works of public utility," and among these "A canal to connect Lake Ontario with the Georgian Bay of Lake Huron, via Lake Simcoe and the valley of the Humber, was pressed by him as an immediate necessity, years ago; and at his own expense he examined the route and published thereon a report which has furnished to later theorizers on the same subject much valuable information."

The originator and promoter of the scheme as it finally took shape was the late Mr. F. C. Capreol, who proposed to construct a ship canal for vessels of the type then used, from Toronto, entering at Humber Bay, via Newmarket, Holland Landing and Lake Simcoe, to the Georgian Bay, a distance of 100 miles, with, it was claimed, only 60 miles of canal proper to be constructed. Mr. Capreol expended much time and money endeavoring to launch the project, and had even succeeded in enlisting English capital for it. The Toronto papers of Sept. 10, 1868, gave glowing accounts of a reception accorded him by the citizens on his return from a financing trip to the Old Land. Reports favorable to the project were presented by select committees of both the Legislative Assemblies in 1857 and 1864, and in the House of Commons of 1869, but the project died what may be termed a natural death.

4. Mention might here be made of another scheme which had its origin in Toronto,

THE GEORGIAN BAY CANAL AND POWER AQUEDUCT,

as it was called, the promoter being E. A. Macdonald, who attained the honor of chief magistrate of that city. There now appears to have been little literature published by the promoters, but the files of the Toronto papers of the early 1890's show that a great deal of newspaper controversy was carried on. Apparently the proposal was for a ship canal from Toronto to Georgian Bay, somewhat after the Capreol plan, and with it to have the city's supply of water brought from Lake Simcoe instead of from Lake Ontario as then and now, the argument being that the supply would be "absolutely pure." The project did not attain much headway, and with the passing of its chief advocate was soon forgotten.

5. In September, 1894, a four days International Convention was held in Toronto, when,

THE INTERNATIONAL DEEP WATERWAYS ASSOCIATION

was formed, to secure the improvement of the waterways from the St. Lawrence to the head of the Lakes. The first President was O. A. Howland, then M.P.P. for Toronto, and the Canadian Vice-President James Fisher, M.P.P., Winnipeg. The late John H. Boyle, of Toronto, was one of the men who gave much attention to this project, and he gathered a large amount of statistical and other information on the subject, most of which is still in existence. A second convention was held in Cleveland in Sept., 1895, and as a result of the agitation an International Deep Waterways Commission was formed, in 1895, the U.S. representatives being Messrs James B. Angell, of Michigan, John E. Russell, of Massachusetts, and Lyman B. Cooley, of Illinois. The Canadian representatives to co-operate with them were Messrs. O. A. Howland, of Toronto, Thomas C. Keefer, C.E., of Ottawa, and Thomas Monro, C.E., of Coteau Landing. The report submitted by the U.S. representatives to their Government was published under date Jan. 18, 1897, and covers over 260 pp. and 25 profile maps. The official report of the two International Conventions was published in Cleveland under date November 6, 1895. Both these reports have a large amount of statistical and other information, valuable still for the consideration of the Great Waterways subject.

6. The next movement in order which attained to a considerable degree of publicity was,

THE GREAT WATERWAYS UNION OF CANADA,

formed in Kitchener (then Berlin), on January 11, 1912, the leading spirit in which was the late Mr. D. B. Detweiler, who may also be said to have been the founder of the original union of municipalities which is now the Hydro-Electric Municipal System. Mr. Detweiler was a man with a far-seeing and patriotic vision of what could be accomplished in the development, not only of his native province, but of the waterways and water powers of the Great West. With untiring energy he co-operated with leading engineers and others, both in Canada and the U.S., hastening the formation of the Waterways Association in the latter country as well as completely organizing the Canadian Association, which but for his untimely death in the early part of 1919, would have been carrying on the project now. The almost entire correspondence in this movement for about six years, has been compiled and indexed, and is now in the Public Archives Department at Ottawa.

7. In January, 1914, a conference was held at Windsor, one of its leaders being Mr. Henry Olay, then mayor of that city, and later on

THE NATIONAL WATERWAYS ASSOCIATION OF CANADA

was partly organized, complete action and further activity being interrupted by the Great War. In March, 1921, a convention was called for Toronto, and although this was only partially successful owing to causes which need not be mentioned here, the Secretary-Treasurer, Mr. J. H. Duthie, of Toronto, says the work will be continued, and endeavors made to co-operate with the other Associations having the same object in view, viz., a Deep Waterway from the Atlantic to the Head of the Lakes.

8. In November, 1919, a large gathering took place at Windsor again, this time under a call from the Border Cities Chamber of Commerce, and here

THE CANADIAN DEEP WATERWAYS AND POWER ASSOCIATION

was formed, O. E. Fleming, K.C., of Windsor, being the President, and Major Alex. C. Lewis, of Toronto, Sec.-Treas. This organization held its first annual meeting in Toronto in Dec., 1920, and besides co-operating with the American Association (The Great Lakes-St. Lawrence-Tidewater Association), it has published considerable literature in support of the great Deep Waterways project, "An Open Waterway to the Ocean."

9. Another effort to promote this object is called

THE GREAT LAKES AND ATLANTIC CANAL AND POWER COMPANY,

promoted and incorporated in 1914 by Mr. N. M. Cantin, who for some years a couple of decades ago was prominent in his attempt to build up a "City of St. Joseph" on the east shore of Lake Huron, a project in which not a few scores of thousands of dollars were expended, the only now visible results of which form a "deserted village." Mr. Cantin's literature in advocacy of his waterways scheme includes two interesting pamphlets with a good map, and his proposal differs from that of the other Associations in that he wants an alternative or connecting link from the St. Lawrence to Ottawa, and if not, a new and shorter Welland Canal from Jordan Harbor on Lake Ontario to Moulton Bay on Lake Erie, a distance of 19 miles; then a canal from Port Talbot on Lake Erie to a point called Port Franks on Lake Huron, a distance of 43 miles, thus saving, he alleges, on the whole round trip from Ocean to head of the Lakes, between 400 and 500 miles.

I mention this proposal not because of its probable accomplishment, but as one of the evidences of a public demand for greater Waterways which must ultimately be carried out.

10. A movement which must not be overlooked in this summary, though not properly a great Deep Waterway Project, is what is known as

THE FRENCH RIVER IMPROVEMENT.

This asks for the creating of a navigable waterway from Georgian Bay to Lake Nipissing, and it is claimed that, in addition to the development of the growing traffic from the natural resources of the great Northern Ontario, it would shorten the distance and effect a saving in the grain haulage from the West, and develop North Bay, which is a railway centre for all the Transcontinental Railway lines, into a great lake port. Besides all this, cheap electric power development would be made possible up to 40,000 or 50,000 h.p. Thus far the repeated appeals to the Dominion Governments to undertake the work have not been successful, the principal difficulty, it is claimed, being that of undertaking at present the great financial obligation necessary.

11. This sketch would be incomplete, and indeed unfair, without a tribute to the organization in the United States, known as

THE GREAT LAKES-ST. LAWRENCE-TIDEWATER ASSOCIATION,

with Executive headquarters at Duluth, Minn. As a result of the agitation carried on for years, a meeting was held in Chicago, in 1914, in which an organization was formed called the "Great Waterways Conference," representing the cities and ports in the U. S. bordering on the lakes, which kept up its efforts until, following a conference at the Rivers and Harbours Congress, in Washington, in December, 1918, the present Association was formed, and has since carried on with great activity and energy. It is composed of representatives of 15 member States, and its publicity literature is valuable for the information supplied and the force of its argument, besides the case presented at the several meetings of the International Joint Commission.

Of course the efforts for a project so vast as this "Deep Waterway to the Sea," have not been carried on thus far without opposition, and that on both sides of the international boundary. In the Eastern States the canal and a large section of the commercial interests profess to fear such a diversion of trade as will be disastrous to the canals on which so much money has been expended, and on the Canadian side there is strong opposition by a considerable section of Montreal opinion, alleging the impracticability of such an "Ocean to the Lakes Waterway," and the injury to Montreal interests if that port be not continued as the one trans-shipping centre on the St. Lawrence. All these opposing interests, as well as the advocates of the Deep Waterway project, have been heard before the International Joint Commission, and the report of that body will be awaited with keen interest in both countries and by both parties to the controversy.

X.

AN OLD PROVINCIAL NEWSPAPER.

BY THE HONOURABLE WILLIAM RENWICK RIDDELL, LL.D., F.R.S.C., ETC.

One S. P. Hart, in 1836, during the troublous times before the Rebellion, started in Belleville a small newspaper called the *Plain Speaker*. One account says:

"It was friendly to the rebels, and the editor was put in Kingston Penitentiary for attempting a raid on a bank at Cobourg. The soldiers (volunteers) afterwards marched to the office of the *Plain-Speaker,* upset the type fonts and trailed the manager in the snow and slush. This movement occurred because the paper appeared one morning with the British coat-of-arms turned upside down in its columns." [1]

In 1838, after the fiasco of a rebellion at Toronto, Hart began to publish at Cobourg a newspaper with the same name—the first number appearing June 5—of which there were at least thirteen issues. The only number I have seen is Vol. 1, No. 13, of Tuesday, August 28, 1838[2]: to me as an old resident of Cobourg, it has proved very interesting and I propose in this paper to give some account of it.

This No. 13 is a quarto of four pages, paged 49 to 52—the paper and ink are both good and the proof-reading is fair.

On the first page appears the announcement:—"The *Plain Speaker*, devoted to the diffusion of News, and the Advancement of Agriculture, Commerce, Domestic Manufactures and Science in general will be published every Tuesday Evening, at the Trades' Printing Office, Corner of Main [3] and First Street.

By S. P. Hart.

"Terms—Town subscribers and those who call at the office for the paper will be charged Two Dollars, when sent by mail Three Dollars. No paper will be forwarded except the money accompany the order. All letters must be post paid.

"Advertisements will be inserted at reduced prices and with few exceptions no advertising will be continued above a month."

The remainder of the first page and part of the first column of the second is taken up with an instalment of a continued story, "The Conscript Brothers."

Then follows the editorial, "Who compose the Producing Classes"—the animus of the editor is abundantly manifest throughout. He writes:—

---

[1] Belden's Atlas of Hastings and Prince Edward Counties, Toronto, 1878, p. iii— I have no means of verifying the story.

[2] Kindly loaned to me by Mr. James Mitchell, the Assistant Archivist of Canada, stationed at Goderich.

[3] "Main Street" sometimes printed "the Main Street," was King Street.

"The Mechanic . . . all those labourers who exercise their physical powers whether they hold the plough, swing the axe, shove the plane, shoulder the hod, throw the shuttle, trail a net or follow any of the various avocations which supply the comforts and necessities of life and contribute to increase the wealth of the community are Producers and 'eat their bread by the sweat of their brow.'"

But "others . . . who wallowing in luxury call themselves the 'Professional Class' . . . pretending to exalted excellence, superior endowments, great personal worth and deep knowledge . . . arrogate to themselves the right of *governing* and directing all the affairs of the Province, of telling people what to think and how to act . . . lovers of *exclusive privileges* . . . high sounding titles . . . given to base lucre and . . . very much intoxicated with power . . . are not the Producing Class in any other sense than this—they produce discord—engender strife—create rebellions—foster disease and fatten upon the miseries of their fellow creatures."

After the editorial, we find printed in parallel columns accounts of two visits— one by Governor Ritner of Pennsylvania, to a farm near Northumberland, Pa., and the other by Governor Arthur,[4] to Cobourg, Thursday, Aug. 23, 1838. The Pennsylvania Governor had cradled in the harvest field having "pulled off his coat, jacket, shoes and stockings," whereas the Canadian had received "a hole and corner address read to him by Sheriff Ruttan, and a humble mechanic was very much maltreated by the bystanders because he refused to take off his hat in respect to the man who disregarded the prayers of thirty thousand of the men [5] whom he is sent a distance of 4,000 miles to govern and the earnest petition of heart broken wives and daughters. He left town Friday morning cheered by the Office keepers and Sycophants and the boarders of the *Caroline*. The industrious farmer, mechanic and labourer reserving their three 'hearty huzzas' [6] for a *Farmer Governor*."

Then follows an editorial item.

"The Farmer, Mechanic, and labourer" are called upon to unite their energies and "with a long and a strong pull and a pull altogether, bring down those who are hanging upon their shoulders and eating up their substance."

This, of course, is sheer balderdash—there was no question of economic tyranny, all that was complained of was political. But we have matter not unlike in certain publications at the present time, some openly Bolshevik, some under other more or less specious names.

---

[4] Sir George Arthur, Lieutenant-Governor of Upper Canada, March 23, 1838, to February 9, 1841.

[5] Sir George Arthur had refused to commute the sentence of death pronounced on Lount and Matthews for High Treason, though petitions for clemency numerously signed were presented to him—one signed by over 5,000 persons was personally presented to him by the wife of Lount, who went on her knees and begged her husband's life—in vain.

[6] A quotation from the account of the American Governor's visit.

The same sort of thing is seen in an item on Rev. A. N. Bethune, [7] and the prefix "Reverend," "the greek word, Aidesimos is used in that language for *reverend* and signifies *awful, venerable, respectable, reverend, compassionate, pitiful*. Either of these titles appended to A. N. Bethune would appear ridiculous in the extreme, particularly if that of *pastor* be added."

The horrors of slavery are recalled by half a column of advertisements in U. S. papers of runaway negroes.

Hart seems to have intended to remove to Belleville again, as a letter to "Monsieur Plain Speaker," says that he in the paper of Aug. 21, had stated that he was going to Belleville, and an item at the bottom of page 3, reads: "We are going to leave Cobourg, and a good many are following our example, some going East, some West, some North, some South. Mr. Joseph Wood goes to Whitby, where he intends to continue the Mercantile business on the Cash system."

An item on page 3 gives us the information: "The N. Y. *Albion,* says that Henry Boulton, 'has been *sacrificed* to the Radicals.' The meaning of this is, he has been dismissed from office upon the petition of the Reformers of Newfoundland; and what is very just, the expenses of removing him are saddled upon him."

This was Henry John Boulton, who had been Solicitor General of Upper Canada, tried for murder [8] because he was a second in a fatal duel, acquitted, dismissed from office in 1833, made Chief Justice of Newfoundland, and in 1838, resigned after a quarrel with the Roman Catholic Bishop; he then came back to Upper Canada, and re-entered public life in a quiet way.

Then follows this item from the *Niagara Reporter:*

"A respite has been granted to Chandler, Waite and McLeod, till the 31st inst. George Buck and Murdock McFadden—sentence commuted—Penitentiary. All the rest are to be transported to a penal colony. Jacob Beamer has been found guilty, and sentenced to be hanged on the 31st inst."

These men had been convicted of Treason. Samuel Chandler, Benjamin Waite and Alexander McLeod were transported for life, as was Jacob Beamer; Murdock McFadden got three years in Kingston Penitentiary: George Buck had the same fate.

As indicating the facilities for trans-Atlantic travel in those days, an item from the NewYork *Commercial Advertiser* is interesting.

The N. Y. *Commercial Advertiser* quotes a letter from Toronto, of Thursday, Aug. 9, containing a statement that the steamer *Transit* had that day arrived from Lewiston, with passengers only 18 days out from England, having arrived in N.Y. by the *Great Western* on Sunday and one of them having remained one day at Oswego on his way up. "Truly this is an age of wonders. . . . To show you

---

[7] Dr. Alexander Neil Bethune, born at Williamstown, Upper Canada, 1800, the son of a Presbyterian Minister; he was ordained deacon in 1823, priest in 1824, and was appointed to Grimsby—in 1827 he was appointed to St. Peter's, Cobourg, and in 1841 founded the Theological School in that town. He became Archdeacon in 1846, and second Bishop of Toronto in 1867, dying in 1879 universally respected. He was held in the highest esteem by all classes and creeds during his life in Cobourg; but he was loyal and did not please Mr. Hart.

[8] See my article "The Solicitor General tried for Murder," 40 Can. Law Times (August, 1920) pp. 636, sqq.

the feeling of people in reference to a trip across the Atlantic, I have this very evening heard perhaps twenty persons say they have made up their minds for a passage in some of the splendid steam-packets in the course of the year. I heard one of the passengers by the Great Western, declare, that he had frequently suffered more inconvenience in crossing our Lake, than he did in his late passage across the Atlantic."

In those days, the traveller went from Toronto to Niagara or Lewiston, then by stage or other conveyance to Albany, then to New York by vessel, or stage—and sometimes taking a week on the way.

The item: "Dr. John Rolph, late M.P.P., is publishing an account of the Revolt," reminds us that Dr. Rolph, fled to the United States on the outbreak of the Rebellion, and lived and practised for some years in Rochester. He received a pardon and returned to Toronto, in 1843, and was still a somewhat prominent feature in political life.

Hart recommended Dobson's Superior ale; his views as to the public houses of the neighbourhood will appear from this article:

"The public houses in the country are conducted as well as can be expected from the support they get. In one particular they are getting more *cute* than formerly.

"Editors should always pass *free*. And on our east tour, many of them refused to take anything from us. Treating us to the best the house afforded, and when we were leaving, slipped the amount of the subscription for the *Plain Speaker* into our hands, with 'don't forget us.'

WE WILL NOT

"Mr. Vanalstine of Grafton, Mr. Ford and Mr. Yarrington, of Colborne, Mr. Ketchum of Brighton, Mr. Harris and Mr. Bullock of Murray are deserving of a liberal support. The Keepers of Public Houses, at the River Trent and Belleville, shall have a chapter to themselves if they behave."

What effect such a recommendation by a bribed editor would have would seem very doubtful.

Taverns are advertised in the newspapers.

E. Shelly's Cobourg Hotel, on the corner of King and Division Streets, "Baggage conveyed to and from the wharf free of charge."

S. H. MacKenzie's North American, "in the immediate vicinity of the Steamboat Landing," from which Hotel "a daily line of stages will be continued to the Rice Lake from whence passengers and baggage will be conveyed to Peterboro."

Other advertisers are George Sutherland, Tailor, who now will sell for cash only so that "GOOD CUSTOMERS shall no more pay for . . . BAD ONES"—W. S. Conger, "one door east of the Albion Hotel," sells groceries, Brandy, Gins, Spirits, Scotch and common Whiskies, Port, Madeira, Teneriffe and Sherry Wines, London Porter, Teas, Sugars, Tobacco, Snuff, Crockery and Glass-ware, Stationery (it is called "Stationary"), Salt, Plaster and Ploughs for Cash only.

"Morrison's Pills, the Hygeia Vegetable Universal Medicines"[9] are advertised by Robert Murray, Agent. Edward Hale had removed his "Stone Yard to the street leading from the main street to the Windmill." [10] W. Gibbons wanted to sell a house and lot on the Main Street, and F. Sprague, to sell or exchange his brick house on Division Street, 38 x 26, quite new, and the lot containing half an acre with a well and a living brook. [11]

A couple of feeble jokes enliven the journal.

"The weather continues hot and sultry. The butchers of Cobourg kill *half* an ox at a time."

"A new idea. We understand that an order has passed the Board of Education which provides that Teachers of Common Schools must be able to *read* and *write their own certificates.*"

The latter was not much of a libel on the ordinary run of teachers at the time.

And so we leave Mr. Hart, Radical Editor, and his *Plain-Speaker*—a very plain speaker in truth.

---

[9] A well-known proprietary remedy of that time—now quite forgotten. Morrison was an Englishman, and founded quite a school of medicine.

[10] I cannot identify the site of the windmill. Hale had a brick yard; and afterwards removed back of Port Hope.

[11] I presume Tannery Creek, still very lively at some seasons of the year.

XI

SOME REFERENCES TO NEGROES IN UPPER CANADA.

BY THE HONOURABLE WILLIAM RENWICK RIDDELL, LL.D., F.R.S.C., ETC.

The report to the Lieutenant-Governor of Upper Canada by Chief Justice William Dummer Powell dated Niagara, 25 September, 1821, contains the following:—

"In the Western District [the Assize Town of which was Sandwich] an indictment for a Riot disclosed certain transactions which may affect the general peace of the district.

* "It appears that runaway slaves from the United States receive great encouragement from the inhabitants of that quarter; and are residents there in great numbers, cultivating for Hire or on Shares excellent Tobacco equal to the growth of the Ohio or the Mississippi. The protection afforded by our laws to the personal freedom of all who live in the Province without offence induced a number of slave owners to employ an active agent to recover their property and this agent failing in many attempts to seduce his victims into the Territory of the U.S. engaged assistance, crossed the Streight in the night and attacked a house in Sandwich occupied by runaway negro slaves. The riot and panic occasioned by this attack created alarm and the assailants fled to their boats; but in the course of the day one of the principals ventured to cross again. was recognized, made prisoner and indicted.

Upon the fullest conviction he was sentenced to fine, imprisonment and the pillory. It is said that the owners purpose a Deputation to his Excellency, the Lieutenant-Governor, for relief on failure of which application is to be made to the Government of the U. S."

Such an application was made, accompanied with a complaint against the Chief Justice's charge to the Grand Jury. He transmitted to His Excellency a copy of his charge which was to the effect that kidnapping was a serious offence but an attempt at kidnapping, which was unsuccessful, could be punished only as an aggravated assault. (Canadian Archives, Sundries, U.C., 1821). Of course the indictment for a riot was at the common law.

Perhaps the most interesting of all the papers in that series is the following petition:

To His Excellency Sir Peregrine Maitland Knight, Commander of the most Honourable Military Order of the Bath, Lieutenant-Governor of the Province of Upper Canada, and Major General Commanding His Majesty's Forces therein, etc., etc., etc.:—

The Petition of Richard Pierpont, now of the Town of Niagara, a man of Color, a native of Africa, and an Inhabitant of this Province since the year 1780.
Most humbly showeth,

That Your Excellency's Petitioner is a Native of Bondou in Africa;—that at the age of sixteen years he was made a Prisoner and sold as a slave; that he was conveyed to America about the year 1760; and sold to a British officer; that he served his Majesty during the American Revolutionary War in the Corps called Butler's Rangers; and again during the late American War in a Corps of Color raised on the Niagara Frontier.

That Your Excellency's Petitioner is now old and without property; that he finds it difficult to obtain a livelihood by his labor; that he is above all things desirous to return to his native country; that if His Majesty's Government be graciously pleased to grant him any relief, he wishes it may be by affording him the means to proceed to England and from thence to a Settlement near the Gambia or Senegal Rivers, from whence he could return to Bondou.

Your Excellency's Petitioner therefore humbly prays that Your Excellency will be graciously pleased to take his case into your favorable consideration, and order such steps to be taken to have him sent as to Your Excellency may seem meet; or to afford him relief in any manner Your Excellency may be graciously pleased to order.

And Your humble Petitioner as in duty
bound will ever pray
his
RICHARD x PIERPONT.
mark

York, Upper Canada,
   21st July, 1821.
   A true Copy,
      James FitzGibbon.

Adjutant General's Office,
York, 21st July, 1821.

I do hereby certify that Richard Pierpont, a man of color, served His Majesty, in North America, during the American Revolutionary War, in the Provincial Corps called Butler's Rangers.

I further certify that the said Richard Pierpont, better known by the name of Captain Dick, was the first colored man who proposed to raise a Corps of Men of Color on the Niagara Frontier, in the last American War; that he served in the said corps during that War, and that he is a faithful and deserving old Negro.

N. COFFIN,
Adjt. Genl. Militia,
Upper Canada.
Upper Canada Sundries (1821).

It does not appear what was done on this petition; but that a Negro Corps was raised at Niagara during the war of 1812 is certain, e.g., there is in 1821 a petition by the widow of Peter Lee, who had been "a private soldier in a colored corps raised by Captain Robert Runchey . . . in the course of the late war, he received an . . . injury to his shoulder."

XII

"WAS MOLLY BRANT MARRIED?"

BY THE HONOURABLE WILLIAM RENWICK RIDDELL, LL.D., F.R.S.C., ETC.

"Sir William Johnson . . . married Molly Brant by Indian custom, and later, to legitimize his children under British law, had the marriage sanctioned and celebrated by the Church."

This passage is found in an official publication by the Province of Ontario.[1] It contains by implication at least two errors and as I think one serious misstatement of fact.

In the first place there is no such thing as "British Law": there is English law, and there is Scottish law; but they are not the same. The English law is based upon the Common Law of England; the Scottish law, upon the Civil Law of Rome.[2]

Again it is indicated that if Sir William Johnson married Molly, even upon his deathbed, their previously born children would be legitimized. The different rules of English and Scottish law in that regard are perfectly well known to every lawyer.

As is generally believed, Constantine, on the urgent advice of the higher clergy, made a temporary law that subsequent marriage should legitimize offspring born previously thereto; his successors renewed the law from time to time and it was made perpetual by the Emperor Justinian, in his memorable codification[3] The doctrine made its way into most of Continental Europe; and it was introduced into Scotland before the Reformation.

In England, as elsewhere, the Canon Law of the Church took over the principle from the Civil Law; and in 1235, there was a memorable attempt on the part of the Bishops to have it adopted as the Law of England. Parliament met at the Priory of Merton, in Surrey, about nine miles from London and there *In Crasino Sancti Vincentii* (i.e. January 23) was passed the famous Statute of Merton, which confirmed the Common Law rule that for a child to be legiti-

---

[1] "Thirty first Annual Archæological Report, 1919 . . . printed by Order of the Legislative Assembly of Ontario," Toronto, 1919, p. 50. On p. 37 appears the statement concerning Sir William Johnson, "Molly Brant, the sister of Captain Brant, became his housekeeper and later, his wife."

[2] Of course, in many matters, especially commercial matters, the rules of the two systems are the same or almost the same; and there is much statutory law which applies to both countries.

[3] The object of the law was to put a decorous end to the concubinage widely prevailing, which was looked upon by most as wholly creditable and by the law as semimarriage.

The law of legitimation *per subsequens matrimonium* was declared by Constantine in a Constitution now lost, renewed by Zeno (Code v, 27.5) and confirmed by Anastasius and Justin (Code v, 27, 6 and 7) Justinian's Code is Code, v. 27, 9 and 11. See the very able and interesting work on Parent and Child by Lord Frazer, a Scottish Judge, 2nd Edition, 1866, p. 32. This work is very accurate and may be confidently relied upon.

mate his parents must have been married before his birth.[4] When England took possession of the New Netherlands, and New Amsterdam became New York (1664), to the extent that her possession was thoroughly established the law that prevailed was the Common Law of England.[5]

William Johnson came to New York in 1738, and to the Mohawk Valley in the following year, buying his estate "Mount Johnson" in 1741, and finishing his mansion there in 1743. From that time until his death, July 11, 1774, he was domiciled in the Mohawk Valley; and it is quite beyond question that the Common Law was in full force in that part of the Colony of New York. His children by Molly Brant were there born; and under the Common Law the legitimacy of a person was determined by the law of the country in which he was born. The conclusion then is irresistible that a marriage of Sir William upon his death bed to her would be wholly ineffective to legitimize her children.[6]

---

[4] Provisiones de Merton (1235) 20 Henry III, c. 9, Statutes at Large, Ruffhead's ed. vol. 1, p. 19, Chapter 9 (8 in the Cotton MSS) is worth quoting in full for its quaint vigor.

"Ad breve Regis de Bastardis, utrum aliquis natus ante matrimonium habere poterit hereditatem, sicut ille qui natus est post, Responderunt omnes Episcopi quod nolunt, nec possint, ad illud respondere quia hoc esset contra formam ecclesiae, Ac rogaverunt omnes Episcopi, Magnates ut consentirent, quod nati ante matrimonium essent legitimi, sicut illi qui nati sunt post matrimonium, quantum ad successionem hereditariam, quia ecclesia tales habet pro legitimis. Et omnes Comites et Barones una voce responderunt, quod nolunt leges Angliæ mutare quae usitate sunt et approbate." The last clause has been quoted and approved thousands of times—the "Common lawyer" delights in it and considers it one of the most glorious if not the most glorious of all the many splendid declarations of the Parliament of England. But the glory of the "Comites et Barones" seems to be dimmed even in England. Bills for the legitimation *per subsequens matrimonium* in England were introduced in Parliament in 1893 by Walter McLaren, M.P., and later by Joseph King and Dr. Chapple, M.P's: the War prevented anything being advanced in that direction for a time but emphasized the necessity of some action in view of the large number of "War babies." In the present year Nevil Chamberlain introduced a Bill of many sections dealing with Bastardy, one clause enacting legitimation *per subsequens matrimonium.* This particular clause was received favorably by the Government and the House; and it is possible that in another year or two, the change will be made. The change has already been made in many of the United States and in some parts of Australia; and the rule prevails in all Civil Law Countries.

Much information is to be found in Sir Dennis Fitzpatrick's article "Legitimation by Subsequent Marriage." 6 Journal Comparative Legislation (1904) p. 22.

The Common Law rule seems doomed with many other Common rules once and for long considered the perfection of human reason.

The Canon Law which adopted the Civil Law principle as early as the twelfth century was applied by the Bishops as part of the Ecclesiastical law certainly down to the Reformation and probably later—Maitland's "Roman Canon Law in the Church of England" (1898) pp. 53 sqq. This was so far effective as to permit an illegitimate to take Holy Orders notwithstanding the stern injunction of Deuteronomy 23:2.

[5] Except that of course, the Courts recognized the rights which had become vested under the modified Civil Law in force under Dutch posssesion.

[6] It was not until 1895 that legislation was passed by the State of New York introducing the Civil Law Rule—See Laws of New York, 1895, Chap. 531, sec. 1 and Laws of New York, 1896, Vol. 1. Chap. 272, sec. 18. The case of Olmsted v. Olmsted (1907) 118 App. Div. 69; 190 N.Y. 458; 216 U.S. 386 discusses the law of New York in that regard.

What I believe to be a misstatement of fact is the allegation that Sir William Johnson had a marriage with Molly Brant, "sanctioned and celebrated by the Church."

The main facts of Sir William Johnson's life are wholly beyond dispute. Born in Ireland, in 1715, he came to the continent toward the end of 1737, and arrived in the Mohawk Valley Region in the following spring; he married in 1739, Katherine Weisenberg [7] who in the next five years bore him three children. She died in 1745, and he took as a companion, Caroline, daughter of Chief Abraham, Sachem of the Lower Castle Mohawks and consequently a niece of the well-known Chief Hendrick. She bore him three children before her death in 1753.

Within a short period, not more than a year, he took in the same capacity, Mary or Molly Brant, sister of the celebrated Joseph Brant, Thayendanegea, with whom he lived until his death, July 11, 1774, and who bore him nine children. [8] Whether anything in the nature of a marriage ceremony took place between them at the beginning of their intimacy, we need not enquire. There may have been something of the kind, but it certainly was not such as anyone considered a marriage binding in law. Molly Brant, of course, considered herself his wife, "in Indian fashion," and must be held ethically and morally innocent of wrong.

There are three stories of a legal marriage. The first is given currency by Jeptha R. Simms in his "Frontiersmen of New York," Albany, 1882, Vol. 1, p. 205, The author speaks of certain memoranda by Henry Frey Yates in a communication to his son, Bernard F., and proceeds: "With reference to this woman, says the memoranda of Yates, 'It is true that Sir William was married to Molly according to the rites of the Episcopal Church but a few years before

---

[7] The contemptuous reference to Johnson's wife by Parkman, "Montcalm and Wolfe," Vol. 1, p. 298, "Here presided for many years a Dutch or German wench whom he finally married" is unworthy of that eminent writer. He is rather more courteous in his "Conspiracy of Pontiac," Vol. 1; at page 95 he says: "Johnson supplied the place of his former (Irish) love by a young Dutch damsel who bore him several children; and, in justice to them, he married her upon her death-bed." The story of this alleged death-bed marriage will be spoken of later in this article.

[8] It is not unlikely that he had other and less creditable liaisons of a temporary or occasional character with women, white and Indian. If half the gossip of the neighborhood was true he should have required to enlarge "Johnson Hall" to the dimensions of the Palace of old Priam—Quinquaginta illi thalami, spes tanta nepotum—for the old commentator tells us "Liberos habuit ex utroque sexu duos ac sexaginta e variis uxeribus." While current stories attributed to Sir William the fatherhood of over one hundred children.

In a fairly common and well known work, "Trappers of New York or a Biography of Nicholas Stoner and Nathaniel Foster; . . . and some account of Sir William Johnson and his style of living, By Jeptha R. Simms . . . Albany, J. Munsell, 78 State Street, 1860," we find it stated on p. 44 that:

Sir William was "on very intimate terms with the Woodward girls, but the most so with Susannah after she became a grass widow—at which time she was about twenty years old" and that he had one or the other as "an agreeable companion for the night," adding a somewhat salacious anecdote. There is no mention of Molly Brant by Simms.

The date of his first association with Molly Brant is very uncertain—different writers give it as about 1746 (Stone, Max Reid), 1754 (Buell), 1759 (Griffis) &c. &c. It is quite immaterial to the present enquiry and I do not pursue the question.

his death. The Baronet feeling his life drawing to a close and abhorring living longer in adultery, to quiet his conscience privately married Molly to legitimize his children by her, as he had done those by the German girl, who was the mother of Sir John and his sisters.'"

This story is quite obviously incorrect at least in detail. Johnston made his will, afterwards properly proved, in January, 1774, much less than a year before his death; and in it speaks of Catharine as his wife, whose remains were to be beside his own, but Molly he calls his housekeeper, and her offspring his "natural" children. It is impossible that she could have been so described had the marriage ceremony been performed between them.

That story failing, it is asserted that the marriage took place on his death-bed;[9] but it is well known that while he had been suffering from dysentery for some time, his death was sudden and unexpected. On July 11, 1774, he made a long and impassioned speech to a number of Indians, Iroquois for the most part, a speech which lasted nearly two hours and called for great mental and physical exertion; shortly after the close of the speech he was stricken with cerebral hemorrhage which resulted in his death within two hours of the termination of his speech. He had no time to think of marriage; and Joseph Brant, Molly's brother, to whom his last words were addressed, and who assisted to carry the stricken Baronet into Johnson Hall, never said or suggested that any marriage was solemnized or spoken of.

Then the story is told that it was after the will and a short time before his death that he had the ceremony performed. [10] To quote again from Simm's "Frontiersmen of New York," *ut supra;* "Among the few who witnessed the ceremony of the Baronet's second marriage, which is said, instead of years, to have been but a short time before his death and after his will was drawn, the memoranda names Robert Adams, a merchant of Johnstown, and Rebecca Vansickler. To the last he accredits his authority . . . ." The utter improbability of this story must strike everyone. If Johnson from any feeling of decency and regard for his companion, made her his wife he certainly would have seen to it that the fact was placed beyond all controversy. He would never have let the will stand which sharply distinguished his wife from his concubine, when a short codicil would make everything clear. The woman had lived long enough among the Whites to know the magic virtue of "marriage lines," and would treasure her marriage certificate. In a word there would be some written evidence at some time, and even if by chance or accident that should be destroyed, there would be some account of it somewhere. Not a scrap of anything approaching evidence or anything but the merest gossip has ever been produced.

---

[9] Phelps & Graham, 1852 p. 72. "A legal marriage took place when Sir William was on his death bed, which ceremony had reference to the descent of property."

[10] In Ketchum's "History of Buffalo," Buffalo, N.Y. 1864, at p. 126, occurs the note "It is said he was married to Molly Brant, a short time before his death according to the rites of the Protestant Episcopal Church, in order to legitimize his children by her." No authority is given.

The strongest kind of negative evidence is, however, available, which would destroy even a prima facie case if such were made out—and that evidence is furnished by the records in the Canadian Archives at Ottawa.

She was held in the highest respect by the authorities in Canada and looked upon as a valuable ally: if she had been married to Sir William, she would have been Lady Johnson and would have been spoken of as Lady Johnson—she never was.

The children of Johnson by his wife, Katharine, were by no means prejudiced against her but rather the contrary—and the same is true of the whole family connection—they never speak of her except as Molly Brant, or some similar name, never Lady Johnson.

Colonel Daniel Claus, who married Anne (Nancy), daughter of Johnson by his first wife Katharine, became a prominent officer in Canada—he must have known of the marriage of Molly if there was one. We find him writing officially to Sir Frederick Haldimand from Montreal, August 17, 1779:

"Sir John (Johnson) and I arrived here Saturday morning. . . . As soon as Molly Brant heard of my arrival, she paid me a visit and gave me a full detail of her adventures and misfortunes since the Rebellion began, but in particular in the Fall of 1777, after our Retreat from Fort Stanwix, when she was insulted and robbed of everything she had in the world by the Rebels and their Indians . . .

"She had a pointed conversation in publick Council at Canadusegy reminding him [i.e., the Headman of the Senecas], of the former great friendship and attachment which subsisted between him and the late Sir William Johnson, whose memory she never mentioned without tears in her eyes, which affects the Indians greatly . . They promised henceforth truthfully to keep their engagements with her late friend the Baronet, for she is in every respect considered and esteemed by them [i.e., the Indians], as Sir William's Relict, and one word from her is more taken notice of by the five Nations than a thousand from any white man. [11] (Claus goes on to speak of her great influence among the Indians and her indisposition to leave her mother and other Indian relatives on Haldimand's invitation).

In another letter from Montreal, September 6, 1789, Claus says: "Miss Molly, since hearing of the movement of the Indians, is very anxious to return among the Six Nations, and says that her staying away at this critical time may prove very injurious to her character hereafter, being at the head of a Society of Six Nations, who have a great deal to say among the young men in particular in time of war." [12].

To this Haldimand replied from Quebec, September 9, 1779, "As to Miss Molly, if she thinks her presence necessary above, she must be suffered to depart. Col. Johnson will of course provide for her journey and give her whatever Presents may be necessary." [13].

---

[11] Can. Arch., Haldimand Papers, B. 114, pp. 63 seq.—the letter is more fully quoted in Buell's "Sir William Johnson," New York, 1903, pp. 267, 268.
[12] Can. Arch., Haldimand Papers, B. 114, pp. 68 seq.
[13] Can. Arch., B. 114, p. 70.

And Claus, September 13, 1779, informs Haldimand that "Miss Molly" accompanied a band of twenty Mohawks he was sending to join Captain Fraser.[14]

April 23, 1781, Haldimand reports to Powell, "representations from Miss Molly."[15]

Three months later, July 26, 1781, Claus writes to Haldimand from Montreal, "Mrs. Mary Brant has been here for some days and yesterday set off for Carleton Island again, taking away her son George and Susan and Mary, two of her daughters, who were here at schools near two years. Margaret, another sister, left this place about a year ago. The schoolmaster tells me the girls sufficiently read and write English and the boy to my knowledge has greatly improved in that respect. . . At Molly's leaving she entreated me to offer her most sincere and hearty respects and thanks to His Excellency. . . She seemed to be happy in her childrens' improved state. . . There are left at school two of Brant Johnson's children, whose mother is daily expected to take them away; the eldest a fine genius and great arithmetician . . ."[16]

Col. Matthews, answering from Quebec, July 30, 1781, says: "His Excellency is pleased to find his intention to the education of Miss Molly's children has so well succeeded and that she appears sensible of the Benefit they have received, it being His Excellency's wish as well on account of the Regard he bore the late Sir William Johnson as to reward the services of Her Family, to show her every friendly attention in his power."[17].

On May 27th, 1783, Haldimand writes from Quebec to Sir John Johnson: "In consideration of the early and uniform fidelity, attachment and zealous services redered to the King's Government by Miss Molly Brant and her famly, I have thought fit to settle on her a yearly pension of £100 currency .. ..."[18] More important still, Haldimand wrote on the same day to Captain Joseph Brant that he had granted a pension of £100 to "Mrs. Molly Brant" for the zealous services of herself and her family.[19]

---

[14] Can. Arch., B. 114, p. 71.
[15] Can. Arch., B. 104, p. 212.
[16] Can. Arch., B. 114, p. 192.
Colonel Daniel Claus had been Deputy Superintendent of Indians from 1761: he was married to Anne (Nancy) elder daughter of Sir William Johnson: Col. Guy Johnson to Mary, the younger.
[17] Can. Arch., B. 114, p. 195.
[18] Can. Arch. B. 115 p. 116. Sir John Johnson had been from March 14, 1782, and was at this time Superintendent General and Inspector General of Indians by Royal Commission—he so remained until the office was abolished, March 25, 1828: he had succeeded his cousin and brother-in-law Col. Guy Johnson, who was suspended on certain charges, February, 1782. Sir John was absent from Canada in England leaving Canada September, 1792, and not returning until October, 1796. The ship "Lady Johnson" sailing with articles for the use of the Indians as mentioned in Haldimand's letter to Sir John Johnson from Quebec, June 14, 1784, Can. Arch., Hald. Papers B. 63, pp. 407 sqq. was called after the wife of Sir John.
Haldimand was about the time of the granting of the pension insisting on the reduction of the expenses of the Indian Department—see e.g. his letter to Sir John Johnson from Quebec, January 26, Hald. Papers, B. 63, p. 57.
[19] Can. Arch., B. 105, p. 358.

November 1, 1784, Haldimand made a standing order that the houses to be built at Cataraqui for Joseph Brant and "Mrs. Mary Brant" were to be considered entirely their property. [20]

In official correspondence within a few years after Johnson's death by and between persons who would be expected to know of her marriage if a marriage had taken place, the Governor and all concerned spoke of her as Molly Brant—the Governor to her brother more formally as Mrs. Mary Brant and at no time is there the slightest suggestion that she was really Lady Johnson.

Perhaps of even more importance is the fact that Joseph Brant, who was pressing the claims of the Indians and of his own family never suggests a marriage, and if negative evidence could be conclusive the fact that at least twice claims were urged upon the Administration by her or on her behalf[21] and not one word is said to indicate that she was other than a person who had been a wife only according to Indian custom.

Then we have the proceedings before Colonel (afterwards Major-General) Thomas Dundas and Mr. Jeremy Pemberton, Special Commissioners on the claims of the United Empire Loyalists. [22]

Sir John Johnson, in 1788, appears as a witness on "the claim of the Children of Mary Brant": and, "says that Mary Brant has received. Compensation for her own losses".—he gives evidence concerning Elizabeth, Magdaline, Margaret, George and Mary—and Peter deceased—there being, he says, "Seven of the children now alive"[23]—Peter Warren Brant, the eldest, being dead.

And "Mrs. Mary Brant" appears as a witness some months afterwards.[24]

Now all this is negative evidence of course: it is proverbially difficult to prove a negative and it would yield to even a small amount of positive evidence. What positive evidence is there?

We have seen that Simms in his "Frontiersmen of New York," asserts the fact positively: he repeats the story in a letter dated at Fort Plain, N.Y., November 20, 1877—he there said that he had not seen the Yates MSS, for many years, that Bernard F. Yates was dead but that he, Simms, had talked with old Mr. Yates, then an old man 30 years ago, who "expressed himself as believing what I stated . . . about Sir William marrying Mary Brant"—the few years perhaps should have been a few months or even days but I gave full credence to his story as

[20] Can. Arch., B. 64, p. 382.
Other letters about this time referring to her are to be found B. 114, p. 63 "Molly Brant" (Claus to Haldimand) B. 114. pp. 66, 70, 115 "Miss Molly" (Haldimand to Claus): B. 114, pp. 68, 71. "Miss Molly." (Claus to Haldimand)
[21] See B. 104, p. 212; B. 114, p. 63.
[22] The commissioners came to Canada and took the evidence in person; this was contained in a number of volumes of manuscript which were retained by Col. Dundas and after his death in 1784 were sold by his family to the American Government. A full copy has been printed in a very convenient form by the Ontario Archives as Second Report (1904).
[23] Sitting of Commissioners at Montreal, March 3, 1788. Rep. (1904) p. 472.
2 Ont. Arch. Rep. (1904), p. 472. Susanne and Anne are not mentioned. There is a somewhat amusing error in the indexing of this volume p. 1384. "Kingsland" is taken for the first name of one of Molly's children instead of the name of a place.
[24] August 30; 2 Ont. Arch. Rep. (1904) p. 983.

he informed me he had the facts of his marriage from a credible witness present—nor was he the only one who told me of the same marriage to Miss Brant."[25] Hearsay upon hearsay without document or probability. There are some fugitive statements made early in the last century to the same effect, but there are quite as many or more to the opposite. [26]

My own enquiries go back some years: I have traced several positive assertions to their source and have always found that there was no foundation for the story.

---

[25] Draper MSS., State Historical Society of Wisconsin, 13 F. 175—the letter is from J. R. Simms to L. C. Draper, Esq.

[26] From the Draper MSS., I select the following: I F 98 (2) "Mrs. Grant who was for many years a resident of Albany and intimate with Sir William Johnson, says, "After the decease of Lady Johnson, Sir William married Mary, the sister of Brant, by whom he had several children, three girls of which afterwards married Colonels in the Army." But in her entertaining book, "Memoirs of an American Lady," she says that Sir William "connected himself with the daughter of an Indian Sachem, who . . . whether ever formally married to him according to our usage or not, continued to live with him in great union and affection all his life." See John Ross Robertson's Diary of Mrs. Simcoe, p. 247. Kirby, in a letter from Niagara, September 9, 1889, says, "She was not married to Sir William by English form of marriage," Draper MSS. 11 F. 207. Draper MSS. 14, F. 100 (5) "They were never legally married though such a statement has been made."

I quote also works more or less generally known: William Elliot Griffis, "Sir William Johnson and The Six Nations" . . . New York, Dodd, Mead and Company, Publishers, n.d., at p. 21 speaks of "Catharine, a daughter of a German Palatine settler named Weissenberg or Wisenburg," and says in a note, "The local gossip and groundless traditions like those set down by J. R. Simms are in all probability worthless"—and indeed "groundless traditions" are generally "worthless." Griffis says "Kate was the only woman with whom he lived in wedlock." He truly says that "no record of the marriage ceremony has yet been found," and suggests that they were married by "some one of the Dutch or German clergymen of the Valley as is most likely," or if not, by the Rev. Thomas Barclay, an English Episcopal Minister at Fort Hunter. Griffis says that when the bones of Johnson were disturbed in 1862, a plain gold ring was found inscribed on the inside "June 1739.16" and suggests that that date was that of his marriage to his own lawful wife.

P. 22 "of Molly Brant, his late mistress, he spoke and wrote as his housekeeper: of the Palatine German lawfully wedded to him, as his beloved wife." Of Molly Brant Griffis says, p. 180, that she "was undoubtedly a woman of ability and with her Johnson lived happily. . ."

P. 206 "Mary Brant, though not only an Indian but a Mohawk Indian, in spirit was to her dying day in the old English and Hebrew sense of the word a virtuous woman."

Augustus C. Buell, "Sir William Johnson" New York, D. Appleton and Company, 1903 pp. 16, 17 speaking of Katherine," daughter of Jacob Weisenburg, a Lutheran clergyman," says, " in 1739 . . . he married her; the ceremony, according to Mr. Max Reid, was performed by the Rev. Mr. Barclay, rector of Queen Anne's Chapel at Fort Hunter." p. 46: "Late in 1745, his white wife Katherine died suddenly . . ." leaving three children. p. 48: "In the fall of 1747 he astonished all his friends by employing a young Indian woman as housekeeper . . . . not Mary Brant . . . . Caroline, daughter of Chief Abraham, Sachem of the Lower Castle Mohawks," a niece of Hendrick, who had three children by him and died giving birth to the third in 1753. About a year after he offered his protection and affection to Mary Brant. She accepted and outlived him, they lived together twenty years, 1754-1774: she bore him nine children, two boys and seven girls, but one of the latter died in infancy.

Buell discredits the romantic story of Mary Brant's first introduction to Johnson and says Johnson had known her from the time she was ten years old.

Not long after Caroline's death (p 57) "the arrangement was made by which Mary became the mistress of his household."

p. 59 "the baronet lived in a morganatic fashion with two Indian women at different times."

For example I have within the year been positively assured of the existence at Albany of written proof of the alleged marriage: On enquiry made of the gentle-

p. 46 (n) Buell properly rebukes Parkman "Wolfe and Montcalm" vol. 1, p. 298, for saying "Here presided for many years a Dutch or German wench whom he finally married."

p. 52 quotes Reid that Johnson married neither Indian girl.

Stone in his "Life of Joseph Brant—Thayendanegea, New York, 1836, vol. 1, p. 18, says that about 1748 "Johnson employed as his housekeeper, Mary Brant, or Miss Molly as she was called, a sister of the celebrated Indian Chief, Thayendanegea with whom he lived until his decease and by whom he had several children."

Note I: "That Molly Brant was not the wife of the baronet is finally proved by his last will in which after desiring to have the remains of his beloved wife Catherine interred beside him he speaks of the children of my present housekeeper, Mary Brant" as his "*natural* children." It is, however, but justice to Molly Brant to state that she always regarded herself as married to the baronet after the Indian fashion."

Stone in his "Life of Joseph Brant—Thayendanegea," New York, 1836, vol. I p. 18, quotes from Mrs Grant's daughter's book, "Memoirs of an American Lady," chapter 39, that "the Indian maiden whether ever formally married to him according to our usage or not continued to live with him in great union and affection all his life."

No suggestion of a marriage is made in this work.

W. Max Reid, "The Mohawk Valley" . . . New York and London, 1901—quotes Griffis' "Life of Sir William Johnson"; gives the date of Johnson's first association with Miss Molly as more nearly 1746 (with Stone), than 1759 (with Griffis), but while quoting Simms "Frontiersmen of New York" on another matter, he says nothing of an alleged marriage.

E. M. Chadwick: "Victorian Families," Toronto. 1894. p. 67, under the heading "Brant" "Mary, or Molly as she was usually better called (died 1805) who became the second wife of Sir William Johnson Baronet (died 1774)." But on communicating with my old friend and former partner, Major Chadwick informs me:—

"In reply to yours of 29th ult., I do not think Sir William Johnson was ever married to Molly Brant according to white man's law but she was certainly his wife according to Indian custom. You will notice that the children (daughters) of this marriage were fully recognized socially, for they all married persons socially prominent." Letter, Toronto, October 1st, 1920.

In the Parliamentary Library of Canada there formerly was a MSS. quarto volume of 347 pages, with additions of 9 and 14 pages, entitled "Canadian Letters, Descriptive of a Tour thro' the Provinces of Lower and Upper Canada in the course of the years 1792 and 1793." (the author's name is not given and the volume is now lost).

"Captain Brant had a sister at Cataraqui who was known by the name of Miss Molly. Sir William Johnson left some children by this squaw with whom he had cohabitated for many years. They are, I believe, with the exception of one son, all daughters. Sir William bequeathed handsome fortunes to the whole family. The Misses Johnson are married respectably in the country. It is with regret that I have heard, since my return to England, of the death of the eldest, Mrs. Kerr. For many minute attentions which in Colonial life are highly valuable to the passing or unsettled stranger, I have now to lament that from this event I must ever remain indebted." Draper MSS, F, 193.

Appleton's Cyclopædia of American Biography:
Sir William Johnson, bart., b. 1715; d. 1774.

"In 1739, he married Catherine Wisenburgh, daughter of a German settler on the Mohawk, who died young leaving three children, a son, John, who was knighted in 1765, and two daughters, Anne and Mary, who married respectively, Col. Daniel Claus and Col. Guy Johnson. Sir William never married again. He had for some years afterwards many mistresses, both Indian and white, and one of his earlier ones, a German, has been the probable cause, from being confounded with his wife, of the erroneous statement that has been made that none of his children were legitimate. Mary, or as she is generally called "Molly" Brant the sister of Thayendanegea, or Joseph Brant, the Mohawk sachem, whom later he took to his house, and with whom he lived happily till his death, has sometimes been termed his wife; but they were never married. He had eight children by her, whom he provided for by his will, in which he calls them his 'natural children.'"

man [27] said to be in possession of it, he stated that he had made considerable enquiry but that he had never seen anything of the kind. About the same time I was informed that an Indian Chief of Caledonia [28] had seen at Johnstown, N. Y., a wedding ring given to Miss Molly by Sir William Johnson, in the possession of a Historical Society there. Enquiry disclosed the fact that the ring was one given by the Baronet to his wife, Catharine Weisenberg, and is in the Historical collection at Johnson Hall; no record of any marriage ceremony has ever been heard of.

Nothing is known of the supposed marriage in the Libraries of Congress, at Washington, of Parliament at Ottawa, of New York, of Boston, of Buffalo, in the Archives at Ottawa and at Toronto, in the Indian Department of the Dominion, or in any place at which I have thought it possible that a record might be found, and I have neglected no known or suggested source of information. [29]

The story of the deathbed marriage perhaps had its origin in that of the marriage on her deathbed to Catharine Weisenberg, a curious story with some semblance of evidence which deserves to be more carefully examined. The state-

---

[27] Dr. Arthur C. Parker, Archæologist of the State of New York, Albany, N.Y., who has Indian blood in his veins.

[28] Chief W. D. Loft, Caledonia, Ontario. *ex relatione* A. G. Chisholm, Esq., Counsel for the Six Nation Indians: my information as to the fact is from the Reverend Wolcott W. Ellsworth, Rector of St. John's Church, Johnstown, N.Y.—his letter is dated from Johnstown, N.Y., October 27, 1920.

Another story coming from modern Indian sources is that the Rev. John Stuart married Sir William to Miss Molly at the Mohawk Village, in 1770; but this was long before his death (1774), and consequently the story is morally impossible.

[29] I copy here a letter from an acknowledged authority, Dr. James Sullivan, State Historian of the State of New York.

"September 27, 1920.

"Hon. Mr. Justice Riddell,
 "Supreme Court of Ontario, Osgoode Hall,
  "Toronto, Canada.

Dear Sir,—

"Up to the present time there has been absolutely no documentary evidence in any form presented to show that Sir William Johnson was married to Molly Brant. In his will, which was drawn up in 1774, he speaks of her as his housekeeper, and certainly if he were married either by regular marriage ceremony prevailing in Christian countries, or even by an Indian rite, he would not have thus spoken of her in his last will and testament.

"We know that various persons have persisted in spreading, or starting rumours to the effect that Sir William Johnson was married to Molly Brant. The most recent of these that this office has tried to run down was one appearing in the *Oneida Despatch* for November 21, 1919. This was given on the authority of DeWitt C. Haddock, who said that he had in his possession a diary of his grandfather, Daniel Haddock, the contents of which bore witness to the fact that Sir William Johnson had been married to Molly Brant, in July, 1769. The newspaper article was such a tissue of misstatements and inaccuracies that on the very face of it no credence could be placed on it. We immediately got into communication with Mr. Haddock and he promised to let us see this diary. Three letters written to him subsequent to such promise have failed to bring any results whatsoever and we believe that the whole thing is a fake.

"These rumours, as you know, are started by a certain kind of person whose moral sense is somewhat shocked by the fact that Sir William Johnson cohabited with Molly Brant, and they therefore try to hatch up some sort of marriage ceremony to make the thing appear highly moral according to a 19th century code."

"Very truly yours,
"JAMES SULLIVAN."

ment that there was a marriage at all seems to be the creation of some who imagined that there was something improper or degrading in the union—improper and degrading it may have been in the man, only the narrow-minded or uncharitable can see impropriety or degradation in the woman. From her own point of view and that of her people, she was a pure and faithful wife, fit to stand before Kings, a virtuous woman whose price was far above rubies. And so it is to Johnson's credit that he always treated her with respect and insisted that others should do the same.

The following copied by me from the original, seems to settle the matter at least as to Peter Johnson, one of the sons of Molly Brant. Why, or for what purpose the affidavit was taken does not appear. John Ray was a prominent citizen of New York.

"City of New York, to wit. Alexander Ellice of London, in the Kingdom of Great Britain, merchant, at present residing in the City of New York, being duly sworn deposeth and saith that he was personally acquainted with Peter Johnson, the natural son of Sir William Johnson, Baronet, deceased, by Mary Brant, his house-keeper; that the said Peter Johnson entered the British Army as an Ensign and for some time in the year of Our Lord one thousand seven hundred and seventy-six sailed with the said army for America, where he died or was killed some time in that year or the year following; that the said Peter Johnson never married to the knowledge of this deponent, and this deponent verily believes died without leaving any lawful issue, and further his deponent saith not.
(Signed)   ALEX'R ELLICE"

Sworn this fourth day of March, 1795,
before me, John Ray, M. Ch'y.
Extract from *Magazine of American History.* Volume VI, 1881.

XIII.

THE REV. ROBERT ADDISON AND ST. MARK'S CHURCH
By Professor A. H. Young.

Though the first missionary at Niagara and the first rector of St. Mark's church, the Rev. Robert Addison was not the first clergyman of the Church of England to officiate at the old capital of Upper Canada. That honour fell to the Rev. John Ogilvie of Albany, N. Y., chaplain to the Mohawks, who accompanied Sir William Johnson and General Prideaux on the expedition which resulted in the reduction of Fort Niagara in the year 1759.

In 1784, the Rev. John Stuart, like Ogilvie a "servant" of the Society for the Propagation of the Gospel in Foreign Parts, paid a visit or prospecting tour to Niagara, but he decided to settle in Kingston, which he did in the summer of 1785. In his correspondence is to be found an account of this visit, which was remarkable mainly for his renewal of relations with his former parishioners of Fort Hunter, N. Y., the Mohawk Indians.

The Indians were fellow-Loyalists and they had removed from their old home on the banks of the Mohawk River in order to remain within British territory. This intention being frustrated by the award of the right bank of the Niagara River to the United States, by the Treaty of Versailles, they left the church and other conveniences which had been provided for them, and again removed, this time to the Grand River, where Stuart continued to visit them occasionally until that duty was taken over by Addison.

The Society (commonly called the S.P.G. for short) had up for consideration at its meeting held on the 15th of March, 1790, a letter from the Right Rev. Charles Inglis, first Bishop of Nova Scotia, on the subject of Niagara. Having jurisdiction ecclesiastical over Canada as well as Nova Scotia, New Brunswick, Bermuda, and Newfoundland, he was anxious to obtain a missionary for Niagara. In this letter he told of Col. Butler and the Hon. Robert Hamilton, together with ten other "principal inhabitants," giving a bond to pay a hundred pounds a year for seven years "to any clergyman appointed by the Bishop or the Society, from the time of his arrival, unless a legal provision is made in the same time." This was about a year before the passing of the Constitutional Act, with its clause concerning "a Protestant Clergy." "The Clergyman will have," the letter continued, "a glebe and house, and, if he chuse it, may easily procure land for his own private property."*

---

*Twelve hundred acres were commonly granted to clergymen of any denomination, as to lawyers, Legislative Councillors, and other persons of consideration, on application to the Executive Council of Upper Canada (and Lower Canada also) in the early days of the Province. There are not a few cases recorded of grants of six hundred acres to wives of barristers and to merchants.

The Bishop was under no illusion as to the religious inclinations of the population, "many leading men," he said, "being Dissenters, who have no Clergymen." He describes them as "generous and public-spirited," and "the Magistrates in each Township" as setting on foot a subscription for building Churches and supporting Ministers;" and the first Protestant Clergymen that shall arrive, of whatever denominations, are to be first provided for out of those subscriptions." He adds: "The state of the country, it seems, requires this latitudinarian scheme . . . . and Government has not interfered in the business."

Col. Butler and Mr. Hamilton represented the Inhabitants as being "1,000 men, 700 women, and 1400 children, half of which are of the Church, and a very few Papists." To give the Society all the information necessary in selecting a missionary, the Bishop informed them that "the climate is mild, rather warmer than New York; the soil exceedingly good through the whole district, which is almost insulated, bounded on the North by Lake Erie, on the South by Lake Ontario, on the West by the River, which runs out of the former into the latter of those Lakes, and in which is the greatest cataract of Niagara."

In response to this appeal, the Rev. Robert Addison, who was recommended by the Bishops of Ely and Peterborough, was sent out by the Society in 1791. Like Lieutenant-Governor Simcoe, who came out in the same year, he arrived too late in the season to proceed to the "Upper Country." Mr. Toosey (or Tousey),[1] who was a missionary in what was soon to be called Lower Canada, advised him to winter in Quebec, which he did. In a letter dated October 31st, "Messrs. Forsyth & Co., Merchants at Montreal, thought it proper to mention to him that the season was too far advanced to admit of almost a possibility of reaching Niagara; and were it even probable, he would find the travelling, which must be by water, exceedingly uncomfortable, and that they thought it his safest plan to delay his journey till Spring; about the end of April."

It was June or July of 1792 before he arrived in Niagara, which was to be the scene of his labours for thirty-seven years. Writing home three months later, "he could say but little concerning the place. He is the only Clergyman of any denomination, and has always preached to a pretty large Congregation. They have no Church, but hope that the Governor, who is to winter with them, will assist them in the building one. He has officiated in various parts of the Settlement near 30 miles apart, but has been prevented by sickness from baptizing and preaching at much greater distances, to which he was invited. He has already baptized 47—married 2 [couples]—buried 7."

This was a great change from Trinity College, Cambridge, of which he had been a member. In return for all that he had given up he received a salary of fifty pounds "to commence at Midsummer next (1791), and the Treasurer was directed to advance him half a year's salary"—presumably for travelling

---

[1] Mr. Toosey, the first English-speaking Church of England rector of Quebec, had been tutor to Lord Dorchester's sons in Quebec. He aspired to be Bishop of Canada, as also did the Revd. Samuel Peters, D.D., when the preferment went to Dr. Jacob Mountain. From 1789, he was Bishop's Commissary or Official for Lower Canada.

expenses. Besides the charge of the white settlers from Dunnville to the "Head of the Lake," now Hamilton, Ontario, he undertook that of the Mohawks on the Grand River, when Dr. Stuart relinquished it, in or soon after 1792.

Stuart, being the Bishop's Official for Upper Canada, informed the Society on the 12th of October of that year that "the people were disposed to make Mr. Addison's situation as comfortable as circumstances will admit, that Col. Butler assured him that 200 pounds currency would be annually paid him by the Parishioners . . . that the Actual Members of the Church of England in that Quarter are not very numerous, but that a Man of Mr. Addison's character and talents, will doubtless greatly increase their number."

The latter statement proved to be true, but the money part of the prognostication failed of fulfilment, even though "The Governor" (Simcoe), again to quote Dr. Stuart, "seems determined to put the Church of England on as respectable a footing as possible . . . from whose countenance much may be expected."

In 1793 the Society is requested to grant an increase in Mr. Addison's allowance "for the keeping of an horse to visit the Indians and the distant parts of the neighbourhood." But the Society could not comply with the request and gave him a gratuity only—"on account of his extraordinary services."

Thanks to the intervention of Dr. Stuart, the "great Chief" Joseph Brant, and Dr. Jacob Mountain, the first Bishop of Quebec, who had just been consecrated as Bishop of Quebec, £20 were added to his annual allowance for visiting the Mohawks. This was indeed a boon, considering the expensiveness of travelling and the dearness of everything in the Settlement. "But by great frugality and some little private possessions," he bravely adds, "he is free from actual want." Friends of his own in England were ready to make contributions toward furthering his work.

"The humble Settler who labours on his land is kind to him," Mr. Addison remarks, "the rich Trader endeavours to be polite, but he is sorry to say that their subscription is likely to end in words. As they, however, still continue to promise fair, he would wish the Society not to remonstrate with them at present." So he continued to make excuses for the parishioners' forgetfulness till the end of the seventh year mentioned in their bond. Then, deprived of the countenance of the Lieutenant-Governor, who had gone home on leave of absence in 1796, "he wishes" (on the 15th of July, 1799, when the Lieutenant-Governor's commission had expired) "to have the Society's interference to require Mr. Hamilton, etc. to comply with their engagements to the Bishop of Nova Scotia to pay the Missionary 100 pounds, which they have never done. The whole amount of the subscription in the eight years he has been there is only 209 pounds, and for two or three years past it has ceased." In one year they gave him £35 and in another £45. *A propos* of the latter he says, "the collection . . . . would have been better if Mr. Hamilton had been there."

Mr. Hamilton (the Hon. Robert Hamilton), the founder of Queenston, Ontario, a sometime partner in business of the Hon. Richard Cartwright of Kingston, and, like the latter, a member of the Legislative Council of the Province, " promised (in 1799) to apply to Government for some wild land to make up all arrears." Withal the Rector goes on to add that "the farm he has purchased in the Parish is very productive." In the same year 1799 he had hopes of " being at the head of a Grammar School at Niagara" and therefore "he should be unwilling to leave the place." He had as early as 1795 entertained thoughts of seeking a transfer to Nova Scotia, to the jurisdiction of his former Bishop, where he should be in a more civilized and a more settled district.

Addison's own applications for lands had not been very successful. Why he did not press them before Simcoe's departure from the province, it is impossible now to learn. Apparently they were dealt with after that event by the Land Board or Committee of the Council, under the chairmanship of the arch-land-grabber, Mr. President Russell, who seems to have been very careful only for himself and his friends.

A petition bearing date June 21, 1796, states that he "has a Grant of only 45 Acres, and therefore humbly requests, that the above, which being near his present Dwelling place, are valuable & desirable to him, he may have an additional Grant of Lands in what Quantity and Situation Your Excellency shall kindly think fit to appoint." In another (No. A.30), read officially on March 29, 1797, he sets out "That his Family consisting of one Son and two Daughters are likely in consequence of such disappointment (the failure of Government to provide for him the salary which he had been led to expect) to be worse provided for." Yet, though it was a kind of request which had been often granted when preferred by men of influence and standing, the endorsement of March 31 reads: "The Board with pain refuses the Prayer of the Petition—being contrary to the general Rule they have laid down for their Conduct in the land granting Department. [Peter Russell]."

There was a slight grain of comfort vouchsafed to him on the same day, however, in that his sister Mary was granted 400 acres on a petition dated at Newark, West Niagara, on the 28th day of the month.

Nothing daunted by the various refusals which he had encountered, he returned to the attack on July 27 and August 14, 1797. On the latter date, as a means of supplementing his income, he was ordered to be given a lease of the salt springs in the township of Ancaster at a rental of five shillings Currency "for such time as he shall continue to officiate as a Clergyman of the Church of England at Niagara," Mr. Alexander McDonell, the former lessee, having given them up.

In 1807, McDonell thought better of his surrender and made claim to Council for compensation for "various utensils left there" by him and used by Addison. The latter, in answer to Mr. Secretary Small's letter on the subject, wrote to him as follows:—

"Lieutenant-Governor Simcoe a few days before he left Upper Canada, offered me the Salt Springs as an Addition to a scanty Income. On his going away he directed Mr. President Russell to put me in possession, by whose direction I Petitioned the Council, and the Springs were ordered to be mine while I remained Minister of Niagara.—I have been at considerable Expence in Covering the Works, and sending out for Salt Pans, &c., and hardly now receive Interest for what

I have disbursed, the whole Income being a Dollar a Week, and that but poorly paid. If the Honorable Council have it in Contemplation to rescind their order in my favor, I trust their Justice will prevent my being a sufferer in this business. For any farther information I refer you to Mr. Russell." . . . .

The Provincial Secretary's letter in reply runs in part as follows:—" I am therefore directed to inform you, that you are required to satisfy Alexander McDonell, Esquire, who had made a demand upon Government for these Utensils, in which you may obtain a Lease of the Salt Springs. Or consider this as a Notice to quit the same."

From the record in Land Book C (in the Public Archives at Ottawa) it appears that the Rector had purchased land from Ralph Clinch (sic) and Robert Kerr, the title to the lot in the former case being disputed by Angus McDonell. The petitioner received on this occasion an Order in Council for three lots in the Township of Flamborough.

Formerly a petition had been presented for a "certain Spot of Land," which apparently lay eastward of the Four Mile Creek in the Township of Newark. This tract, consisting of thirty five acres, had formerly been granted to a man named Snow, who had died intestate, without heirs in Canada. On August 15th, 1795, Addison had been informed that it was not within the Committee's power to recommend that the prayer of the petition should be granted. In June, 1796, the same petition, in amplified form, was again presented, with the further request that he should be "admitted, as Administrator, to the Effects of one John Snow." At the same time he cast eyes upon "any vacant Lands that might be between the Lands occupied by Danl. Servos, and the Lands granted to one Cackle, lying westward of the Four Mile Creek." "The above," the petition recites, "which being near his present Dwelling place, are very valuable & desirable to him."

In making these requests, Mr. Addison, it must be repeated, was doing only what other professional men, business men, Legislative Councillors, Members of Parliament, retired officers, and others were doing—and what a great many people of the present day would do, if they had similar opportunities of enriching themselves at the public expense.

Returning to the hopes which, in 1799, he entertained of becoming head of the Grammar School, these also were doomed to disappointment for the time being. Not for eight years longer (1807) was any established in the Province. Then there were some very interesting enquiries instituted into the suitability or unsuitability of the house of the Hon. D. W. Smith for the purposes of the school at Niagara.

Notwithstanding these disappointments Mr. Addison had had the satisfaction of writing to the Society in 1798 that he was "one of the four Clergymen appointed for Upper Canada under the Constitutional Act with an Allowance from Government of 100 pounds per annum." He had been quite envious of Mr. Stuart and of Mr. Raddish at York because of the liberality of Government toward them, so the new order of things was decidedly welcome to him, but he adds: "And if every article of life were not extravagantly dear, he would think himself well provided for." In 1811 his own and Mr. Stuart's situation was such that Mr. Pollard of Sandwich longed to be placed on an equality with him and the Rector of Kingston.

When the Government was about to be removed to York because of the cession of Fort Niagara to the United States, it had been supposed by the Duke of Portland that there would not be anything for Mr. Addison to do in Niagara. Yet for many a year following 1796, Niagara was a much more important town commercially than York, and a more populous one, apparently.

In the letter last quoted Mr. Addison states that "The Bishop of Quebec mentioned to Mr. Stuart that Chaplains of Regiments were to be abolished, and Clergymen residing in the vicinity of Forts, who could attend the garrison, were to be allowed for it. If so, he wishes to be mentioned as residing close to Fort George, Niagara, and at present doing duty there without any emolument." This desire was fulfilled under the governorship of General Craig, as is shewn by a letter of June 28th, 1811.

For the eighteen months, January, 1795, to June, 1796, the 5th Regiment had allowed him ten guineas; but, like the Lieutenant-Governor, "they are also gone." The Lieutenant-Governor in his time had not been able to give him anything for this kind of service, notwithstanding the fact that a certain Mr. Drewe, in England, received for many years £100 annually as Chaplain to the Forces at Niagara, which he never saw.

On the 18th of November, 1811. Addison was appointed as Assistant Chaplain to the 2nd Battalion of the Royal Canadian Volunteers, "the [Roman Catholic?] Bishop not having sent a Chaplain conformable to his Promise."

In 1812 he was Chaplain at Fort George, receiving pay at the rate of £25 per annum with the allowance of a subaltern. He wanted to be put on an equality with the Rector of York (Dr. Strachan), who also was doing Chaplain's duty.

In 1813 his Chaplain's pay amounted to £60, his rectorial income from Government in that year being £200.

As early as June, 1796, he had made known the fact that he was Chaplain to the Commons' House of Assembly at a salary of $100. In 1793 a minute of the Executive Council of the Province records, on the 13th of July, that the House had fixed the salary at £25—currency, not sterling.

The Lieutenant-Governor is stated to have allowed him £10 a year—presumably as his own chaplain—but Mrs. Simcoe makes no mention of him in her Diary, in which, however, she speaks highly of sermons by Dr. Stuart and the Bishop of Quebec. She merely says, "There's no Church here, but a room has been built for a Freemason Lodge, where Divine Service is held."

In 1798 the scale of fees to which he was entitled in the exercise of his clerical functions is given. "The Surplice fees amount to nothing. Two dollars are usually paid for a wedding; nothing for Christening or Burials." Once more there is a note of discouragement at the smallness of the amount the people had given him that year, £30, with the pathetic sentence added—"A man seems to lose his liberty and consequence in proportion to what he thus receives from the Public."

A year earlier, 1797, encouragement was found in the fact that "The Magistrates of Niagara have applied to the Duke of Portland in his behalf," (all these matters being settled then, not in Canada, but at the Colonial Office), which was the more acceptable, as it was done without his solicitation or knowledge." Encouragement was needed, for "his mission is very laborious, and he must either neglect his duty, or make a circuit several times in the year of more than 150 miles through a wild country; . . . . . he has performed his duty with humble and conscientious assiduity."

Wrestling with the difficulties of the situation, he had enlisted the sympathies of his Bishop, who wrote to the President of the Council, as follows, on the 14th of July, 1798, as recorded in State Book B, PP. 191: "I have been requested by Mr. Addison, to mention to you his wish to be allowed Rations, as a sort of Chaplain to the Indians. I am no Judge of the propriety of this application, and beg leave to refer it to you; not doubting but you will have the goodness to comply with it, if it seems to you to be reasonable."

The postscript was very much to the point:—"Wherever subscriptions are entered into, for an annual payment towards the support of a Clergyman, I believe you will think it expedient that legal security should be given for such payment to him and his Successors until (sic) they shall be otherwise provided for by Law."

Looking forward a twelvemonth from the date of writing in 1797, Addison begged the Society to grant him leave to visit England, as he would then have been seven years in their service. He had been reprimanded upon one occasion for not transacting his business through the Bishop of Quebec rather than with the Society direct, but formalities were dispensed with on this occasion and permission was given, without any thought as to the irony of the terms in which it was couched—" provided he can get a clergyman to supply his place." Even in York (Toronto), which, though a village, was the capital of the province, a clergyman could not be induced to stay, much less to take duty for anybody in another town, distant some thirty miles by water and eighty, or thereabouts, by land.

Again and again, the same question of leave of absence comes up, in 1801 permission being sought to go home "to embrace an old, honoured father before his departure hence." In 1802 he " would like to have the permission though he hardly knows how to support the voyage, having a perfect hatred to the sea." But the Bishop had expressed a " wish that he would not leave Niagara at present," so the visit was once more put off. In the next year the Bishop desired him "to give up the thought of it at present." Apparently the Bishop did not answer letters promptly, for Mr. Addison adds, in writing to the Society, "that he is pleased that his request at last has been noticed: but he has never made up his mind to set off at any particular time."

Once more there is hope of building a Church. It had not been done in Major-General Simcoe's time, as Mr. Addison had hoped it would be, service being held, after the Lieutenant-Governor's departure at least, in the Court House, which is described as "a good room." In December, 1803, they are "talking of building a Church." In June, 1804, there is a subscription list. In July, 1805, the Church is begun and half up. He "will write more particularly by Captain Brant, the Mohawk Chief, should he go to England in the fall."

On the 29th of January, 1807, he has to report that " The Church at Niagara is not yet finished. They began on too large a scale for their means, but have entered into a fresh subscription, and hope to compleat it in the course of next summer." Apparently this subscription did not change the situation materially, for in July of the same year the "Church advances slowly," albeit "the floors are laid and the windows are nearly ready for glazing." "But," he adds, "it is not to be wondered at that it goes on no faster, as almost all the settlers about Niagara are Presbyterians."

This remark does not presuppose any feeling of hostility toward Presbyterians, as may be judged from a letter of 1795, to mention no other. On the 27th of August in that year he wrote: "A Presbyterian Minister is settled among them, and is much caressed by the common people; but I still and heartily wish he may be of use, as he seems liberal and well informed, and must lessen my toil of travelling about the country, as the greatest part is Presbyterians."

At midsummer, 1804, two interesting items of information are given: firstly, that two Presbyterian Ministers are licensed to perform the marriage ceremony, one in Niagara and one in the next township; and, secondly, that "Most of the Settlers from the States are Dissenters."

Without formal license this right of solemnizing marriages could be exercised only by the clergy of the Church of England. Presently it was granted also to the clergy of the Established Church of Scotland and after several years to the Methodists, whose "riding preachers" proclaimed their message as frequently as circumstances and the watchful Lieutenant-Governor allowed.

Between 1792 and 1796 Lieutenant-Governor Simcoe encouraged settlers from the States to migrate to Canada, offering them liberal grants of land, to the dissatisfaction of the Loyalists, who thought that these good things should be confined to themselves and their children.

In the letter of 1807 already quoted from, request is made for Prayer Books and a "Church Bible," evidently for his lectern, "as his eyes begin to fail, and he can only read good print with glasses."

A year later accounts of the Church are not so cheering. "Nothing has been done to the Church, the expence having disheartened his good hearers; but it has gone too far to be neglected, and the next effort will finish it." On the 2nd of January, 1809, which a *lapsus pennae* of the Secretary's clerk who was writing up the Journal made 1808, there is a hope that "it will be ready for [Divine] Service toward the end of the summer," the first coat of plaster having been already put on. January, 1810, saw the building finished and "service performed in it since the previous August." The pews are described as handsome and as having sold for more than £300.[2] He declares it to be the best church in the

---

[2] These sales gave a freehold of the pews, conditional upon the payment of an annual rental to the Wardens.

Province, adding that he hopes to "compleat" it next Spring, "if their funds do not fail." Just how a "finished" church was to be "compleated," it is difficult to understand.

There was recourse to the Provincial Parliament in 1807 in order to obtain funds. The Legislative Council had risen before the House of Assembly, and the Councillors had gone home. On the last day of the Assembly's meeting, when the few members left had been considering the purchase (at a cost of £50) of two pews in the Church at York for the use of the two Houses of the Legislature, it had been proposed to vote a like sum to several districts, among others to Niagara, for the purpose of finishing their churches. An address upon the subject had been presented to the Lieutenant-Governor and had been "in Part, if not wholly, acceded to by him."

Mr. Cartwright, who took seriously his legislative responsibilities and the dignity of the Council, is the authority for this transaction. Writing to Mr. Hamilton, he says, "We shall, I suppose, be called upon to sanction all this, as mere Matter of course in an appropriation Bill at the next Session. But, unless we take some measure to put a stop to such irregularities, we shall very soon become what Mr. Thorpe already calls us—'mere Lumber'." To which, so far as Niagara was concerned, Mr. Hamilton replied: "I had not before heard the Reasons for the *Liberality* of the *Legislature* to the Church at Niagara, but, as it came in very good Time to assist in finishing it, we were thankful without asking Questions."

Large congregations were assembling in the new church in July, 1810; and "two small convenient chapels" were in use ten or twelve miles from Niagara, service being performed in them alternately on the first Sunday in every month "to crowded audiences." Communicants were "rather encreasing," being "in the whole Settlement something more than 56."

There was a gallery in the church, as is indicated in the letter of January 16th, 1811, when the church was nearly finished, "except a few seats in the gallery." The congregation, "which is large," was said to be "well accommodated for Public Worship."

But the war, which for twenty years had been expected, was gathering to a head. In August, 1812, "they were all in bustle and confusion from the declaration of war by the American States." Added to that, the Rector had been ill and the draft for his allowance for the last half year had come back protested, "although he had never failed to write whenever he drew."

A couple of months later he says: "That the Baptisms are so few (only 11), is owing to the distress of the times. The enemy, after taking Niagara, sent most of the respectable inhabitants as prisoners of war into the States two or three hundred miles into the interior. He was put upon his parole, and supposed to remain in his own house. But, when our army advanced towards Niagara, they found a line about four miles from the Town, and his house (which is nearly that distance) was sometime the headquarters. Then he performed Divine Service in the separate divisions of the army alternately, and visited the sick, who were very numerous."

Of the victories at Detroit and Queenston there is no mention in the letters. Nor is there any of the death of Major-General Brock, at whose funeral, at Fort George he officiated, according to *The Kingston Gazette,* on the 16th of October, 1812. He recorded the General's death in the register of St. Mark's.

The next letter was written only on the 7th of January, 1814, for reasons that become apparent on perusal of it. "During the last half year the enemy being in possession of Niagara, he could not perform his duties as usual. The Town and Church are burnt, and the Enemy have crossed to the other side of the River. It is not possible to describe the horrid scenes he has witnessed. He has reason, however, to be very thankful. For, though he has been plundered, made prisoner of war, and harrassed till he was dangerously ill, yet his house, which is about 3 miles from the town, has escaped, and afforded an Asylum to several unhappy Sufferers who fled from the flames. They hope for happier times, and to see the Church, which was fortunately built of stone, repaired."

Thirteen months later, February 16th, 1815, he sends word home that "The Church is covered and used as a Commissary's store." Such it continued to be for a considerable part of that year, Divine Service being performed meanwhile in the General Hospital.

In the same letter he records that "He has witnessed during the last Campaign allmost all the sad scenes of Distress which a Country subject to the Ravages of War can suffer." True Englishman that he was, he received comfort from the knowledge that "The English troops, however, by the blessing of heaven, though greatly inferior in Number to the Enemy, have driven them beyond the Frontier."

At midsummer he was able to move freely about in the neighbourhood once more and to perform service in various places. In the following January (1816) "by means of subscription the Church has been sufficiently repaired for the performance of Divine Service, though it is by no means so comfortable as before its destruction by the "Americans." Though repaired, it was fit for use only in the summer, some other place having to be provided for the winter.

As late as 1818 the restoration was incomplete and hope was again reposed in the Government. In July of that year there was "some expectation of procuring assistance from Sir John Sherbrooke," the additional information being conveyed that during the war the Church had been used also as "a Barrack."

In the preceding year there had evidently been sent to him some expression of appreciation of his conduct, for, in writing on the 17th of January, 1817, "he is most happy to hear that the Society have approved his exertion." Two years before, at a general meeting of the Society, his salary had, upon recommendation of the Bishop of Quebec and of the committee, been continued to him during his enforced absence from his mission owing to the war.

During the same period the President of Upper Canada, there being no Governor in the province at the time, had permitted him to retain his allowance from Government, in "consideration of the dearness and difficulty of the Times," seeing that it was not through any fault of his own that he was not discharging the duties of his cure. He found employment during this period at the hands of Admiral Sir James Yeo, as "Chaplain to the St. Lawrence."

The Bishop of Quebec, in whose letter dated January 30th, 1815, these particulars are contained, informed the Society that "Mr. Addison expresses a hope, should he live to see Peace restored, of resuming his station at Niagara." This he did; but three years afterwards he begged to have the care of the Indians on the Grand River transferred to Mr. Leeming of Ancaster together with the £20 which he had been receiving for this duty. He spoke of them as the "Anandagas," though now they are called Onondagas.

Before relinquishing the care of the Indians, he took measures for the translation of the Gospels into Mohawk and for a fresh supply of Indian Prayer Books to replace those destroyed in the war. The former was to be done by the great chief, Major Norton, who received from Addison this commendation: "He is the only person capable of such work. And, if he undertakes it, he will execute it well."

Norton, it appears from a later letter, was living on the Reserve and was cultivating his land. Mr. Addison hopes his example in so doing will be beneficial to the Indians in leading them also to agricultural pursuits. As Norton understood printing, Mr. Addison suggested that the Society should send him a press, "as no compositor can be tolerably correct in a difficult and unknown language without constant inspection." If the suggestion were not accepted, "it will be necessary for him to attend the press which is at a distance of 30 miles."

Former translators were Dr. Stuart and the Great Chief Captain Joseph Brant, already mentioned. Connected by ties of affinity with Sir William Johnson and by bonds of gratitude with Dr. Stuart, Brant had led his people from the province of New York to Upper Canada, and had settled one half of them on the Grand River, where their descendants still occupy the lands then granted near the present city of Brantford. His was the first church built in the province and thither he brought half of the Communion service "presented by Queen Ann to her loyal Mohawks." He was ever anxious, even amid his dreams of a great Indian confederacy, with which he was occupied in 1792, to promote the interests of the Church. He promised Mr. Addison a conveyance over the seventy miles that separated them, if he would visit his band, and he subsequently acted as his interpreter when he preached.

Dr. Stuart, who knew Brant thoroughly, did not approve of his assertion that "the Indians will be better pleased with 3 or 4 visits from Mr. Addison in the year, than to have a Residential Missionary." His own opinion was that "they are afraid of the restraint which the Continual residence of a Clergyman would necessarily lay them under," and he was "verily persuaded, that occasional visits are to be considered more as matters of form, than [as] productive of any lasting good effect." Yet Brant's views prevailed and his Indians were for many years without a resident missionary before the New England Society provided one. In the interval a schoolmaster looked after them, Brant himself often reading the service.

In 1799 Mr. Addison states that Brant wants a resident missionary, he having, apparently, changed his mind, and that he is inclined to take a Roman Priest.

This difficulty, though subsequently overcome, was disheartening, for an earlier report, in 1799, had informed the Society that "his (Addison's) success with the Indians is very encouraging, considering the little time that he can spend among them." He had at the same time to communicate the fact that "The Indian Church was struck with lightening and the steeple damaged last summer."

Satisfactory relations with Brant were re-established, for, as has been already pointed out, he was to be the bearer of a letter to the Society if he should go to England, which, apparently he did.

In 1806 the Chief is reported to be of great assistance in the endeavours "to bring these wandering tribes to any attention to the Christian Doctrine." In 1807 "many of them have given up the ruinous habit of drinking spirituous liquors."

The Rector says, in communicating to the Society the news of his death, that "he was a man of uncommon intelligence" and that "we shall miss him much in his visits to the Mohawk Church."

Bad roads in autumn and winter, excessive heat in summer, and occasional ill-health prevented the Rector at times from paying his visits to the Indians. Therefore, he was glad in 1818 to place upon younger shoulders the responsibility for this portion of his work. In the Society's Report for 1816 is a note to the effect that, owing to his illness Dr. Strachan of York had paid the Indians a visit in his stead.

In 1818, according to the First Report of the Bible Society of Upper Canada, Addison was in York (Toronto) for the annual meeting, which was held in the district school-house early in November of that year. He moved "That the thanks of this Society be transmitted to the British and Foreign Bible Society, through the medium of the Right Honorable Lord Teignmouth, its president, for their munificent donation (of Bibles), and that his Excellency the Lieutenant Governor (Sir Peregrine Maitland) be requested to transmit the same." In the speech which he made upon the occasion he joined patriotism with religion by saying: "Every good and loyal subject feels a glow of gratitude to the great disposer of events, that he so signally went forth with our hosts, when the convulsions and conflicts of the civilized world were ended by the last great victory—every real Christian feels a still warmer sentiment of praise, when he observes that the same Almighty power has raised up men in our parent country, who unite to diffuse the light of truth through every part of the world."

For eleven years more the Rector went about his work in his parish, which grew gradually smaller by reason of the appointment of more missionaries to parishes lying between Ancaster and Chippawa. In 1826 he held service in his own house during a period of illness, after which he was given an assistant. This assistant, Mr. Creen, is mentioned as taking duty in 1827 also at Queenston, which had previously been served by the Army Chaplain,* then removed to York.

From 1823 to 1829, the year of his death, Mr. Addison was a member of the Provincial Board of Education, under the presidency of Dr. Strachan, Archdeacon of York.

Some eleven years later, Strachan, then Bishop of Toronto, who had known him well from 1812, the year in which he himself became Rector of York, wrote about Addison thus, in the Journal of the First Visitation of his Diocese:—

"He was a gentleman of commanding talents and exquisite wit, whose devotedness to his sacred duties, kindliness of manners, and sweet companionship, are still sources of grateful and fond remembrance. He may justly be considered the missionary of the western part of the province. In every township we find traces of his ministrations, and endearing recollections of his affectionate visits.

"He was also Missionary to the Indians on the Grand River; and, although, from the great distance of his residence at Niagara, he could visit them but seldom, yet by the blandness of his address and his peculiar facility in communicating the most important truths, he acquired over their untutored minds a prevailing influence."

---

* This Chaplain was the Rev. B. B. Stevens, as shewn by the S.P.G. Reports and as pointed out by Mrs. Thompson, who kindly indicated the site of the small, convenient Chapel at Queenston referred to by Mr. Addison.

XIV.

THE REV. ROBERT ADDISON.

Extracts from the Reports and (Manuscript) Journals of the Society for the Propagation of the Gospel in Foreign Parts,* With notes by Professor A. H. Young.

REPORT, 1784-1785, p. 47.
Quotation from a letter from the Revd. John Doty, of William Henry (Sorel).
"A part of the Mohawks had removed the preceding summer from La Chine to Niagara; the remainder went last May to the Bay of Kenti, 40 miles from Cataracqui, to take possession of lands assigned (sic) them by the Government. It is not yet determined whether the whole tribe together with their brethren of Conajoharee, will unite in this new settlement, as Captain Brant with a number of the Mohawk and Conajoharee chiefs, have it in contemplation to form a grand settlement on a river, 40 miles above Niagara, on the Canada side of the lake being incoraged (sic) to this by the mildness of the climate, fertility of soil, and convenience for hunting.

"On the 2nd of June last Mr. Stuart** himself set out on a visit to these Mohawks, taking in his way all the New Settlements of Loyalists on the river and Lake, and on the 18th of the same month he arrived at Niagara.

"On the following Sunday he preached to the garrison, and in the afternoon to satisfy the eager expectation of the Mohawks, he went on horseback to their village, about 9 miles distant and officiated in their Church. After a short intermission, they returned to the Church, where he baptized 78 infants & 5 adults; the latter having been previously instructed by his Indian Clerk, who regularly reads prayers on a Sunday, and lives a very sober and exemplary life. The whole was concluded with a discourse on the nature and design of baptism. It

---

* The Society,—which now conducts operations in all parts of the world, was founded in 1701 for the purpose of securing church services to English-speaking people in the Colonies and Plantations. In Algoma and other Canadian Dioceses its beneficent work is still carried on.

** The Revd. John Stuart, M.A., D.D., often called "the Father of the Church in Upper Canada," was born at Paxton, Pa., on February 25th, (O. S.) 1740; was educated at the College of Philadelphia, now the University of Pennsylvania; was a schoolmaster in Lancaster, Pa., from 1763 to 1770; missionary to the Mohawks at Fort Hunter, N. Y., from 1770 to 1781; schoolmaster and military chaplain at Montreal 1781 to 1785; missionary at Cataraqui, Kingston, 1785 to 1811; schoolmaster there 1786; Bishop's Official 1789 to 1811; chaplain to the Legislative Council of Upper Canada, 1792 to 1807. For further details see *The Revd. John Stuart, D.D., U. E. L., of Kingston, U. C. and his family*, and *The Parish Register of Kingston, U. C. 1785-1811*, by A. H. Young.

was a very affecting scene to Mr. Stuart to see those affectionate people, from whom he had been separated more than seven years, assembled together in a decent and commodious church, erected chiefly by themselves and with the greatest seeming devotion and gravity. Even the windows were crowded with those who could not find room within the walls. The concourse of Indians was unusually great, owing to the circumstance of the Oneidas, Cayugas, and Onondagas being settled in the vicinity.

"Before Mr. Stuart left them he baptized 24 children & married 6 couple."
JOURNALS. 1781-1784.
Vol. 23, p. 409.

Letter dated Montreal, July 17th, 1784, acquainting the Society, that on the 2nd of June, he [Stuart] set out & visiting on his way all the New Settlements of Loyalists on the River and Lake, on the 18th arrived at Niagara.

On the Sunday after he landed he preached in the Garrison, and on the afternoon of the same day, to satisfy the eager expectations of the Mohawks, he proceeded on horseback to their village, nine miles distant, and officiated in their church. After a short intermission, they returned to the church, where he baptised 78 infants and 5 adults; the latter having been previously instructed by his Indian clerk, who regularly reads prayers on a Sunday, and lives a very sober and exemplary life. The whole ceremony was concluded with a discourse on the nature and design of baptism. It was very affecting to Mr. Stuart to see those affectionate people, from whom he had been separated more than seven years assembled in a decent commodious church, erected principally by themselves, with the greatest seeming devotion and a becoming gravity. Even the windows were crowded with those who could not find room within the walls. The concourse of Indians on this occasion was unusually great; owing to the circumstance of the Oneidas, and Cayugas and Onondagas, being settled in the vicinity. All those people speak different dialects of the same language. Before Mr. Stuart left their village, he afterwards baptized at different times, 24 children, & married 6 couple.

On his way home being determined to visit every settlement of Loyalists, he remained some time at Cataraqui and baptized all the children that were presented for that purpose; & buried one.

JOURNALS. 1787-1792,
Vol. 25, pp. 120-1.

Letter dated Kingston Cataraqui, July 2nd, 1788, in which he [Stuart] acquaints the Society that . . . . Finding he should necessarily be detained at Niagara some days for a passage and that no regular Clergyman had been in that extensive settlement since he had been there in 1784, he gave notice of his intention to preach on the Sunday Morning following, when he preached to a crowded audience & baptized 37 infants, which, with those baptized in private houses during his stay there, amounted to 72, of which 7 only were adults, and he thinks a still greater number remain unbaptized from the impossibility of collecting the children at such a distance on so short notice. That on the day before his departure from Niagara, the Commanding officer, in conjunction with the principal inhabitants of the adjoining settlement, represented to him their want of a Clergyman and, as they wished to have some previous personal knowledge of one to be appointed & many of the inhabitants had formerly been Mr. Stuart's parishioners at Fort-Hunter, they promised that, if the Society would allow him to accept their invitation, they would make him a liberal subscription, & give proper security for the due payment of it. That Mr. Stuart gave them no encouragement to expect him at least till the Society's pleasure should be known, but advised them to invite Mr. Frazer, formerly the Society's missionary at New Jersey, and, if he should prove acceptable, & they would make a reasonable subscription for his better maintenance, Mr. Stuart would recommend their case to the Society

VOL. 25, 1787-1792, p. 360.

An application was made by the Revd. Robert Addison, A.M., late of Trinity College, Cambridge, to be taken into the Society's service, recommended by Edward Montagu, Esq., and Mr. Humphreys, Lecturer of Hampstead. Agreed that he may be a proper person to send to Niagara, if the Bishops of Peterborough and Ely should give a satisfactory account of him.

Ibid. May 20th, 1791, p. 366.

The Secretary read 2 Letters; one from the Bishop of Ely, and another from the Bishop of Peterborough; in which the account of the Revd. Robert Addison was so satisfactory that the Board agreed to appoint him their missionary to Niagara, with a salary of Fifty pounds, to commence at midsummer next, and the Treasurer was directed to advance him half a year's salary.

VOL. 26, 1792-1795, p. 45.

A letter dated Quebec, April 29th, 1792, which came by Mr. Toosey,* to whom he refers for an account of himself, and who advised him to stay the winter there, and to a letter he had received from Messrs. Forsyth & Co., merchants at Montreal, dated October 31st, 1791, wherein they write that they thought it proper to mention to him that the season was too far advanced to admit of almost a possibility of reaching Niagara; and were it even probable, he would find the travelling, which must be by water, exceedingly uncomfortable, and that they thought it his safest plan to delay his journey till spring; the navigation being open about the end of April.

VOL. 26, 1792-1795, p, 180.

Niagara, October 3rd, 1792.

That, as he had only arrived the July preceding, he could say but little concerning the place. He is the only Clergyman of any denomination, and has always preached to a pretty large Congregation. They have no Church, but hope that the Governor,† who is to winter with them, will assist in the building one. He has officiated in various parts of the settlement near 30 miles apart, but has

---

* Mr. Toosey had gone to England to see if it were possible to obtain the appointment of Bishop of Quebec, he being Rector of that city.

†This Governor was of course Col. (afterwards Major-General) John Graves Simcoe, first Lieutenant-Governor of Upper Canada, 1792-1799.

been prevented by sickness from baptizing and preaching at much greater distances, to which he was invited. He has already baptized 47—married 2—buried 7. VOL. 26, 1792-1795, p. 77.

Letter dated Kingston October 12th, 1792, in which he [Stuart]* acquaints the Society that he had been at Niagara, where he was detained near 4 weeks, as Chaplain to the Upper House of Assembly, that he found the people were disposed to make Mr. Addison's situation as comfortable as circumstances will admit, that Col. Butler assured him, that £100 currency should be annually paid him by the Parishioners.

He observes, that the Actual Members of the Church of England in that quarter are not very numerous, but that a man of Mr. Addison's character and talents will doubtless greatly increase their number. During his stay at Niagara, Captain Brant, with the chief Men and Warriors of the Mohawks, went to Detroit, to assist at a General Council of the Western Nations; which circumstance rendered his intended visit to their village unseasonable. Mr. Addison, however, promised to perform this duty for him, as soon as the Indians returned home. The Governor, he says, seems determined to put the Church of England on as respectable a footing as possible in that province, from whose countenance much may be expected. He mentions the arrival of a Mr. Boultellier, who had preached at Quebec, Montreal, etc., having said that he was sent by the Society as their Missionary to Detroit—that he had demanded a sight of his Letters of Orders, upon which he said that he was only in Deacon's Orders, having been Ordained, immediately before he left England, by Dr. Douglas, Bishop of Salisbury, and that he had left all his papers in a trunk at Quebec. Upon further enquiry, he acknowledged, that he had no appointment from the Society and in several particulars prevaricated so much as to give Mr. Stuart a very unfavourable opinion of him. He appears to Mr. Stuart, rather to want common sense and prudence, than to have any premeditated design of acting the part of an impostor.

Ibid, pp. 180-181: Niagara, April 6th, 1793.

That it is not possible to send an account in the form of the Notitia Parochialis drawn out in the Society's Instructions, the boundaries of the parish not being fixed, & the number of Inhabitants increasing daily. That his [Addison's] congregation is very considerable, though his Communicants have not yet exceeded 17, but that, if the Governor continues with them, much may be expected from his presence and example. He has been at several places in the Settlement to the distance of 20 or 30 miles, preaching and baptizing, and has been strongly solicited to visit the Mohawks, who are about 70 miles distant. He has promised to go, if his health will permit, which has been for some time indifferent, and the Indians will find a conveyance. He wishes that the Society's Funds would allow of some additional salary for the keeping of a horse to visit them and the distant parts of the neighbourhood. He is requested to travel 10 or 15 miles to preach and baptize, almost every week. Baptisms since his last 70—Marriages 8—Burials 10.

---

* It will be remembered that since 1789, Stuart had been Bishop's Commissary or Official.

Agreed in opinion that the Society cannot comply with Mr. Addison's request; but on account of his extraordinary services, recommend that a Gratuity be given him.

Ibid, p. 199.

Letter dated Kingston, October 10th, 1793, acknowledging the secretary's letter of the 7th of May last, which he [Stuart] received the day before. That he spent 8 days at Niagara, in the Month of June, but finding his presence there [as Chaplain to the Legislative Council] only a matter of form, he requested and obtained leave of absence, thinking his time might be employed to better purpose at home, & that it is not likely he may attend on any future occasion.* That Mr. Addison, through the intercession of Capt. Joseph Brant, has desired him to solicit the Society for some small allowance for visiting the Mohawks on the Grand River. Mr. Brant thinks that the Indians will be better pleased with 3 or 4 visits from Mr. Addison, in the year, than to have a Residential Missionary; but Mr. Stuart's opinion is—that they are afraid of the restraint which the Continual residence of a Clergyman would necessarily lay them under, and he is verily persuaded, that occasional visits are to be considered more as matters of form, than productive of any lasting good effect. The Society will judge. Mr Boultellier proved to be an imposter. He wintered at Niagara, and occasionally performed the functions of a Clergyman, notwithstanding Mr. Stuart's Injunctions to the contrary. He quitted the Settlement a few days before Mr. Stuart arrived there in June. He is now, he believes, at New York. But he has had various applications from different settlements to forward their Petitions to the Society, for Missionaries, to which his uniform answer had been, "If you comply with the standing rules of the Society, a copy of which is in my possession, I will give you all the Assistance in my power, otherwise I will not interfere." For Mr. Addison, he says, has not received the sallary promised by the people, nor has he obtained the £100 allowance from Government, so that he has nothing certain than the Society's bounty† and Mr. Stuart's own appointments, Civil & Ecclesiastical, are all honorary only.

Agreed in opinion that Cols. Butler and Hamilton be requested to inform the Society why the terms on which they desired a Missionary have not been complied with."

Ibid, pp. 217-218: Niagara, October 23rd, 1793.

That since his last in April he has preached and baptized in various parts of the Settlement. He went as far as the Mohawk village near 70 miles distant, & was much pleased with their regular and devout attention. He baptized 19, & was joined in celebrating the Lord's Supper by 12 women and 2 men. Their great Chief Captain Brant interpreted. He was solicited to go over frequently

---

* He did attend in later years at both Niagara and York till 1807. In that year he resigned in favor of his son, the Rev. George Okill Stuart, Rector of York, who had occasionally performed the Chaplain's duty for him.

† This "bounty" was £50 sterling per annum. It was payable in England and was there subject to the income tax. Hence it was much decreased before Mr. Addison received it.

and he intends it as often as he conveniently can; but the expense of travelling is felt by a man of very small income. He wishes the Society would add something to his salary as Missionary to the Mohawks, & he will endeavour to qualify himself by learning to read the language at least. Every thing is very dear in the Settlement; but by great frugality and some little private possession he is free from actual want. The humble settler who labours on his land is kind to him; the rich Trader endeavours to be polite; but he is sorry to say that their Subscription is likely to end in words. As they, however, still continue to promise fair, he would wish the Society not to remonstrate with them at present. The worst circumstance is that they have no Church—nor have they any Clerk, so that he has the unpleasant task of going through the Morning Service without a pause and sometimes without responses being made in an audible manner. He has written to some of his acquaintances in London to set on foot a little private subscription to enable him to alter these matters. Since his last 97 Baptisms. Marriages 9. Burials 15.

Ibid, p. 306: General Meeting at Lambeth Palace, January 16th, 1795.

The Archbishop communicated to the Board a letter which his Grace had received from the Bishop of Quebec [the Rt. Rev. Jacob Mountain] respecting the state of religion in his Diocese of Canada, in which his Lordship recommends that £20 a year should be added by the Society to Mr. Addison's salary, Missionary at Niagara, to aid him in the expense of travelling to the Mohawks at Quenti [which ought, of course, to be the Grand River].

Resolved to agree to the same.

Ibid, pp. 376-377: Niagara, January 15th, 1795.

In which he returns his sincere thanks to the Society for the Gratuity, which was very acceptable. That he has hitherto had very little pecuniary assistance from his People, but hopes in future that he shall receive more; should it be otherwise, he shall be happy to avail himself of the Society's permission to remove to Nova Scotia, although the only objection to his present situation is too small an income for so dear a place.

Vol. 27, 1796-1799, pp. 113-114: June 27th, 1796.

That he considers himself much obliged to the Society for the permission to leave Niagara, and remove to Nova Scotia, though he is inclined to wait the event of the Bishop's application to the Ministry in his favour, which General Simcoe * has promised to support. That he had applied before to Governor Simcoe respecting his officiating for the Regiment in the Fort without any emolument, and he said it was not in his power to help him. That what he received from the Society is the principal part of his income. He has been Chaplain to the House of Assembly, for which he has 100 dollars a year. Governor Simcoe allowed him £10 a year, but he has left, and the 5th Regiment for the 3 last half-years allowed him 10 guineas, but they are also gone. Surplice fees amount

---

* The Lieutenant-Governor was on the eve of going to England on leave of absence which, though intended to be brief, lengthened out to almost three years. Clergymen's salaries had to be provided for in the Imperial budget. Hence the reference to the ministry.

to nothing. Two dollars are usually paid for a wedding. Nothing for Christening or Burials. His subscription in the last year but one amounted to little more than £30. The last year they made no collection, & when the Provincial Secretary, Mr. Jarvis,** mentioned it to him, he seemed disinclined to it. 'Tis, he observes, at best but a pitiful means of support. A man seems to lose his liberty and consequence in proportion to what he thus receives from the Public.

That in his last journey to the Mohawks he baptized 18 Indians, 3 Negroes, and 32 Whites. Captain Brant interprets for him, & the serious deportment and devotion of these poor creatures is exemplary. He has 18 communicants as fine and conscientious as can be found, he is persuaded, in any Christian congregation. The whole of his Baptisms since his last amount to 121; Marriages 4; Burials 16. Communicants at Niagara 14.

Ibid., pp. 237-238, May 29th, 1797.

In which he writes that since his last letter by Major Littlehales *** he had baptized 110, married 11, & buried 7. That his Communicants increase both in the Settlement & among the Indians. That the Magistrates of Niagara have applied to the Duke of Portland **** in his behalf, which was the more acceptable, as it was done without his solicitation or knowledge. That his Mission is very laborious, & he must either neglect his duty, or make a circuit several times in the year of more than 150 miles through a wild country. That he has performed his duty with humble and conscientious assiduity, & struggled with very narrow circumstances. He fully expected £100 a year from Government, as the Secretary said he might depend upon it. He thinks his case the more hard, as Mr. Raddish,* by whom he sends this Letter, is allowed it. He requests the Society's permission to come to England next summer, as he shall then have been seven years in their service. But should any thing be done for him before that time, which will make his situation easier, he believes he should not venture on the journey, as he dislikes the sea extremely.

Agreed that Mr. Addison may have leave to come over to England next summer, provided he can get a Clergyman to supply his place.

(Agreed with the Committee).

Ibid., pp. 372-373: Niagara, May 3rd, 1798.

That since his last by Mr. Raddish he has baptised 141, married 15 couple, & buried 4. He has the satisfaction of acquainting the Society that he is one of the four Clergymen appointed for Upper Canada with an allowance of £100 Per Annum. And, if every article of life were not extravagantly dear, he should think himself well provided for. He says that the Bishop of Quebec mentioned

---

** Mr. Secretary Jarvis, whose wife was Hannah, daughter of the Revd. Samuel Peters, D.D., recommended by Col. Simcoe for the proposed bishopric of Upper Canada, was the founder of the Jarvis family of Toronto.

*** Major Littlehales, the Lieutenant-Governor's Secretary, withdrew from the Province with his chief.

**** The Duke of Portland was the Secretary of State for the Colonies.

* Mr. Raddish had come out with Mr. Chief Justice Elmsley, late in the autumn of 1796, to be Rector of York and had gone home in the following midsummer. He remained in England, whence, in March, 1799, he resigned his Canadian living.

to Mr. Stuart that Chaplains of Regiments were to be abolished, Clergymen residing in the vicinity of Forts, who could attend the Garrison, were to be allowed for it. If so, he wishes to be mentioned as residing close to Fort George, Niagara, & at present doing duty there without emolument. The good people of Niagara have forgotten their subscription. His Indian Mission goes on well—20 Communicants. There are about 550 belonging to the Church, & they are increasing, as he has some friendly serious Indians, who, under his direction, persuade the neighbouring villagers to be baptised and teach them the principles of Christianity as well as they are able.

Vol. 28, 1799-1804, p. 99.

December 29th, 1799.

Brant * wants a missionary, he reports, and is inclined to take a Roman Catholic priest.

Ibid., pp. 194-5.

June 5th, 1801, at York† where he then was attending the Legislature as Chaplain to the Assembly, having an opportunity of writing by a young man, & therefore cannot be exact as to his Notitia. But he ventures to state the Christenings at 60 & weddings & burials much as before. He requests the Society's leave to come home to embrace an old and honoured father before his departure hence, as he has been 10 years at his Mission.

Agreed in opinion that Mr. Addison have leave to come home, if the Bishop of Quebec shall approve of it, and any provision can be made for the care of his mission during his absence.

Agreed with the Committee.

Ibid., p. 259.

January 10, 1802, in which he writes that his baptisms since his last amount to 57. Marriages 19. Burials 4. Communicants much the same. That in most of his late letters he has requested leave to come home for a few months. He would like to have the permission, though he hardly knows how to support the voyage, having a perfect hatred to the sea.

Ibid., p. 296.

July 20, 1802, to acquaint the Society that since he wrote last his Baptisms have been 48. Marriages 9. Burials 3. Comm. much the same & both his

---

* At the time that he was negotiating for the alienation of a portion of the Mohawk lands to Davenport Phelps, Samuel Street, William Jarvis, and Thomas Beasley, Brant was very anxious to have Phelps ordained and made his missionary. To this the Bishop of Quebec ('Mountain) appears to have committed himself, without first making full enquiries. Having made them, he withdrew his consent, whereupon Brant is said to have replied: "Very well, then I shall turn Methodist." Phelps, whose name is found on the Roll of Barristers, at Osgoode Hall, returned to the United States, and, having been ordained, did duty as a missionary in New York State.

† There is some very interesting correspondence relating to the removal of the government and the legislature to York, Mr. Chief Justice Elmsley, being strongly opposed to removal, which had been enjoined by the Lieutenant-Governor, upon his representative, Mr. President Russell. A year before the date of this letter the Revd. George Okill Stuart, a graduate of Harvard, had been ordained and placed in charge of the mission of York.

congregations as large as usual. The Bishop of Quebec has expressed a wish that he would not leave Niagara at present. As he intends to visit them next summer, he hopes to obtain leave once more to come to England, though, as he mentioned before, he is a very bad sailor.

Ibid., p. 397.

April 3, 1803, acquainting the Society that, since his last, he had baptized 57; married 14 couple; & buried 7. His Congregation and Communicants continue much the same as before at Niagara. Among the Indians he has more Baptisms, & an Increasing Congregation. He has had a letter from the Bishop of Quebec respecting his leave of absence, who wishes him to give up the thought of it at present. He is pleased that his request has at last been noticed; but he had never made up his mind to set off at any particular time, and he has no doubt of his Lordship's leave when he finds it necessary.

Ibid., p. 419.

October 1, 1803, acquainting the Society that, since his last he has baptized 55; married two couple; & buried 4. He accounts for his having fewer than before from the arrival of a Scotch gentleman, a Dr. Young, from Montreal, by special invitation, he supposes. He is said to be a good preacher, but he has the misfortune of poverty, and (if report be right) deserves it, being a slave to liquor.* To show the disposition of his parishioners, he says they gave $500 a year for 3 years to a minister who is since turned trader, & he believes they will give this something more. At the same time they absolutely refuse to give him [Addison] one shilling. He is however about trying to bring them to a settlement, and will acquaint the Society with the issue of it in his next.

Vol. 29, 1804-1809, p. 14.

December 27, 1804 [1803], in which he writes that he has been ordered by the Bishop of Quebec to send his Notitia regularly every time he draws for his Salary. This he observes will occasion expence of postage, which he has hitherto avoided by sending his letters by private hands. His Congregation rather Encreases, and they begin to talk seriously of building a Church. Since his last, which he sent by a Mr. Hubb, about three months before, his Baptisms amount to 27. Marriages 1. Burials 1. The Indians continue very attentive.

Ibid., p. 46.

June 6, 1804, in which he transmits this Notitia. Since Christmas, 75 Baptisms; 2 Marriages; & 1 Burial. He says that he once before accounted for the few Marriages and Burials, since which two Presbyterian Ministers have been licensed to marry,† one of whom lives in Niagara, the other in the next Township. Most of the settlers that come in from the States are Dissenters. His congregation, however, rather encreases, & is sometimes crowded. They are about

---

* This is rather severe on Mr. Young, who had suffered from the social customs prevalent in Montreal during the period of his residence there, but who appears to have recovered himself, as many another man has done, by removing to a new place of abode.

† At this time the right of performing the marriage ceremony was restricted to clergymen of the Church of England, though those of other communions might obtain a license so to do on application to the magistrates in their Quarter Sessions.

subscribing for a Church. The Court House, which is now used, is a good convenient room. His success among the Indians is very satisfactory. He sometimes baptises 20 when he visits them, & he has had some Tusgaroras [Tuscaroras] offer for Baptism. He had prepared an address, and intended to visit the nation when he was among the Indians a month before, but was prevented by the indisposition of his interpreter.

Ibid., p. 129.

July 1st, 1805. That since his last (which was sent some time after Christmas) his Baptisms amount to 61. Marriages 4. Burials 2. His Congregation encreases. The Church is begun and half up. He will write again, more particularly by Capt. Brant, the Mohawk Chief, should he go to England in the fall.

Ibid., p. 209.

July 5, 1806, that since his last, his Baptisms amount to 70—Marriages 7 & Burials 3. He has baptized several Indians of different tribes on Grand River, about 70 or 80 miles to the west of Niagara, among which was a Chief of the Cayuga nation & his wife. They had been man and wife many years; but thought it more decent and respectable to be united after the Christian form. That he is greatly assisted by Captain Brant, Chief of the Mohawks, in his endeavours to bring those wandering tribes to pay any attention to Christian Doctrine.

Ibid., pp. 269-270.

Head of the Lake Ontario [Hamilton], 50 miles from Niagara, January 29, 1807—where he was upon a visit to the Indians & took the opportunity of writing by a gentleman on his way to England, and therefore could not send an exact account of Baptisms. He had baptized 19 Indian children, & married 3 couples. His Congregation was uncommonly large. He sent to the neighbouring villages, and went himself to one of them, where he understood a great number of Indians were assembled to partake of an entertainment given by an Indian lately married. He had the satisfaction to add, that several from the other Six Nations besides the Mohawks have become Christians, and many of them have left off the ruinous habit of drinking spirituous liquors. The Church at Niagara is not yet finished. They began upon too large a scale for their means, but have entered into a fresh subscription; and hope to complete it in the course of next summer.

Ibid., p. 291.

July 5, 1807, in which he acquaints the Society that since the 1st of January he had baptized 75; married 7; and buried 9. He had been amongst the Indians, & baptized 10, tho' he could not stay his usual time. He was requested to fix a time for baptizing several Anandagas [Onondagas] who have for a time forborne the use of spirituous liquors. The church [St. Mark's] advances slowly. The floors however are laid, & the windows ready for glazing; but it is not to be wondered at that it goes on no faster, as almost all the settlers about Niagara are Presbyterians. He says, that he is often asked for Prayer Books

& told that there are none in the shops. A Church Bible too would be very useful to him, as his eyes begin to fail, and he can only read good print with glasses.

Agreed to recommend that some Prayer Books, and a Quarto Bible be sent to Mr. Addison.

Agreed with the Committee.

Ibid., p. 368.

July 10, 1808, that since he wrote last, his Baptisms have amounted to 48, Marriages 6, Burials 3. That he had been prevented visiting the Indians on account of heavy rains & excessive heats. He hoped, however, soon to be with them. That nothing has been done to the Church, the expence having disheartened his good hearers; but it has gone too far to be neglected, and the next effort will finish it. Every part of his Mission is as prosperous as before. He has drawn as usual.

Ibid., pp. 412-413.

Jan'ry 2, 1808, by which the Society is informed that since his last, the Baptisms have been 62—Marriages 6 & Burials 5. That Capt. Brant, the great Chief of the Mohawks, died about a month ago. He had translated part of the New Testament,* was a man of uncommon intellect; but fell a victim to drunkenness.** Mr. Addison says that he shall miss him in his visits to the Mohawk Church. The Church at Niagara advances but slowly. It has gotten the first coat of plaister, & he hopes that it will be fit for divine Service toward the end of the summer. The number of Communicants is the same, but among the Indians they encrease. He had 20 the last time he was with them.

Ibid., p. 421.

January 14, 1809, acquainting the Society that, since his last, the Baptisms have been 97—Marr. 10—Burials 13. At his last visit to the Indians he baptized upwards of 50. He understood that they were sober and well disposed, and had written to some tribes which live near 20 miles from the Mohawks down the Grand River. Norton, a very extraordinary young man, was his interpreter. They seemed to him to offer themselves candidates for Baptism from a persuasion of the truth & value of our holy faith, & without something of that sort, he has no wish to baptize any of them. At the Mohawk Church he has generally 20 Communicants. He had 18 at a Settlement 30 miles from him, and at Niagara 12 or 14. He does his best among a people to whom he was sent, & he believes his labour is not quite in vain.

Vol. 30, 1810-1814, p. 87-88.

Jan'y 5, 1810, in which he acquaints the Society, that since his last the Baptisms amount to 65—Marriages 7—Burials 9. They have so far finished their Church at Niagara that Divine Service has been constantly performed there since last August. The pews are handsome, & sold for more than £300. It is the

---

* This translation was done in collaboration with the Revd. John Stuart. See *The Parish Register of Kingston.* (Brant's death occurred Nov. 24th, 1807).

** Stone's "Life of Brant" gives a different view of the case and takes to task Dr. Strachan for having given expression to the view here set forth by Mr. Addison.

best Church in the Province, and they hope to complete it next spring if their funds do not fail. His communicants rather increase. Among the Indians there were 22 last time. He was not able to visit them during the winter on account of the very bad state of the roads, but hoped to do so in a very few days, should the weather permit. He has drawn as usual.

Ibid., p. 119.

July 2, 1810, in which he acquaints the Society that since his last, Baptisms have amounted to 83—Marriages 6—Burials 6. That in the new Church, where Service is now performed, he has large Congregations; & in two country places 10 or 12 miles from Niagara, the inhabitants have erected two small convenient chapels,* where he alternately performs Divine Service on the first Sunday in every month to crowded audiences. The Communicants rather encrease, being in the whole settlement something more than 56. But he is most satisfied with his success among the Indians, several of whom belonging to the least cultivated tribe on the Grand River have been lately baptized.

Ibid., p. 158.

January 16, 1811, to acquaint the Society that since his last, he has baptized 57, married 8 couple, & buried 7. That the very bad state of the roads prevented his visiting the Indians in the autumn, which will account for his Baptisms being fewer than usual; but he intends to set out on a visit to them in a few days. That the Church is now very neatly finished, except some seats in the gallery; and the Congregation, which is large, is well accommodated for Public Worship. The Communicants continue rather to encrease.

Ibid., p. 198.

June 28, 1811, in which he acquaints the Society that since his last, the Baptisms have amounted to 64—Marriages 5—Burials 7. That in his last visit to the Indians, he baptized 20, and married 4 couple. His communicants rather increase, and the Mission continues to be prosperous.

Ibid., p. 264.

Two letters. .... of the respective dates of May 20, and August 11, 1812. In the first of which he encloses this Notitia:—Baptisms 79; Marriages 7; Burial 1. Communicants rather encrease. He has large Congregations. It gives him pain to mention that the draft for his allowance for the last half year came back protested, although he has never failed to write whenever he drew.** He has been very ill.

They were all in bustle and confusion from the Declaration of War by the American States.

Ibid., p. 349.

---

* One of these Chapels was apparently at Queenston. The foundation of it, on which a shed now stands, is pointed out on the left hand, in ascending the Heights on the Electric Railway.

**A quotation from a letter written by Bishop Mountain, on November 5th, 1813, confirms what has been already said about the costs of drafts:—"In the Upper Province, the Clergy are subject to a deduction of the Income Tax, & of a Discount on their drafts of 20 or 25 per cent."

October 14th, 1812. That since he wrote last, the Baptisms have been 26—Marriages 6 and Burials 11. That the Baptisms are so few is owing to the distress of the times. The enemy, after taking Niagara, sent most of the respectable inhabitants as prisoners of war into the States 2 or 300 miles into the interior. He was put upon his parole, and suffered to remain in his own house. But when our army advanced towards Niagara, they found a line about four miles from the Town, & his house (which is nearly that distance) was sometime the headquarters. Then he performed Divine Service to the separate divisions of the army alternately, & visited the sick, who were very numerous. They expected to fall back when the winter sets in.

Ibid., p. 395.

January 7th, 1914. That since he wrote last, his Notitia stands thus: Baptisms 21. Burials 7. Marriages 2. That during the last half year, the Enemy being in possession of Niagara, he could not perform his duties as usual. The Town & Church are burnt, and the Enemy have crossed to the other side of the river. It is not possible, he says, to describe the horrid scenes he has witnessed. He has reason, however, to be very thankful. For, though he has been plundered, made prisoner of war, & harassed till he was dangerously ill, yet his house, which is about three miles from the Town, has escaped, and afforded an asylum to several unhappy sufferers who fled from the flames. They hope for happier times, and to see the Church, which was fortunately built of stone, repaired.

Ibid., p. 412.

July 11th, 1814. Encloses following Notitia:—Baptisms 54, Marriages 12, Burials 3. This part of the Province is again the seat of war, a battle was fought six days since within ten miles of his residence, in which the British Force was obliged to retire. In consequence the whole country is open to the Enemy, and nothing is to be expected but scenes of wickedness & desolation.

Vol. 31, 1815-1818 p. 37.

Niagara. February 16th, 1815. Baptisms 42. Marraiges 7. Burials 10. He has witnessed during the last Campaign almost all the sad scenes of Distress which a country subject to the Ravages of War can suffer. The English troops, however, by the blessing of heaven, though greatly inferior in number to the enemy, have driven them beyond the frontier. The Church is covered and used as a Commissary's store. Mr. Addison performs Divine Service in the General Hospital.

Ibid., p. 87.

July 10, 1815, in which he reports that he had performed divine Service in various places in the neighbourhood of Niagara, the Church is still used as a Commissary's Store but it will soon be emptied, as a new Store House is in great forwardness. His Notitia contains Bapt. 86, Marriages 5, Burials 2.

Ibid., p. 161.

Jan: 30th, 1816, in which he writes that by means of a subscription the Church has been sufficiently repaired for the performance of Divine Service, though it is by no means so comfortable as before its destruction by the Americans. He is requested by the Indians to apply to the Society for a further supply of Mohawk Prayer Books. His Notitia contains Baptisms 105, Marriages 7, Burials 9.

He has drawn upon the Treasurer to the amount of £90, which he hopes will prove correct, £25 due last July, £50 last Christmas, £10 for visiting the Indians, £5 Income Tax.

Agreed to recommend.

That 25 Bibles, 50 Testaments, 50 Prayer Books, & some Indian Prayer Books be sent to Mr Addison.

Agreed with the Committee.

Ibid., p. 185.

Aug. 3d, 1816, in which he reports that by means of a private subscription they had been enabled to repair the Church, so that they could make use of it in the summer, but during the winter some other place must be prepared for the Congregation. At the Bishop's last visitation 54 of his Congregation were confirmed—this number would have been almost doubled had not the enemy been so long in possession of the Country & destroyed the Town. He earnestly requests some Mohawk Prayer Books may be sent.

Ibid., p. 243.

January 10, 1817, in which he writes that they have long been in expectation that Government would give them some assistance in repairing their Church, which was used as a Government Store House previously to its being burnt by the enemy—should these expectations be disappointed, he is fearful that a considerable time must elapse before the building will be put in proper state for divine Service. The Notitia contains Baptisms 41, Marriages 12, Burials 5. He is most happy to hear that the Society have approved his exertions.

Ibid., p. 318.

September the 6th, 1817, in which he reports that he had applied to Mr. Norton, the great Chief, to translate the remainder of the Gospels into Mohawk. He is the only person capable of such a work & if he undertakes it, he will execute it well. Some Indian Prayer Books would be very acceptable. The last sent were lost during the war—he acknowledges the receipt of a box of books—the Notitia contains Baptisms 55, Marriages 5, Burials 5.

Agreed to recommend.

That 30 Indian Prayer Books be sent to Mr. Addison and that he be authorized to communicate to Mr. Norton the readiness of the Society to encourage their undertaking.

Agreed with the Committee.

Inserting the words the great interest which the Society feel in the proposed undertaking and their perfect readiness to afford it every encouragement.

Ibid., p. 362.

January 4, 1818, in which he writes that the state of his health and the badness of the roads had prevented him from visiting the Indians during the last summer tho' he is now in hopes of seeing them within a week or 10 days. He has just received a box of books but he is in want of some for the Mohawks. The last sent were lost—he has often expressed his concern that the Indians have no better means of Instruction than the short and occasional visits which the great distance of Niagara from their settlement will allow Mr. Addison to afford—he is happy to observe that Mr. Leeming, missionary at Ancaster, has been induced to extend his care to them—his distance is only eighteen miles, while Niagara is ninety miles from the Mohawk country—he ventures to suggest to the Society, the expediency of making some allowance to Mr. Leeming for this extra duty, as independent of the additional expense of travelling—appeals are frequently made to the charitable feelings of the missionary, which his slender income will not allow him to meet.

Mr. Addison will continue to visit until he hears of Mr. Leeming's appointment and afterwards (whether his allowance of £20 per annum is continued or not) he will take every opportunity of visiting them, as his health will permit—that his attention to the Indians is of some importance will appear from the Circumstance that the Annual Baptisms amount to 100—it is probable other Tribes may be induced by the example of the Mohawks to profess Christianity. The Notitia contains Baptisms 38, Marriages 8, Burials 6.

Agreed to recommend.

That an additional salary of £20 be given to Mr. Leeming upon his undertaking to visit the Indians once each month. That 20 Indian Prayer Books, 100 Primers, together with 10 English Bibles, 50 Testaments, 50 Common Prayers be sent to him—that Mr. Addison's Allowance be continued in consideration of the length of his services, and, in the hope that he will visit the Indians as often as circumstances will permit—that in consequence of the statement in Mr. Addison's letter a separate mission be established in the Mohawk country, where there is already a Church and that a Communication be opened with Mr. Addison and Mr. Leeming on that subject.

Ibid., pp. 415-416.

July 15th, 1818. That he has lately seen Major Norton, who has promised to translate some further parts of the New Testament into Mohawk. He is at present much occupied in improving his lands and, as he lives among the Indians on the Grand River, he hopes his example and influence will be of essential service to those poor wanderers, and induce them to cultivate their lands; it will be necessary for him to attend the press which is at a distance of 30 miles—as no compositor can be tolerably correct in a difficult and unknown language without constant inspection. Mr. Norton is acquainted with printing and perhaps the Society will take it into consideration, whether it would be advisable to send him out a press. The Church has been twice repaired by subscription, but they cannot make use of it in winter. They have some expectation of procuring assistance from Sir John Sherbrooke—as it was used for a barrack during the war.

Vol. 32, 1819-1820, p. 137.

July 1st, 1819, in which he writes that he had transmitted by Col. Grant, of the 70th Regiment, some observations of Mr. Norton's on the subject of civilizing the native Indians—some impediments have checked the progress of the translations in consequence of the removal of the Printer. At a meeting with Mr. Norton which he has proposed, it is hoped these difficulties will be obviated.

Ibid., p. 297.

Janry 10th, 1820, in which he transmits the Notitia, containing Baptisms 31; Marrs. 4; Funerals 9. The Church which had been so dilapidated during the war that it could not be used in cold weather, will soon be thoroughly repaired, as the Lieut.-Governor * has appropriated £500 for that purpose. Mr. Norton had promised to undertake the translation of the remaining part of the Gospel in the Mohawk Language as soon as his other occupations would permit. Mr. Addison had intended to urge the prosecution of it in person—but his own state of health and the bad Condition of the Roads prevented his visit—when he has made any progress and prepared for the Press, Mr. Addison will advance what money may be required for his expenses.

Agreed to recommend.

That Mr. Norton be again urged to complete the translation of the Gospels in the Mohawk Language and that an assurance be given him that all reasonable expenses shall be paid.

Ibid., p. 381.

July 4, 1820, in which he writes that since his last the Notitia contains Bapts 33; Marrs 4; Burls 3. Mr. Norton has been very ill & by exposing himself too soon has suffered a relapse, which has prevented his progress in the Translation. When Mr. Addison saw him two months since, he had only finished four chapters of St. Matthew—it is probable by this time he has completed that Gospel, as he purposed to devote all his leisure time to it—he [Addison] intended to have been with him but the excessive heat rendered travelling very inconvenient and he has been much occupied in superintending the repairs of the Church and preparing for a confirmation by the Bishop in the course of a few days—he intends to pass over to Mr. Norton when the heat has subsided.

Vol. 33, 1821-1822, p. 74.

Janry 28, 1821, in which he writes that Mr. Norton had nearly finished the Gospel of St. Matthew, but he is unwilling to proceed with that of St. Luke, as the prospect of its extended usefulness is not very encouraging at present. He considers the establishment of a certain number of National Schools would be productive of more advantage—among the Indians he baptized 3 and received 2, who had been previously baptized by Mr. Norton—the Church [St. Mark's] will be finished in the course of the spring.† The Notitia contains population 900, mostly Presbyterians, but the most respectable part attend the church. Baptms 24; marrgs 2; Burls 7; Comms. 42.

Agreed to recommend

---

* This Lieutenant-Governor was Lieutenant-General Sir Peregrine Maitland, whose summer residence was situated near Stamford.

† Apparently the Church was not consecrated till August, 1828, the same month in which those at Stamford and Chippawa were consecrated, by Bishop Stewart. Sir Peregrine Maitland, the Report for 1829 states, attended the ceremony.

That Mr. Addison be informed that the Society are perfectly disposed to establish schools in the Indian territory wherever they may be found useful.

Ibid., p. 175.

July 2, 1821, in which he writes that, as the service is performed in the Church every Sunday by the Military Chaplain,* he avails himself of the opportunity to visit the neighbouring villages, where he preaches to full congregations and baptizes the Children.

Mr. Norton has finished the Translation of St. Matthew and has promised to proceed till the Indians are furnished with the four Gospels. It would be very desirable that the inspired comment and illustration of the Christian Doctrines contained in the Acts of the Apostles & the Epistles were added. Should Mr. Norton's other pursuits prevent his performing this good work, he has mentioned an Indian whom he thinks capable of undertaking it. His name is Aaron Hill, reader and interpreter to Mr. Leeming. Mr. Norton will correct the manuscript. The Notitia contains Bapts 30, Marrs 3, Burs 13, Communts 33.

Agreed to recommend

That enquiries be made of Mr. Addison respecting the practicability of printing the version of St. Matthew and the probable expence attending it.

Ibid., p. 277.

Febry 1, 1822, in which he writes that he has been so unwell that he was not able to undertake the journey to the Mohawk Indians—he has, however, written to Mr. Leeming to point out a proper person for the conduct of a school and, should the roads prove good in the winter, and his health permit, he will endeavour to accomplish his usual visits. Mr. Norton seems fearful that the translation of the Gospels into Mohawk would be of little use. He writes that he could hardly undertake the whole, considering the little attention the Mohawks pay to literary improvements in their own language. He has reason to believe that, in this respect, they have retrograded and certainly it would be too great an undertaking to attempt without some assurance of benefitting thereby the cause of Christianity. Most of the Mohawks speak and understand English and have applied to him for English Bibles.

Mr. Norton looks not to remuneration, but is deterred from the work from the consideration that it would occupy more of his time than his other avocations would allow him to devote to it. Aaron Hill, an Indian and the Society's catechist, is fully capable of the work and Mr. Norton will engage to look over it. The Notitia contains Baptisms 15, Marriages 2, Burials 6, Communts 33.

Ibid., p. 412.

Augt 12, 1822, in which he writes that Aaron Hill, the Catechist, has proceeded in the translation of St. Luke's Gospel as far as the 11th Chapter. His own health has lately suffered considerably. The Notitia contains Baptisms 13, Marriages 2, Burials 8.

Vol. 34, 1823-1824, pp. 104-105.

---

* This Chaplain was the Revd. B. B. Stevens. *Report for 1821.*

The Bishop [of Quebec] submits to the Board an application from Mr. Addison for permission to retire upon his full salary, with an intimation that, should such an arrangement be admitted in any case, the present would claim the most favourable consideration, as Mr. Addison has been in the service of the Society more than 30 years.

Agreed to recommend

That the Bishop of Quebec be informed that in no instance has the Society accepted the resignation of a Missionary claiming the full allowance of £200 per annum, and that the pension of £100 is restrained to those Missionaries whose age and infirmities render them incapable of performing the duties of their situations.

Ibid. January 14, 1823, in which he reports that the first Sunday in every month the Chaplain to the forces * performs the services at Niagara & he avails himself of the opportunity to go out into the neighbouring Villages when the Roads and Weather will allow him, where he meets large congregations.

At St. Catherines (sic),** distant 22 miles, there is a Church and they intend to build a parsonage forthwith, but the pressure of the times will delay its completion—he has also been at Grimsby, 30 miles distant, in the hopes of settling some disputes which had arisen respecting their Church and Parsonage, of which good prospects—he was on the road to the Indians when he met Mr. Leeming, who had just been in their country and told him they were much dispersed. The Notitia contains Bapts 15; marr 6; Bur 6.

Ibid., p. 233.

July 1st, 1823, in which he writes that on his road towards the Indians he met Mr. Leeming, who had just left their settlements where few of them were to be found, the greater part being gone on a hunting expedition—he continued his route along the lake and preached at Grimsby—the weather was very severe and he was detained at York by a very bad cold, from which he is not yet recovered, although he is able to officiate in the Church—he is doubtful whether Mr. Norton has finished the translation, but he is disposed to think that he has; it is probable Mr. Norton will go to England for a short time and he would then superintend the printing. The notitia contains Bapts 27, Marr 6: Bur 4.

Ibid., p. 368.

Jan 1, 1824, in which he writes that he has intended to have visited the Indians to have given some advice and direction to the missionary but on his road he ascertained that Mr. Morley [Mosley?] was not arrived—he would not-

---

* From the Report of 1822, this Chaplain would seem to have been Mr. Frith, of Queenston.

** According to the Report of 1824, St Catharines was one of nineteen places at which it was proposed to establish a missionary. In that of 1826 Mr. Bethune, of Grimsby, and Mr. Leeming, of Chippawa, officiated there once a month. "A good congregation assembles, and there is a prospect of the population rapidly increasing, as the formation of the canal which is to connect Lake Erie with Lake Ontario at that place is now in progress." In the Report for 1828, mention is made of a military establishment as well as of the canal in connection with St Catharines. In the Report for 1829 is noted an improvement in the behaviour of the congregation. There were much fever and destitution that year.

withstanding have pursued his way, had not the roads within 20 miles of the village been entirely broken up, he was compelled to leave his sleigh and return by a waggon, which is a very inconvenient mode of travelling, especially for an old man. Aaron Hill has nearly finished the translation of the Gospels, but it will be of no service till it has been corrected by Mr. Norton, who is at present absent and likely to continue so for a time.

VOL. 35, 1824-1826, p. 114.

July 1, 1824, in which he reports that Mr. Mosley paid him a visit on his way to the Indian Settlements on the Grand River. Aaron Hill, the Interpreter, was at that time with him and he was happy in the opportunity of explaining to him the Character of the People with whom he was to reside. Mr. Mosley appeared much disheartened, and has been unwell since he reached his destination. Aaron Hill has nearly finished the translation of the Gospel, and waits only for the correction of Mr. Norton, when the Work will be ready for the Press.

It may be doubtful whether it may be desireable to print it in England and Mr. Norton thinks it probable that he shall have occasion to go to that Country in the course of the next Summer, when he would willingly superintend the printing.

Mr. Addison has great reason to be thankful for the Restoration of his health, which enables him to attend to the duties of his mission with the same regularity as in former years.

The Notitia contains Baptms 26, Marr 7, Burials 8.

VOL. 36, 1826-1827, p. 380.

[Letter from the Bishop of Quebec, 21st August, 1826] . . . . Mr. Addison's health, although he is still very infirm, has perceptibly improved within the last year.

Ibid., p. 408.

March 30th, 1826, in which he [Addison] says—He is sorry to inform the Society that he has a long and severe illness, which has reduced him to a very weak state of health.

During the time of his illness he had the service in his own house, being happily free from pain.

His Notitia is as follows: Baptms 34; Burials 16; Marriages 11.

He has performed the duty in Church for some months past.

If Mr. Creen,* the District School Master, could be ordained to officiate at Queenston, and be his Assistant, the appointment would be very acceptable to him (Mr. A.)

He has frequent communication with the Indians, and he understands the School about 7 miles above the Village is in a very flourishing State.

---

* Thanks to the vigorous missionary policy of the second Bishop of Quebec, the Rt. Revd. and Hon. Charles James Stewart, Mr. Creen was ordained, apparently in 1826, and was ordained priest in 1827, judging from the Society's Report for 1828.

The Indians have made a requisition to him for a supply of Books; and he is quite without English Prayer Books, Bibles and Testaments, which are frequently asked for by poor people.

If a small package was sent to Mr. Archdeacon Steward ** at Kingston for him, it would be better than if forwarded to Niagara.

Dr. Strachan *** has been up among the Indians and, if Mr. Leeming does not come early in the spring, he will request Mr. Bethune **** to visit them, that they be not quite without the Sacrament.

The Communicants are about 50.

The Town of Niagara contains upwards of 1,000 inhabitants, and the rest of the parish better than three times as many.

Agreed to recommend

1. That Mr. Addison be authorized to procure from the District Committee, in aid of the Society P.C.K. at Kingston, Bibles to the amount of £20.

2. That the Society do avail themselves of the kind offer of Dr. Strachan to superintend the Printing of the Mohawk Testament when prepared for the Press.

3. That 500 Copies be printed, and that he be authorized to draw on the Treasurer for the expense incurred thereby.

VOL. 38, 1828, p. 64.

24th August, 1827, in which he says: He is much pleased that Dr. Strachan has promised to see to the Printing of the Mohawk Testament himself, which he hopes will be ready for him in the beginning of the Winter. He saw Aaron Hill, the Translator, in Spring, who said he had nearly finished the Corinthians and promises to proceed with all diligence.

He is much gratified in stating that Mr. Hough is highly respected among the Indians and is likely to be very useful in his mission.

He can say the same of Mr. Creen, who is much esteemed by his hearers. The Town of Niagara contains upwards of *1,100 Souls,* and the rest of the Township about *3,000.*

His Notitia is as follows: Baptisms 13; Burials 5; Marriages 4.

** This was George Okill Stuart, already mentioned. After his father's death, in 1811, he became Rector of Kingston and Bishop's Official for Upper Canada, 1812. The latter title was changed to Archdeacon of Upper Canada (or York), in 1821. On the creation of the Archdeaconry of Kingston in 1827, he was given jurisdiction over it. In 1862, he year of his death, he became Dean of St. George's Cathedral, in the then new Diocese of Ontario.

*** Dr. Strachan (1778-1867), Bishop of Toronto from 1839, to 1867, was a schoolmaster in Kingston (1799-1803), in Cornwall (1803-1812), in York (1812-1823); missionary at Cornwall (1803-1812), Rector of York and Toronto (1812-1847), Archdeacon of York (1827-1847); President of the Provincial Board of Education (1823-1832) and of King's College, now the University of Toronto (1827-1849).

**** The Revd. Alexander Neil Bethune (1800-1879), was missionary at Grimsby, (1823-1828), Rector of Cobourg (1828-1867), Archdeacon of York (1847-1867), Principal of the Theological Institution at Cobourg (1842-1852), Editor of The Church (1837-1857, more or less), Co-adjutor Bishop of Toronto, under the title of Bishop of Niagara, (January-November, 1867), **Bishop of Toronto (1867-1879).**

Mr. Creen, who performs most of ye occasional services, will send the account of all that has taken place in the Township since his Appointment.
Vol. 40, 1830, p. 89.
Read a letter from the Lord Bishop of Quebec, dated Dec 10, 1829.

He begs now to communicate thro' the Society the loss sustained by them in one of their Missions by the death of the Rev. R. Addison, in October, 1829, whose Age was greater and the period of whose labour in the Service of the Society was longer than that of any other Clergyman in the Diocese at the time of his decease. He had administered to the Congregation of Niagara nearly 40 years and died in his 75th year, beloved and regarded by all. The Board will recollect that, in consideration of his long services, they were pleased to appoint the Rev. T. Creen to be his Assistant with the salary of £100 in the year 1826. This gentleman made full proof of his Ministry to the entire satisfaction of his rector and Congregation. They have now unanimously solicited that Mr. Creen may be appointed to the vacant mission and he has accordingly given him the nomination, subject to the approbation of the Board. He has ventured to sanction his resigning the District School, and he (the Bishop) has authorized him to draw upon the Treasurer on the 1st of Janry for an increase in salary, viz: £200 per annum from the time of Mr. Addison's demise. Being executor to the deceased, he (Mr. Creen) will draw for the remainder of the salary due to Mr. Addison. He begs to recommend the widow of Mr. Addison to the usual Pension.

Agreed to recommend

6. That the appointment of Mr. Green to the mission of Niagara, vacated by the decease of the late Mr. Addison, the exemplary & highly respected Miss. of that place be confirmed, and that the additional salary to which he will be entitled to do commence from Oct., 1829.

7. That the usual pension of £50 be granted to the widow of Mr. Addison, to commence from Jan. 1, 1830.

www.ingramcontent.com/pod-product-compliance
Lightning Source LLC
Chambersburg PA
CBHW022107230426
43672CB00008B/1307